Impersonals and other Agent Defocusing Constructions in French

Human Cognitive Processing (HCP)
Cognitive Foundations of Language Structure and Use
ISSN 1387-6724

This book series is a forum for interdisciplinary research on the grammatical structure, semantic organization, and communicative function of language(s), and their anchoring in human cognitive faculties.

For an overview of all books published in this series, please see
http://benjamins.com/catalog/hcp

Volume 50

Impersonals and other Agent Defocusing Constructions in French
by Michel Achard

Impersonals and other Agent Defocusing Constructions in French

Michel Achard
Rice University

John Benjamins Publishing Company

Amsterdam / Philadelphia

The paper used in this publication meets the minimum requirements of the American National Standard for Information Sciences – Permanence of Paper for Printed Library Materials, ANSI z39.48-1984.

DOI 10.1075/hcp.50

Cataloging-in-Publication Data available from Library of Congress:
LCCN 2014039899 (PRINT) / 2014041384 (E-BOOK)

ISBN 978 90 272 4666 0 (HB)
ISBN 978 90 272 6907 2 (E-BOOK)

John Benjamins Publishing Co. · P.O. Box 36224 · 1020 ME Amsterdam · The Netherlands
John Benjamins North America · P.O. Box 27519 · Philadelphia PA 19118-0519 · USA

Table of contents

Preface

I first encountered impersonality during childhood. Growing up in France, as early as I can remember, I was amazed at the force of some very specific expressions that ruled my daily interactions with an iron fist. The dreaded *Qu'en dira-t-on?* 'What will they say?' kept me under the ever-watchful eye of an unsympathetic judge whose negative comments would reduce me to social dust. Equally worrisome, the peremptory *Ça ne se fait pas!* 'This isn't done!' invariably slammed the door on any attempt at dialogue following the denial of such legitimate requests as "Why can't I drink coke for breakfast?" In both cases, in addition to their sheer power, the faceless character of these expressions terrified me. There was no presence with whom one could negotiate, no authority to appeal to; there was nothing to add. The forces at work dwarfed anything human; the social gods had spoken.

This book represents an attempt to show that French culture cares so deeply about these maximally general statements that describe the structure of our physical and social world that the language has developed a sophisticated set of "impersonal" constructions to describe them. It is dedicated to my parents, Georges and Josette Achard, who patiently taught me not to be afraid of the *Qu'en dira-t-on?*, and to my wife Melanie, who never accepted *Ça ne se fait pas* as a legitimate response.

I am grateful to the faculty and students in the Linguistics Department at Rice University, as well as my colleagues at numerous national and international conferences for providing moral support, as well as much welcome discussion at various stages of this work. The editing team of the Human Cognitive Processing series, in particular Klaus-Uwe Panther, Linda Thornburg, and Esther Roth deserve a special mention for their patience and kind guidance throughout the process. Finally, I am very much in the debt of two anonymous reviewers whose extremely thorough reading of the manuscript went well beyond the call of duty, and whose helpful suggestions much improved this final version.

CHAPTER 1

Narrow and broad impersonals
Definitions and scope of analysis

This chapter defines the scope of the analysis developed throughout the monograph. It argues that no theoretical model currently available in the literature provides an adequate representation of impersonal constructions in French. Syntactic accounts have restricted the impersonal domain to the sole *il* 'it' construction on the basis of the pronoun's structural specificity as a semantically vacuous placeholder. However, the pronoun's exclusively syntactic role cannot be maintained in the face of several analyses that have successfully described its semantic import. The impossibility of a purely syntactic treatment of impersonals opens the door to a more-inclusive interpretation of the category that includes a number of other constructions. Functional accounts have long attempted to expand the impersonal domain, but have had difficulty isolating its distinguishing criteria except for the fact that impersonals tend to have defocused agents. This sole criterion is unsatisfactory because it does not distinguish impersonals from other constructions such as passives or middles that also have defocused agents. The account developed in the following chapters follows the functional tradition in expanding the scope of French impersonals beyond the *il* construction, but it also provides a way of constraining the category to the kind of constructions that describe a class of highly general events that cannot be imputed to a specific cause.

1. Beyond structural analyses

A monograph-length investigation of French impersonals may appear unnecessary because these constructions have been studied extensively, and no longer seem to present any particular difficulty. Morphologically, French possesses a specific pronoun *il*, which does not function as an indefinite neuter similar to its English gloss 'it', but appears strictly in situations where a nominal or an infinitival or finite clause follows the predicate.[1] As an illustration, *il* is impossible in (1.1) where the neuter demonstrative *ce* alone can anaphorically refer to the situation described in the preceding context, but it is felicitous in (1.2) where a subjunctive clause follows the predicate *être juste* 'be fair':[2]

---

1. The weather predicates such as *il pleut* 'it is raining' are the only ones not followed by any entity.

2. Throughout this monograph the presence of a pound sign indicates a manufactured example.

(1.1) #*Tu ne me laisses jamais sortir, ce/*il n'est pas juste!*
'You never let me go out, it's not fair!'

(1.2) #*Il n'est pas juste que tu ne me laisses jamais sortir*
'It is not fair that you never let me go out!'

Semantically, *il*'s "pleonastic" character (Chomsky 1981: 26) keeps it separate from other pronouns. Jones (1996: 120) most eloquently expresses this very common position: "Intuitively, we know that *il* … does not refer to anything – it does not represent an argument of the verb which can be characterized in terms of a theta-role such as Agent, Experiencer, etc. Rather, its function appears to be purely syntactic, satisfying a requirement that all finite clauses must have a subject". The current syntactic literature uses *il*'s morphological distribution and its semantic emptiness to provide a structural definition of impersonals: "Impersonal sentences are constructions in which the subject position is occupied by a *dummy* pronoun *il*, which does not refer to anything." (Jones 1996: 120, emphasis in the original, but see also Gledhill 2003: 131; Perlmutter and Postal 1983: 101; Rowlett 2007: 133 for similar claims for French, as well as Chomsky 1981; Blevins 2003; Radford 2004: 291 ff; Mendikoetxea 2008 among many others for other languages).[3]

The requirement that the subject be semantically empty restricts the French impersonal domain to two main construction types determined by structural criteria. The intrinsically impersonal predicates illustrated in (1.3) are lexically specified as lacking an external argument, so their theta roles [theme in (1.3)] are assigned to their complements. The predicate's lexical entry therefore has an empty slot in subject position, to be filled at a later stage by the dummy *il* (Jones 1996: 66). In the "derived" constructions in (1.4), the dummy pronoun is inserted as the result of the gap created by the movement of the real subject *que ma mère vécût sans moi*. The existence of the possible alternative *que ma mère vécût sans moi était possible* 'that my mother lived without me was possible' is offered as justification for posing the alternative option as the base form (Jones 1996: 66).

(1.3) a. *Il **faut** un marteau*   (adapted from Jones 1996: 120)
'A hammer is necessary [it is necessary a hammer]'

  b. *Il **s'agit** de notre avenir*   (from Jones 1996: 120)
'It is about our future'

---

3. These analyses are quite different from each other because they are conducted under different frameworks, or they reflect different stages of development and sophistication of the Generative model. These differences will not be presented in this introduction because they are less directly relevant to our immediate concerns than their shared insight of a dummy subject inserted to address a structural necessity. Jones's analysis is selected as an illustration because of its clarity, even though several more current syntactic solutions have been proposed.

(1.4)   *Pour la première fois je sentais qu'il **était possible** que ma mère vécût sans moi*
                                    (Proust, M. *A l'ombre des jeunes filles en fleurs*: 648)
        'For the first time I felt it was possible for my mother to live [that my mother
        live] without me'[4]

The structural specificity of the *il* constructions offers the welcome advantage
of clearly delineating the French impersonal domain. In particular, it provides a
rigid distinction between impersonals and other structures with which they share
important semantic similarities. For example, *il*'s pleonastic nature allows us to
distinguish the impersonal construction in (1.4) from the demonstrative structure
in (1.5), even though *il* and *ça* are both possible in both contexts and could be
substituted for each other with little observable semantic difference:

(1.5)   *Dubreuilh t'attend avec impatience. Ne te laisse pas embarquer dans son
        machin… – j'y suis déjà plus ou moins embarqué, dit Henri. – eh bien! Dépêche-
        toi de t'en sortir. Henri sourit: non. Ça **n'est plus possible** aujourd'hui de rester
        apolitique.*   (Beauvoir, S. de. *Les mandarins*: 101)
        'Dubreuilh is waiting for you impatiently. Don't let him drag you into his
        plan. – I am already more or less part of it, Henry said. – well get out of it as
        soon as you can. Henry smiled: no. It [this] is no longer possible to remain
        outside of politics these days'.

Importantly, the impersonal quality of (1.4), and hence the validity of the structural
distinction between impersonal and demonstrative constructions, rests solely on
the semantic distinction between *il* and the demonstrative pronoun *ça*.[5] While *il*

---

4.   Throughout the monograph, the translations are mine, although some of the literary works
from which the examples are taken have been translated professionally. This choice was made to
emphasize the particularities of the French constructions under investigation, sometimes to the
detriment of English colloquial usage. When a very close translation would yield incomprehen-
sible results, the word-for-word form is given in brackets following a more natural translation.

5.   *Ce* and *c'* are also possible in this construction, as the following examples illustrate:

(i)   *bien sûr que la journée ne se passera pas sans pluie. Ce **n'était pas possible** que ça reste
      comme ça, il faisait trop chaud*   (Proust, M. *Du côté de chez Swann*: 101)
      'Of course the day will not finish without rain. It [this] was not possible that it [this] the
      weather would stay like this, it was too hot'

(ii) *dis tu m'entends, que je t'aime bien? … tu te rends compte de ce que j'ai fait pour toi au
      moins? … c'était peut- être pas la peine que je vienne aujourd'hui? … tu m'aimes pas quand
      même un petit peu Léon? C'est **pas possible** que tu m'aimes pas du tout…*
                                    (Céline, LF. *Voyage au bout de la nuit*: 600)
      'Eh can you hear me, that I love you a lot? … you realize what I did for you at least?
      maybe I shouldn't have come today? … you don't love me at least a little bit Leon? It
      [this] isn't possible that you don't love me at all…'

is assumed to be semantically empty, demonstratives are analyzed as "referential expressions which refer forward to the finite or infinitival clause" (Jones 1996: 128). Constructions such as (1.5) are therefore treated as dislocated constructions: "It is postulated that the constructions with *ce* or *ça* are not impersonal constructions, but dislocated constructions analogous to *elle est arrivée, Marie*" (Jones 1996: 128). If this semantic distinction between the different kinds of pronouns is accepted, there is little else to add. *Il*'s vacuous character validates a structurally distinct impersonal class, and that relatively narrow class is clearly delineated from other semantically related constructions. The situation, however, is not as clear cut as the structural analyses claim. In fact, the rigid semantic difference between pleonastic *il* and cataphoric *ça* proves difficult to maintain under careful scrutiny because (1) *il* can legitimately be claimed to be meaningful, and (2) *ça* does not strictly refer forward to the complement clause.[6]

With respect to (1), it is worth noting that the very idea of meaningless elements, whose sole function is to fulfill a syntactic need, represents a theoretical assumption that many linguistic models do not share. In Cognitive Grammar (CG), for instance, in which the analyses presented in this monograph are conducted (to be presented in detail in Chapter 2; see also Langacker 1987, 1991, 2008), all linguistic forms symbolize the association of a conceptual content and a phonological form and should hence be considered meaningful, even when their meaning is quite abstract. Second, researchers of various orientations have long recognized

---

6. In a similar manner, positing that the placeholder *il* is inserted as a structurally required subject is not entirely convincing, given the large number of expressions where it is missing. These include *si bon me semble* 'if I so desire', *vaut autant partir tout de suite* 'might as well leave right away', *d'où vient que vous rentrez si tard?* 'how come you are coming back so late?', or *faut pas y aller* 'one shouldn't go' (Grevisse 1986: 340–342). These expressions cannot summarily be dismissed as frozen remnants of an earlier form of the language in which subjectless impersonals were the norm. Zero impersonals are still frequently attested in contemporary French, most notably following epistemic and evaluation predicates, as illustrated in the examples below. The presence of these constructions seriously calls into question the stringent structural need for a place holding subject in French, and thus the purely syntactic function posited for *il*. This issue will be examined further in Chapters 3 and 5.

(i) *Il y avait aussi le fermier Boissinot, dont le sommeil était léger: **possible que** Boissinot n'eût pas été fâché de savoir Raboliot en campagne…*   (Genevoix, M. *Raboliot*: 69)
   'There was also Boissinot, the farmer, who slept lightly. [It was] possible that Boissinot wouldn't have minded knowing Raboliot was on the prowl'

(ii) *vous êtes un gaillard, Monsieur Krafft. **Dommage que** vous ne soyez pas des nôtres!*
                     (Rolland, R. *Jean-Christophe: dans la maison*: 1053)
   'You are a sturdy fellow Mister Krafft. Pity you are not one of us!'

that potential subjects do not exclusively refer to participants in the predicate's argument structure, but may also describe more general and diffuse considerations pertaining to the general atmosphere that surround the depicted scene:

> Tel sujet psychologique peut être une donnée plus complexe qu'une idée de chose ou de personne, un fait par exemple, quelque chose qui se passe, ou bien une situation dans le temps ou l'espace déterminée de quelque façon mais en elle-même vide de représentation précise. Cette situation qui encadre le prédicat peut même se réduire à l'idée toute vague et inexprimable d'une ambiance quelconque.

> 'Such psychological subject can be a more complex entity than that of a thing or person, a fact, for example, something that happens, or a situation in time or space determined in some sense but by itself deprived of specific representation. This situation that surrounds the predicate can even be reduced to the very vague and difficult to express idea of some kind of ambiance'.
>
> (Sechehaye 1950: 45, translation mine)

Consequently, despite its centrality to the structural accounts, *il*'s semantic emptiness has frequently been questioned. French grammarians (Wartburg and Zumthor 1958; Sechehaye 1950; Galichet 1968 inter alia) as well as more recent researchers in the functional/cognitive linguistics tradition have convincingly argued, using different but related constructs, that impersonal pronouns in a variety of languages should not be considered dummy placeholders, but referential (albeit general) expressions. To provide just a sample of the proposals found in the literature, Bolinger (1977: 84–85) calls the English *it* "a definite nominal with almost the greatest possible generality of meaning" while Langacker (1993) argues that the same pronoun denotes "an abstract setting". Kirsner (1979: 81) argues that the Dutch *es* codes "general presence or availability", while Lakoff (1987: 542) and Smith (1985, 2000) suggest that the English *there* and German *es* both indicate "a mental space". Closest to our current concerns, I have previously argued that the French *il* refers to "the abstract setting identifiable as the immediate scope for the existential predication" (Achard 1998: Chapter 7). The analysis developed in this monograph follows the aforementioned researchers in treating the impersonal pronoun as a meaningful expression; a precise characterization of its semantic import is developed in the following chapters. At this introductory stage, however, it is important to preview the analysis in order to validate the claim that *il* is indeed meaningful, and that consequently a strictly structural account of French impersonals is difficult to maintain.

Following the CG tradition (to be presented in detail in Chapter 2), impersonals are considered "abstract locational constructions" (Achard 2010), closely related to the kind of structure illustrated in (1.6):

(1.6) *À partir du xviiie siècle, un sourd travail devient perceptible. ...* **La France**
*voit une école bourgeoise renouer avec la tradition interrompue de ses propres
"peintres de la réalité"*   (Huyghe, R. *Dialogue avec le visible:* 154)
'Starting in the 18th century, an obscure current begins to surface. ... **France**
witnesses the emergence of a bourgeois school that reconnects with the interrupted tradition of its own "reality painters"'

In (1.6) the subject of *voir* 'see' (France) represents the temporal and spatial setting
within which the event that the predicate describes unfolds. Impersonals resemble
these "setting subjects constructions" (Langacker 1991: 345) in that they also select
a kind of setting as their subject, but that setting is much more abstract than the one
illustrated in (1.6). In order to characterize it with some precision, we need to bear
in mind that in any interaction a fundamental distinction can be drawn between
the participants and the area or domain within which their interaction develops.
Langacker (2002, 2004, 2009) calls this area the "field" (to be presented more extensively in Chapters 2 and 3). In the physical domain, the field represents the area
within which agents have the perceptual and kinesthetic potential to capture their
target. By analogy, in the epistemic domain the field can be characterized as the
mental reach within which some concept can be identified, or in other words the
abstract area defined by the knowledge structures necessary to reach a conclusion
about the epistemic status of a given entity. In (1.7), for instance, the alternative
edition of a book unknown to the hearer (underlined in the example) constitutes
the target whose epistemic status is being determined. In order to conceptualize
this target and assert its existence, the speaker relies on a knowledge base that at the
very least includes the immediate circumstances that surround the publication of
the work. In Cognitive Grammar that knowledge base constitutes the field within
which the profiled interaction can be conceptualized.

(1.7) *le désespéré que vous avez eu tant de peine à vous procurer, dites-vous, est, sans
doute, l'édition Soirat.* **Il en existe** <u>une autre</u> *qui vient de paraître, à mon insu
et sans mon autorisation.*   (Bloy, L. *Journal:* 74)
'The desperate [person] you say you had such trouble finding is most likely
the Soirat Edition. There exists an alternative edition that was just released,
unbeknownst to me and without my permission'.

Langacker (2009) suggests that the English impersonal *it* specifically refers to that
knowledge base: "I thus propose, as a general characterization, that impersonal
'it' profiles the relevant field, i.e. the conceptualizer's scope of awareness for the
issue at hand" (Langacker 2009: 139). If this proposal is adopted for French (to
be developed in Chapter 3, see also Achard [2010]), *il* in (1.7) is not a pleonastic
placeholder but a referential construct that represents the conceptual base that allows the speaker to assert the existence of the alternative edition. Importantly for

our purposes, the speaker's use of an impersonal construction in (1.7) indicates that the field within which the alternative edition of the book is identified does not merely represent his own mental reach but that of anyone placed in similar conditions, who would invariably reach the same conclusion. Because it is available to a "generalized conceptualizer" (Langacker 2009:115), the event coded in the complement is presented at the highest level of generality, namely an intrinsic property of the abstract scene within which it is experienced.

The recognition of *il*'s semantic import makes it hard to maintain that it is radically different from *ça* because its import is strictly structural. Furthermore, a careful examination of the meaning of *ça*, (*c'*) further narrows the semantic gap between impersonal and demonstrative pronouns, and therefore eliminates the need to posit different structures for the constructions illustrated in (1.4) and (1.5). In order to evaluate the claim that *ça*, *ce*, and *cela* "refer forward to the finite or infinitival clause" (Jones 1996:128), Achard (2010) compared these pronouns to *ceci* 'this' and found that if *ceci* truly has a "strictly cataphoric" sense illustrated in (1.8) where the pronoun unambiguously refers to a forward entity but *ça* and *cela* do not (Achard 2010:465).

(1.8)   *Revenant l'autre soir du théâtre avec Robert, nous passons près d'un groupe d'agents qui causent entre eux à mi-voix, et **ceci** parvient jusqu'à nous dans le grand silence de la rue déserte: "il lui a filé un coup de lame".*

(Green, J. *Journal. T. 5. 1946–1950*:210) (from Achard 2010)
'On the way back from the theater with Robert the other night, we walked past a group of policemen talking to each other in low voices, and this comes to us in the silence of the deserted street: "he cut him with a blade"'.

In *ceci*'s strictly cataphoric sense, the entity to which the pronoun refers (henceforth the referred entity) is completely independent semantically from the surrounding context. In (1.8), nothing in the preceding discourse allows the reader to semantically anticipate the nature of the upcoming utterance beyond the benign observation that an unknown policeman is responsible for it. *Ceci* therefore unambiguously refers forward to "*il lui a filé un coup de lame*", and can be considered a strict cataphoric pronoun (to be developed further in Chapter 6).

While strict cataphorics account for almost 50 percent of the overall examples involving *ceci* (Achard 2010:463; see also Chapter 6), *ce*, *ça*, and *cela* never exhibit this specific sense. With these pronouns the referred entity is always closely semantically integrated into the surrounding context. In the most obvious cases it explicitly repeats a lexical item from the previous discourse, as in (1.9) where the shared lexical elements are underlined. In this case the postverbal entity is so clearly semantically integrated within the surrounding (preverbal) context that it could be viewed as lexically redundant and easily left out:

(1.9)   *"Promenons-nous. <u>Amusons-nous</u> tant qu'il nous reste de la chair sur les os." Il*
        haussa les épaules: "tu sais bien que ça n'est pas si facile de <u>s'amuser</u>".

                                                    (Beauvoir, S. de. *Les mandarins*: 93)
        '"Let's go for a walk. Let's have fun while we still have flesh on our bones." He
        shrugged: "you know that it [this] is not so easy to have fun'".

In other instances the referred entity expresses the reformulation or reanalysis of
the previous context as in (1.10), where *le péché par omission* 'a sin by omission'
provides the recapitulation and generalization of the situation described in the
preverbal context:

(1.10) *quand on pense à tout ce qu'on pourrait faire et qu'on ne fait pas! Toutes les*
        occasions qu'on laisse échapper! On n'a pas l'idée, pas l'élan; au lieu d'être ouvert
        on est fermé; c'est ça le plus grand péché: <u>le péché par omission.</u>

                                                    (Beauvoir, S. de. *Les mandarins*: 70)
        'when you think about all you could do and don't do! All these opportunities
        we waste! For lack of imagination, of energy; we are closed instead of being
        open; this is the greatest sin: a sin by omission'.

The shared semantic content between the context that precedes the pronoun and
the one that follows it sheds some doubt on the legitimacy of analyzing *ça* as strictly
cataphoric. It seems more insightful to simply note that the ambiguity between
anaphoric and cataphoric reference precisely constitutes one of the pronoun's distinguishing characteristics (to be developed further in Chapter 6). This ambiguity
is most dramatically expressed in (1.9) where an anaphoric or cataphoric interpretation yields the same entity as the referent. Similarly, a cataphoric interpretation
of *ça* in (1.10) where *le péché par omission* is the referent seems just as plausible as
its anaphoric counterpart where the pronoun refers back to the previous context,
namely *toutes les occasions qu'on laisse échapper! On n'a pas l'idée, pas l'élan; au*
lieu d'être ouvert on est fermé.

    The difference between *ceci* and *ça* underscores the necessity of an analysis
that incorporates the strict cataphorics illustrated in (1.8) and the ambiguous ones
presented in (1.9) and (1.10). In order to provide a unified account of the different configurations these pronouns describe, Achard (2010) suggests expanding the analysis proposed by Smith (2000, 2004) where cataphoric pronouns in
examples such as (1.11) in English and German (respectively [1a] and [1b] in
Smith [2000: 483]) serve a "space designating function" (Smith 2000: 486, see also
Fauconnier 1985). As such, they "anticipate the mental spaces set up by space
builders" by "designating the spaces themselves in the grammar" (Smith 2000: 487).

(1.11) a. *I despise (it) that John voted for the governor*
        b. *Wir bedauern (es) daß Hans so dumm ist*
            'We regret (it) that Hans is so stupid'

Smith's analysis directly accounts for strict cataphorics such as *ceci* in (1.8). *Ceci* profiles the abstract nominal entity that announces the direct quote to follow, and the following quote elaborates this abstract setting. Examples such as (1.8) constitute a limiting case because the mental space that announces the upcoming entity is maximally abstract and devoid of specific contextual content. There are, however, no limits to the possible internal structure of this space, and it seems reasonable to imagine that it may be contextually elaborated to different degrees. Achard (2010) suggests that the ambiguous cases in (1.9) and (1.10) only differ from strict cataphorics in the level of contextual elaboration of the mental space that the pronoun designates. Rather than empty and maximally abstract, it is fully inclusive of the discourse context from which the referred entity is extracted for specific purposes. It is therefore reductive and misleading to analyze *ça* as referring forward to the complement clause. To the contrary, the pronoun also crucially refers back to an abstract region that contains the immediate discourse circumstances that the entity that follows the pronoun repeats, generalizes, or summarizes.

We are now in a position to reconsider the two constructions introduced in (1.4) and (1.5), repeated here for convenience:

(1.4)   *Pour la première fois je sentais qu'**il était possible** que ma mère vécût sans moi*
                    (Proust, M. *A l'ombre des jeunes filles en fleurs*: 648)
         'For the first time I felt it was possible for my mother to live [that my mother live] without me'

(1.5)   *Dubreuilh t'attend avec impatience. Ne te laisse pas embarquer dans son machin… – j'y suis déjà plus ou moins embarqué, dit Henri. – eh bien! Dépêche-toi de t'en sortir. Henri sourit: non. Ça n'est plus possible aujourd'hui de rester apolitique.*   (Beauvoir, S. de. *Les mandarins*: 101)
         'Dubreuilh is waiting for you impatiently. Don't let him drag you into his plan. – I am already more or less part of it, Henry said. – well get out of it as soon as you can. Henry smiled: no. It [this] is no longer possible to remain outside of politics these days'.

The previous discussion made it clear that the semantic distinction between *il* and *ça* that constitutes the cornerstone of the structural analyses of impersonals is untenable. First, the pronoun *il* is not a meaningless dummy with a strictly structural function, but refers to the field within which the situation that the complement describes can be entertained. In (1.4) that field is composed of the narrator's sensations, feelings, and more analytical thoughts about his relationship with his mother, which led him to the conclusion that she may be able to have a life without him. Second, the position that demonstrative pronouns (*ce, ça, c'*) cataphorically refer to the postverbal complement clause also needs to be reexamined because it fails to capture their additional anaphoric value. In (1.5), for instance, the postverbal infinitival clause *rester apolitique* constitutes Henry's explicit reformulation of his interlocutor's previous informal advice *Ne te laisse pas embarquer dans son machin*, and consequently *ça*'s reference needs to incorporate the previous context. The analysis of the pronoun's referent as the abstract region that contains the immediate circumstances from which the postverbal entity is extracted, captures its ambiguous nature.

The recognition of *il*'s semantic import eliminates the motivation for treating the impersonals and demonstratives respectively illustrated in (1.4) and (1.5) as structurally different. To the contrary, the analysis developed in Chapter 6 further underscores the semantic proximity between *il* and *ça* by showing that each pronoun represents a slightly different kind of abstract setting (see also Achard, in press). Consequently, in the context of the copular complement construction [*c*' + *être* + ADJECTIVE + COMPLEMENT CLAUSE] (developed in Chapter 6) in which the two kinds of pronouns participate, both are indeed impersonals and their specific distribution reflects both their closeness and subtle differences in meaning.[7]

Another objection to the similar treatment of *il* and *ça* in (1.4) and (1.5) comes from the pronouns' respective distribution in other environments. In this view *ça* cannot be considered an impersonal because it does not occur in all the contexts where *il* is attested. For example, Jones (1996: 128) notes that it is impossible with intrinsic impersonals as illustrated in (1.12) and (1.13), and it cannot have a left-dislocated counterpart as illustrated in (1.14) and (1.15). The examples in (1.12)–(1.15) are adapted from Jones (1996: 128):

(1.12)   *Il/*ça faut que tu viennes*
         'It/*this is necessary that you come'

(1.13)   *Il/*ça semble que Pierre aime Marie*
         'It/*this seems that Peter loves Mary'

(1.14)   *Ça/Il me plaît de voyager*
         'This/It pleases me to travel'

(1.15)   *Voyager, ça/*il me plaît*
         'To travel, this/*it pleases me'

This argument is not very convincing. The fact that *il* and *ça* are not always interchangeable certainly does not imply that they cannot overlap in some contexts. The claim that *ça* is always impersonal would obviously be untenable, but the imperfect

---

7.   Recall that *il* denotes the field, i.e. the knowledge structures that allow the conceptualizer to assess the entity in the complement. *Ça* refers to the abstract setting, namely the immediate context from which that entity is extracted. The difference between the two pronouns therefore essentially pertains to the salience of the conceptualizer's role in the epistemic evaluation of the entity that the complement clause describes. *Il* emphasizes the required mental effort, while *ça* is more directly concerned with the immediate context itself. This distinction is examined in detail in Chapter 6.

overlap between the two pronouns provides no serious challenge to the alternative proposal that demonstratives do have impersonal value in some environments.[8]

In fact, *ça*'s recognition as an impersonal pronoun in the construction illustrated in (1.5) appears quite natural, given the diachronic development of impersonals. In Old French both *ço* and *il* occur with impersonal meaning in very comparable timeframes. Impersonal verbs are attested with *ço* (or Ø) in *La vie de Saint Alexis* (middle of eleventh century), while the first examples of impersonal *il* are attested in the *Chanson de Roland* (1090) (Bruno 1936: 286). The relevance of these historical facts to the synchronic landscape of contemporary French is difficult to assess outside of a specific study well beyond the scope of this introduction. The impersonal construction has indeed changed quite radically over the years, and a careful investigation needs to be undertaken before the contemporary French *ce/ça* can be interpreted as the unquestioned reflexes of the Old French *ço*. Nevertheless, despite these valid objections the presence of a demonstrative in Old French impersonal constructions does provide some validity to the analysis of demonstratives as impersonals in specific contexts, and argues against their treatment as strictly distinct classes. Additionally, the impersonal *il* finds its contemporary roots in its earlier value as a neuter-demonstrative pronoun, so close in meaning to *cela* that the two forms have been considered semantically equivalent:

> Soit le type "Il est arrivé un malheur". Son origine nous reporte à l'époque où il était un démonstrative neutre (latin illud). "Il est arrivé" signifiait "cela est arrivé". On ajoutait en épexégèse: "(Ce qui est arrivé est) un malheur".

> 'Let's take an example such as "Il est arrivé un malheur". Its origin comes from a time when it was a neuter demonstrative (Latin illud). "Il est arrivé" meant "cela est arrivé". One added in an epexegesis: "(Ce qui est arrivé est) un malheur"'.
>
> (Bally 1932: 199, translation mine)

Some recent analyses have also treated the two pronouns together. For instance, Perlmutter and Postal consider both *il* in *il est évident qu'il est coupable* 'it is obvious that he is guilty' and *c'* in *c'est étonnant le nombre de gens qui croient tout cela* 'it is amazing the number of people who believe all this' as "dummy nominals" (Perlmutter and Postal 1983: 101). Olsson's (1986) account discussed in the next paragraph also treats both *il* and *ça* as impersonal pronouns. The account proposed in this monograph follows these proposals in analyzing *il* and *ça* as impersonal pronouns (in the appropriate contexts described in detail in Chapter 6), but it diverges from them in the recognition of their semantic import.

---

8.   In fact, a large part of the analysis developed in the upcoming chapters on different kinds of structures consists of precisely delineating the conditions under which these structures deserve the impersonal label.

The similarities between *il* and *ça* in copular complement constructions invalidate the claim that French impersonals are structurally distinct. This position has profound consequences because it forces us to abandon the narrow, syntactic account in which the impersonal domain is restricted to the structural confines of the *il* construction, to the benefit of a broader category that incorporates, at the very least, the demonstrative constructions illustrated in (1.5). A possible alternative to the syntactic position consists of treating the category in purely morphological terms. For example, Olsson (1986) suggests analyzing as impersonal:

> les verbes et les locutions précédés d'un pronom sujet neutre (*il, ce,* ou *cela/ça*) qui n'a aucun rapport avec ce qui précède dans le contexte, ni avec un mot particulier, ni avec le contenu total.

> 'the verbs and locutions preceded by a neuter subject (*il ce,* or *cela/ça*) which has no connection with the preceding context, either with a specific word or the global content'.   (Olsson 1986: 29, translation mine)

This solution successfully broadens the scope of French impersonals by incorporating the demonstrative constructions, but it also faces a number of difficulties. First, Olsson's definition of the class of neuter-subject pronouns is difficult to maintain in light of the previous discussion of the respective meanings of *il* and *ça*. If *il* can reasonably be considered relatively independent from the previous context, the anaphoric/cataphoric character that *ça* commonly displays seriously challenges the claim that it has no connection to the preceding discourse. Second, a purely morphological account fails to take into account the different kinds of constructions in which demonstratives participate, and thus includes some that may not deserve the impersonal label. For example, intuitively for now but arguments will be provided in the following section (as well as Chapter 6), the single predicate construction in (1.16) differs from its copular counterpart in (1.5) by the degree of generality of the event the complement describes. Whereas the complement content in (1.5) is available to a "generalized conceptualizer" (Langacker 2009: 115, see also Section 3), the content of the complement in (1.16) represents the exclusive conception of the hearer, explicitly coded by the second-person singular object pronoun *te* (*t'*).[9] Consequently, because it lacks the level of generality commonly expected of impersonals it seems difficult to accept the single predicate construction in (1.16) as an impersonal, even though it respects Olsson's morphological criteria:

---

9. Note that in the situations illustrated in (1.16), the presence of *il* would be impossible. Chapter 6 argues that this impossibility represents a further argument in favor of not analyzing them as impersonals.

(1.16)   *et toi, mauvais gredin, que je t'y reprenne à courir les routes en faisant le conspi-*
         rateur!... ça t'étonne que je t'aie tiré de là, hein?

                                                    (Adam, P. *L'enfant d'Austerlitz*: 280)

         'As for you good-for-nothing scoundrel, don't let me catch you running around
         doing mischief! It [this] surprises you I got you out of this doesn't it?'

The brief overview presented in this introduction shows that French impersonals cannot adequately be characterized using syntactic or morphological criteria. If French does indeed possess a distinctive impersonal class (to be discussed further in the next section), it therefore needs to be defined in functional terms. The notion of a functional category will become clearer as the analysis unfolds, but in this introduction it is important to contrast it with morphological and syntactic categories. Using the structures described in this introduction as an example, *il* constructions are morphologically distinctive because of the specific form of their initial pronoun, but the previous discussion showed that they are not syntactically distinctive because *il*'s semantic import makes it impossible to treat it as a mere structural placeholder. Despite their morphological differences, the *il* and *ça* constructions presented in (1.4) and (1.5) are functionally similar because they describe the same kind of event (to be developed in Chapter 6).

The analysis developed in the following chapters argues that French impersonals constitute a functional category in which participating constructions recruited from various morphosyntactic origins describe a specific kind of event (to be developed in the next section). The functional nature of the impersonal category has two important ramifications. First, no morphological category (not even *il* constructions [to be explained in the next section as well as Chapter 3]) is exclusively composed of impersonal constructions. Second, a complete inventory of the morphological origin of all French impersonals is extremely difficult to provide since the category is largely independent from morphological criteria. The analysis developed in this monograph considers these two points in turn. Chapters 3 to 5 show that if a large majority of *il* constructions do meet the functional definition of impersonals, a small minority does not, and thus cannot be considered impersonal despite their morphological form. Chapters 6 to 8 illustrate how some constructions from other morphological categories (demonstratives in Chapter 6, middles in Chapter 7, and indefinite *on* in Chapter 8) can also deserve the impersonal label, and how they can be distinguished from their morphologically similar counterparts that do not. As a starting point, the next section introduces the functional category of impersonals cross-linguistically, and provides an overview of the French impersonal domain.

2. Toward a French impersonal functional category

In the functional view, the impersonal category is bound together by a number of shared semantic functions. As opposed to the narrow impersonal domain of syntactic investigation, the functional impersonal category represents a broad area composed of a (potentially) large set of constructions that may not have any morphological or syntactic traits in common. The discovery of the set of functional commonalities that these constructions share, however, has proven difficult. To date, the only universally accepted observation is that all impersonals "lack a definite human agent as subject", and "may all be seen as a means of agent backgrounding or defocusing" (Siewierska 2008a, note 3; see also Sansó 2005; Słoń 2007, as well as Shibatani 1985 about defocusing).

This broad impersonal category is obviously difficult to delineate, both language internally and typologically. Within a single language, different researchers use the label to describe entirely different constructions (Siewierska 2008a, 2008b). Typologically, since impersonals only unanimously share the presence of a noncanonical subject, i.e. a subject that does not possess the morphological, semantic, and syntactic reflexes commonly exhibited by subjects of transitive clauses (Langacker 2006; Helasvuo and Vilkuna 2008; Divjak and Janda 2008; Creissels 2008a; Malchukov and Ogawa 2011), the category is most often defined negatively, as the departure that the constructions that compose it exhibit from the coding of a prototypical transitive clause. Malchukov and Siewierska's description of the paper by Malchukov and Ogawa in their edited volume provides a clear illustration of that negative definition: "Building on the work of Keenan (1976), they propose to distinguish R-impersonals (with a notional subject lacking in referential properties), A-impersonals (with a notional subject lacking in agentivity), and T-impersonals (with a notional subject lacking in topicality)". In the current functional view, impersonals constitute an eclectic category composed of "various types of predicative constructions that do not show the canonical manifestations of a subject" (Creissels 2008a: 4; see also Helasvuo and Vilkuna 2008), and the category is best represented as a "set of features" rather than a "coherent concept" (Helasvuo and Vilkuna 2008: 242). Most researchers recognize the usefulness of this kind of definition typologically, but some are more skeptical about its relevance to the description of individual languages. For instance, Helasvuo and Vilkuna (2008: 242) suggest that "impersonality may be a useful tool for cross-linguistic comparison because it directs the analyst's attention to a broad field of phenomena that share the same properties; but it does not seem to us to be a necessary notion in the description of individual languages." The analysis proposed in this monograph challenges Helasvuo and Vilkuna's pessimism for at least one language. The following chapters show that (1) the impersonal category does represent a useful concept to describe French grammar because it groups together a coherent kind of event, and (2) it is possible to delineate a class of French impersonal constructions.

3.   The French impersonal category

French impersonals represent a coherent natural class because they systematically code highly general and predictable events available to anyone in the appropriate circumstances, the occurrence of which cannot be imputed to a specific, well-delineated source. This position will be elaborated throughout the following chapters but as an introduction to its most relevant concepts; befitting the understanding that impersonals radically diverge from transitives, it is useful to compare the two types of clauses in some detail.

Transitive clauses prototypically describe the energetic interaction between at least two participants (Hopper and Thompson 1980; Langacker 1987; Lazard 1998 among many others). Transitivity involves several parameters "each of which suggests a scale according to which clauses can be ranked" (Hopper and Thompson 1980: 251). For example, the clause in bold print in (1.17) reaches the highest level of transitivity because it ranks highest on a scale of agency, volition, and kinesis (soldiers intended to perform the highly kinetic action of killing), but also in affectedness and individuation (the dead soldiers are obviously totally affected, and easy to delineate).[10]

(1.17)   *En quinze jours, **la 1ère armée a tué 10000 allemands**, fait 18000 prisonniers, enlevé 120 canons.*   (Gaulle, C. de. *Mémoires de guerre, le salut*: 136)
          'Within two weeks, the first army killed 1000 Germans, took 18,000 prisoners, removed 120 guns.'

Its individual parameters taken together, the clause in (1.17) describes a highly specific energetic interaction occurring within precise time limits between a well-delineated highly volitional agent (the soldiers) and an equally well-individuated terminally affected patient (the 18,000 Germans). The event the predicate describes is therefore highly specific in the sense that its occurrence is not likely to be repeated again in exactly the same manner, the responsibility for its accomplishment rests strictly on the agent, and the patient represents the sole affected entity. The strict delimitation of the two participants renders the action that the predicate describes inaccessible to any other potential parties. More precisely, no person other than those involved in the interaction may have any direct experience of that action.

The conceptual organization of a transitive clause strongly contrasts with its impersonal counterparts (also in bold print) illustrated in (1.18):

---

10. Hopper and Thompson's (1980: 252) complete list of transitivity parameters includes kinesis, aspect, punctuality, volitionality, affirmation, mode, agency, affectedness of O, and individuation of O.

(1.18)   *Bien que vêtu de sa seule chemise de nuit, Mathias ouvre la croisée.* **Il ne fait pas froid. Il pleut** *encore, mais à peine; et* **il n'y a pas de vent.** *Le ciel est uniformément gris. Rien ne subsiste de la brusque risée qui chassait le grain contre les carreaux, il y a quelques minutes. Le temps est désormais très calme.* **Il tombe une petite pluie, fine, continue, sans violence.**

(Robbe-Grillet, A. *Le voyeur*: 234)

'Although he wore only his nightgown, Mathias opened the window. It is not cold. It is still raining, but hardly so; and there is no wind. The sky is gray all over. Nothing remains of the sharp breeze that pushed the rain against the glass a few minutes ago. The weather is now very still. A little sustained drizzle falls quietly [it falls a little rain, continuously, without violence]'.

The impersonal clauses in bold print in (1.18) present a very different conceptual organization. The weather predicates do not code an interaction but a continuous state that involves no participants. The predicate is exclusively concerned with setting the atmospheric scene, and that scene is available to any person being at the right location. In that sense, and unlike the transitive interaction illustrated in (1.17), the processes in (1.18) are available to a "generalized conceptualizer", namely anyone present at the appropriate location (Langacker 2009: 115) who would enjoy the same experience. Weather predicates may describe the most generalized form of impersonal events because atmospheric conditions are independent of any external presence, but other impersonal constructions similarly involve a generalized conceptualizer even though their predicate may contain at least one participant in its lexical semantic structure. For example, in (1.7) repeated here, the speaker assesses the presence of an entity *une autre [édition]* 'an alternative edition' in reality. That entity is not only available to the speaker but to anyone in possession of the relevant knowledge base that allows them to assert its existence. The predicate *exister* describes a stable and hence highly predictable configuration shared by anyone with the appropriate information:

(1.7)   *le désespéré que vous avez eu tant de peine à vous procurer, dites- vous, est, sans doute, l'édition Soirat.* **Il en existe** <u>*une autre*</u> *qui vient de paraître, à mon insu et sans mon autorisation.*   (Bloy, L. *Journal*: 74)

'The desperate [person] you say you had such trouble finding is most likely the Soirat Edition. There exists an alternative edition which was just released, unbeknownst to me and without my permission'.

One of the main claims of this monograph is that the French impersonal class should include any structure that describes events at the highest level of generalization and predictability, regardless of their morphological realization. As initial selection criteria, let us suggest that any structure should be considered impersonal provided that (1) it defocuses or backgrounds the agent of the predicate, and (2) its predicate describes a situation at a degree of stability and prediction that makes it available to a generalized conceptualizer, or in other words virtually anyone in the appropriate situation. It should be noted, however, that the diagnostic value of these two criteria is only posited for French and seeks no further typological validity. The only claim this monograph makes is that French recognizes a functional impersonal class to code highly general and predictable events that cannot be imputed to a specific cause, and that the different structures that describe those events should be considered members of that class. In addition to the *il* impersonals investigated in Chapters 3 to 5, Chapters 6 through 8 show that demonstrative, middle, and indefinite subject (*on*) constructions are recruited from their own morphosyntactic classes because they serve similar functions.

In addition to *il* impersonals, the two aforementioned criteria are met in a number of structures, such as the demonstrative in (1.19), the middle construction in (1.20), and the indefinite pronoun structure in (1.21), all indicated in bold print in their respective contexts. The basic insight elaborated in the following chapters is that these four constructions should be considered impersonals because they are functionally equivalent.

(1.19) *D'ailleurs il n'est pas tout à fait vrai que le chemin de fer ait un tracé aussi raide, aussi indifférent et brutal qu'on veut bien le dire. Ainsi que tu me le faisais remarquer l'an dernier, en haut de La Sèche, c'est **étonnant** de voir comme il s'est incorporé au paysage*
        (Alain-Fournier, H. *Correspondance avec J. Rivière*: 28)
'Anyway, it is not quite true that the railroad track cuts such a steep, indifferent and brutish path as people have said. As you were indicating to me last year, at the top of La Séche, it [this] is surprising to see how well it blends [itself] into the landscape'

(1.20) *Il note que le pain sans levain est cuit sur des plaques de tôle et ressemble à de la galette ou aux crêpes de carnaval, que **le saucisson d'Arles se fait avec de la viande de mulet**.*   (Durry, MJ. *Gérard de Nerval et le mythe*: 82)
'He notes that yeast-free bread is cooked on flat metal sheets and resembles biscuits or the pancakes of carnival time; that the sausage from Arles is made [makes itself] with mule meat'.

(1.21) ***On** ne trouve pas toujours facilement, en Espagne, un endroit pour camper, à cause de l'absence de bois, et de la culture intensive.*
        (T'Serstevens, A. *L'itinéraire espagnol*: 16)
'One cannot always easily find a place to camp in Spain, because of the lack of forests, end extensive agriculture.'

The notion of functional equivalence is intuitively simple and narratively powerful, as illustrated in (1.22) in which different constructions (in bold print) code a
single semantic configuration:

(1.22)   A *l'US Air Force*, **il a été demandé** *de retarder la mise au point du futur chasseur*
          F-22. L'Armée de Terre **s'est vue fermement prier** *de trouver une alternative à*
          son futur hélicoptère Comanche. Les Marines ont dû imaginer leur avenir sans
          l'avion-hélicoptère V-22 "Osprey" et **on a conseillé** *à la Navy de ralentir son*
          programme de mise au point du nouveau sous-marin d'attaque.   (AFP)
          'The U.S. Air Force [to the U.S. Air Force, it] was asked to delay the design of
          its future combat fighter F-22. The Army was [saw itself being] firmly asked
          to find an alternative to its future Comanche helicopter. The Marines had to
          imagine their future without the plane-helicopter "Osprey", and the Navy was
          advised [one advised the Navy] to slow down its program of designing a new
          attack sub-marine'.[11]

The paragraph in (1.22) describes the requests for frugality that budget cuts have
forced the four branches of the U.S. armed forces to endure. The author's narrative strategy maintains perfect symmetry across the four victims in an effort to
underscore the drastic character of the measures and the impossibility of eluding
them. The conceptual/semantic structure of each clause is identical. As the agent,
the American government represents the source of the orders in each instance,
and individual branches of the military constitute the patient or affected entity, the
nature of the affectation coming in the form of a program to be eliminated. This
semantic organization, however, is represented by different syntactic constructions.

---

11. The two impersonal criteria can obviously be satisfied by the predicate's lexical semantic
structure. In particular, this is the case for the weather verbs illustrated in (1.18) where the agent
is naturally defocused and the process obviously available to anyone. It is also worth noting
that even though the four constructions illustrated in (1.7), (1.19), (1.20), and (1.21) constitute
the focus of the analysis proposed in this monograph, they are certainly not exhaustive of the
impersonal category in French. As indicated at the beginning of this section, any construction
that satisfies the two aforementioned criteria can legitimately be called impersonal. This includes
at the very least some passive constructions, as well as many other structures more difficult to
precisely enumerate. For example, in (1.22), *les Marines ont dû imaginer leur avenir sans l'avion-*
hélicoptère V-22 "Osprey" 'the Marines had to imagine their future without the plane-helicopter
"Osprey", is obviously equivalent to impersonal #*il a été demandé aux Marines d'imaginer leur*
futur sans l'avion-hélicoptère V-22 "Osprey". If the construction *avoir dû* + INFINITIVE exhibits
this equivalence reliably, it should indeed be analyzed as possessing an impersonal sense. The
issue of a possible complete inventory of French impersonals is left for further research. The four
constructions investigated in this manuscript are simply intended to provide a methodology to
approach it.

In the impersonal (first) and the indefinite *on* (third) construction, the patient is coded as oblique, introduced by the preposition *à*. The agent is not explicitly specified in the impersonal but is coded as subject (albeit in a very general way) in the indefinite construction. Finally, in the highly specific (second) *se voir* construction, the patient is coded as subject and the agent is left implicit. Despite their syntactic differences, these three constructions are commonly treated as different kinds of passives because they serve the same semantic function.

One of the goals of this monograph is to provide justification for the functional equivalence of the *il, ça*, middle, and indefinite impersonals. The analyses conducted in the following chapters investigate the precise conditions under which they can legitimately be called impersonal. At this introductory stage, however, the plausibility of treating these four constructions as functionally equivalent can be illustrated in two ways. First, each can be substituted for the other almost freely, with minimal semantic alteration. For instance, the attested *il* impersonal in (1.23) can be replaced by a demonstrative in (1.24), a middle in (1.25), and the indefinite pronoun on in (1.26) without noticeable meaning difference:[12]

(1.23)   *Miguel Mejia Baron a succédé au poste d'entraîneur à l'Argentin Cesar Luis Menotti à la fin de l'année 1992 et a qualifié l'équipe nationale pour la phase finale du Mondial. Selon le président de la Fédération, "**il était nécessaire** de poursuivre cette collaboration".*   (AFP)
‘Miguel Mejia Baron took over the coaching position from Argentine Cesar Luis Menotti at the end of 1992, and he qualified the team for the final phase of the World Cup. According to the President of the Federation, "it was necessary to continue this collaboration"’.

(1.24)   #*C'était nécessaire de poursuivre cette collaboration*
‘it was necessary to continue this collaboration’

(1.25)   #*Cette collaboration devait **se poursuivre***
‘This collaboration had to continue itself’

(1.26)   #*(L') **on** se devait de poursuivre cette collaboration*
‘One (we) had to continue this collaboration’

Similarly, the substitution of the attested middle in (1.27) by an *il* and *c'* impersonal in (1.28) or an indefinite pronoun construction in (1.29) also preserves an overwhelming part of the original meaning:

---

12. The notion of functional equivalence does not imply that these sentences are exactly identical in meaning. The subtle variations that exist between the different constructions are considered in the course of the various analyses.

(1.27) *A la fin il explique à mon amie américaine que **le livre en question ne se trouve pas en magasin**, mais qu'il en a cependant un exemplaire qu'il pourra lui céder*
(Green, J. *Journal. T. 5. 1946–1950*: 55)
'In the end, he explains to my American friend that the book in question cannot be found [doesn't find itself] in a store, but that he nonetheless has a copy he will be able to give her'

(1.28) *#il /c'est impossible de trouver le livre en question en magasin…*
'it is impossible to find the book in question in a store…'

(1.29) *#on ne trouve pas le livre en question en magasin…*
'one cannot find the book in question in a store…'

Second, the functional equivalence of the four impersonal constructions is confirmed by their behavior in translation. For instance, while English 'it' most frequently corresponds to French impersonal *il* in parallel corpora as illustrated in (1.30), demonstrative *ça* in (1.31), middle *se* in (1.32) and indefinite *on* in (1.33) and (1.34) also constitute attested equivalents to the English impersonal:[13]

(1.30) **It is** therefore **necessary** that the Commission should now do some tightening up.

(1.30′) **Il est** dès lors **nécessaire** que la Commission fasse des efforts de son côté.

(1.31) **It is true** that the problem of the forestry sector is an extremely complex one.

(1.31′) **C'est vrai** que le problème du secteur du bois est terriblement complexe.

(1.32) The Commission should use these proposals to prioritise its reaction to the slump in wood sales, for what we had feared is actually taking place, and **it is becoming impossible** to sell wood.

(1.32′) Au titre de celles – ci, la Commission se doit de réagir en priorité à la mévente du bois, car voilà que ce que l'on redoutait arrive, **le bois ne se vend plus**.

(1.33) Indeed, **it is debatable** whether this could be carried through at all without amending the Treaty.

(1.33′) **On peut** également **se demander** si c'est seulement possible sans modification du Traité.

(1.34) It is a question of doing what is technically possible; obviously **it is not possible to do anymore**, but we must be sufficiently ambitious.

(1.34′) Il s'agit bien de faire tout notre possible techniquement. **On ne peut** certes **pas** demander plus, mais nous devons être suffisamment ambitieux.

---

13. The examples in (1.30)–(1.34) come from a parallel corpus of EEU parliament deliberations. The English and French examples in parallel corpora are numbered individually using prime numbers rather than glossed because it is often difficult to know which constitutes the original.

It is important to note that each construction satisfies the two criteria of impersonality proposed at the beginning of this section in its own idiosyncratic way. Starting with the agent, perhaps the most common defocusing strategy selects an alternative entity to the agent as subject. Although it is investigated more thoroughly in Chapters 3 to 5, this introduction already mentioned that *il* and *ça* constructions both select some abstract location (respectively the field and setting in Achard [2010]) as their subject. Similarly, the middle construction illustrated in (1.20) also defocuses its agent by selecting an alternative participant as the main figure in the relation the verb codes. In (1.20) the agent (the cook) is not explicitly mentioned, and the final product is selected as subject.[14] However, the selection of an alternative entity as the subject does not constitute the only way of defocusing the agent of the predicate. Another strategy consists of construing that agent at a level of generality sufficiently high to include any conceptualizer in a position to experience the process that predicate describes. This is the case in the indefinite pronoun construction in (1.21), where *on* refers to the agent of the traveling process, but that agent is so general that it includes virtually any traveler or potential traveler to Spain. In this case, to be further developed in Chapter 8, the agent's low "delimitation" (Langacker 2009: 123, see also Chapter 8), i.e. the level of specificity at which the nominal that describes the participants in the verbal process is described, serves as defocusing strategy.

The four constructions diverge more radically with respect to the second criterion, namely the availability of the process the predicate codes to a generalized conceptualizer (Langacker 2009: 115; Achard 2010). First, none of the constructions considered in this monograph are consistently functionally impersonal. Even the *il* construction, the most consistently impersonal among them, includes instances that do not meet the category's functional definition, as in (1.35) for instance, where the event that the predicate describes is too specific to be generally available (to be developed shortly, as well as in in Chapter 3):

(1.35)   *Entends- tu ce que je te dis? Joseph hocha la tête. – tu attendras dans les bois que la nuit tombe. À ce moment, tu descendras dans le ravin et tu rejoindras la route. Tu attendras encore, une heure s'il le faut.* **Il passera** <u>une voiture</u> *qui ralentira et s'arrêtera à la hauteur du ravin pour te laisser monter.*

(Green, J. *Moïra: roman*: 244)

'Can you hear what I am telling you? Joseph nodded. You will wait in the woods until nightfall. At that time, you will go down the ravine toward the road. You will wait again, one hour if you have to. A car will come [there will pass a car]. It will slow down and stop by the ravine to let you in'.

---

14. This strategy is obviously also used in passives. These constructions are not discussed at length in this monograph.

The situation is even more extreme for the demonstrative, middle, and indefinite impersonals because they are recruited from much larger morphosyntactic classes, most instances of which are not general enough to share the impersonal label. The identification of an impersonal subset within these larger categories therefore needs to show not only that the predicate in some constructions is indeed more generally available than in others, but also how these constructions acquire their level of generality. The remainder of this section concentrates on the generality of the impersonal subset; the next section examines these constructions' position within their own morphosyntactic classes.

The difference between the specific demonstrative in (1.16) and its impersonal counterpart in (1.19) predominantly resides in the higher level of generality of the impersonal construction:

(1.16)   *et toi, mauvais gredin, que je t'y reprenne à courir les routes en faisant le conspi-rateur!... **ça t'étonne** que je t'aie tiré de là, hein?*

                                                     (Adam, P. *L'enfant d'Austerlitz*: 280)
          'As for you good-for-nothing scoundrel, don't let me catch you running around doing mischief! ...It [this] surprises you I got you out of this doesn't it?'

(1.19)   *D'ailleurs il n'est pas tout à fait vrai que le chemin de fer ait un tracé aussi raide, aussi indifférent et brutal qu'on veut bien le dire. Ainsi que tu me le faisais remarquer l'an dernier, en haut de La Sèche, **c'est étonnant** de voir comme il s'est incorporé au paysage*

                                          (Alain-Fournier, H. *Correspondance avec J. Rivière*: 28)
          'Anyway, it is not quite true that the railroad tracks cuts such a steep, indifferent and brutish path as people have said. As you were indicating to me last year, at the top of La Séche, it [this] is surprising to see how well it blends [itself] into the landscape'

In (1.16), the internal state that *étonner* describes occurs at a precise temporal and spatial location among precisely outlined participants, namely the speaker and hearer, specifically mentioned by the second person pronoun *t'*. Importantly, the hearer is the only person concerned with the occurrence of the verbal process in the sense that no one else shares his surprise. Furthermore, that process only takes place once and cannot be expected to be available at a different time, another location, or between different participants. Because it is strictly confined to the specific instance that the sentence in (1.16) describes, *étonner* can be characterized as a specific process. The situation is entirely different in (1.19). The surprise the predicate *étonner* describes is not restricted to a specific participant but shared by anyone who happens to look at the described landscape. The process that *étonner* codes is thus general enough for the construction it participates in to be called impersonal.

The middle and indefinite pronoun constructions respectively illustrated in (1.20) and (1.21) also exhibit a high level of generality. *Se faire* 'is made' in (1.20) is not restricted to a particular time, location, or set of participants, but refers to any situation in which the recipe is implemented. Consequently, it cannot only be apprehended in one specific instance but is available to a general conceptualizer, i.e., anyone in a position to experience a valid instantiation of the profiled process. In the context presented in (1.20), *se faire* can thus be repeated, and even expected to occur any time the conditions are right. In this sense, it is considered general enough to be called impersonal. Similarly, the example in (1.21) does not describe a specific excursion to Spain but the expectation that should accompany any potential traveler to that country. In the case of (1.21), this level of generality is a direct consequence of the low level of delimitation of the indefinite subject. This point is considered in further detail in Chapter 8.

4.   A constructional proposal

How do the subsets of demonstrative, middle, and indefinite subject (*on*) impersonals emerge out of the context of their respective morphosyntactic categories? More precisely, since generality is a scalar notion, how can specific instances that possess it in the required amount be precisely identified? Let us first note that it is not always be possible to draw the line between impersonal and nonimpersonal structures with surgical precision, but that the fuzzy boundaries of the impersonal category are not particularly problematic. In the cognitive linguistics tradition, linguistic categories in general are overwhelmingly fuzzy. Furthermore, and more interestingly, the evaluation of the two criteria within specific structures, and thus the treatment of these structures as impersonals, is greatly facilitated by the clustering of closely related senses into specific constructions (Goldberg 1995, 2006; Langacker 1987a, 1991, 2005). In some cases these constructions are easily identified by morphosyntactic criteria. For example, Chapter 6 (see also Achard 2010) shows that demonstratives reliably acquire the level of generality required of impersonals within the confines of the copular complement construction (*c' + être* + ADJECTIVE + COMPLEMENT CLAUSE). In other words, the difference in status between (1.16) and (1.19) can be attributed to the latter's constructional structure. Other constructions are not so easily recognized, but they can nonetheless always be identified by the presence of some semantic or pragmatic features that allow us to distinguish them from their structurally similar neighbors (to be illustrated shortly, see also Fillmore [1982], Lakoff [1987]). Given the fluid nature of the proposed criteria, these constructions provide islands of regularity within which impersonals can reliably be identified, and therefore constitute one of the main organizing principles of the impersonal category in French.

The centrality of the notion of construction to the organization of French impersonals emerges from the following chapters, but in order to introduce its scope and anticipate the direction of the upcoming analyses it is useful to briefly consider an example of the kind of clustering effects around which French impersonals are organized. These effects obviously do not concern *il* impersonals that are specialized in that function, but they are attested in the three other morphosyntactic classes investigated in this monograph. The case of the middles briefly presented in the remainder of this section anticipates the analysis proposed in Chapter 7, and serves to illustrate the more general principle at work in the three separate classes.

As indicated in Section 3, the middle construction illustrated in (1.20) satisfies the first impersonal requirement by definition because it naturally defocuses the agent by selecting an alternative participant as subject. In order to meet the second criterion, however, the verbal process needs to be evaluated along a continuum of generality in order to determine if the structure that contains it can be called impersonal. The presence of stable configurations renders the decision more systematic. These configurations constitute constructional islands within which different instances exhibit specific pragmatic characteristics that distinguish them from their morphosyntactically similar neighbors.

The example illustrated in (1.36) represents a valid instance of the middle category, but it cannot be accepted as an impersonal because the event the verbal process codes is too specific to be generally available. Its occurrence is clearly restricted to a particular place and time, and the uniquely identifiable participants it involves make it unlikely to be reproduced in a similar fashion for other conceptualizers to experience.

(1.36) Hero, brusquement: *Tu m'as compris! (Il serrait son verre dans sa main, le verre se casse.* Ils regardent le verre tous deux dans la main de Héro qui dit doucement. *Excuse-moi, mon vieux. J'aime casser.*

(Anouilh, J. *La répétition: ou, l'amour puni:* 75)
'Hero, suddenly: You understood me! (He was holding his glass in his hand, the glass breaks [itself]. Both of them look at the glass in Hero's hand, and Hero says softly: Excuse me, Old Man. I like to break [things]'.

The processes that the middle construction describes become progressively more general if the agent and the circumstances responsible for its realization can be clearly identified as stable so that future occurrences can be predicted with confidence, and hence be potentially available to everyone. Consequently, middles are more likely to have impersonal value when their subjects can, in some sense, be shown to facilitate the occurrence of the described process. Importantly, this facilitating capacity does not represent a semantic role (such as agency for example), but a pragmatic feature associated with the subject at various levels of strength in different circumstances. The example in (1.37) illustrates the difference between facilitation and agency. The agent of the writing process can logically only be the author, but the very topic of his work nonetheless prominently figures in its success. In this sense, the book itself (or more precisely its topic) can be said to facilitate the writing task:

(1.37) *Mais tu as eu une critique étonnante, dit Louis d'un ton encourageant; il sourit.*
        "Il faut dire que tu es tombé sur un sujet en or; pour ça tu es verni; quand on
        tient un pareil sujet, **le livre s'écrit tout seul**".
                                                        (Beauvoir, S. de. *Les mandarins*: 249)
        'But your reviews were surprising, Louis said in an encouraging tone; he smiles.
        "You have to admit you came across a golden topic; you were lucky that way;
        with a topic like that, the book writes itself"'.

This pragmatic notion of facilitation plays a critical role in assessing the reliability and expectability of the described process because it neutralizes the idiosyncratic characteristics of individual agents. From the standpoint of the syntax and semantics represented in the construction's argument structure, middle impersonals are thus perfectly similar to other middles, but their subject's role in facilitating the occurrence of the profiled process renders the latter easier to expect and thus available to everyone.

The subject's role in the occurrence of the described process is a flexible and gradual notion, and consequently the impersonal status of middle constructions can also only be evaluated along a continuum. However, some specific environments (or constructions) can be identified where middles unquestionably deserve the impersonal label. These environments distinguish themselves from the rest of the middle class by the specific set of semantic/pragmatic features they contain, and thus constitute stable constructional islands. In the first one already illustrated in (1.20) and also in (1.38), the verbal process is constitutive of the subject in the sense that it represents an integral part of the definition of the entity that the subject codes.

(1.38) *Elle secoua la tête: "j'ai trente-sept ans et je ne connais aucun métier. Je peux*
        me faire chiffonnière; et encore! – Ça s'apprend, un métier; rien ne t'empêche
        d'apprendre".   (Beauvoir, S. de. *Les mandarins*: 283)
        'She shook her head: "I am thirty seven years old and I have no skills. I could
        be a rag picker, if that! – A trade, you can always learn it [that learns itself a
        trade]; nothing prevents you from learning"'.

In the examples in (1.20) and (1.38), the verbal process can clearly be expected because its occurrence is fully subsumed in the definition of the entity that the subject represents. In (1.20) mule meat constitutes a necessary ingredient of the saucisson d'Arles, without which the latter would not deserve its name. Its presence is thus fully predictable because it constitutes a critical part of the recipe. Similarly, in (1.38) mastering a trade necessarily entails an apprenticeship period, and that period represents a legitimate part of what a trade is. This definitional characteristic of the examples in (1.20) and (1.38) or, in other words, the way in which the verbal process is constitutive of the subject's semantic definition constitutes the pragmatic feature that groups together a large amount of middles and allows them to acquire impersonal status. In terms of the methodology adopted here, this feature anchors a middle impersonal constructional island.

In the second island illustrated in (1.39), the occurrence of the verbal process can also be expected because it is required by a set of social norms or conventions. In this construction the predicates pertain to the precise way in which things should be done by anyone involved in specific activities. Because social norming applies to everyone, the occurrence of the process that the predicate codes is available to any conceptualizer, and the construction can rightfully be called impersonal.

(1.39)   *Dans les livres, les gens se font des déclarations d'amour, de haine, ils mettent leur cœur en phrases; dans la vie, jamais on ne prononce de paroles qui pèsent.* **Ce qui "se dit" est aussi réglé que ce qui "se fait".**

(Beauvoir, S. de. *Mémoires d'une jeune fille rangée*: 119)
'In books, people claim their love or hatred for each other, they pour their hearts in their words; in life, no one ever pronounces words with any weight. What "is said [says itself]" is as tightly regulated as what "is done [does itself]"'.

The quotation marks around *se dire* and *se faire* in (1.39) represent the highly conventionalized character of these predicates that indicate the strict social codes that govern how people act and what they say. Their deontic character is obvious. The example in (1.39) does not describe what people do and say, but what society allows them to do and say. The specificity of this deontic construction is clearly illustrated by the difference between *se dit* in (1.39) and the identical lexical form in (1.40) that merely describes the surrounding discourse and has no deontic value. The difference in meaning between (1.39) and (1.40) when the two predicates are lexically identical clearly shows that the construction itself contributes to the deontic value that the sentence in (1.39) conveys.

(1.40)   *– Nous sommes en 1920, Jo. Vos idées sont d'un autre temps. Il faut vous réveiller, sortir de vous-même, écouter ce qui se dit autour de vous.*

(Green, J. *Moïra: roman*: 173)
'– We are in 1920, Jo. Your ideas belong to another time. You have to wake up, get out of yourself, listen to what people are saying [says itself] around you'.

The deontic value of this constructional cluster allows the verbal process to be expected because everyone is subject to the same social norming, and is therefore bound to act in a similar manner. The process is thus general enough to warrant the impersonal label because the social rules that require its occurrence and thus ensure its expectability make it available to any conceptualizer. In the kind of cases illustrated in (1.39), the deontic pragmatic feature provides the motivation for a second constructional island within which middles can be considered impersonal.

This brief example merely intends to illustrate two points developed throughout the following chapters for the demonstrative, middle, and indefinite pronoun constructions. First, the impersonal sense of these constructions represents a well-attested semantic extension from its more basic senses. Second, impersonal senses cluster within morphosyntactically distinct (demonstratives) or pragmatically determined (middles and indefinites) into constructional islands that predominantly constitute the organizing principle of the French impersonal category.

5.   Recapitulation and discussion

This introduction has emphasized the difficulty of finding the right properties to precisely delineate a French impersonal class. Syntactic criteria need to be abandoned because the recognition of *il*'s meaning not only critically challenges its purported pleonastic status, but also highlights its semantic similarity with the demonstrative pronouns *ce* and *ça*. A successful account of the impersonal category therefore needs to expand its scope beyond the narrow confines of the *il* construction. Morphological criteria fare no better because they allow the inclusion of structures not general enough to be considered impersonals, and also wrongly exclude functionally related constructions with different morphology. This introduction suggests two functional criteria to define a French impersonal class: a structure is called impersonal if (1) the agent of the verbal process is defocused, and (2) that process is presented at a level of generality that makes it available to anyone in a position to experience it. The account proposed in this monograph follows the broader functionalist and typological traditions (Malchukov and Siewierska 2011; Siewierska 2008a, 2008b; Sansó 2005; Słoń 2007 inter alia) because the demonstrative, middle, and indefinite pronoun constructions have been argued to have similar status in many other languages. However, the present account elaborates on their initial insight in three major ways. First, it provides a methodology for precisely delineating the conditions under which these constructions truly have an impersonal value. While the two suggested criteria are general and scalar, their evaluation within the four structures investigated in the following chapters is rendered possible by the clustering of related senses into

specific constructions. Because of the flexibility of the criteria, these constructional clusters constitute the main organizing principle of French impersonals.
Second, the impersonal criteria combine to provide a positive definition of the
category, namely a coherent class of stable configurations that can reliably be
observed and anticipated by anyone in a position to do so. Third, it shows that if
the French impersonal category is not delineated by morphological or syntactic
criteria, it is nonetheless structured around specific constructions that exhibit
semantic similarity and functional equivalence.

The hypothesis presented in this introductory chapter raises a number of questions and possible objections. The first pertains to the validity of attempting to
delineate a French impersonal class. Given the fluid nature of the proposed criteria,
and the fact that no syntactic or morphological features can reliably be used to
identify it, then perhaps the whole enterprise is simply misguided. To a certain
extent, this objection is valid. Each of the structures under investigation in this
monograph possesses a clearly recognizable morphosyntactic form that determines category membership. Demonstratives are reliably coded by *ce* or *ça*, the
presence of the *se* marker identifies middle structures, and *on* allows us to identify
indefinite pronoun constructions. If these three morphosyntactic categories are
described in sufficient detail, one could argue that labeling a subset of them as
impersonal provides little additional insight (Helasvuo and Vilkuna 2008:242).
This objection, however, does not bear scrutiny. French grammar does include *il*
constructions, which predominantly code impersonal events, and which exhibit
a great deal of functional equivalence with a much more limited set of morphologically unrelated constructions. Whether or not these structures are grouped
together under a single label, this functional equivalence needs to be investigated.
The fact that a subset of these different structures would emerge out of their respective environments to form stable functionally equivalent islands is important
because it reveals the sensitivity that French grammar exhibits toward a class of
highly general, stable, and expectable events whose mere occurrence, as opposed
to their precise origin, is at issue.

The particularity of the French impersonal class is that it includes at the same
time the large, overwhelmingly impersonal *il* construction, and an array of morphosyntactically distinct constructions, each of which emerges from the larger
classes of demonstratives, middles, and indefinite pronoun structures. The status
of each of these structures as impersonal has long been noted in the literature. As
we saw in the previous section, Perlmutter and Postal (1983) as well as Olsson
(1986) treat indefinite demonstratives as impersonals. Kemmer (1993) indirectly
recognizes the impersonal value of some middles (to be considered in detail in
Chapter 7), and Creissels (2008b) as well as Cabredo Hofherr (2008) illustrate a
large body of research on impersonal indefinite subject pronouns. Collectively,

however, no attempt has been made to integrate them into a more general model of impersonal constructions, and show how a subset of each class comes to be functionally equivalent with a subset of the other classes. The integration of these seemingly disparate structures into a coherent model of impersonality that systematically codes highly general and predictable events captures an important aspect of French grammar. We therefore need a clear understanding of the processes by which *il* impersonals, demonstrative, middle, and indefinite pronoun constructions come to code such events. One might argue that the term "impersonal" is not required to describe this broad category, and that we should respect tradition and reserve it for the strictly morphological *il* construction. However, I believe that using the label to describe the larger functional category underscores the similarities between the four constructions considered in this monograph. Furthermore, the term impersonal appears appropriate to describe a class of events maximally distant from the dynamic interaction that a transitive clause describes. It should be noted, however, that the interest of French in maximally general events is not necessarily shared by other languages, and consequently the definition of impersonals followed throughout the analysis is restricted to French. Other languages may organize the category differently, or even have no use for it at all.

The distributed structure of the impersonal category requires two separate steps in the analysis. The first, a detailed exploration of the *il* construction, is developed in Chapters 3 to 5. The second one developed in Chapters 6 through 8 shows how demonstrative, middle, and indefinite impersonals emerge from the rich ecologies of their respective morphosyntactic categories, and therefore need to be described in that broader context. This necessity constitutes one of the major difficulties of the analysis. Ideally, a thorough description of each kind of impersonal should only be undertaken within the full context of the entire category from which it originates, but this scenario is obviously well outside the scope of this monograph. The methodological compromise consists in providing sufficient background about the broader morphosyntactic class to clearly illustrate how its impersonal subset relates to its overall internal organization.

6. Outline of the following chapters

Chapter 2. A cognitive approach to French impersonals

This chapter presents the theoretical framework in which the analyses of the four impersonal constructions are developed. It introduces the major tenets of Cognitive Grammar (Langacker 1987a, 1991, 2008), with particular emphasis on the conceptual basis of clause structure. In particular, it shows how a transitive clause codes an event where the agent of the process that the predicate describes is also selected as the clause's most focal entity and thus selected as subject. The four impersonal constructions investigated in this monograph are shown to use different strategies to defocus the agent. Middle impersonals choose an alternative participant as subject, while *il* and *ça* impersonals select an element of the setting. Indefinite *on* impersonals select the agent as subject, but the selectional restrictions placed on that agent (its delimitation) are so low that any person can be viewed as a potential agent. Finally, the notion of construction is discussed in detail, and its relevance to the internal organization of French impersonals is evaluated.

Chapter 3. The semantic range of impersonals

This chapter provides an overview of the main issues involved in the description of *il* impersonals. It first addresses the need to treat simple impersonals, namely constructions where a nominal follows the predicate, separately from their complex counterparts where the predicate is followed by an infinitival or finite clause in the indicative or subjunctive. The semantic function of the construction is discussed in detail. Overall, *il* impersonals are treated as presentational structures that identify and locate the entity coded in the postverbal expression with respect to a specific facet of experience, and the pronoun *il* codes the field, i.e. the knowledge structures that allow the conceptualizer to assess that location. The distribution of the predicates in the construction is shown to reflect the semantic overlap that exists between its individual components. The most frequently attested predicates crucially invoke the setting in their lexical semantic structure, and the analysis and evaluation of that setting represent a large part of the mental structures required to determine the location of the postverbal entity. This semantic analysis of predicate distribution is shown to provide better results than syntactic accounts based solely on the structural properties of the predicate.

Chapter 4. Simple impersonals: Patterns of usage

While Chapter 3 describes the different semantic classes of predicates that participate in the simple impersonal *il* construction and hence that construction's semantic range, Chapter 4 focuses on the fine-grained usage patterns that develop with some of the most frequent predicates such as *exister* 'exist', *rester* 'remain', *manquer* 'lack', *arriver* 'arrive', *venir* 'come', and *passer* 'pass'. This in-depth analysis of individual predicates represents the necessary complement to the more general account provided in the previous chapter, and both are equally essential to obtain a clear understanding of *il* impersonals' usage. Not only are those predicates semantically compatible with the impersonal construction, but their association has developed into preassembled complex units that reliably and systematically describe specific kinds of scenes. For example, *il existe* 'there exists' represents the exclusive choice to introduce the presence of a new entity in reality, even though alternative forms of the predicate are potentially available. Overall, the individual analyses provided in this chapter reinforce the account introduced in Chapter 3 by showing how the semantic overlap that exists between the construction itself and the predicates that participate in it has created complex meaningful units that specialize in the description of highly specific scenes.

Chapter 5. Complex impersonals

This chapter addresses complex *il* impersonals. Unlike simple constructions that pertain to the identification of an entity, complex impersonals ascertain the existence of events. Once this distinction and its correlates are taken into account, complex impersonals are also presentational constructions that evaluate the presence of the process in the complement in reality. Different clause types are shown to represent different levels of reality. Infinitival and subjunctive complements reflect the "effective" level of basic reality where the mere occurrence of events is assessed. By comparison, indicative complements reflect the more inclusive level of "elaborated" reality that contains a set of epistemically assessed "propositions". Here again, the distribution of the different predicates with these complement types reflects their respective semantic import. For instance, deontic predicates such as *il faut* and *il est nécessaire* 'it is necessary' are solely compatible with infinitive and subjunctive complements because they are merely concerned with the effective changes necessary in order to reflect the conceptualizer's view of the world. By comparison, the complement of epistemic predicates reflects the conceptualizer's level of confidence in the reality of the event that the complement clause evokes. Consequently, positive predicates such as *il est certain* 'it is certain' or *il est clair* 'it is clear' are followed by an indicative clause, but *il est douteux* 'it is doubtful' only occurs with a subjunctive clause.

Chapter 6. Demonstrative (*ça*) impersonals

This chapter shows that in the context of the copular complement construction (*être possible* 'be possible', for example), French possesses two impersonal constructions, respectively introduced by *il* and *ça* 'this' (*c'*). *Ça*'s impersonal status directly reflects its properties in other contexts, namely its flexible reference, its dual anaphoric/cataphoric character, and the subjective construal it imposes on the scene it profiles. However, these characteristics only allow the pronoun to deserve the impersonal label within the copular complement construction because that construction alone provides the required level of generality. In this particular context the demonstrative pronoun's semantic import is very similar to that of *il*, described in preceding chapters. Whereas *il* profiles the field, *ça* profiles the abstract setting within which the event or proposition in the complement can be identified, the difference pertains essentially to the salience of the conceptualizer's effort in that identification. The distribution between the two forms reflects their semantic proximity, and also crucially depends on the meanings of individual predicates.

Chapter 7. Middle (*se*) impersonals

This chapter shows that the so-called passive middles or *Moyennes* 'middle' *se* constructions are impersonal, and investigate the conditions under which this small section of the French middle domain can receive this label. While some middles such as "spontaneous event" predicates (*se briser* 'break', for instance) are too specific to be impersonal because they describe a process restricted to a particular place and time between clearly delineated participants, the process profiled by the middle impersonals increasingly gains in generality if the circumstances responsible for its realization can be identified as stable; future occurrences can therefore be predicted with confidence and hence available to everyone. Middle constructions are thus more likely to have impersonal value when their subject bears some responsibility for the occurrence of the profiled process. Subject responsibility is well established and stable in two constructions that can therefore rightfully be called impersonal. In the first, the profiled process is definitional of the entity the subject codes in the sense that it is completely incorporated in what it means for that entity to be what it is. In the second constructional cluster, the profiled process is also predictable because its occurrence is required by a set of social norms or conventions. Because social norming applies to everyone, that process is available to any conceptualizer. These two patterns constitute stable constructional islands because the responsibility of their subject for the occurrence of the profiled process sets them apart from their morphosyntactically similar neighbors.

Chapter 8. Indefinite (*on*, *ils*) impersonals

Impersonal *on* is well attested in the literature, but its connections to its other senses are not always spelled out clearly. This chapter shows that impersonal *on* needs to be distinguished from both its referential and passive counterparts. It demonstrates that if personal *on* is distinguished by two specific characteristics, namely (1) the identifiability of its referent, and (2) that referent's exclusive responsibility for the realization of the event the predicate profiles, the passive and impersonal values arise when one or both of these characteristics are missing. Passive *on* emerges when the pronoun's referent is not identified, but nonetheless remains solely responsible for the event coded by the predicate. Impersonal *on* emerges when both characteristics of the pronoun's personal sense are missing, namely the referent is not only unidentified but also maximally inclusive of all relevant conceptualizers. This chapter also investigates the two constructional islands in which the referent of indefinites obtains the degree of generality required of its impersonal status, namely the homogenization and virtualization of experience.

Chapter 9. Recapitulation and conclusion

This chapter summarizes the results obtained in the previous chapters. It also considers the relation that exists between the impersonal and passive categories, as well as generic statements. Finally, it concludes this monograph by presenting several instances of the functional equivalence of the four constructions, which confirms the relevance of the impersonal category for the French language.

7.   A note on the methodology and data

The demonstrative, middle, and indefinite pronoun constructions have been selected for investigation because of their functional equivalence with *il* impersonals. However, these structures do not claim to exhaustively represent the impersonal category. It is quite possible that other constructions not considered here also meet the proposed definition of impersonals. In particular, the relation between impersonals and generic statements, such as *un chat, ça dort toute la journée* 'a cat [that] sleeps all day' for example, will not be considered in detail in this monograph. The focus on a small number of constructions within one single language fills an important gap in our understanding of impersonals for several reasons. First, a careful analysis of individual constructions affords a clear view of the functional equivalence of a subset of those constructions in specific circumstances. Second, because it is considerably narrower in scope than typological accounts, it provides an understanding of how the different constructions meet the impersonal criteria. This allows us to consider at the same time the general ecology of the category, i.e. the source of the possible candidates, as well as the precise context (syntactic, semantic, or pragmatic) in which specific impersonal constructions emerge.

The data on which the analysis is based come from three sources. The first is the Internet-based FRANTEXT database of literary French (novels, essays, journals, and so on) made available by the Project for American and French Research on the Treasury of the French Language (ARTFL), and most specifically the 760 texts that constitute its twentieth-century offerings. The second is a corpus of journalistic prose composed of approximately 70 million words from the *Agence France Press* (AFP) news agency (1993–1995). The distribution of French and English constructions is investigated within a parallel corpus of European Union parliament deliberations collected using Michael Barlow's parallel concordance program Paraconc. The few manufactured examples are preceded by the # sign. The data sources clearly indicate that written French constitutes the sole focus of this monograph. Importantly, the conclusions reached in the course of the analysis cannot be directly extended to spoken language. For example, the distribution of *il* and *ça* impersonals in the copular construction presented in Chapter 6 may be entirely different for spoken French, where *ça* is undoubtedly much more frequent.

The reliance on both literary and journalistic data constitutes an attempt to reduce the genre bias inherent to all single-genre corpora, and provide a representative picture of French written usage. For example, the distribution of predicates in the simple impersonal construction presented in Chapter 3 relies on 303 literary examples from FRANTEXT and 307 journalistic occurrences from AFP. Taken together, the 610 tokens nonetheless show remarkable consistency. While the 307 AFP tokens instantiate 16 different predicates, 39 predicates are represented in the literary examples. However, all but two of the predicates found in the journalistic texts are also attested in the literary corpus, and the remaining two have very close synonyms among the attested verbs. The juxtaposition of the two corpora therefore allows us to delineate a grouping of core predicates that transcend the specificity of a particular genre, but also to capture the precise manner in which the creative nature of literary prose extends this core group to a large number of related predicates. Both kinds of information are shown to provide critical insight into the meaning of simple *il* impersonals.

Some sections of the overall corpus (FRANTEXT, AFP, or any of their relevant subparts) are also invoked at different points of the analysis when their specificity provides important insight into the observed phenomena. For example, Chapter 6 investigates the distribution of *il* and *ça* impersonals in copular complement constructions, and shows that the selection between the two constructions reflects alternative construals of the conceptualized scene. Because construal is fluid by definition, the best illustrative contexts come from situations in which the author's narrative intentions can be evaluated through the presence of the various strategies that conspire to produce the desired effects. With respect to our example, the semantic import of *il* and *ça* is all the more noticeable when the specific construal each pronoun imposes on the conceptualized scene it describes can be shown to partake in the author's overall narrative strategy. In order to capture at the same time the overall distribution of the two constructions, as well as their respective relevance to the overall narrative strategy of a specific novel, the whole corpus is first examined, but the results of this investigation are then compared to the situation observed within the context of Simone de Beauvoir's *Les mandarins*. The discrepancy between the distribution within the novel (where *ça* is overwhelmingly more frequent) and within the corpus at large (where *il* represents the most frequent alternative by far) can be imputed to the independently attested "spoken" style of De Beauvoir's narrative, and confirms the analysis of the two constructions developed in the chapter.

CHAPTER 2

A cognitive approach to French impersonals

This chapter introduces the most basic tenets of the Cognitive Grammar model (Langacker 1987, 1991, 2008) in which the analysis of French impersonals is developed. It first explores CG's fundamental claim that grammar is symbolic in nature, and that consequently the lexicon and syntax form a continuum of symbolic units. Second, it presents the two kinds of strategies the four French impersonal constructions adopt to reduce the agent's inherent salience. *Il* and *ça* impersonals as well as the middle constructions select an alternative entity as subject while *on* impersonals decrease the agent's delimitation (the way the pronoun restricts its reference to individuated participants) to the point where it includes humanity in general. Third, it shows how the notion of construction provides the organizing principle of the French impersonal category.

1.   A symbolic view of language

In Langacker's words, "CG's most fundamental claim is that grammar is *symbolic in nature*" (Langacker 2008: 5, emphasis in original). If a symbol is described as the pairing of a semantic structure and a phonological shape, the symbolic value of lexical items is unproblematic. For example, the word "cat" straightforwardly represents the symbolic association of a semantic content (the meaning of the term) and its phonological representation (phonologically represented as /kæt/). More controversially, however, the study of grammar, which one could define as the combination of simple elements (words) into conventional complex expressions, requires no further apparatus than symbolic structures to characterize at the same time the general schematic patterns (the rules) and their specific instantiations (the actually occurring forms). In other words, "*lexicon and grammar form a gradation consisting solely in assemblies of symbolic structures*" (Langacker 2008: 5, emphasis in the original).

1.1   Conceptual semantics

Because grammar "resides in schematized patterns of conceptual restructuring and symbolization" (Langacker 2008: 27), grammatical constructions are meaningful by definition and their description necessarily begins with a careful investigation of the conceptual structures they incorporate. CG therefore strongly relies on a model of conceptual semantics in which "linguistic meaning resides in conceptualization" (Langacker 2008: 43), and includes at the same time some conceptual content (the scene selected for the purposes of linguistic coding) as well as a particular way of construing that scene, i.e. the conceptualizer's decision to structure and present it in a specific fashion.

More specifically, meaning is characterized by the psychological operation of imposing a profile on a conceptual base. The base consists of the knowledge structures relevant to the conception of a given expression; the profile selects the part of the base that expression designates, i.e. renders more salient. For example, the word "roof" uses as its base the conception of a building and its profile consists of the upper part of the structure, as the bold lines in Figure 2.1 indicate. Note that different expressions such as "window" or "door" profile different substructures of the same base.

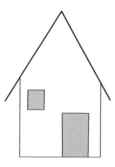

Figure 2.1 Profiling: "roof"

The imposition of a profile on a base is crucial in CG because it provides the basis for a large number of linguistic constructs, and in particular the grammatical categories (nouns, adjective, verbs, and so on). The grammatical category of an entity is not determined solely by its conceptual content but by the nature of its profile. According to the nature of their profile, linguistic entities are divided into "things" and "relations". "A thing is a set of interconnected entities which function as a single entity at a higher level of conceptual organization" (Langacker 2008: 107). The interconnected entities can be spatially contiguous, as in "rock", for example, which describes a contiguous region in physical space, but they needn't be. For example, the entities that compose a team are not necessarily contiguous at any point of time but they are nonetheless connected by more general considerations of common goals and strategy (not to mention possibly similar jerseys). Importantly, things are "autonomous" elements, i.e. their conception does not necessarily make reference to another entity. It is certainly possible to imagine numerous activities pertaining to rocks (picking them up, lifting them, throwing them for example), but none of these activities in which rocks usually partake is necessary for entertaining the concept of a rock.

Unlike things, relations profile the interconnections between entities. These interconnections can describe stable configurations such as the prepositions "in" or "on". In these configurations, illustrated with "in" in Figure 2.2a, the position of the most focal entity (the "trajector" or tr) is being assessed with respect to that of another (second focal) entity, namely the "landmark" (lm). Other expressions describe dynamic configurations. In Figure 2.2b for example, the preposition "into" profiles the different spatial configurations that the trajector and landmark respectively adopt at different points of time on their way to the final state of inclusion. The dashed lines indicate that the trajector and landmark remain the same throughout the different stages of the movement. Complex prepositions are also scanned in a summary fashion with the entirety of the conceptualized episode available at the same time. Finally, verbs also profile different spatial configurations between their trajector and landmark. At the clausal level the most focal figure in the profiled relation (tr) is coded as subject. If the verb is transitive, the landmark (secondary figure) is coded as the object. For example, the predicate illustrated in (2.2c) represents a number of situations in which a participant crosses the boundaries of a location ("John entered the room", "the police entered the building", etc.). The participant ("John", "the police") is coded as the subject, the location ("the room", "the building") as the object. Verbs also differ from other complex expressions by the temporal nature of their profile. Unlike prepositions, they are processed sequentially, that is, one episode at a time. Sequential scanning is indicated by the bolded arrow in (2.2c). The differences in profile between these three configurations are recapitulated in Figure 2.2 (from Langacker 2008: 117).

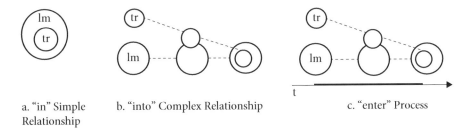

a. "in" Simple   b. "into" Complex Relationship   c. "enter" Process
Relationship

Figure 2.2 Profiling: Grammatical categories

Relations differ from things in that they make necessary reference to the abstract entities that participate in them. For example, it is impossible to envisage an episode of eating without making implicit reference to an entity responsible for the eating (the agent), as well as an entity eaten (the patient), even if both entities remain very abstract. This difference allows us to consider things as "autonomous" and relations as "dependent" expressions (Langacker 2008: 104).

1.2   The conceptual base of clause structure

The CG symbolic view of language dictates that any linguistic structure at any level of complexity or abstraction is meaningful. The semantic import of different types of clauses can thus also be characterized as the specific profile they impose on a conceptual base. Because all language forms are ultimately grounded in human experience, the base relative to which clause structure is best described consists of a relatively small number of very general models and archetypes (Langacker 2008: Chapter 11) that represent specific aspects of our conceptual organization and can be exploited for linguistic purposes. The first of these archetypes pertains to "the organization of a scene into a global *setting* and any number of smaller, more mobile *participants*" (Langacker 2008: 355, emphasis in original) that interact with one another, and can occupy different locations at different times. The notion of interaction between the participants makes necessary reference to the "billiard-ball model" that represents "our conception of objects moving through space and impacting one another through forceful physical contact" (Langacker 2008: 355), as well as our knowledge that some objects possess the inner resources to provide the necessary energy while others merely transmit or absorb it. Based on this model, the archetypal conception of an "action chain" represents "a series of forceful interactions, each involving the transmission of energy … from one participant to the next" (Langacker 2008: 355–56).

In addition, the roles of the participants in the described event are understood relative to different kinds of conceptual "archetypal roles" that can also be exploited linguistically. To provide just two examples, "an *agent* is an individual who willfully initiates and carries out an action, typically a physical action affecting other entities. It is thus an 'energy source' and the initial participant in an action chain" (Langacker 2008: 356, emphasis in original). By contrast, the opposite role of "patient" is defined as "something that undergoes an internal change of state. … Typically inanimate and nonvolitional, a patient usually changes as the result of being affected by outside forces. It is then an 'energy sink' and the final participant in an action chain" (Langacker 2008: 356, emphasis in the original). The other roles will be considered as needed in the course of the analysis.

Another archetype required for the characterization of clausal structure pertains to the manner in which we make mental contact with the different facets of the world around us. The analogy here is that the conceptualization of the scenes we apprehend for the purpose of linguistic expression proceeds in a manner analogous to the special case of spectators watching a play. This "stage model" captures how we focus our attention on different aspects of a scene to enhance the perceptual experience. First, from the maximal range of their perception (maximal scope), viewers select their general focus of viewing attention (immediate scope). Within this immediate scope, they further narrow their attention to specific participants or elements of the surroundings (profile). Langacker expresses the analogy as follows: "The maximal field of view, the onstage region, and the focus of attention correspond respectively to an expression's maximal scope, immediate scope, and profile" (2008: 356).

Closely related is a group of archetypes that pertain to the speech event itself, and involves models of speaking, listening, and engaging in social interaction, as well as different models of viewing arrangement that pertain to the perceptual asymmetry that exists between the subject of perception (conception) and the perceived (conceptualized) object. This analysis considers specific configurations at different points, but for now we will simply note that the default viewing arrangement consists of "two interlocutors being together in a fixed location, using a shared language to describe occurrences in the world around them" (Langacker 2008: 357).

The "canonical event model" (Langacker 2008: 357) represents a way of integrating these different interconnected archetypes into "what is arguably the most typical kind of occurrence" (Langacker 2008: 357). More specifically, "this occurrence is identified as a bounded, forceful event in which an agent (AG) acts on a patient (PAT) to induce a change of state. This event is the focus of attention within the immediate scope (the onstage region), being apprehended from offstage by a viewer (V) not otherwise involved in it. All of this unfolds within some global setting" (Langacker 2008: 357). The canonical event model is illustrated in Figure 2.3 (from Langacker 2008: 357):

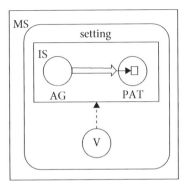

Figure 2.3 Canonical event model

Finally, in order to describe a large number of perceptual, physical, social, or mental control events, Langacker (2002, 2004) describes the "control cycle". At any given moment (the baseline), an actor (A) has control over a certain number of entities that collectively constitute his dominion (D). In the next phase, a target (T) enters his field of potential interaction (F), thus creating a state of tension that needs to be resolved. One way of resolving this tension brings the target into the actor's dominion by exerting force onto it. The outcome of this action phase is a modified static dominion that incorporates the newly acquired element. The different phases of the model are illustrated in Figure 2.4 (from Langacker 2004: 536):

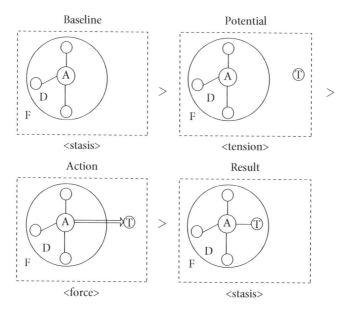

Figure 2.4 The control cycle

Although different manifestations of this cycle perpetually unfold in the different domains of human experience, this monograph is particularly interested in epistemic and social control. Epistemic control pertains to the "acquisition of propositional knowledge" (Langacker 2009: 131). The actor is a conceptualizer, the target a proposition that represents a facet of the world around her, and the dominion is her view of reality, composed of the propositions she holds true (Achard 1998, 2002). Social control pertains to the manipulation of other individuals' behavior, according to a set of expectations and obligations. The situation presented in the previous chapter and repeated here for convenience provides an instance of epistemic control:

(2.1)   *Pour la première fois je sentais qu'**il était possible** que ma mère vécût sans moi*
        (Proust, M. *A l'ombre des jeunes filles en fleurs*: 648)
        'For the first time I felt it was possible for my mother to live [that my mother
        live] without me'

In (2.1), the impersonal predicate *il était possible* 'it was possible' profiles the author's formulation (Langacker 2002, 2004) of the proposition *ma mère vécût sans
moi* 'my mother live without me' as a possible candidate for insertion into his conception of reality (his dominion). In this example, the adverbial *pour la première
fois* 'for the first time' serves to highlight the initial entry of the propositional target
in the author's sphere of awareness. Predicates also profile different stages of the
epistemic process that results in the modification of the conceptualizer's dominion. For example, in the modified (2.1'), the predicate *savoir* 'know' profiles the
result of the mental process by which the author has incorporated the proposition
ma mère pouvait vivre sans moi 'my mother could live without me' as part of his
conception of reality.

(2.1') #*Je **savais enfin** que ma mère pouvait vivre sans moi*
        'I knew at last that my mother could live without me'

The difference between (2.1) and (2.1') also shows that epistemic control predicates
can be both personal and impersonal, but this monograph is obviously predominantly concerned with the impersonal predicates.

1.3   The prototypical coding of clause structure: The transitive clause

In order to be communicated our conceptualizations need to be linguistically
coded, and because grammar is composed of conventionalized composite units,
certain types of clauses are particularly well suited for expressing certain types
of events. Among all the possible types, the transitive clause, which codes the
interaction between an agent selected as the focal figure (trajector) of the profiled
relation and thus marked as subject, and a patient chosen as the secondary figure
(landmark) and thus coded as object, is perhaps the most common because it
allows the participants with the highest degree of cognitive salience, namely the
agent and patient, to also be treated as the two most focal figures in the linguistic
representation of the conceptualized event. This alignment between semantic roles
and focal prominence is illustrated in (2.2), repeated from Chapter 1:

(2.2)   *En quinze jours, **la 1ère armée a tué 10000 allemands**, fait 18000 prisonniers,
        enlevé 120 canons.*   (Gaulle, C. de. *Mémoires de guerre, le salut*: 136)
        'Within two weeks, the first army killed 1000 Germans, took 18,000 prisoners,
        removed 120 guns'.

The example in (2.2) describes the outcome of several battles in which the first army was involved in during a two-week period. If we focus exclusively on the first clause in bold print, the agent *la 1ère armée* 'the first army' is the most cognitively salient participant in the interaction that the predicate *a tué* 'killed' profiles. It is also treated as the most focal figure linguistically by being selected as the trajector of the profiled relation, and hence as the clausal subject. The first army's victims (*10000 allemands* '10,000 Germans') are also salient participants in the profiled interaction. This salience is linguistically recognized by their selection as the landmark of the profiled relation, and their consequent marking as direct object. The coding of a prototypical transitive clause such as the one in (2.2) is illustrated in Figure 2.5 (from Langacker 2008: 385):[1]

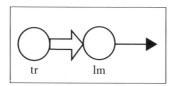

Figure 2.5 Coding of a transitive clause

A transitive clause may represent the unmarked, possibly even prototypical, way of coding events such as that depicted in (2.2), but it by no means constitutes the only alternative. Linguistic coding is a matter of construal and therefore of speaker choice, and speakers have the possibility of giving focal prominence to any entity they choose. Nothing inherent to the conceptualized scene imposes the selection of any entity as a focal participant, and conversely "the elements made prominent linguistically need not be the most salient on non-linguistic grounds" (Langacker, 2009: 112). The multiple clause types available in any language illustrate the flexibility of construal because they provide conventionalized alternatives for the description of scenes with similar conceptual content. Human beings possess both the cognitive flexibility to construe a scene in alternate ways and the symbolic resources to express this flexibility linguistically.

---

1.   For convenience, the notation used in Figure 2.5 is simplified to the contents of the immediate scope of predication IS in the canonical event model presented in Figure 2.3. A more complete representation would also include the conceptualizer and the viewing arrangement illustrated in Figure 2.3. This simplified notation is also used for all the figures in the remainder of this chapter.

2. Defocusing strategies

The term "defocusing the agent" as it was used in the previous chapter captures the various strategies speakers use to break the natural alignment between the inherent salience of the agent in the conceived event and its importance in that event's linguistic representation. The constructions investigated in this monograph achieve this break in two different ways. The first involves the selection of an alternative entity as the focal figure in the profiled relation (the subject); the second consists of increasing the level of generality at which the nominals that describe the participants in the profiled process are described (delimitation).

2.1 Alternative trajector selection

Despite its intrinsic cognitive salience, speakers often have good reasons to not select the agent as the linguistically focal figure in the profiled relation. They may ignore its real nature, find it irrelevant to the description of their conceptualization, or perhaps even want to protect it from undesirable consequences. Whatever their reasons are, speakers of all languages have at their disposal an inventory of different clause types that allow them to represent their conceptualization in ways that decrease the agent's role. One of the simplest ways of defocusing the agent is to select another participant as subject. In French, the passive construction illustrated in (2.3) makes use of that strategy by selecting the patient as the focal figure of the main relation:

(2.3) *Toute la Russie saura que le grand-duc Serge **a été exécuté** à la bombe <u>par le</u>*
       <u>groupe de combat du parti socialiste révolutionnaire</u> pour hâter la libération du
       peuple russe.   (Camus, A. *Les justes*: 310)
       'Everyone in Russia will know that Grand-Duke Serge was executed with a
       bomb by the fighting group of the revolutionary Socialist party to speed up
       the liberation of the Russian people'.

The specific assignment that represents the semantic import of the passive construction (Langacker 1982) selects the patient *le grand-duc Serge* as the focal figure and thus codes it as subject. The agent *le groupe de combat du parti socialiste révolutionnaire* is defocused (Shibatani 1985) because it is not treated as a clausal participant. In French as well as in English and a number of other languages, the agent can be demoted to an oblique complement introduced by a *par* 'by' phrase.[2] In (2.3), the name of the agent represents a relevant part of the message; it is

---

2. This demotion is not possible in all languages. See Lazdina (1966) for Latvian, as well as the other languages illustrated in Keenan and Dryer (2007: 307).

therefore still specifically mentioned even though its position outside the clausal core alongside other oblique complements defocuses its role in the profiled process. In what Keenan and Dryer call "basic passives" (2007: 307), however, the defocusing is complete and the agent is not even explicitly mentioned. This is illustrated in (2.4) in which the predicate *blesser* 'injure' obviously has an agent, which we might for example hypothesize as being another person, but which, for whatever reason, the speaker chooses to leave implicit:

(2.4)   *Sa lettre ne me dit rien d'autre, sinon sa détermination de ne pas me revoir non plus. Elle **a été blessée** sans doute et plus gravement que nous le supposons.*

      (Anouilh, J. *La répétition: ou, l'amour puni*: 120)

'Her letter doesn't mention anything else, beside her determination not to see me again either. She was hurt, probably more seriously than we think'.

Figure 2.6 illustrates the trajector/landmark assignment of passives. Note that English and French passives designate "the entire agent-theme interaction" (Langacker 2008: 385).[3]

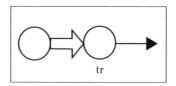

Figure 2.6 Passive construction (from Langacker 2008: 385)

Middle constructions illustrated in (2.5)–(2.7) resemble passives in that they both evoke "an agentive process but selects the theme as its trajector" (Langacker 2008: 385).

(2.5)   *La comtesse est une femme de tête, elle lui passe ses maîtresses comme il lui passe, de son côté, ses amants, pourvu que **le jeu se joue** dans leur monde, avec des cartes qu'elle connaît.* (Anouilh, J. *La répétition: ou, l'amour puni*: 59)

'The countess is a smart woman, she will let him have his mistresses as he also lets her have her lovers, provided that the game takes place [plays itself] in their world, with cards that she knows well'.

---

3.   The notation in Figure 2.6 is simplified. Since only prototypically transitive clauses passivize (Hooper and Thompson 1980; Rice 1987; Lazard 1998), and because "the primary function of the passive is to provide an alternative to the default agent orientation of canonical transitives" (Langacker 2008: 385), a full representation would include the conception of a transitive verb. See Langacker (2008: 383), in particular Figure 11.5.

(2.6) Hero, *brusquement: Tu m'as compris!* (*Il serrait son verre dans sa main, **le verre*** ***se casse**. Ils regardent le verre tous deux dans la main de Héro qui dit doucement.*) *Excuse-moi, mon vieux. J'aime casser.*

(Anouilh, J. La répétition: ou, l'amour puni: 75)

'Hero, suddenly: You understood me! (he was holding his glass in his hand, the glass breaks. Both of them look at the glass in Hero's hand, and Hero says softly): Excuse me Old Man. I like to break [things]'.

(2.7) *Jetable, certes, mais indémodable: **la fameuse pointe Bic qui a fait la fortune*** ***du baron Bich, décédé lundi,** se vend toujours à 15 millions d'exemplaires par jour dans le monde.*

(AFP)

'Disposable, sure, but never out of fashion: The famous Bic pen that made Baron Bich, who died on Monday, rich still sells to the tune of 15 million a day in the world'.

The examples in (2.5)–(2.7) present different kinds of middles that will be considered in detail in Chapter 7. Concentrating on their similarities for the moment, the three predicates (*jouer* 'play', *casser* 'break', and *vendre* 'sell') are generally transitive. In the middle construction, however, the presence of the middle marker *se* renders them intransitive, and the theme is selected as the trajector in the profiled relation and thus coded as subject, while the agent is not expressed.[4] Consider for example the clause *le verre se casse* 'the glass breaks' in (2.6), repeated from the previous chapter. The agent is not mentioned, and the theme *le verre* 'the glass' is selected as the trajector. The nature of the agent is not in doubt, since it is explicitly mentioned in the following independent clause *j'aime casser* 'I like to break [things]'. However, it is not treated as a clausal participant. Similarly in (2.7), the theme *la fameuse pointe bic* 'the famous Bic pen' is selected as subject while the agent, namely the different people who sell the pen throughout the world, is only recoverable pragmatically.

The main difference between the passive in Figure 2.6 and the middle construction illustrated in Figure 2.7 is that if passives profile the complete interaction between the agent and the theme, "the middle profiles only what happens to the theme" (Langacker 2008: 385). In other words, a middle "does invoke causation but leaves it unprofiled" (Langacker 2008: 385).

---

4. French possesses another "absolute intransitive" (Langacker 2008: 385) that does not include the middle marker *se*. A possible alternative of (2.6) using that construction would be #*le verre casse* 'the glass breaks'. For a comparison of the two constructions see Achard (2009).

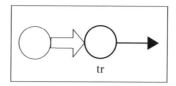

Figure 2.7 Middles (from Langacker 2008: 385)

In both passives and middles, agent defocusing is accomplished by selecting another participant, namely the theme as the focal figure of the profiled relation.
There are, however, no constraints on the nature of the entity that can be chosen
as focally prominent for linguistic purposes. In particular, any aspect of the setting
such as the spatial or temporal frames within which the participants interact can
be selected and thus marked as subject. The examples in (2.8) and (2.9) illustrate
the shift in construal that results from the respective selection of the agent (2.8) or
the setting (2.9) as the clausal figure, and its consequent subject marking:

(2.8)   *Le silence se faisait pesant. La flamme de la lanterne pétillait et charbonnait
        dans l'air nauséeux, des ombres douteuses* **grouillaient** *sur les voûtes souillées.*
                                        (Gracq, J. *Le rivage des Syrtes*: 299)
        'The silence was becoming heavy. The flame of the lantern was sparkling and
        darkening the foul air, dubious shadows were crawling on the soiled vaulted
        ceilings'.

(2.9)   *La chambre, ou cellule, où il se trouvait,* **grouillait** *d'hommes et de femmes de
        blanc vêtus. Ils se pressaient autour de son lit, et ceux qui étaient au deuxième
        rang se haussaient sur la pointe des pieds et allongeaient le cou, afin de mieux
        le voir.*   (Beckett, S. *Malone meurt*: 137)
        'The bedroom, or the cell, where he was located was crawling with men and
        women wearing white. They were huddling near his bed, and those in the
        second row were standing on their tiptoes and craning their necks to see him
        better'.

The predicate *grouiller* 'crawl' in (2.8) and (2.9) is intransitive. Since French is a
nominative/accusative language, in (2.8) the single participant *des ombres douteuses* 'dubious shadows' is selected as the focal figure in the profiled relation and
thus coded as subject. The setting within which the profiled process occurs is coded
by the oblique *sur les voûtes souillées* 'on the soiled vaulted ceilings'. The example
in (2.9) describes a scene that contains very similar elements, namely a group of
participants *des hommes et des femmes de blanc vêtus* 'men and women dressed in
white' participating in an interaction described by the same predicate (*grouiller*) as
in (2.8). However, the linguistic coding of that scene reflects an entirely different
construal where the setting, *la chambre, ou cellule, où il se trouvait* 'the room or

the cell where he was located' is selected as the focal figure, while the participants are coded as an oblique complement introduced by the preposition *de*. Another example of setting subject construction where the setting is temporal rather than spatial is illustrated in (2.10):[5]

(2.10)   *L'année 1945* **voit** *refondre entièrement et étendre à des domaines multiples le régime des assurances sociales. Tout salarié en sera obligatoirement couvert.*
(Gaulle, C. de. *Mémoires de guerre, le salut*: 97)
'The year 1945 witnessed the total reorganization and expansion of the social security system. Every employee will necessarily be covered'.

In the constructions illustrated in (2.9) and (2.10), the setting is a well-delineated spatial or temporal location. In the CG tradition, impersonals are sometimes called "abstract setting constructions" (Smith 1985) because they also select a setting as their subject, albeit one much more abstract. In order to describe this abstract setting we need to recall the control cycle presented in Figure 2.4 where the agent's effort to incorporate the target into her dominion manifests itself within her zone of potential interaction or field. In other words, the field can be viewed as defining the range of the agent's reach for the interaction that the sentence depicts.

---

5.   The setting construction illustrated in (2.9) and (2.10) should not be confused with other constructions in which the setting is treated as a participant, as illustrated in (i) and (ii). This is particularly obvious in (ii) since the clause is in the passive voice, and only participants can passivize (Hooper and Thompson 1980; Rice 1987; Langacker 2009):

(i)   *La salle entière* **chavira** *sous ses yeux, glissant avec lenteur de droite à gauche comme le pont d'un navire sur une mer démontée.*   (Green, J. *Moïra: roman*: 42)
'The whole room sank under his eyes, slowly gliding from right to left like the deck of a ship in the rough sea'.

(ii)   *La salle des séances de la cour* **fut** *d'ailleurs* **envahie**, *au cours de l'audience, par une foule tumultueuse et même menaçante.*   (Gaulle, C. de. *Mémoires de guerre, le salut*: 461)
'During the trial, the court's audience room was invaded by a tumultuous, even threatening crowd'.

In (iii) and (iv) the setting metonymically represents an agent, and thus cannot be considered an instance of setting subject construction:

(iii)   *"L'aide porte atteinte à l'honneur de la nation", a encore estimé le Star, qui pense que "en bref* **tout le pays** **doit retourner** *au travail et travailler dur, avec efficacité et assiduité".*
(AFP)
'"The assistance is detrimental to the nation's honor", also claimed the Star, who thinks that "in short, the whole country must get back to working hard, diligently and efficiently"'.

(iv)   *Toute la salle, toute l'île, se passionnait pour l'accident tragique.*
(Robbe-Grillet, A. *Le voyeur*: 222)
'The whole room, the whole island was fascinated by the tragic accident'.

The field can have many different manifestations in different domains; some of those manifestations are presented in Chapter 3. For now, we simply note that in the case of epistemic control, of particular relevance to the issues investigated in this monograph, the field described as the conceptualizer's scope of awareness (or "mental reach" [Langacker 2009: 139]) at the moment of epistemic evaluation. For example, in (2.1) repeated once again, the field represents the scope of the evidence that leads the narrator to consider the possible truth of the proposition evoked in the complement. That evidence includes the totality of the mental efforts, deductions, and analyses required to access the event in the complement.

(2.1)   *Pour la première fois je sentais qu'il était possible que ma mère vécût sans moi*
            (Proust, M. *A l'ombre des jeunes filles en fleurs*: 648)
         'For the first time I felt it was possible for my mother to live [that my mother live] without me'

As mentioned in the previous chapter, I have previously adopted Langacker's (2009: 139) proposal that the English impersonal pronoun "it" profiles the field, or "the conceptualizer's scope of awareness for the issue at hand" (Achard 2010). Consequently, the semantic function of *il* in (2.1) is to profile the author's mental range with respect to which the possible truth of the proposition *ma mère vécût sans moi* can be entertained.

Impersonals therefore resemble setting constructions in selecting a nonparticipant as their main clausal figure, but they differ in the precise nature of the selected entity. To illustrate the difference between the different possible construals, Figure 2.8 represents the profile assignments of the three examples in (2.11)–(2.13), where (2.11) is extracted from the attested example in (2.8) while (2.12) and (2.13) are adapted:

(2.11)   ...*des ombres douteuses grouillaient sur les voûtes souillées*
            '...dubious shadows were crawling on the soiled vaulted ceilings'

(2.12)   #*Les voûtes souillées grouillaient d'ombres douteuses*
            'The soiled vaulted ceilings were crawling with dubious shadows'

(2.13)   #*Il grouillait des ombres douteuses sur les voûtes souillées*
            'There crawled dubious shadows on the soiled vaulted ceilings'

The examples in (2.11)–(2.13) present the same objective scene. A group of participants (the shadows or P in the diagrams) are perceived as crawling (represented by the solid arrow) within a specific setting (the vaulted ceilings represented by the solid outside box). Furthermore, the agent's perception of the crawling occurs within the latter's visual field (indicated by the dashed box labeled F in the diagrams). Note that the setting and the field do present some overlap, but they

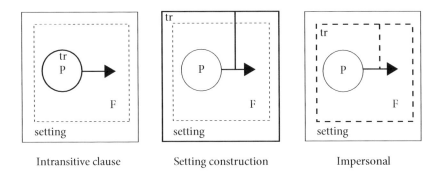

Figure 2.8 Alternative construals: Intransitive, setting, and impersonal constructions in (2.11)–(2.13)

are not coextensive. For one thing, it is doubtful that the agent's field of vision can encompass the entirety of the ceilings at any given time. Furthermore, while the setting represents a well-delineated physical area, the field depicts a more abstract region defined primarily by the agent's perceptual abilities at any given time. The three constructions illustrated in (2.11)–(2.13) structure this base in different ways by selecting alternative entities as the focal figure in the profiled relation. As we saw earlier, in an intransitive clause the participant is chosen as more focal and thus marked as the clausal subject. In a setting subject construction, the setting is selected as the most prominent clausal figure and therefore coded as subject. Finally, in an impersonal construction the field is selected as the most focal figure and coded as subject. In the intransitive clause the agent is presented as initiating the profiled process. In the setting and impersonal constructions, however, the pro-filed process is somehow associated with the setting or the field (to be developed further in Chapters 3 and 4). This is indicated in the diagrams by the solid line between the setting and the process, and the dashed line between the field and the process. Chapter 6 argues that *il* and *ça* impersonals can be respectively analyzed as impersonal and (abstract) setting constructions (see also Achard [2010]). The following chapters investigate impersonals in further detail, but this very brief overview should suffice to show that these constructions present no particular structural anomaly. On the contrary, they take their natural place in the inven-tory of clause types that speakers have at their disposal to linguistically capture the relative salience they want to give to the various elements that compose their conceptualizations.

2.2   Identification and delimitation

The brief description of the structures presented in this section suffices to emphasize the connection that exists between *il* impersonal, demonstrative, passive, and middle constructions since they all depart from a prototypical transitive clause in selecting an entity other than the agent of the profiled relation as their most focal figure. However, this alternative trajector choice cannot be invoked to describe the impersonal value of the indefinite *on* constructions because in that case the agent is indeed selected as the trajector of the profiled relation.

In order to understand the defocusing strategy involved in *on*'s impersonal value, we need to revisit some of the aspects that make the kind of transitive clause illustrated in (2.2) prototypical, with particular focus on the reasons for the salience of the agent/subject.

(2.2)   *En quinze jours, **la 1ère armée a tué 10000 allemands,** fait 18000 prisonniers, enlevé 120 canons.*   (Gaulle, C. de. *Mémoires de guerre, le salut*: 136)
'Within two weeks, the first army killed 1000 Germans, took 18,000 prisoners, removed 120 guns'.

The transitive clause illustrated in (2.2) profiles an interactive process (*tuer* 'kill') initiated and carried out by an agent (*la 1ère armée*) to the detriment of a patient (*10000 allemands*). The inherent salience of the agent can be attributed at the same time to its situation with respect to the viewing arrangement (the ground) and to its role with respect to the profiled process. First, *la 1ère armée* is a well-defined participant, easy to delineate and distinguish from the other participants. Furthermore, the presence of the definite article *la* indicates that "there is only one instance of that specified type in the current field of awareness" (Langacker 2009: 171), so the narrator assumes that the reader will have no problem identifying it. The agent's role relative to the profiled process is also clearly identifiable since *la 1ère armée* is clearly and unambiguously the only entity responsible for the killing. The agent in (2.2) therefore possesses the two characteristics that provide a prototypical agent with its intrinsic salience, namely (1) individual identifiability, and (2) clear and exclusive responsibility for the realization of the profiled process. The second defocusing strategy consists of selecting as subject an agent that has low intrinsic salience because it lacks one of these characteristics.

Chapter 8 shows that in its impersonal sense, *on* has a very low level of intrinsic salience because (1) its referent is not identifiable, and (2) the responsibility for the realization of the profiled process is too diffuse to be assessed with precision. With respect to (1), the pronoun can never be considered impersonal in its definite sense illustrated in (2.14), where it refers to a group of two people whose existence is independently attested:

(2.14)   *J'envoyai un mot au jeune Bresson que je retrouvai un soir vers six heures au*
          *Stryx; **on parla de Jacques**, qu'il admirait; mais le bar était désert et il n'arriva*
          rien.   (Beauvoir, S. de. *Mémoires d'une jeune fille rangée*: 268)
          'I sent a note to young Bresson whom I met one evening around 6 o'clock at
          the Stryx; we talked about Jack whom he admired; but the bar was empty and
          nothing happened'.

On is definite in (2.14) because its mention is sufficient to identify the intended referent in reality. In its indefinite sense illustrated in (2.15), however, the pronoun's referent is indefinite because its referent cannot be identified with precision. The director is describing the necessities that all actors face, and the pronoun's referent constitutes a "virtual instance" of the actor category (Langacker 2008: 36) conjured up in order to illustrate his point:

(2.15)   "***Quand on joue***, *il faut se concentrer et se relaxer, il faut oublier les problèmes*
          techniques", *a déclaré le cinéaste, qui tourne actuellement* "*La jeune fille et la*
          mort".   (AFP)
          "'When you play [one plays], you have to be concentrated and relaxed [it is
          necessary to concentrate and relax yourself], you must [it is necessary to]
          forget the technical problems", the director who is currently shooting "the
          young lady and death" declared'.

With respect to (2), the pronoun's referent in (2.14) is clearly identifiable because it is composed of two well-delineated entities. In this case, the pronoun's "delimitation" or in other words its "projection to the world" (Langacker 2007: 179) is very high or precise in the sense that it eliminates any individual except the narrator and Bresson. *On*, however, possesses a large range of delimitation, from a single entity (to be developed in Chapter 8) to groups of various sizes that can extend to notions as vague as "people in general". This decreasing delimitation is illustrated in (2.16) and (2.17):

(2.16)   "*Quand **on a fait le film**, les images des massacres de notre siècle nous sont*
          revenues en mémoire, on ne les a pas refusées", *a ajouté le réalisateur.*   (AFP)
          "'When we shot the film, the images of the massacres of our century came
          back to our minds, we didn't refuse them", the director added'.

(2.17)   *Dans un entretien avec la presse jeudi après-midi, le Pr. Grimaud rappelé que*
          "*tout pronostic concernant son état est extrêmement réservé, dans les heures*
          *qui viennent. **On ne peut jamais dire qu'il n'y a plus d'espoir**, cependant il y*
          a toujours des risques de complications secondaires à craindre", *a-t-il indiqué.*
                                                                                (AFP)
          'In an interview with the press on Thursday afternoon, Pr. Grimaud reminded
          us that "any prognosis concerning his condition in the coming hours is
          extremely reserved. One can never say that there is no hope, but there are
          always risks of secondary complications", he indicated'.

The example in (2.16) describes the choices made during the shooting of a movie. *On*'s delimitation extends to the group of individuals connected to the movie in a creative fashion. That group is large, but still relatively restricted. In contrast, in (2.17) the surgeon's statement applies to mankind in general. The universality of hope and its maximally inclusive scope confers to the pronoun an almost proverbial value with unlimited reference and thus minimal delimitation. Because the only restriction *on* imposes on its referent is that it be human (to be developed in Chapter 8), the pronoun is a perfect candidate for general statements that involve humanity at large, as illustrated in (2.18) that describes a universal philosophical stance. Examples like (2.17) and (2.18) clearly show that when *on*'s delimitation is low, the agent's responsibility relative to the realization of the profiled process is largely irrelevant since that process is available to everyone.

(2.18)   *Il faudrait oser; **on** n'ose point. Mais sait-**on** bien? La doctrine du libre jugement est profondément enterrée.*   (Alain. *Propos sur des philosophes*: 20)
          'We should be daring [it would be necessary to dare], we don't [one doesn't] dare. But do we [does one] know? The free judgment doctrine is deeply buried'.

The selection of indefinite *on* when it has low delimitation therefore constitutes a defocusing strategy because in that condition the pronoun possesses very low intrinsic salience. In fact, we can legitimately say that an entity's inherent salience decreases incrementally with its delimitation. In terms of the general approach to impersonals developed in this monograph, the relation between indefinite pronoun constructions, *il/ça* impersonals, passives, and middles is clear. Despite its selection as trajector in the profiled relation, the agent in the indefinite construction is so diffuse and general that it can merely be equated with human presence, and any conceptualizer in a position to experience the profiled process would have the same experience. Consequently, the indefinite *on* construction allows the speaker to express her linguistic conceptualization at a level of generality comparable to the previously described impersonals, passives, and middles. Chapter 8 analyzes *on* constructions in further detail and describes the precise conditions under which "with a low degree of delimitation, the plural pronouns are effectively impersonal, referring to people as an undifferentiated mass instead of as identified individuals" (Langacker 2007: 179).

The introductory chapter presented the defocusing of the agent as the first impersonal diagnostic criterion; it is now clear that the four constructions investigated in this monograph implement the two defocusing strategies presented in this section. Middle impersonals, illustrated in the previous chapter and repeated in (2.19), decrease the inherent salience of the agent of the conceived event by selecting the patient as the focal figure in its linguistic representation:

(2.19)   *Il note que le pain sans levain est cuit sur des plaques de tôle et ressemble à de la galette ou aux crêpes de carnaval, que **le saucisson d'Arles se fait avec de la viande de mulet**.*   (Durry, MJ. *Gérard de Nerval et le mythe*: 82)
'He notes that yeast-free bread is cooked on flat metal sheets and resembles biscuits or the pancakes of carnival time; that the sausage from Arles is made [makes itself] with mule meat'.

Il and *ça* impersonals illustrated in the previous chapter and repeated in (2.20) and (2.21) also select an entity other than the agent as linguistically most important, but that entity is not a participant.

(2.20)   *Miguel Mejia Baron a succédé au poste d'entraîneur à l'Argentin Cesar Luis Menotti à la fin de l'année 1992 et a qualifié l'équipe nationale pour la phase finale du Mondial. Selon le président de la Fédération, "**il était nécessaire** <u>de poursuivre cette collaboration</u>".*   (AFP)
'Miguel Mejia Baron took over the coaching position from Argentine Cesar Luis Menotti at the end of 1992, and he qualified the team for the final phase of the World Cup. According to the President of the Federation, "it was necessary to continue this collaboration"'.

(2.21)   *D'ailleurs il n'est pas tout à fait vrai que le chemin de fer ait un tracé aussi raide, aussi indifférent et brutal qu'on veut bien le dire. Ainsi que tu me le faisais remarquer l'an dernier, en haut de La Sèche, **c'est étonnant** <u>de voir comme il s'est incorporé au paysage</u>*   (Alain-Fournier, H. *Correspondance avec J. Rivière*: 28)
'Anyway, it is not quite true that the railroad track cuts such a steep, indifferent and brutish path as people have said. As you were indicating to me last year, at the top of La Séche, it [this] is surprising to see how well it blends [itself] into the landscape'

Finally, indefinite (*on*) impersonals illustrated in Chapter 1 and repeated in (2.22) do not select an entity other than the agent as the trajector of the main relation, but the very low level of delimitation of the subject/agent decreases its intrinsic salience by reducing its distinguishability and specificity.

(2.22)   ***On** ne trouve pas toujours facilement, en Espagne, un endroit pour camper, à cause de l'absence de bois, et de la culture intensive.*
                                                      (T'Serstevens, A. *L'itinéraire espagnol*: 16)
'One cannot always easily find a place to camp in Spain, because of the lack of forests, end extensive agriculture.'

The conceptual mechanisms by which the four constructions presented here satisfy the first impersonal criterion are now clear. In order to fully understand the conditions under which the second criterion, namely the high degree of generality of the profiled process, can be achieved, the next section introduces the notion of "construction" more precisely.

3. Grammatical constructions

In the CG model the grammar of a language (the lexicon, morphology, syntax) "can be characterized as a *structured inventory of conventional linguistic units*" (Langacker 1987: 57, emphasis in original). Some units are simple, i.e. they integrate a phonological and semantic pole into a symbolic representation, but others are symbolically complex. The function of grammar is to allow speakers to produce symbolic expressions at any degree of complexity, and "constructional schemas" (Langacker 2009: 5) provide the templatic instructions to integrate simple symbolic units into progressively more complex ones. Cognitive Grammar resembles the different strands of Construction Grammar (Fillmore, Kay, and O'Connor 1988; Goldberg 1995, 2006; Croft 2001) in that it "takes constructions, rather than 'rules', to be the primary objects of grammatical description" (Langacker 2009: 2). In CG: "A *construction* is defined as either an expression (of any size), or else a schema extracted from expressions to capture their commonality (at any level of specificity)" (Langacker 2009: 2, emphasis in original).

In a typical construction, component structures are integrated to form a composite structure both at the phonological and the semantic pole. At each pole, integration is indicated by correspondence lines that equate particular elements within the component structures. At the composite level the corresponding elements are merged (or "unified") (Langacker 2009: 11). The integration of the two component structures "smart" and "woman" into the composite "smart woman" is represented in Figure 2.9:

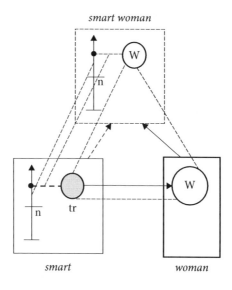

Figure 2.9 "Smart woman" (from Langacker 2009: 11)

This figure illustrates the view that a construction "is an assembly of symbolic structures linked by correspondences and categorizing relationships" (Langacker 2009: 12). The correspondence (dotted) lines indicate the semantic overlap between the different aspects of the component and composite structures, which leads to their integration. For example, the semantic integration of the trajector of the relation that the adjective "smart" profiles and the specific entity that the noun "woman" profiles yields the composite entity of a woman evaluated as above the norm on a scale of intelligence. The arrows describe categorizing relationships. The first connects the schematic trajector of "smart" and the noun "woman". Since "woman" is completely compatible with the more schematic trajector, the relation is one of elaboration. The other two categorizing relationships connect the two component structures and the composite assembly. The relationship between "woman" and "smart woman" is one of elaboration because the two structures are fully consistent in their specifications (both profile things, the composite expression being more specific). However, the categorizing relationship between "smart" and "smart woman" is one of extension (dashed arrow) because the specifications of the two structures do not match perfectly (the adjective profiles a relation, but the composite structure profiles a thing). The difference between the two categorizing relations captures the asymmetry typically observed between the component structures. Only one of the components (the profile determinant) provides its own profile to the composite structure. Importantly, the construction itself has its own meaning, independent in some measure from that of its component constituents. For instance, it is the constructional meaning, i.e. the semantic properties of the composite structure, that determines that the expression "smart woman" designates the woman (rather than the property of being intelligent), or that the woman is the trajector of "smart". These characteristics constitute the semantic contributions of the composite assembly to the overall meaning of the composite expression.

Obviously, the complex assembly "smart woman" instantiates the larger constructional schema illustrated in Figure 2.10 that more generally pertains to the combination of adjectives and nouns in English. Importantly, abstract constructional schemas such as that described in Figure 2.10 also contain semantic information. For example, the heavy box around the noun component indicates that it provides the profile for the composite expression, and that the latter will thus invariably designate a noun. It also specifies that the noun component elaborates the trajector of the relation that the adjective profiles. It is important to bear in mind that the grammar of a language is composed of a very large array of similar constructions ranging from specific expressions to the most schematic, but that each of them provides its own meaningful contribution to the overall meaning of the utterance.

Because grammatical constructions are symbolic, they are also necessarily meaningful. Congruent with the principles of conceptual semantics, each construction's

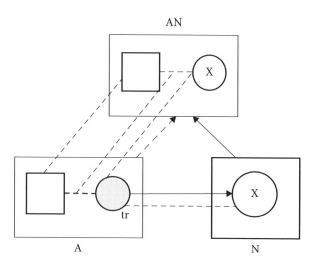

Figure 2.10 Adjective Noun combination (from Langacker 2009:14)

meaning can be characterized as the specific profile it imposes on the scene it describes. It should therefore be clear that the four constructions investigated in this
manuscript do not have the same meaning. The discussion of their "functional
equivalency" can only be taken to mean that they are often available to describe the
same conceptual base, but each construction competes with the others to structure
that base in its own individual manner. The selection of a particular construction is
determined by the speaker's evaluation of the best possible fit between her conceptualization and the array of linguistic resources she has at her disposal.

The assembly instructions presented in this section are appropriate and necessary to explain the morphosyntactic form of a construction, but in their current
formulation they do not allow us to distinguish between different subconstruction
types. For example, the previous chapter showed that the deontic character of the
example repeated in (2.23) distinguishes it from its counterpart in (2.24) in spite
of their similar form. More precisely, *se dit* (and *se fait*) in (2.23) refer to what is
socially acceptable, while the same predicate in (2.24) merely describes the issues
currently being discussed:

(2.23)   *Dans les livres, les gens se font des déclarations d'amour, de haine, ils mettent
leur cœur en phrases; dans la vie, jamais on ne prononce de paroles qui pèsent.
Ce qui "se dit" est aussi réglé que ce qui "se fait".*

(Beauvoir, S. de. *Mémoires d'une jeune fille rangée*: 119)
'In books, people claim their love or hatred for each other, their pour their
hearts in their words; in life, no one ever pronounces words with weight. What
"is said [says itself]" is as tightly regulated as what "is done [does itself]"'.

(2.24) – *Nous sommes en 1920, Jo. Vos idées sont d'un autre temps. Il faut vous réveiller,*
        sortir de vous-même, écouter **ce qui se dit** *autour de vous…*

                                                           (Green, J. *Moïra: roman*: 173)

        '– We are in 1920, Jo. Your ideas belong to another time. You have to wake up,
        get out of yourself, listen to what people are saying [says itself] around you'.

It is very important for the purposes of this monograph to realize that the instructions for putting together the kind of complex symbolic structure that constructions constitute can be extremely specific and include a variety of semantic
and pragmatic elements that cannot be observed with the sole consideration of
their morphological shape. These fine-grained aspects of constructions are more
difficult to represent, but their symbolic significance is nonetheless important.
Despite their similar morphological shape, the middle structure in (2.23) should
be considered a different construction from that in (2.24) because it alone contains
the pragmatic property of obligation imposed on speakers to restrict themselves to
specific topics. This pragmatic feature constitutes an integral part of the instructions the construction provides to integrate its various component parts.

The CG view of constructions needs to be understood within what has been
called the usage-based character of the model (Langacker 1988, 2000; Kemmer
and Barlow 2000). This conception of language organization and processing contains several related facets, but this monograph is primarily interested in two of
its main tenets. The first is the fact that usage shapes the structure of the linguistic
system and thus determines which symbolic structures are available for linguistic
expression. The construction in (2.23) represents a good example. The systematic
association of a specific pragmatic feature in a predictable middle construction
gets conventionalized and hence reliably available as a separate, more specific construction. The second aspect of the usage-based model relevant to our purposes
is its maximalist approach to language structure. Any structure is included in the
grammar whether or not it can be subsumed under a more general statement.
This position yields a very large inventory of constructions, each potentially available for the linguistic expression of the speaker's conceptualization. The notion
of construction is thus relevant to the analysis presented in this monograph at
two separate levels. The first is obviously at the morphosyntactic level (the level
at which the adjective noun construction in Figure 2.10 is presented) in terms of
the specific instructions required to assemble the four different constructions. As
the previous chapter has shown, this level is too coarse for the identification of
a class of impersonal constructions in French. At a more specific level, however,
similar cases cluster into constructional islands in which exemplars are bound
together by a specific morphosyntactic context (*ça* impersonals in the copular
complement construction) or pragmatic considerations. It is at this second level
of constructional islands that French impersonals can be successfully identified.

This maximalist approach also recognizes that every level of schemas is relevant to linguistic organization. The investigation in Chapter 4 reveals the surprisingly systematic low-level associations that exist between the *il* impersonal construction itself and six of the most frequently attested predicates.

4. Recapitulation and conclusion

This chapter presented the concepts developed within the model of Cognitive Grammar whose most fundamental claim is the symbolic character of all areas of linguistic representation, including the lexicon and syntax. The symbolic nature of grammatical constructions makes them meaningful, and their meaning is characterized as the specific profile they impose on a conceptual base. The strategies that the four impersonal constructions described in this monograph use to defocus the agent of the event they describe have been presented, and the mechanisms that facilitate the emergence of constructional islands have been introduced. The next chapters investigate them in further detail within the context of each construction, and show that individual constructional islands provide the French impersonal category with its internal structure despite its morphosyntactic discontinuity.

The events that the four constructions that constitute the French impersonal class code all possess similar characteristics, namely agents that are difficult to precisely identify and generalized processes that cannot be imputed to specific agents. These events, which represent the way things are, sharply contrast with the ones that transitive clauses code, which explains the negative definition impersonals often receive. In a nutshell, transitive clauses profile dynamic interactions, whereas impersonals describe the current state of things. These two different semantic clause types (since impersonals do not have a single syntactic form) stand in complete opposition on every facet of their representation. Whereas a transitive clause presents clearly delineated participants, impersonals describe a minimally delimited agent. The transitive agent is solely responsible for the occurrence of the profiled process but the impersonal process is available to all conceptualizers. Furthermore, if the transitive clause maximizes the asymmetry between the conceptualizer and the scene conceptualized, impersonals blur this distinction since the speaker is also part of the described reality. Finally, while dynamic predicates are most frequently attested in transitive clauses, impersonals show a preference for verbs of observation or epistemic evaluation (more on this in Chapter 3). The consistency of the opposition, however, does not mean that impersonals can only be described negatively, but that French speakers have found it symbolically relevant to linguistically group together an array of structurally eclectic constructions that code the exact opposite of a transitive event.

CHAPTER 3

The semantic range of *il* impersonals

The analysis of *il* impersonals is carried out over three chapters. Chapters 3 and 4 discuss simple impersonals, namely structures where the predicate is followed by a nominal, while Chapter 5 analyzes complex constructions where a finite or infinitival clause follows the predicate. This chapter focuses on the semantic import of the construction itself. It shows that impersonals are presentational constructions whose semantic function is to locate a given entity in some domain, and the individual components elaborate the relevant aspects of this general meaning. Impersonal *il* profiles the field, namely the knowledge structures on which the conceptualizer relies to assess that location, and the predicate specifies the process by which the conceptualized entity arrives at its location. The relationship between the construction itself and the participating predicates is investigated over two chapters. Chapter 3 defines the semantic contours of the simple impersonal category by evaluating the range of predicates attested in the construction, while Chapter 4 concentrates on the specific usage patterns that the most frequent predicates exhibit. Taken together, they illustrate at the same time the large amount of semantic overlap that exists among the construction's individual components, as well as the highly specific usage patterns that each predicate develops in its impersonal usage.

1. Introduction

Despite the claim made in the introduction that the French impersonal class should be broadened to include at least four different morphosyntactic constructions, *il* constructions nonetheless constitute the core of the category because they are overwhelmingly impersonal (see note 4 in the next section, as well as Section 6.1 in Chapter 4). Furthermore, since the *ça*, middle, and indefinite pronoun constructions are argued to exhibit impersonal value on the basis of their functional equivalence with *il* impersonals, it is important to clearly understand the latter's semantic and functional properties to subsequently determine the range of similarities the other constructions need to demonstrate to deserve a similar status. This chapter begins the investigation of *il* impersonals. Its main goal is to show that the consideration of the meaning of *il*, and hence the construction's own semantic/functional import, provides a convincing account of the overall structure of the category with particular respect to the distribution of predicates that participate in it. However, several different aspects of the construction need to be discussed before this position can be clear enough to be convincing, and this chapter is organized around these specific issues. Section 2 discusses the distinction introduced in Achard (1998 Chapter 7) between simple and complex impersonals according to the nature of the entity that follows the predicate. Section 3 focuses on the pronoun *il* itself, investigates the semantic hypothesis briefly mentioned in the introduction in further detail, and places this analysis in the context of the French tradition of impersonal research. Section 4 investigates the distribution of predicates in simple constructions, and shows that the results based on the semantic overlap that exists between the construction and individual predicates more adequately represent attested usage than syntactic accounts based on the predicates' structural properties. Finally, Section 5 recapitulates the results and concludes the chapter.

2. Simple and complex impersonals

In the French tradition, the term impersonal has predominantly been used to describe constructions in which the pronoun *il* 'it' does not refer to any participant in the discourse but nonetheless determines the third-person singular verb agreement on the following predicate, and where that predicate in turn is followed by a "postverbal expression" (Brunot 1936) that frequently codes the agent of the event the predicate profiles.[1] In the example in (3.1), the impersonal pronoun and predicate are in bold print and the postverbal expression is underlined:

(3.1)   *J'aurais cru à une foule de parents et de curieux.* **Il est venu** <u>très-peu de gens</u>.
(Bloy, L. *Journal*: 396)
'I would have thought a crowd of parents or spectators would be there. Very few people came [There came very few people]'.

In (3.1) the pronoun *il* 'it' is called an impersonal subject because it does not refer to any participant in the discourse but determines verb agreement, as reflected by the third-person singular agreement on the predicate *est venu* 'came'. The postverbal noun phrase (*très peu de gens* 'very few people') codes the agent of the coming event, but it does not determine verb agreement. This broad structural definition covers a large array of constructions that raise widely different kinds of issues for the analyst. It is thus necessary to group them together in ways that facilitate concentrating on specific issues at any given time. For example, structural

---

1.   Not all impersonal predicates are followed by a postverbal expression. For example, weather verbs, as in *il pleut* 'it is raining', are most frequently not.

investigations of impersonals have invariably focused on the derived predicates, i.e. those that can be preceded by a variety of subjects in different contexts (Jones 1996; Gledhill 2003; Rowlett 2007), to the detriment of intrinsic ones that can only be preceded by the impersonal pronoun *il*, because the impersonal realization of derived predicates results from some syntactic operation while that of intrinsic predicates is simply specified in their lexical semantic structure.[2]

I have suggested in previous work (Achard 1998: Chapter 7) that the distinction between simple and complex constructions according to the morphosyntactic nature of their postverbal expression provides useful insights about our overall understanding of impersonals. To briefly review this distinction, the constructions illustrated in (3.1), where the postverbal expression is a noun phrase, were called simple. By contrast, those presented in (3.2) and (3.3), where the postverbal expressions are respectively an infinitival and finite complement clause, were referred to as complex impersonals.

(3.2)   *L'entretien avec M. Lake a duré une trentaine de minutes. **Il n'a pas été possible** d'obtenir de détails sur la teneur des discussions.*   (AFP)
'The interview with M. Lake lasted approximately thirty minutes. It was not possible to obtain information about the content of the discussions.'

(3.3)   *"**Il est possible** que nous annoncions d'autres révisions, néanmoins nous devrions nous rapprocher du montant définitif," a déclaré le directeur adjoint de State Farm, Roger Lehman.*   (AFP)
'It is possible that we may announce further revisions, but we should be getting closer to the final amount, State Farm's Deputy Director Roger Lehman declared.'

---

2.   *S'agir* in (i) is an intrinsic impersonal predicate because it can only be preceded by impersonal *il* as the contrast with (ii) indicates:

(i)   *Aucune femme parmi nos anciennes malades n'a eu lieu, à ma connaissance, de se plaindre de nos soins... **il s'agit** sans doute encore d'une pauvre égarée...*
(Céline, L.F. *Voyage au bout de la nuit*: 577)
'No woman among our former patients has had, to my knowledge, any reason to complain about our treatment. It is probably another poor lost soul...'

(ii)   **Une pauvre égarée s'agit sans doute*
'A poor lost soul probably is'

Although the distinction between intrinsic and derived predicates is interesting and important, I believe it has been overstressed in order to justify the real subject role of the postverbal expression, and hence the dummy status of the impersonal pronoun (see Chapter 1). Intrinsic predicates are not considered specifically in this chapter, but certain predicates (*il faut, il s'agit*) are discussed in Chapter 4.

Despite the presence of the pronoun *il* in both instances, the simple and complex impersonals are distinguished by their distribution patterns and by the semantic function of grounding that they both serve in different manners. In terms of distribution, the majority of predicates can only participate in one construction or the other. For example, *venir* 'come' in (3.1) can only be followed by a nominal, whereas *être possible* 'be possible' in (3.2) and (3.3) only occurs with an infinitive as in (3.2), or a subordinate finite clause as in (3.3). Further examples of exclusively simple and complex impersonals are respectively illustrated in (3.4) and (3.5):[3]

(3.4)   *Entends- tu ce que je te dis? Joseph hocha la tête. – tu attendras dans les bois que la nuit tombe. À ce moment, tu descendras dans le ravin et tu rejoindras la route. Tu attendras encore, une heure s'il le faut.* **Il passera** <u>une voiture</u> *qui ralentira et s'arrêtera à la hauteur du ravin pour te laisser monter.*

(Green, J. *Moïra: roman*: 244)[4]

'Can you hear what I am telling you? Joseph nodded. You will wait in the woods until nightfall. At that time, you will go down the ravine toward the road. You will wait again, one hour if you have to. A car will come [there will pass a car]. It will slow down and stop by the ravine to let you in'.

(3.5)   *Il suffit que nous voyions deux ou trois personnes causer et s'agiter derrière une fenêtre, sans entendre ce qu'elles disent, et déjà* **il** *nous* **est** *bien* **difficile** <u>de deviner la pensée qui les mène</u>.   (Maeterlinck, M. *La vie des abeilles*: 43)

'Even when you see two or three people behind a window talking to each other and gesticulating, it is really hard to guess the thought process that governs their interaction'.

In fact, only a relatively small number of predicates participate in both simple and complex constructions, as illustrated in (3.6)–(3.9) with *arriver* 'arrive' and *rester* 'remain':[5]

---

3.   Complex *venir* 'come' is only possible in the interrogative form, as in #*d'où vient-il qu'il soit ici?* 'how come he is here?' for example.

4.   This example is repeated from Chapter 1 (1.36), where it was claimed that the *il* construction did not deserve the functional impersonal label because the event it describes is too specific to be generally available. The difference between morphological and functional impersonals is set aside for the moment because this chapter is mainly concerned with the semantics of the morphological *il* construction. However, it is taken up again in Chapter 4, Section 6 after the entire morphological category has been investigated.

5.   It is worth noting that the predicates that occur in both simple and complex constructions such as *falloir* (*il faut*) 'be necessary', *manquer* 'lack', *rester* 'remain' are also among the most frequently attested overall. This will be considered in detail in Chapters 4 and 5.

(3.6)   *Je n'aurais sans doute pas dû te dire tout ce que j'ai dit, fit-il d'un ton plus calme,*
        *mais c'était plus fort que moi. Pendant des mois, je me tais et **il arrive** <u>un jour</u>*
        <u>où je n'en peux plus</u>.   (Green, J. *Moïra: roman*: 192)
        'I probably shouldn't have told you all that I told you, he said in a calmer tone,
        but I couldn't help it. I will be silent for months and there comes a day when
        I can't hold it any more'.

(3.7)   ***Il arrive** <u>que les touristes passent plus de temps bloqués sur la piste</u> qu'ils ne*
        voyagent dans le ciel pendant la durée du vol.   (AFP)
        'It happens that tourists spend more time stuck on the runway than actually
        up in the air'.

(3.8)   *Quand j'aurai payé la roulotte et le cheval, **il** nous **restera** donc au moment du*
        départ <u>quinze cents francs à distribuer aux pauvres</u>.
                                                     (Aymé, M. *Clérambard*: 191)
        'When we leave, after paying for the car and the horse, there will be fifteen
        hundred francs left for us to give to the poor'.

(3.9)   *Henri regarda Dubreuilh d'un air interrogateur: – Si ce qui existe a toujours raison,*
        *il ne **reste** <u>qu'à se croiser les bras</u>.*   (Beauvoir, S. de. *Les mandarins*: 554)
        'Henry looked at Dubreuilh with a question in his eyes: – If what is is always
        right, the only thing to do is do nothing [there only remains to keep your arms
        folded]'.

Furthermore, the competition between *il* and the demonstrative *ce/ça* presented
in the introduction and further illustrated in (3.10) and (3.11) is only attested with
complex impersonals. The difference between (3.10) and (3.11), as well as the specific
importance of the copular environment (*être* + ADJECTIVE) for the *il/ça* alternation
constitutes the topic of Chapter 6 and will therefore not be considered further here,
but the fact that the competition between the two pronouns only occurs with complex impersonals constitutes a valid reason to consider these constructions separately.

(3.10) ***Il** n'est pas **nécessaire** <u>que ma pensée s'accorde avec la vie</u>…*
                                    (Barres, M. *Mes Cahiers T. 6 1907–1908*: 270)
        'It is not necessary for my thoughts to agree with life…'

(3.11) *#**Ce** n'est pas **nécessaire** <u>que ma pensée s'accorde avec la vie</u>…*
        'It is not necessary for my thoughts to agree with life…'

In addition to their different distributions, simple and complex impersonals are also
distinguished by their respective semantic functions that directly result from the
very nature of their postverbal expressions. With simple impersonals the predicate
is followed by a nominal; the construction is therefore concerned with identifying
the proper instance of the noun type that the speaker has in mind, and the determiners and other nominal "grounding expressions" (Langacker 2009: 167–181)

provide directions for narrowing down the scope of possibilities to just the right individual. By contrast, complex impersonals are followed by a complement clause; the expressions of "clausal grounding", namely tense and modality (Langacker 2009: 162–165), provide the resources necessary to assess the existence of the process described in the complement. Nominal grounding therefore pertains to the reference of the entity coded by the postverbal expression, while clausal grounding provides an epistemic assessment of the process profiled in the complement clause. The two constructions of simple and complex impersonals should therefore be kept separate initially so that the issues they individually raise can be thoroughly examined before a unified analysis is attempted. For this reason Chapters 3 and 4 are exclusively concerned with simple impersonals, while Chapter 5 discusses complex constructions. The first step in the analysis, however, concerns the status of the pronoun *il*, which obviously represents the distinguishing feature of the entire category.

3.   Status of impersonal *il*

The syntactic and semantic status of the pronoun is critical to any treatment of impersonals because it conditions the analysis of all the other components of the construction. This section shows that the CG solution briefly introduced in the previous chapters constitutes a natural extension of the well-established French psychological tradition (Sechehaye 1950; Galichet 1968).

Impersonal *il* is unquestionably the grammatical subject of the sentence since it possesses the three characteristics of French subjects. First, it is located before the predicate; second, it can be inverted in question formation, and finally, it dictates verb agreement. However, these formal properties have not traditionally been sufficient to treat it as the sole subject of the predicate. In earlier analyses that often confuse the concepts of "subject" and "agent", the majority of grammarians attempted to distinguish the *sujet grammatical, formel, logique, or morphologique* 'grammatical, formal, logical, or morphological subject' from the *sujet réel* 'real subject' of the predicate coded by the postverbal expression (Lauwers 2004: 293).[6] This

---

6.   The various positions within the two-subject approach are too numerous to be exhaustively presented here. We will simply note that some extreme positions have even refused *il* the status of grammatical subject, even though no alternative is suggested: "Il *parfois* ce *qui accompagne les verbes impersonnels n'est pas un sujet mais un pronom neutre qui ne joue aucun rôle et qu'on ne peut analyser*" (Bruneau and Heulluy 1937: 293) '*Il*, sometimes *ce* which accompanies impersonal verbs is not a subject but a neuter pronoun that does not play any role, and which cannot be analyzed'. The two-subject analysis lost its popularity by 1935 (Lauwers 2004: 294).

"two-subject solution" remained unassailable until Brunot (1936) pointed out that the postverbal expression should never be considered a subject but a complement:

> Dans l'expression actuelle – fort ancienne – *il faut de la vertu*, il est impossible de considérer *de la vertu* autrement que comme un complément et non point un sujet.

> 'In the current – very old – expression *il faut de la vertu*, it is impossible to consider *de la vertu* as anything else than a complement, and not a subject'.
> (Brunot 1936: 290, translation mine)

It necessarily follows that *il* is the only subject of the predicate:

> Quant à *il*, il ne désigne point assurément un sujet auteur de l'action. Il est analogique et ne représente rien; il n'en est pas moins le sujet, et ne joue en aucune façon le rôle qu'on lui a attribué d'annoncer un vrai sujet qui viendrait derrière. Ce sujet qui suit est un objet.

> 'As for *il*, it certainly does not designate a subject who performs the action. It is analogical and represents nothing; it is nonetheless the subject, and certainly does not play the part it was given to announce a real subject that would follow the predicate. This subject that follows is an object'. (Brunot 1936: 290, translation mine)

Brunot's insight about the structure of impersonals is still prevalent. Current syntactic theories have essentially adopted his analysis by treating *il* as a dummy in charge of satisfying the structural requirements of the French language (a modern twist on the grammatical subject solution). The position in Chomsky's 1981 Government and Binding theory is representative of a syntactic solution. Elements such as *it*, *there*, and "their counterparts in other languages (French *il* and, we will later suggest impersonal PRO in such languages as Italian and Spanish)" (Chomsky 1981: 26) are treated as "pleonastic elements" that get inserted by a structural requirement specific to the language: "Obligatory insertion of the NP α follows from the fact that the constructions illustrated require subjects for some structural reason" (Chomsky 1981: 26). The mechanisms adopted in the more recent Minimalist program (Chomsky 1995; Rowlett 2007) do not change the spirit of the analysis very much, even though the insertion mechanisms are quite different. Other nongenerative syntactic theories analyze impersonals with different theoretical tools but similar initial insight. Relational Grammar, for example, treats the French *il* and *ce* "dummy nominals" (along with their counterparts in various languages) as "final subjects" of the clause, also inserted to meet strictly structural requirements (Perlmutter and Postal 1983: 101).

3.1 "Dummy" *il*?

The very motivation for calling *il* an analogical or pleonastic form is to attend at the same time to its grammatical significance and its purported semantic vacuity.[7] Tesnière clearly expresses the pronoun's lack of meaning when he discusses the expression *il pleut* 'it is raining':

> *il* n'est en réalité que **l'indice** de la troisième personne et ne désigne nullement une personne ou une chose qui participerait d'une façon quelconque au phénomène de la pluie.

> '*il* is in reality only the mark of the third person and in no way designates a person or a thing which would participate in any way to the phenomenon of the rain.'
> (Tesnière 1959: 106, emphasis in the original, translation mine)[8]

Since the pronoun offers no semantic contribution it naturally follows that its import is exclusively syntactic. However, while essentially agreeing with this position, some authors nonetheless express it in a slightly more nuanced fashion. For example, Wartburg and Zumthor note that:

> Les verbes impersonnels sont des verbes expriment un procès dépourvu de sujet: dans *il pleut*, la langue exprime le procès de la pluie, en l'actualisant quant au temps et au mode; mais ce procès n'a pas de sujet à proprement parler (tout au plus le sujet est rejeté dans de vagues circonstances générales parmi lesquelles se dessine le procès).

> 'Impersonal verbs are verbs that express a process deprived of subject: in *il pleut*, the language expresses the process of raining while actualizing it in terms of tense and mood; but this process has no subject so to speak (at the most the subject is rejected in vague and general considerations among which the process unfolds)'.
> (Wartburg and Zumthor 1958: 193, translation mine)

The final parenthesis of Wartburg and Zumthor's quote contains the most distinctive aspect of their position, namely the idea that the subject of an impersonal can be represented by the vague circumstances from which the event coded by the predicate emerges. This recognition, however, has important consequences

---

7. Statements that express this position abound in the literature. For example, Hilty (cited in Wilmet 1997: 274) calls the impersonal pronoun "une forme vide qui n'a pas de signification en elle-même et ne renvoie à rien" 'an empty form which has no significance by itself and refers to nothing' (Hilty 1959: 250). The quotes by Brunot and Chomsky presented in the previous section clearly indicate that *il*'s analysis as a semantically vacuous placeholder possesses both a long tradition and significant lasting power.

8. Consequently Tesnière calls these predicates "verbes avalents" 'zero valency verbs' (Tesnière 1959: 106).

because it critically expands the range of possible subjects and allows certain authors to treat impersonal *il* as a full-fledged member of the category. This position is clearly stated in Sechehaye:

> Tel sujet psychologique peut être une donnée plus complexe qu'une idée de chose ou de personne, un fait par exemple, quelque chose qui se passe, ou bien une situation dans le temps ou l'espace déterminée de quelque façon mais en elle-même vide de représentation précise. Cette situation qui encadre le prédicat peut même se réduire à l'idée toute vague et inexprimable d'une ambiance quelconque. Nous le verrons à propos du verbe impersonnel latin (*pluit*, 'il pleut').

> 'Such a psychological subject can be a more complex entity than a thing or person. It can be, a fact, for example, something that happens, or a situation in time or space that we can recognize in some manner but deprived of any specific representation. This situation that surrounds the predicate can even be reduced to the very vague and difficult to express idea of some kind of ambiance. We will see this in the case of the Latin impersonal verb (*pluit* "il pleut")'.

> (Sechehaye 1950:45, translation mine)

Galichet considerably expands on Sechehaye's insight and notes that the impersonal construction represents a choice by the speaker to present her conceptualization in a precise way to express a specific nuance:

> car il est mille façons d'exprimer une idée, et, si l'on choisit un type de phrase plutôt qu'un autre, c'est bien pour marquer une nuance particulière.

> 'For there are thousands of ways of expressing an idea, and, if a type of sentence is selected rather than another one, it is indeed to express a specific nuance'.

> (Galichet 1968:140, translation mine)

Galichet illustrates his position with Valéry's phrase: "Il court sur La Fontaine une rumeur de paresse et de rêverie" 'There runs throughout La Fontaine a rumor of laziness and reverie' (Galichet 1968:139) and claims that:

> Le "il" exprime justement l'ambiance dont parle M. Sechehaye [see Sechehaye's quote above]. Quant à "rumeur de paresse et de rêverie", ce membre de phrase désigne en quelque sorte l'agent qui crée cette ambiance.

> 'The "il" expresses precisely the ambiance which M. Sechehaye is referring to. As to "rumeur de paresse et de rêverie", this sentence segment designates the agent who creates the ambiance so to speak'.

> (Galichet 1968:139, translation and insertion in brackets mine)

Importantly, Galichet concludes that grammatical constructions should be investigated in the context of the author's choice rather than relative to the logical relations their components may exhibit in other, perhaps more frequently attested contexts (i.e. when the agent of the predicate occurs in subject position):

> En préférant le tour impersonnel: "il court sur La Fontaine une rumeur de paresse et de rêverie...", Paul Valéry a cherché un effet de style, il a voulu mettre le verbe en évidence et donner à son affirmation un caractère volontairement vague. C'est donc dans ce type de phrase spécialement choisi par l'écrivain qu'il faut analyser les rapports syntaxiques des éléments et non dans un autre, plus commode à analyser sans doute, mais différent.

> 'In his selection of the impersonal structure "il court sur La Fontaine une rumeur de paresse et de rêverie...", Paul Valéry sought a specific stylistic effect, he wanted to highlight the verb and give his statement a purposefully vague character. It is thus in these kinds of sentences specifically chosen by the author that the syntactic connections between the components should be analyzed, and not in any other one, certainly easier to analyze, but different'.

> (Galichet 1968: 140, translation mine)

The recognition of the possibility of coding the general circumstances that surround the predicate or, in other words, the general ambiance of the impersonal scene opened the door to the treatment of the impersonal pronoun not only as the grammatical subject of the predicate, but also as a referential expression rather than a meaningless dummy (Bolinger 1973). To the possible objection that a notion such as "atmosphere" is too general to be considered meaningful, Bolinger rightfully points out that "our mistake has been to confuse generality of meaning with lack of meaning" (Bolinger 1977: 85). Consistent with this statement, he claims that English *it* should be analyzed as "a definite nominal with almost the greatest possible generality of meaning, limited only in the sense that it is 'neuter'. ... It embraces weather, time, circumstance, whatever is obvious by the nature of reality or the implications of context". Other researchers have followed the same insight and treated impersonal pronouns in various languages as meaningful as well. For example, Kirsner (1979: 81) claims that Dutch *er* has the meaning of "low situational deixis" or "mere sceneness" – i.e. an entity is "on the scene" but "the identity of that scene is immaterial".[9]

---

9.   In a different tradition (Gustave Guillaume's psychomécanique), Moignet treats impersonal ("unipersonal" in his terminology) verbs as "une sémanthèse dont la personne d'univers est incapable de s'assimiler à la personne humaine du moi – incapable en un mot de sortir d'elle-même" 'a sementhesis where the person of the universe is incapable to assimilate to the human person of the self – incapable in a word to get out of itself' (Moignet 1974: 63, translation mine). Consequently, the impersonal pronoun represents the *personne d'univers* 'person of the universe': "Le pronom personnel il du verbe unipersonnel est donc le pronom de la personne d'univers, immanent au plan verbal, indétachable de la sémanthèse..." 'The personal pronoun *il* of the unipersonal verb is thus the pronoun of the person of the universe, immanent to the level of the verb, inseparable from the semanthesis...' (Moignet 1974: 64, translation mine).

Finally, even though, as we have seen, the impersonal pronoun has not always been granted semantic meaning, the overall pragmatic function of the impersonal construction was nonetheless recognized early, and many grammarians acknowledge the construction's role of defocusing the agent. In a statement representative of many authors who view the impersonal construction as stylistically distinctive, Grevisse (1936: 332 [cited in Lauwers 2004: 295], translation mine) notes that:

> La construction impersonnelle est un procédé de style qui permet de donner plus de valeur à l'action exprimée par le verbe, en diminuant d'autant l'importance du sujet ou même en l'éludant tout à fait.
>
> 'The impersonal construction is a stylistic process that allows us to give more value to the action expressed by the verb, by decreasing the subject's importance accordingly, or even by suppressing it altogether'.[10]

3.2   The field

The solution proposed within the theory of Cognitive Grammar directly follows in the path that the psychological accounts presented in the preceding section blazed, and is thus largely based on the recognition of the meaning of impersonal pronouns. Recall from Chapters 1 and 2 that in CG impersonals are closely related to the setting subject constructions once again illustrated in (3.12) because they also select an aspect of the setting as the focal figure in the relation that the predicate profiles.[11]

---

10. Other similar statements include the following: "Le tour impersonnel met en relief le verbe" (Grammaire Larousse 1936: 58) 'The impersonal construction highlights the verb'. Furthermore, the German tradition of French grammars often considers the impersonal construction from the standpoint of information structure (Lauwers 2004: 614).

11. Consequently, just like setting subject constructions, impersonals do not passivize since passivizability correlates with transitivity, and the constructions that passivize the most felicitously are those that involve the interaction between the participants in an action chain (or analog) respectively coded as trajector and landmark (Langacker 2009: 118). This is the case in both English and French, as illustrated in (i)–(iv):

   (i)   *Big drops are being rained (by it)*
   (ii) *A natural disaster was witnessed by Georgia*
  (iii) *Une école bourgeoise a été vue par la France*
  (iv) *De grosses gouttes sont plues (par il)*

The parallel behavior of setting and impersonals to passivization has led to the treatment of impersonals as "abstract setting" constructions.

(3.12)   *À partir du xviiie siècle, un sourd travail devient perceptible. ...* **La France**
*voit une école bourgeoise renouer avec la tradition interrompue de ses propres
"peintres de la réalité"...*   (Huyghe, R. *Dialogue avec le visible:* 154)
'Starting in the eighteenth century, an obscure current begins to surface. ...
France witnesses the emergence of a bourgeois school that reconnects with
the interrupted tradition of its own "reality painters"...'

The entity that impersonals select, however, is considerably more abstract than
the temporal or spatial setting within which the process is carried out in (3.12),
and has already been called the field. This section investigates this notion further.
It first presents Langacker's analysis of English impersonals before showing how
it can be adapted to French.

In order to characterize the field with some degree of precision, we need to
recall that in the control cycle model introduced in Chapter 2 agents can only
exert their dominion over their target if the latter is within their reach or, in other
words, contained within the area that permits potential interaction with it. In the
perceptual and physical domains, that field can be respectively characterized as
the perceptual and kinesthetic range within which agents can extend the necessary force to capture their target. In more abstract domains that are much more
inclusive it is more difficult to outline precisely, and its definition is understandably
much more general: "More abstractly, it might be interpreted as indicating the
relevant scope of awareness, i.e. everything invoked in apprehending the situation
described" (Langacker 2009: 138). This scope of awareness obviously depends on
the precise nature of the domain considered. For example, in (3.13) it is mainly
restricted to the perception of the ground, but the emphasis may be placed on more
experiential factors, as in (3.14) and (3.15) where that scope includes all the factors
that allow a generalized conceptualizer to experience the scene described. These
factors may involve perceptual, mental, social, or psychological elements that all
contribute to the experience the scene evokes:

(3.13)   *We can't go through here, **it**'s all wet*

(3.14)   ***It**'s quiet in the countryside*   (from Langacker 2009: 138)

(3.15)   #***It**'s embarrassing when you can't remember somebody's name*

One sort of mental experience consists of making the kind of epistemic judgments
by which we continuously enrich our conception of reality, as illustrated in (3.16)
and (3.17):

(3.16)   ***It is true** that there was a joint decision by the Council and Parliament seeking
to discontinue emergency lines*

(3.17)   ***It is perfectly correct** that we need to apply this in certain cases*

In cases such as those in (3.16) and (3.17), the scope of awareness is maximally inclusive and incorporates everything that the conceptualizer takes into account to make the epistemic judgment the predicate codes. By analogy with the perceptual and physical domains, Langacker (2009: 139) describes the field in abstract domains as a conceptualizer's "mental reach" with respect to a certain entity: "At higher levels of cognition, the field is much harder to delineate, given our extraordinary mental capabilities. But by analogy to the physical and perceptual levels, we can describe the field for higher-level cognitive processes as comprising everything a conceptualizer is capable of apprehending at a given moment, or everything apprehended for a given purpose. Metaphorically, it is the conceptualizer's 'mental reach'". This most inclusive conception of the field constitutes the cornerstone of the CG analysis of impersonals. In a proposal that recapitulates and synthesizes the previous research in the area, Langacker suggests that impersonal constructions select the field as the focal figure in the profiled relation, and that field is represented by the impersonal pronoun: "I thus propose, as a general characterization, that impersonal 'it' profiles the relevant field, i.e. the conceptualizer's scope of awareness for the issue at hand" (Langacker 2009: 139). In my previous descriptions of French impersonals (Achard 1998, 2010), I have adopted Langacker's proposal to French, and claimed *il* also profiles the field.[12] I still believe this position is correct but it needs to be explained further, given the differences that exist between the two languages.

As was mentioned in the introduction, English does not have a designated impersonal form that always fulfills that role. As illustrated in (3.13)–(3.15), "it" is a neuter third-person singular pronoun that potentially refers to any discourse entity even though it may be difficult to precisely delineate, and its impersonal sense constitutes a straightforward extension of its neuter anaphoric value. In French, *il* does not synchronically have a neutral value.[13] This role is assumed by the demonstrative pronoun *ce* (*c'*, *ça*), as the translations of (3.13)–(3.15) in (3.18)–(3.20) show:

---

12. In Achard (1998: 282), I suggested that *il* profiles the "immediate scope of the existential predication, that is the specific part of R [reality] immediately necessary for E's [the event] construal". Langacker's definition adopted here is perfectly compatible with my 1998 statement, but it represents an improvement in that it directly connects impersonals to more general issues of clause structure. For a review of several accounts of the meaning of impersonal pronouns, see Langacker (2009).

13. In addition to its impersonal sense, *il* is also a third-person masculine singular subject pronoun, as (i) illustrates:

(i) **Qui** *ça? – Dutertre. – Je ne me rappelle plus… si, il est venu une fois, mais pas dans les classes…*   (Colette, G. *Claudine à l'école*: 133)
    'Who? – Dutertre. – I don't remember…yes, he came once, but he didn't visit the classrooms…'

In (i) the pronoun *il* anaphorically refers to Dutertre, and marks third-person masculine singular agreement with the predicate. In that use, this subject pronoun needs to be distinguished from its feminine counterpart *elle* 'she'.

(3.18)   *On ne peut pas traverser ici, c'est tout mouillé*

(3.19)   *C'est calme à la campagne*

(3.20)   *C'est gênant quand on ne se rappelle pas du nom de quelqu'un*

Il only represents the French equivalent to "it" with complex impersonals where it is also in competition with *ça*, as the translations of (3.16) and (3.17) in (3.21) and (3.22) illustrate.

(3.21)   *Il/c'est vrai qu'une décision commune du parlement et du conseil visait à supprimer les files d'urgence*

(3.22)   *Il/c'est tout à fait correct que nous devons l'appliquer dans certains cas*

The impersonal usage of English "it" is thus strongly rooted in its neuter (anaphoric) value. Langacker convincingly explains its impersonal uses in terms of a decrease of its delimitation. Recall from Chapter 2 that delimitation refers to "how the profiled instance projects to the world (or the relevant universe of discourse)" (Langacker 2009: 123). More specifically:

> I will merely suggest that impersonal *it* represents the extreme case of vagueness and non-delimitation. It (or *it*) is not only definite but also referential, given that our mental world includes highly abstract entities. What makes it special, compared to straightforward cases of anaphoric *it*, is that its referent is maximally diffuse, being wholly unlimited within the immediate scope of discourse. Its impersonal uses stem directly from its properties and place in the system of English definite. Of all the definite English nominals, it does the least by way of signaling out and identifying a particular, well-delimited referent. As a pronoun, it does not occur with a lexical noun providing a type specification. Its own specification, something like 'neuter' or 'non-human thing' is highly schematic and applicable to the widest possible array of entities.   (Langacker 2009: 129)

The differences between French and English raise two related questions. First, is it possible for *il* and "it" to be characterized in a similar manner since their respective distributions are so different, and *il* has no current neuter sense? Second, how can we account for the difference between *il* and *ça* given their competition with complex impersonals? To dispense with the second question quickly, Chapters 5 and 6 show that French and English are organized differently with respect to the kind of abstract location (Achard 2010) that can receive linguistic prominence. While *il* can indeed be viewed as profiling the field, neuter pronouns can only profile the setting, however abstract (Achard 2010, in press). Competition arises in the cases in which the two notions maximally overlap. This position is explained in detail in Chapters 5 and 6, and will thus not concern us further here. The first question, however, requires more careful examination.

Historically, *il* is quite similar to "it" because it also used to have a neuter sense. In Old French the most common impersonal marker was Ø, but beginning in the twelfth century *il*, from the Latin neuter third-person demonstrative *illud*, gradually became more and more grammaticalized to become "*général*" by the sixteenth century (Brunot 1936: 285). During that time *il* was a neuter pronoun comparable to "it", which did not exclusively mark masculine referents but also more general propositional entities, in a role similar to the one demonstratives (*ce, c', ça*) play in the contemporary language.[14] This neuter sense is illustrated in (3.23):

(3.23)   *C'estoit jadis chose bien rare, Que de voir un abbé ignare: Aujourd' huy **il** est si commun, Que cent mille, aussi bien comme un, Se trouveront:…*

(Marot, C. [1526]. *Les Traductions*: 171)

'It was in the past a very rare thing to see an uncultured abbot: Nowadays it is so common, that you can as easily find one hundred thousand as one'

In (3.23) *il* does not refer to the abbot or any male character in the discourse, and thus cannot be considered a personal pronoun. Neither is it an impersonal, since no postverbal expression is present in the sentence. The pronoun's meaning is that of a neuter expression referring to the event *voir un abbé ignare* 'see an uncultured abbot'. The *Dictionnaire de la langue française* (Émile Littré 1872–1877 made available online by the FRANTEXT project at http://artfproject.uchicago.edu/content/dictionnaires-dautrefois) cites numerous examples of the pronoun's neuter usage in the seventeenth century, including those in (3.24)–(3.28):

(3.24)   *Ayant appris dès le collège qu'on ne saurait rien imaginer de si étrange et si peu croyable, qu'**il** n'ait été dit par quelqu'un des philosophes*

(Descartes, R. *Discours de la méthode* II: 4)

'Having learned since college that one could not imagine anything so strange and unbelievable that it would not have been said by a philosopher'

(3.25)   *Si ce que je dis ne sert à vous éclairer, **il** servira au peuple*   (Pascal, B. *Cousin*: X)

'If what I am saying serves to enlighten you, it will serve the people'

(3.26)   *Une raison première et universelle, qui a tout conçu avant qu'**il** fût…*

(Bossuet. *Connaissances. V*: 2):

'A primitive and universal reason, which has conceived everything before it has occurred'

(3.27)   *Tout cela ne convient qu'à nous. – **Il** ne convient pas à vous-même, Repartit le vieillard…*   (La Fontaine, J. de. *Fables. X*: 8)

'All this is only convenient for us. It is not convenient for yourself the old man replied…'

---

14. A contemporary translation of (3.23) would need to include the demonstrative pronoun *ce*: *'aujourd'hui c'est si commun'*.

(3.28)   *Le premier effet de l'amour est d'inspirer un grand respect; l'on a de la vénération*
         pour ce que l'on aime; ***il*** *est bien juste: on ne reconnaît rien au monde de grand*
         comme cela   (Pascal, B. *Passions de l'amour*: XXX)
         'The first effect of love is to inspire a great respect; one has veneration for the
         object of one's love; it is only fair: one knows nothing in the world as great as
         that'

Furthermore, *il*'s neuter pronoun value has not completely disappeared from contemporary usage, as the examples in (3.29)–(3.35) illustrate:

(3.29)   *De ce chef, initialement, la reproduction apparaît comme un simple procédé*
         imaginé par la nature pour assurer la permanence de l'instable dans le cas des
         vastes édifices moléculaires. Mais, comme ***il*** *arrive toujours dans le monde,*
         ce qui n'était à l'origine qu'un hasard heureux, ou un moyen de survivance, se
         trouve immédiatement transformé et utilisé en outil de progrès et de conquête.
                              (Teilhard de Chardin. *Le phénomène humain*: 110)
         'From this standpoint, initially, reproduction appears to be a simple process
         nature imagined to allow instability to remain permanent in the case of huge
         cell assemblies. However, as it often occurs in the world, what was initially only
         fortunate happenstance, or a means of survival, gets immediately transformed
         and used as a tool for progress and conquest'.

(3.30)   *Peut-être la foule italienne eut-elle instinctivement la notion de mes sentiments.*
         Peut-être, dans son épreuve, la pensée de la France lui était-elle plus familière,
         comme ***il*** *arrive aux pays malheureux.*
                              (Gaulle, C. de. *Mémoires de guerre, l'unité*: 194)
         'Perhaps the Italian crowd understood my feelings instinctively. Perhaps, in its
         ordeal, the French way of thinking was more familiar to them, as it happens
         to countries in distress'.

(3.31)   *Mais à la sortie, la vie est si pressée qu'elle ne prend pas toujours une forme dési-*
         gnée comme celle du levraut et du chameau. Des gravures montrent à la sortie
         d'étranges mélanges d'êtres comme ***il*** *arrive pour ce colimaçon reproduit dans le*
         livre de Jurgis Baltrusaitis (p. 58) "À tête humaine barbue et à oreilles de lièvre,
         coiffé d'une mitre et à pattes de quadrupèdes".
                              (Bachelard, G. *La poétique de l'espace*: 108)
         'But in the end, life is in such a hurry than it doesn't always take a designated
         form like that of a camel or a young hare. Some drawings reveal strange mix-
         tures of animals like it happened with this reproduction in Jurgis Baltrusaitis'
         book (p. 58) of a shape "with a bearded human head and the ears of a hare,
         with a mitre on its head and four legs"'.

(3.32) *L'expédition d'Algérie a été d'un côté une affaire de prestige dynastique; de l'autre une mesure de police méditerranéenne; comme **il** arrive souvent, la défense s'est transformée en conquête.*   (Weil, S. *Écrits historiques et politiques*: 90)
'The Algerian expedition was on the one hand an affair of prestige for the dynasty, and on the other a business of Mediterranean policing; as it often happens, defense became conquest'.

(3.33) *Considère-t-on un produit ou un lot bien déterminé de produits rigoureusement caractérisés, il est possible de dire si, communément, il se négocie sur un marché local, national, pluri-national. Si, à l'échelle du monde, ainsi qu'**il** arrive pour les grandes matières premières et les produits de base, les offres et les demandes se conjoignent dans une bourse ou sur une place principale, on parlera d'un marché mondial.*   (Perroux, F. *L'économie du XXe siècle*: 285)
'For any product or well-determined set of products, it is possible to say if it usually sells on a local, national, or international market. If, at the world level, as it happens for raw materials and basic products, supply and demand meet at an exchange or a centralized location, we will talk about a world market'.

(3.34) *Comme **il** arrive presque toujours, le débat autour du discours s'était développé dans la confusion.*   (Guéhenno, J. *Jean-Jacques. T. 2*: 18)
'As it almost always happens, the debate over the discourse was confusing from the beginning'.

(3.35) *Il est incroyable à quel point je parviens encore à sous-estimer, presque à décompter mes possibilités d'afflux religieux…*   (DuBos C. *Journal T. 3*: 321)
'It is incredible to what extent I still manage to underestimate, almost exclude my potential for religious outbursts…'

The examples in (3.29)–(3.35) show that *il* still occurs where one might expect the more commonly attested *ça/c'*. Although *il*'s neuter value is predominantly restricted with *arriver* (*il arrive*), it is also found with other predicates such as *être incroyable* 'be incredible' in (3.35). The diachronic examples show that the development of French *il* parallels that of "it" up to a certain point, before the two pronouns diverge. The common diachronic paths of *il* and "it" validate a similar analysis of the two pronouns. It seems reasonable to suggest that following a period when it expressed both neutral anaphoric and impersonality (much like "it" does today), *il* became grammaticalized as a specialized impersonal. From this standpoint, even though the French and English systems synchronically diverge, their diachronic similarity, especially their shared characteristic of having a neuter pronoun used as an impersonal at some point in their history, justifies treating *il* in a way parallel to "it". More systematic similarities between impersonals and demonstratives will be explored in Chapters 5 and 6, but at this stage of the analysis it suffices to point out that *il* does not constitute a random form arbitrarily selected to perform a specific structural function. Even though it is not directly observable synchronically, impersonal *il* represents a perfectly well-motivated development of its earlier use as a neuter pronoun.

We can therefore expand Langacker's proposal to French, and claim that in the example presented in Chapter 1 and repeated in (3.36) *il* profiles the speaker's mental reach relative to the existence of the alternative edition, or in other words the knowledge base composed of all the facts that allow him to assert the edition's existence.

(3.36)   *Gêné par la pensée qu'il existe <u>un livre appelé le pêcheur justifié</u>. Je ne l'ai pas encore lu. J'ai cru que cela me troublerait, mais j'en connais le thème.*
                                        (Green, J. *Journal. T. 5.* 1946–1950: 232)
          'Disturbed by the thought that there exists a book called the justified sinner. I haven't read it yet, I thought it would disturb me, but I know what it is about'.

In order to conceptualize this target and address its epistemic status, the speaker's knowledge base needs to include at the very least the precise conditions under which the author came to be aware of the book's existence (how he heard about it, saw it, and so on). This section of the conceptualizer's knowledge base constitutes the field within which the epistemic status of the target can be addressed, and that field, profiled by the impersonal pronoun *il*, is selected as the focal figure in the main relation and thus coded as subject.

The impersonal construction was already included among the configurations presented in Figure 2.8, but it is repeated in Figure 3.1 for convenience:

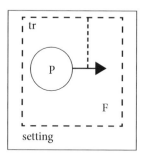

Figure 3.1 *Il* impersonal construction

In Figure 3.1 the field is marked F and indicated with a broken rectangle. The field is coded as the trajector of the process and thus selected as subject. The process [*exister* 'exist' in (3.36)] is also profiled. By contrast, the only participant marked as P [the book in (36)] is left unprofiled. Importantly, the broken line between the process and the field indicates a tight connection between the two entities. The nature of that connection, however, deserves further attention. On the one hand, it seems fairly straightforward. The very definition of the field confers to the latter a high level of responsibility with respect to the process coded by the predicate because that process could only be uncovered against its background. On the other hand, the field was described as a given conceptualizer's scope of awareness with respect to the profiled process, and it is therefore not immediately obvious how one individual's knowledge base concerning a process might be responsible for its occurrence. In order to reconcile these seemingly diverging observations, we need to remember that even though the conceptualizing experience that leads to the discovery of the existing book is indeed that of the speaker (or any relevant conceptualizer), it is not presented as such. Recall from Chapter 1 that the second requirement for impersonals is that the conceptualized scene be available to a generalized conceptualizer. The basic idea is that any person in a similar position would invariably reach the same conclusion. For example, in (3.36) anyone in possession of the same information as the author would invariably have reached the same conclusion. In this sense, the existence of the book can be considered a property of the field. This point is particularly important because this characteristic of *il* impersonals confers to the construction its general character, which alternative impersonal candidates will have to emulate.

At this point of the analysis the field may seem like a rather vague concept because of the difficulty of predicting with precision the mental knowledge base on which each conceptualizer relies to express her conceptualization. However, the analyses of individual predicates developed in Chapter 4 reveal an important level of conventionalization, due in no small part to the constraints imposed by the semantics of individual predicates. With *rester* 'remain' and *manquer* 'lack' (in *il reste/manque des pommes* 'there remains/lacks apples', for example), the field necessarily incorporates the conceptual manipulations that make it possible for the conceptualizer to compare the conceptualized entity to its original or ideal counterpart. Even with predicates such as *il y a* 'there is' that impose no specific restrictions on the postverbal expression, the field nonetheless exhibits a certain amount of regularity provided by the conventionalized individual patterns that each semantic configuration evokes. Chapter 4 shows that once the usage of specific predicates is thoroughly examined the notion of field is not hopelessly nebulous or idiosyncratic, but that the conceptual routines that subtend linguistic expressions are themselves subject to the same conventionalization patterns that those expressions represent.

It is worth noting that the CG solution addresses the issues raised by French grammarians in a clear and straightforward manner. First, the assignment of the subject role to the field poses no particular problem since subject assignment is a matter of construal (i.e. how the conceptualizer chooses to structure her conceptualization for linguistic purposes). Importantly, the assignment of a specific entity as subject is kept strictly separate from the role this entity plays in the process the predicate codes (its thematic role). Consequently, there is no need to consider different kinds of subjects ("real" or "final", for example) and the third-person agreement is naturally accounted for since the field is the only and unquestionable clausal subject. Second, because the process profiled by the predicate is presented as a property of the field in the sense described above rather than the production of its participants, its importance is naturally highlighted while that of the participants is proportionally decreased. Finally, the pragmatic role of the construction is also readily accounted for since the agent is naturally defocused by virtue of the field's selection as the most salient figure in the profiled relation.

3.3   Semantics and information structure

Finally, one might argue against *il*'s semantic import by claiming that the sole function of the impersonal construction is the management of the flow of information within the clause. This aspect of impersonals was emphasized early on in the German tradition of French grammar (Lauwers 2004: 614), and more recently in the work of Lambrecht (1994). In this view, the construction's main function consists of ensuring that the theme follows the predicate if it conveys new information. Exclusive focus on the theme's location diminishes the semantic import of the impersonal pronoun because the latter is only instrumental in the construction's overall function as a placeholder. However, while impersonals undeniably perform an important information management function, their semantic import cannot be reduced to that sole function because alternative strategies such as inversion or Ø impersonals are also available for speakers to manage the flow of information and compete with *il* impersonals in relevant contexts. Consider for instance the example in (3.37):

(3.37)   *Aujourd'hui âgé de 22 ans, l'Américain, qui a obtenu derrière l'inaccessible Pete Sampras les meilleurs résultats de ce début d'année -quatre victoires sur six finales disputées-, est toujours en quête d'un autre titre dans un tournoi du Grand Chelem pour étoffer son palmarès. A cause d'un service manquant de puissance et d'une envergure trop faible au filet, le gazon anglais de Wimbledon ne semble pas la surface où il pourrait y parvenir. **Restent les surfaces rapides**, et la terre battue, une surface a priori faite pour son jeu.*   (AFP)

'Now 22, the American with the best results of the year behind the unreachable Pete Sampras with four victories in his six finals is still chasing another Grand Slam title to improve his record. Because of his relatively weak serve and lack of reach at the net, the British grass at Wimbledon doesn't seem the place where he could get it. Hard courts remain [remain hard courts], as well as tournaments played on clay, a surface that seems well suited to his game'.

In (3.37) the theme of the predicate *rester*, namely *les surfaces rapides* 'fast surfaces', is coded as its subject, as indicated by the plural agreement on the predicate. Note that in this inverted subject construction its postverbal location is identical to the one it would occupy in the impersonal construction *il reste les surfaces rapides*. However, these two constructions are not semantically identical since the impersonal would constitute an awkward choice in this example. Consequently, even though the impersonal and subject inversion constructions are equivalent from the standpoint of information structure, the selection of the impersonal pronoun as subject cannot solely be imputed to the need for the predicate's theme to follow that predicate, and a successful analysis of impersonals needs to carefully investigate the pronoun's own semantic import.

In the same vein, the example in (3.38) illustrates a Ø impersonal rather than a subject inversion construction because of the third-person singular agreement on the predicate when the theme is plural. Here again, the Ø and *il* impersonals are pragmatically equivalent – they afford the same kind of solution to an information management problem – but they are not identical because the pronoun contributes its own meaning to that of the construction:

(3.38) *Plus loin, deux autres divisions blindées, la 12è SS (Hitler-Jugend) et la division Panzer-Lehr, respectivement près d'Evreux et vers Alençon-Le Mans. Trois autres divisions (1è SS, 2è et 16è) se tiennent au nord de la Seine, aux environs de Mons, Peronne et Senlis.–Aviation: moins de 500 appareils, dont une majeure partie viennent d'être envoyés sur le front est. **Reste quelques dizaines de bombardiers et chasseurs.***   (AFP)

'Further, two other divisions of tanks, the 12th SS (Hitler-Jugend) and the Pantzer-Lehr division, respectively near Evreux and around Alençon-Le Mans. Three other divisions (1st SS, 2nd and 16th) positioned north of the Seine, around Mons, Peronne and Senlis. – Air support: fewer than 500 planes, a major part of which had been sent to the eastern front. Several dozens of bombers and fighter planes remain [remain several dozens of bombers and fighter planes]'.

These two examples clearly show that if *il* impersonals share an important pragmatic function with other constructions, their semantic import cannot be reduced to this sole function. *Il* impersonals differ from Ø impersonals and subject inversion constructions precisely because of the presence of the pronoun. As a result, the latter's semantic relevance cannot be denied and needs to be considered carefully to reach a thorough understanding of the construction's semantic function.[15]

---

15. The distinction that exists between the *il* impersonals on the one hand, and Ø impersonals and subject inversion constructions on the other obviously raises the issue of the specific meaning of these constructions. The matter is complicated by the frequent difficulty of distinguishing

4. The semantic range of simple impersonals

The basic insight behind the analysis developed in this monograph is that impersonals are meaningful constructions, and that their individual components exhibit large amounts of semantic overlap. Obviously, because each component contributes its own semantic import the construction's overall meaning can only

---

between Ø impersonals and subject inversion constructions when the theme is in the singular, and the agreement on the predicate is a third singular in both cases, as illustrated in (i)–(iii). Nevertheless, these constructions tend to code "list readings" where the author checks out specific items from a list before specifying the ones that are left over.

(i)   *Ces nouveaux venus seront encadrés par la "légion italienne" de Vogts, des joueurs aguerris mais encore jeunes: Stefan Effenberg (Fiorentina) et Andreas Moeller (Juventus), les fortes têtes de l'équipe, dont le génie créateur ne demande qu'à s'imposer, Thomas Haessler (AS Rome) et Matthias Sammer (passé l'an dernier de l'Inter de Milan au Borussia Dortmund).* **Reste la question du gardien de but.**   (AFP)

'These newcomers will be surrounded by Vogts' "Italian legion", composed of experienced players who are still young: Stefan Effenberg (Fiorantina) and Andreas Moeller (Juventus), the leaders of the team whose creative genius only needs to be unleashed, Thomas Haessler (AS Rome) and Matthias Sammer (transferred from Inter Milan to Borussia Dortmund last year). The question of the goalkeeper remains [remain the question of the goalkeeper]'.

(ii)   *"Pyongyang ne subirait pas de grandes conséquences matérielles si elle confirmait officiellement son retrait" a précisé M. Meyer." L'aide technique non médicale de l'ordre de 275.000 dollars par an a été suspendue vendredi dernier par le Conseil des Gouverneurs de l'Agence.* **Reste l'aide médicale** *qui est modeste et les conseils d'assistance technique dispensés par l'AIEA pour aider les pays-membres à maitriser les technologies nucléaires, at- il dit.*   (AFP)

'"Pyongyang would suffer no great material consequences if they officially confirmed their withdrawal Mr. Meyer added." The nonmedical technical assistance worth around 275,000 dollars a year was suspended last Friday by the agency's Governing Board. Only the modest medical assistance and technical advice dispensed by the agency to help member states to master nuclear technologies remain, he said [remain the modest medical assistance and technical advice dispensed by the agency to help member states to master nuclear technologies remain he said]'.

(iii)   *Après le maigre bilan du Mondiale italien (115 buts seulement, soit 2,21 par match, plus faible moyenne de l'histoire), la FIFA a tout fait pour redonner du plaisir aux joueurs et au public. A cet effet, les arbitres auront eux aussi un rôle essentiel: le tâcle par derrière équivaudra à un carton rouge et le hors-jeu de position ne sera plus systématiquement sanctionné.* **Reste le jeu.** *Et ceux qui le font.*   (AFP)

'After the meager results of the Italian Mondiale (only 115 goals, that is 2.21 per game, the weakest average in history), FIFA did everything to give pleasure back to players and spectators. To that effect, the referees will play a crucial part: a tackle from behind will mean a red card, and an off side position will not necessarily be called. The game remains [remains the game], and those who play it'.

become clear once each component's role has been well understood. Two aspects of the construction's meaning have already been mentioned, and are developed further throughout this chapter as well as in Chapter 4. First, impersonals have been described as presentational constructions because they identify or locate a given entity with respect to some domain. Second, impersonal *il* was shown to profile the knowledge structures that render that location possible. This section and the next chapter focus on the role of the predicate within the construction. The remainder of this chapter establishes the semantic range of the construction by examining the classes of predicates that participate in it. Chapter 4 investigates the specific patterns that each of the most frequent predicates develops in its impersonal usage. Taken together, they provide a complementary view of different aspects of the construction's usage.

4.1   Distribution of predicates with simple impersonals[16]

As mentioned in the previous section, the distribution of predicates in the simple impersonal construction reflects the semantic overlap that exists between its individual components. The way in which the pronoun *il* fits the construction is clear.

---

16. Impersonal predicates may occur with either active or passive morphology, as illustrated in (i) and (ii):

(i) *Mais quand j'ai ouvert la porte, j'ai vu Vincent. Il m'a dit: – Ne vous inquiétez pas! Ce qui m'a tout de suite inquiétée. J'ai dit: "il est arrivé <u>quelque chose</u> à Nadine!"*

(Beauvoir, S. de. *Les mandarins*: 196)

'But when I opened the door, I saw Vincent. He told me: – Do not worry! Which worried me right away. I said: "something happened to Nadine" [there happened something to Nadine]!'

(ii) ***Il a été dit*** *par le physicien anglais Patrick Blackett <u>que l'utilisation de la bombe n'a pas tant été le dernier acte militaire de la deuxième guerre mondiale que le premier acte voulu de la guerre froide avec l'union soviétique.</u>*

(Goldschmidt, B. *L'aventure atomique: ses aspects politiques et techniques*: 58)

'It was said by British physicist Patrick Blackett that the use of the H bomb was not as much the last military act of World War II as the first intentional act of the cold war with the Soviet Union.'

In (i) the predicate exhibits active morphology, namely tense and perfective aspect (*passé composé*). In (ii) the predicate contains the passive marker, namely the auxiliary *être* 'be' inserted between the auxiliary *avoir* 'have' and the past participle *dit* 'said', the two components of the *passé composé* form. In the literature, constructions with active morphology are sometimes called "Extraposition of Indefinites" (EXIs), whereas the structures with passive morphology are referred to as "Impersonal passives" (IPs) (Legendre 1990). As the example in (ii) indicates, impersonal passives often (but not always) involve finite (or infinitival) postverbal expressions, and will thus be investigated in Chapter 5. The remainder of this chapter is exclusively concerned with active simple impersonals.

The knowledge base that it profiles allows a generalized conceptualizer to locate the conceptualized entity in some domain. This section shows that the most frequent predicates in the construction are precisely those that exhibit the most semantic overlap with both the pronoun and the overall construction because they centrally invoke an element of the setting in their lexical semantic structure. To be more explicit, these predicates maximally overlap with the pronoun's meaning because the analysis and evaluation of the setting within which the conceptualized entity occurs represent a large part of the mental effort required to determine its location.

Before we move on to the analysis, a note on the data used in the remainder of this chapter is in order. As mentioned in the introduction, French possesses a class of predicates that can only be preceded by the impersonal pronoun. The presence of these intrinsic predicates complicates the evaluation of the range and frequency of the larger impersonal class that includes optional verbs for two reasons. First, some intrinsic predicates (*il faut* 'it is necessary' and *il y a* 'there is' in particular) are so frequent that their inclusion adds uncomfortable bulk to the data, and thus considerably restricts the range of predicates that can reasonably be examined. Furthermore, the consideration of intrinsic impersonals provides no particular insight into the assessment of the predicates that exhibit most semantic affinity with the impersonal construction (Gries and Divjak 2009), since by definition they can only occur in that construction. Consequently, the intrinsic impersonals *il faut* 'it is necessary', *il s'agit* 'it is about', *il y a* 'there is', as well as the weather verbs (*il pleut* 'it is raining', *il fait froid* 'it is cold') are not included in this part of the analysis. This methodological choice is not detrimental to our overall understanding of the semantic range of simple impersonals because (1) intrinsic impersonals easily fit into the semantic classes uncovered by the investigation (for example, *il faut* is semantically very close to *manquer* 'lack' considered in detail in the next chapter), and (2) the most frequent ones (*il y a*, *il faut*, *il s'agit*) are considered individually in Chapters 4 and 5 respectively. These forms excluded, the data set used in this section consists of a total of 610 tokens of active impersonal constructions, 307 from the AFP corpus, and 303 from 25 texts of the twentieth-century FRANTEXT database searched by construction. More precisely, the searched term was '*il*', and impersonals were extracted manually.[17] The 307 journalistic tokens instantiated sixteen different verbs, while thirty-nine verbs were represented in the 303 literary examples. The data from the two corpora are remarkably similar despite the apparent disparity in number, because all but two of the predicates found in journalistic texts were also attested in the literary corpus and the remaining two have very close synonyms among the attested verbs. Furthermore, the relative frequency of the

---

17. This data set is identical to that used in Achard (2009).

most commonly found predicates is very similar in both corpora. The difference in total number of verb types could be attributed to the wider range of narrative situations covered in the literary texts.

The first striking characteristic that the corpus reveals is the extreme disparity in the relative frequency of the participating predicates. Out of the forty-one attested verbs, *exister* 'exist' and *rester* 'stay' account for 363 tokens, that is, over 50 percent of all instances. Furthermore, only nine predicates, namely *exister* 'exist', *rester* 'stay', *manquer* 'lack', *arriver* 'arrive', *venir* 'come', *être* 'be', *résulter* 'result', *passer* 'pass', and *coûter* 'cost', produce ten or more tokens. On the other hand, fourteen verbs contribute between two and six tokens each, and eighteen only provide one token. Second, the predicates in the simple impersonal construction exhibit remarkable semantic consistency. The forty-one verbs of the corpus easily divide themselves into the five well-defined classes illustrated in (3.39)–(3.43). The number that follows each class indicates the number of tokens for the whole class; the one that follows each verb represents the number of tokens for that verb. An example indicated in prime numbers follows each class as an illustration.

The overwhelming majority of the attested predicates assess the presence or absence of the elements that compose the conceptualized scene. The verbs of this class are given in (3.39):[18]

(3.39)   **Elements that compose a scene (452):** *exister* 'exist' (195), *rester* 'stay' (168), *être* 'be' (16), *manquer* 'lack' (61), *subsister* 'subsist' (6), *suffire* 'be enough' (5), *demeurer* 'remain' (1), *durer* 'last' (1)

(3.39′)   ... *Et puis, j'incarne un modèle de femme qu'on voit rarement au petit écran. Il **existe** de nombreux modèles masculins (Dechavanne, Ardisson, Rapp), mais peu de femmes...*   (AFP)
'....Plus the fact that I represent a type of women you don't often see on TV. There exist many such males (Dechavanne, Ardisson, Rapp), but few women...'

The second most frequent class illustrated in (3.40) includes predicates that denote the appearance/disappearance of a participant on/from a scene:

(3.40)   **Appearance/disappearance on/from a scene (83):** *arriver* 'arrive' (40), *venir* 'come' (21), *naître* 'be born' (3), *sortir* 'go out' (5), *surgir* 'rush' (1), *entrer* 'come in' (4), *revenir* 'come back' (3), *apparaître* 'appear' (2), *survenir* 'occur' (2), *paraître* 'appear' (1), *fuser* 'gush out' (1)

---

18. *Il faut* 'it is necessary', *il y a* 'there is', as well as the weather verbs such as *il pleut* 'it is raining', *il fait froid* 'it is cold', or *il y a du vent* 'there is wind' belong in this category.

(3.40′)   *...il me semble que tous mes livres ont eu pour point de départ le traversin où je pose ma tête, mais dire comment je vois m'est impossible. En tout cas, **il arrive** toujours <u>une seconde</u> où ces images d'une netteté parfois hallucinante se décomposent tout à coup et glissent les unes dans les autres.*

(Green, J. Journal. T. 5. 1946–1950:77)

'It seems to me that all my books started with the pillow where I rest my head, but it is impossible for me to express the way I see. In any case, there always comes one second when these sometimes incredibly sharp images suddenly decompose and fade into one another'.

The third related class illustrated in (3.41) includes predicates that denote a logical result or consequence. The complement of the predicate is presented as an expected occurrence that enters the conceptualized scene.

(3.41)   **Expected consequence (21)**: *résulter* 'result' (15), *s'ensuivre* 'follow' (5), *ressortir* 'come out' (1)

(3.41′)   *Je crois que lorsque cette unité se rompt, **il** en **résulte** <u>des crises</u> qui sont ni plus ni moins que des crises de folie.*   (Green, J. Journal. T. 5. 1946–1950:304)
'I believe that when this unity is broken, there results crises that are no less than crises of dementia'.

The fourth class describes the motion of a participant within a scene. It includes the predicates in (3.42):

(3.42)   **Motion within a scene (29)**: *tomber* 'fall' (6), *monter* 'go up' (4), *passer* 'pass' (10), *couler* 'flow' (1), *courir* 'run' (1), *remuer* 'shake' (1), *descendre* 'go down' (1), *voler* 'fly' (1), *circuler* 'circulate' (1), *glisser* 'glide' (1), *rôder* 'roam' (1), *pousser* 'grow' (1)

(3.42′)   *Entends- tu ce que je te dis? Joseph hocha la tête. – tu attendras dans les bois que la nuit tombe. À ce moment, tu descendras dans le ravin et tu rejoindras la route. Tu attendras encore, une heure s'il le faut. **Il passera** <u>une voiture</u> qui ralentira et s'arrêtera à la hauteur du ravin pour te laisser monter.*

(Green, J. Moïra: roman: 244)

'Can you hear what I am telling you? Joseph nodded. You will wait in the woods until nightfall. At that time, you will go down the ravine toward the road. You will wait again, one hour if you have to. A car will come [there will pass a car]. It will slow down and stop by the ravine to let you in'.

Finally, a fifth and related class is composed of verbs that describe the general sensory impression that the conceptualized scene evokes. The relevant predicates are given in (3.43):

(3.43) **Sensory impression that permeates a scene (13):** *régner* 'rein' (6), *flotter* 'float' (3), *émaner* 'emanate' (1), *filtrer* 'filter' (1), *cuire* 'cook' (2)

(3.43′) ***Il flottait*** *entre ces murs* <u>*une odeur affreusement douce et grisante*</u> *qu'il s'efforça de ne pas respirer, une odeur de lilas.*   (Green, J. *Moïra: roman*: 158)
'There floated between these walls a horribly sweet and enticing odor that he tried not to breathe in, an odor of lilac'.

4.2   Presence of the setting in the predicates' lexical semantic structure

The semantic consistency revealed in the previous section is interesting, but does not per se confirm the hypothesis suggested at the beginning of this section. In order to do so and to better understand how the most frequent predicates overlap with simple impersonals, we need to consider more specifically the lexical semantic structure of different kinds of predicates. Predicates are commonly evaluated along several semantic dimensions. The number of participants in the main relation separates transitives from intransitives. The degree of volition of their subjects as well as their inherent aspectual properties are also routinely invoked to differentiate predicates in numerous contexts. I suggest that verbs can also be distinguished with respect to the relative salience of their participant and the setting within which their interaction takes place in their lexical semantic structure, or scope of predication in CG terminology. This section elaborates on the claim made earlier that the most felicitous impersonal predicates are precisely those that most relevantly and naturally include their setting as part of their scope of predication. More particularly, this semantic distinction allows us to account for the two striking characteristics of the distribution of impersonals, namely the overwhelming frequency of the stative and, to a lesser extent, motion verb classes in the construction, and the possible occurrence of a very large quantity of predicates within the other semantic classes.

As was mentioned in previous chapters, transitive verbs predominantly focus on the interaction between the participants in the main relation. For example, in *Marie a mangé la tarte* 'Mary ate the pie', the verb *manger* 'eat' exclusively profiles the interaction between Mary and the pie. Even though the eating episode necessarily occurs at a given time and place, these circumstances are not necessarily invoked when the verb is conceptualized. The setting is therefore not part of the verb's scope of predication. Intransitives present more diversity. Different classes of predicates widely differ with respect to the respective salience of the participant and the setting in their lexical semantic structure. The verbs of mental activity such as *rêver* 'dream' or *réfléchir* 'think' constitute one extreme where the communicative focus is turned exclusively toward the participant. For example, *Marie a réfléchi* 'Mary thought (about it)' profiles a process internal to the participant Mary, while the setting has little recognized salience. At the other extreme, stative predicates such as *être* 'be', *exister* 'exist', *rester* 'stay', *manquer* 'lack' assess the current state of a specific scene by identifying the elements that compose it. Importantly, that scene represents the setting itself. The latter therefore constitutes a crucial aspect of the scope of predication of those verbs because it provides the search domain within which the elements described in the complement can be identified. For example, in *il reste de la bière (dans le frigo)* 'there is some beer left (in the fridge)', *rester* 'remain' describes the range of mental operations leading to the speaker's conclusion. These operations include a comparison between the original amount of beer available and the actual consumption, as well as the estimation of the difference. The setting (the fridge) represents a necessary component of the verb's lexical semantic structure because it is within its confines that the presence of the leftover beer can be assessed.

In between these opposite cases, a large number of verbs profile different degrees of respective salience between the participant and the setting. For instance, the verbs of physical activity and internal change predominantly focus on their participant, but nonetheless include the setting in their scope of predication. Let us take *courir* 'run' and *grandir* 'grow' as examples. In both cases, the descriptive focus is predominantly placed on the participant to the detriment of the setting. In *Marie a couru* 'Mary ran', *courir* most prominently profiles Mary's activity. Similarly, in *Marie a grandi* 'Mary grew', *grandir* describes the changes internal to Mary herself. However, the processes that these verbs profile are not exclusively internal to the participant, as was the case with the mental activity verbs. Consequently, their meaning involves some interaction with the setting, even though the latter is not always prominently displayed. Finally, the semantic import of some verbs consists precisely of profiling their participant's interaction with the setting. For example, in *Marie est arrivée* 'Mary arrived', the meaning of *arriver* 'arrive' profiles Mary's appearance onto the conceptualized scene. The setting, namely the scene that gets modified by Mary's appearance, thus constitutes a necessary part of the verb's scope of predication.

We can now evaluate the claim that the most frequently attested predicates necessarily include some aspects of the setting in their scope of predication by confronting the distribution presented in the preceding section to the lexical semantic structure of the participating predicates. The semantic overlap between the verbs that centrally invoke the setting in their scope of predication and the impersonal construction should be clear. The field and setting represent different yet related notions. As was discussed in Section 3, the field differs from the setting by incorporating the mental processes necessary to apprehend the conceptualized scene but it crucially includes the relevant aspects of that scene, namely aspects of the setting. It is therefore quite natural for the impersonal construction that selects the field as the main figure in the profiled relation to exhibit maximal compatibility with the predicates that prominently feature the setting in their scope of predication because those aspects of the setting that the conceptualizer uses as the search domain to assess the conceptualized entity are common to both the predicate and the construction itself. This semantic overlap explains at the same time the centrality of the most frequent predicates as well as the specific conditions under which many others can be felicitous in the construction.

The compatibility that results from semantic overlap is particularly obvious for the stative predicates illustrated in (3.39′). In (3.39′) *il* profiles the field where the event described in the complement can be located, that is, the relevant subsection of the French television landscape as well as the analytical skills that enable the speaker to ascertain the presence of male show hosts. *Exister* profiles the presence of the hosts within this search domain. The verbs of sensation presented in (3.43) are quite similar to the stative predicates because they describe the overall atmosphere of the conceptualized scene or, in other words, the presence of specific sensations within that scene. The setting also constitutes a crucial part of their scope of predication because it defines the search domain within which these sensations can be experienced. In (3.43′), for example, *flotter* 'float' profiles the olfactory sensation that permeates the room. The verbs of appearance/disappearance from a scene are equally straightforward. Here again the setting constitutes a necessary part of these verbs' scope of predication because it marks the limit at which the conceptualized entity comes into or disappears from view. Let us turn to (3.40′) for illustration. *Il* profiles the field, that is to say, the section of the author's day when the described phenomenon occurs as well as his awareness of that moment. *Arrive* 'arrive' profiles the way in which that scene is modified by the occurrence of the sensation.

The semantic class presented in (3.42) under the label "motion within a scene" deserves a little more attention because it contains inherently directed motion predicates (*monter* 'go up', *passer* 'pass', *descendre* 'go down'), as well as physical activity predicates (*courir* 'run', *rôder* 'roam', *voler* 'fly'), and an internal change predicate (*pousser* 'grow'). The inherently directed motion predicates are unproblematic because they have already been argued to profile their participants' interaction with the setting. These verbs are therefore perfectly compatible with impersonals because that setting constitutes a necessary part of their scope of predication. In (3.42′), *passer* 'pass' matches up well with *il* because the field that the pronoun profiles, i.e. the general knowledge base that allows the conceptualizer to predict the car's arrival, includes one of its essential characteristics, namely the location that the car will necessarily traverse.[19] On the other hand, the physical

---

19. This example emphasizes the distinction between the setting and the field. The important point is that these two entities greatly overlap semantically.

activity and internal change predicates represent a potential difficulty because they were previously argued to place their descriptive focus on their participant to the detriment of the setting in their scope of predication. However, this difficulty disappears once the specific discourse conditions that favor their impersonal use can be brought to light.

So far, the compatibility between the intransitive predicates and the impersonal construction has been treated as a matter of strict lexical semantics. Specific verbs were considered more directly compatible with the construction because of their lexical structure. However, in CG grammatical relations are first and foremost a matter of construal, and conditions particular to the context of the utterance can easily override any verb's lexical characteristics. This is indeed the case with the attested examples of physical activity and internal change predicates. It was noted in several instances that these predicates place the descriptive focus on their participant. However, it is useful to remember that in each instance the participant's activity or change of state necessarily involves some interaction with the setting, even though the latter is not prominently displayed. For example, the activity predicate *courir* 'run' contains as part of its scope of predication the same motion component as an inherently directed motion verb such as *passer* 'pass'. Both involve their subject's trajectory through some location, but they diverge in the descriptive focus that they each place on different aspects of the conceptualized scene. Activity predicates are more concerned with the participant's role in the process, while inherently directed motion verbs more specifically concentrate on the trajectory through space.

The inherent salience of the participant represents the main reason why activity and internal change predicates are not always felicitous with impersonals. These predicates are too strongly centered on their participant to match up well with a construction that selects the field as clausal subject. However, if due to particular circumstances in the context of the conceptualized situation the participants' salience and individual character decreases to the point that their activity can be construed as a mere feature of the setting, the field can easily be involved as the main figure in the profiled relation. In these conditions the participation of the verbs of activity and internal change in impersonals is perfectly natural, as the examples in (3.44) and (3.45) illustrate.

(3.44)   *le ciel était gris de nuages il y **volait** des oies sauvages qui criaient la mort au passage au- dessus des maisons des quais* (Aragon, L. *Le roman inachevé*: 71)
'The sky was gray with clouds wild geese were flying [there in it flew wild geese] screaming death as they flew above the houses on the pier'.

(3.45) *Quelquefois, derrière la barre de la lagune, un aviron par intervalles tâtait l'eau*
gluante, ou tout près s'étranglait le cri falot et obscène d'un rat ou de quelque
bête menue comme il <u>en</u> **rôde** *aux abords des charniers.*

(Gracq, J. *Le rivage des Syrtes*: 179)

'Sometimes, beyond the edge of the lagoon, an oar intermittently probed the
sticky water, or, close by, arose the dreary and obscene scream of a rat or some
other little creature which roam near mass graves [such as there of it roam
near mass graves]'.

Despite the fact that *voler* 'fly' and *rôder* 'roam' are activity predicates, their use in
(3.44) and (3.45) makes them quite similar to the sensation predicates presented in
(3.43). In a way similar to odors and sounds, motion can also permeate the conceptualized scene if it is construed as one of the features that importantly contribute
to its overall atmosphere. In this sense, the predicates that profile motion within a
scene can be viewed as the visual correlates of the sensation predicates because both
profile a specific facet of the setting's ambiance. In (3.45), for instance, the roaming
of the rats is presented not as an activity that specific rodents are involved in, but as
a distinctive feature that strongly contributes to the unique ambiance of mass graves.

The distinction between setting and participant therefore accounts for the very
large number of stative and inherently directed motion predicates in the distribution presented in the previous section. These verbs are most naturally compatible
with the impersonal construction because they prominently include the setting
in their scope of predication. Any other intransitive verb is only possible in the
construction in the highly specific circumstances described in this section. These
circumstances pertain to the conditions of the utterance, and ultimately to speaker
choice. They are largely independent from the meaning of the predicate and can
thus predictably occur with many predicates but with low frequency.

4.3   Comparison with structural accounts

In the analysis developed in this chapter, the semantic overlap that exists between
the construction's individual components accounts for the distribution of predicates in the simple impersonal construction. This view contrasts with the syntactic
solutions presented in Chapter 1 where the argument structure of the predicate is
held responsible for its felicity in the construction. This section shows that the CG
account is preferable for two main reasons. First, its flexibility is better suited to
describe the frequency effects of the distribution described in the previous section.
Second, because that distribution directly follows from the semantic fit between
the construction's individual components, the CG solution needs none of the ad
hoc constraints that structural accounts unfailingly require.

Because simple impersonal predicates are necessarily intransitive, their analysis and distribution in syntactic frameworks has been dominated by the Unaccusative Hypothesis (UH, Perlmutter 1978), namely the proposal that "certain intransitive clauses have an initial 2 [object] but no initial 1 [subject]" (Perlmutter 1978: 160, insertions in brackets mine). The basic insight of UH is that intransitives can be separated into "unaccusative" and "unergative" predicates depending on their initial syntactic structure. While this hypothesis was proposed within the framework of Relational Grammar (Perlmutter 1983; Perlmutter and Rosen 1984), it has been widely adopted in most syntactic frameworks, and invoked to deal with a large number of issues.[20]

The first step in the evaluation of the syntactic position is to examine the influence of the predicate's structure on its participation in the impersonal construction. Unaccusative predicates are unequivocally recognized as felicitous. The acceptability of unergative predicates, however, is more difficult to assess since their potential presence seems to elicit diametrically opposed responses. Some researchers (Herschensohn 1982, 1996; Postal 1984; Ruwet 1989; Labelle 1992) view the possible participation of a predicate in the construction as a test of its unaccusative structure. Others (Kayne 1979; Grimshaw 1980) claim that unergatives can be felicitous in the construction. Legendre claims that unergatives are fully productive with simple impersonals (Extraposition of Indefinites or EXI in her terminology), and illustrates her statement with examples such as those in (3.46) (from Legendre 1989: 155):

(3.46) a. *Il lui téléphonait de nombreuses personnes à cette époque*
            'Many people used to call him/her in those days [There him/her used to call many people in those days]'
        b. *Il a cédé beaucoup de candidats à ce genre de pression*
            'Many candidates caved in under this kind of pressure [There caved in many candidates under this kind of pressure]'
        c. *Il a éternué beaucoup d'enfants pendant le concert*
            'Many children sneezed during the concert [There sneezed many children during the concert]'

---

20. Although it has been used to describe a wide array of grammatical phenomena in different languages, the relevance of the Unaccusative Hypothesis to French can easily be overstated because the structural tests designed to prove its existence are not particularly convincing. Several of them have been seriously questioned in the literature; others seem to respond to semantic criteria rather than purely syntactic factors (Hériau 1980; Cummins 2000; Achard 2009). More generally, from a theoretical standpoint UH is not an acceptable construct in a CG analysis because it makes reference to an exclusively syntactic level of representation. This is incompatible with CG's position that only phonological, semantic, and symbolic units as well as the categorizing relations between them constitute the possible elements of the grammar of a language.

    d.   *Il a violemment réagi beaucoup de personnes à l'annonce de cette nomination*
'Many people reacted violently when this nomination was announced [There violently reacted many people when this nomination was announced]'

    e.   *Savez-vous qu'il mendie beaucoup de personnes dans les rues de la capitale?*
'Do you know that many people beg for money in the streets of the capital city? [Do you know that there beg many people for money in the streets of the capital city?]'

    f.   *Il a cogné plusieurs imbéciles à la porte*
'Many idiots knocked on the door [There knocked many idiots on the door]'

    g.   *Il a souri beaucoup de personnes à l'annonce de cette nouvelle*
'Many people smiled when this news was announced [There smiled many people when this news was announced]'

Upon closer scrutiny, however, these seemingly irreconcilable positions are considerably tempered by the caveats their proponents introduce in their analyses. The advocates of the possible use as an impersonal as a test of unaccusativity for a given predicate nonetheless acknowledge that the construction sometimes tolerates unergatives. However, their presence is too heavily constrained to seriously challenge the construction's diagnostic status: "While unergatives may be found in impersonal constructions, the availability of this construction for unergatives is much more restricted than it is with unaccusatives" (Labelle 1992: 381). Furthermore, the unergative predicates that appear in active impersonals are claimed to undergo a semantic shift that bleaches them of all semantic content beyond that of "appearance in the world of discourse" (Guéron 1980: 653–654; see also Herschensohn 1982: 211; Labelle 1992: 381). In a similar vein, Jones (1996: 127) suggests that when they occur in an impersonal construction, unergative predicates have an "existential" value and that their semantic meaning is "redundant".

    Similarly, researchers who claim that unergatives are productive with impersonals recognize that they are subject to specific constraints that do not apply to unaccusatives. For example, Legendre (1990) notes that if unaccusatives freely occur with definite (initial) subjects, unergatives are only felicitous with indefinite (initial) subjects. The contrast between the examples in (3.47) and (3.48) illustrates this indefinite subject constraint:

(3.47) a. **Il mange Paul dans ce restaurant*
'Paul eats in this restaurant [There eats Paul in this restaurant]'

       b. **Il travaille Marie dans cette usine*
'Mary works in this factory [There works Mary in this factory]'

    c.   *Il dormait Fido dans un coin de la pièce*
        'Fido slept in a corner of this room [There slept Fido in a corner of the room]'

(3.48) a.   *Il mange beaucoup de linguistes dans ce restaurant*   (from Pollock 1978)
        'Many linguists eat in this restaurant [There eat many linguists in this restaurant]'

    b.   *Il travaille des milliers d'ouvriers dans cette usine*   (from Postal 1982)
        'Thousands of workers work in this factory [There work thousands of workers in this factory]'

    c.   *Il dormait un chat dans un coin de la pièce*   (from Martin 1970)
        'A cat slept in a corner of the room [There slept a cat in a corner of the room]'

Moreover, her claim of the full productivity of unergatives with impersonals is restricted to specific dialects: "There are dialects of French in which EXI is totally productive with unergatives, though the existence of such dialects has never been documented in the literature" (Legendre 1990: 82).[21] The way in which researchers from both camps hedge their analyses reveals the basic agreement that obtains about the facts of the construction, but it also reveals that the binary distinction between unaccusative and unergative predicates is simply too coarse to handle several important aspects of the distribution presented in the previous section. It seems reasonable to suggest that the diametrically opposed statements concerning the presence of unergative predicates in impersonals result in great part from the polarizing nature of the unaccusative/unergative split. The distribution presented in this chapter clearly shows that the participating predicates tend to cluster semantically regardless of their structure, and that positing a structural dividing line between them yields no significant insight in understanding their distribution.

First, structural considerations fail to address the discrepancy in the frequency of the different classes. In particular, it does not explain why such a reduced number of unaccusative predicates constitute the overwhelming majority of the total

---

21. The syntactic correlates of the predicate's assignment to the unaccusative or unergative class depend on the specific framework. Generally, unaccusatives pose no particular problems. Since their only argument is a direct object by definition, the dummy *il* is inserted to satisfy French's structural need for a final subject. The treatment of unergatives is less uniform. For Legendre (1990: 83), "the dummy enters as a 2. It is argued that unergative EXIs involve Antipassive, that is a structure in which the pivot demotes to 2 prior to being put en chômage by a dummy entering as a 2". For Jones (1996: 127), the "existential" semantics of unergative predicates in impersonals somehow make it unaccusative-like: "When the content of the verb is redundant, the Agent is reinterpreted as a Theme, thus effectively converting the verb into an unaccusative verb which expresses the existence of the Theme entity"

instances, while other unaccusatives, most notably internal change predicates, occur so seldom. Second, the semantic bleaching that the activity and internal change predicates have been argued to undergo with impersonals has been exaggerated. For example, it seems difficult to reduce the meaning of *voler* 'fly' and *rôder* 'roam', respectively illustrated in (3.44) and (3.45) and repeated here, to "appearance in the world of discourse" (Guéron 1980: 653–54; Herschensohn 1982: 211; Labelle 1992: 381):

(3.44)   *le ciel était gris de nuages **il y volait** <u>des oies sauvages</u> qui criaient la mort au passage au- dessus des maisons des quais* (Aragon, L. *Le roman inachevé*: 71)
'The sky was gray with clouds wild geese were flying [there in it flew wild geese] screaming death as they flew above the houses on the pier'.

(3.45)   *Quelquefois, derrière la barre de la lagune, un aviron par intervalles tâtait l'eau gluante, ou tout près s'étranglait le cri falot et obscène d' un rat ou de quelque bête menue comme **il <u>en</u> rôde** aux abords des charniers.*
(Gracq, J. *Le rivage des Syrtes*: 179)
'Sometimes, beyond the edge of the lagoon, an oar intermittently probed the sticky water, or, close by, arose the dreary and obscene scream of a rat or some other little creature which roams near mass graves [such as there of it roams near mass graves]'.

There is no arguing that the meaning of these verbs in the impersonal construction differs from the one they have in personal situations. However, rather than the result of some obscure bleaching process, this semantic variance directly and naturally follows from the construal shift characteristic of their presence within an impersonal structure. When the activity and internal change predicates are used in their personal sense, they profile the interaction between their participants. Consider for example the manufactured personal counterpart of (3.45) in (3.49):

(3.49)   #*Des rats rôdent aux abords des charniers*
'Rats roam near mass graves'

In (3.49) the physical energy involved in the roaming act is predominantly anchored in the rats themselves. The speaker's main role is mostly to observe and report that display of activity that comes from a well-delineated concrete source. Her conceptualization of the roaming act can thus be called maximally objective (Langacker 1985, 1990). The same verb in (3.45) evokes a very different construal. The roaming is not contained in the highly individualized source of the rats themselves; it is more diffuse and identified as a part of the scene's atmosphere. Because the construal of the scene, and hence the selection of the movement of the rats as one of its distinguishing characteristics, represents a mental act by the speaker, the roaming is essentially anchored in her conceptualization. The diffusion of the physical energy from a well-defined source contained in the main figure of the main relation to a primarily mental force associated with the construal relation itself and thus located in the speaker reflects its subjectification (Langacker 1985, 1990). The speaker's (mental) energy for conceiving the roaming represents the subjective counterpart of the (physical) energy that emanates from the animals. The specific meaning of the verbs of activity and internal change in impersonals can therefore be attributed to the subjectification of the main relation that becomes more diffuse and associated with the speaker's construal of the conceptualized scene. Importantly, this subjectification represents an intricate part of the meaning of the construction.

Finally, while it is hard to see how the unergative structure of the predicate may determine the necessary presence of an indefinite determiner on its postverbal expression, the presence of an indefinite nominal clearly represents a context that favors the selection of the field as clausal subject with verbs that usually favor their participants. The indefinite subject constraint illustrated in (3.47) and (3.48) is naturally explained by the fact that the presence of an indefinite nominal decreases the inherent salience of the participant in the scene, and therefore favors a construal where the setting holds focal prominence. Let us illustrate this point with the contrast in (3.47a) and (3.48a), repeated here:

(3.47)　a.　*Il mange Paul dans ce restaurant*
　　　　　　'Paul eats in this restaurant [There eats Paul in this restaurant]'

(3.48)　a.　*Il mange beaucoup de linguistes dans ce restaurant*　　(from Pollock 1978)
　　　　　　'Many linguists eat in this restaurant [There eat many linguists in this restaurant]'

In (3.47a) *Paul* is an object of current immediate perception, and the salience of that participant is extremely high. In (3.48a) the object of perception can only be formed over time, and by the consideration of many instances. Furthermore, it is not achieved by observation alone but with the help of other cognitive abilities such as comparison and analysis. The frequent observations required as well as the analysis of those observations are instrumental in considering the presence of linguists as a statement about the restaurant or, in other words, a specific feature of the field itself. This constraint is motivated by the strong natural emphasis placed on participants and their actions, and therefore occurs on both activity (unergative) and internal change (unaccusative) predicates.

The presence of a participant coded by an indefinite nominal does not represent the only context that favors an impersonal construal. The felicity of the verbs of activity and internal change in active impersonals is also greatly enhanced if explicit emphasis is placed on the field in the context. Consider, for example, the pairs in (3.50) and (3.51) where the locational *y* denotes specific focus on the field.

(3.50) a. #?*Il a cuit beaucoup de gigots dans ce four*
            'Many roasts cooked in this oven [There cooked many roasts in this oven]'

      b. #*Ce four est génial, il y cuit un gigot en 45 minutes*
            'This oven is great, it only takes 45 minutes to cook a roast [there cook
            in it a roast in 45 minutes]'

(3.51) a. #?*Il a mariné beaucoup d'olives dans le pot bleu*
            'A lot of olives marinated in the blue jar [There marinated a lot of olives
            in the blue jar]'

      b. #*Ne prends pas le pot bleu, il y marine des olives*
            'Do not take the blue jar, there are olives marinating in it'

In (3.50b) and (3.51b) the oven and the jar are topical, and the presence of the locational pronoun *y* 'there' reinforces the setting function of the two containers. The speaker's mental reach (the field) that *il* profiles is therefore more strongly focused on the respective performance or availability of the oven and the pot respectively than in (3.50a) and (3.51a) where the statements constitute more general commentaries about cooking and marinating. As a result, the examples in (3.50b) and (3.51b) are much more natural than their counterparts in (3.50a) and (3.51a). The contrasts in (3.50) and (3.51) lend further support to the analysis developed in this section where the semantic overlap between the predicates and the impersonal construction depends on the salience of the field in their scope of predication.

As a brief summary, this section showed that a solution based on the semantic overlap between the meaning of the simple impersonal construction and the verbs that participate in it provides a convincing explanation of the distribution of intransitives in that construction. This semantic account presents several advantages over a structural analysis. First, it allows us to group together the verbs of activity and internal change that are structurally different. Second, it is capable of accounting for the overwhelming frequency of some classes of predicates in the construction, as well as for the possible presence of a very large number of verbs under the appropriate conditions. Finally, it sheds some light on the long-lasting debate that surrounds the grammaticality of some activity predicates. For example, the possible felicity of Legendre's example presented in (3.46a) and repeated here depends on the hearer's ability to construct a context in which the calling – an activity usually centered on the participants – could legitimately be construed as a distinguishing characteristic of the described time frame.

(3.46) a. *Il lui téléphonait de nombreuses personnes à cette époque*
            'Many people used to call him/her in those days [There him/her used to
            call many people in those days]'

The examples introduced in (3.46) are therefore not problematic because of the syntactic structure of the predicate, but because of the unconventional matchup between the predicate and the impersonal construction.

5.   Recapitulation and conclusion

This chapter showed that simple impersonals, namely those whose postverbal expression is a nominal, should be distinguished from their complex counterparts where the predicate is followed by an infinitival or finite clause because of their conceptual and functional differences. Simple impersonals were further argued to be presentational in nature, in the sense that their semantic function is to identify or locate the entity coded in the postverbal expression with respect to a specific domain.

Each part of the construction was shown to semantically contribute to this function. In a natural extension of the French psychological tradition, the pronoun *il* profiles the field, or in other words the scope of the conceptualizer's awareness in assessing the status of the postverbal entity. The construction's semantic range, established by the predicates that participate in it, directly follows from the presence of the field in its semantic structure since the most frequent predicates are precisely those that saliently invoke the setting in their scope of predication. Importantly, the predicates that more saliently focus on their participants and their activities can nonetheless participate in the construction if these activities can somehow be construed as characteristic of the scene in which they occur. The fine interplay between the semantic structure of the predicate and the more global properties of the scene described clearly shows that the distribution of predicates in simple impersonal constructions is not a matter of structure but one of construal, and that the semantic properties of any predicate can be overridden by the characteristics inherent to the scene it only partially describes. This semantic analysis was shown to better represent the usage of simple impersonals than its syntactic counterparts where predicate distribution is strictly based on structural criteria.

The semantic range presented in this chapter represents one important aspect of the construction's meaning because it shows that the usage of *il* impersonals clusters around well-delineated semantic areas. However, this observation only describes a very general aspect of the construction's meaning because it cuts across a large number of predicates. Another facet of the construction's meaning is provided by the in-depth examination of the usage patterns that each one of the most frequent predicates such as *exister* 'exist', *manquer* 'lack', or *rester* 'remain' exhibit in their impersonal usage. The next chapter continues the investigation of the meaning of the simple impersonal construction by showing that its association with these predicates creates preassembled chunks that systematically and reliably describe specific kinds of scenes, even though other constructions are potentially available.

CHAPTER 4

Simple impersonals
Patterns of usage

This chapter explores the relation between *il* simple impersonals and the individual predicates most frequently attested in this context. It shows that the construction's association with *exister* 'exist', *rester* 'remain', *manquer* 'lack', *arriver* 'arrive', *venir* 'come', and *passer* 'pass' produces stable preassembled chunks that are reliably and consistently invoked together to code specific experiences. This predicate-centered analysis combines with the construction-centered account presented in the previous chapter to provide a complete overview of French simple impersonal usage.

1. Introduction

The previous chapter established the semantic range of simple impersonals as presentational constructions. It showed that the meaning of the pronoun combines with the lexical semantics of the predicate to locate the entity coded in the postverbal expression with respect to some domain. However, this observation alone does not provide an exhaustive picture of the usage of simple impersonals because it is far too abstract and does not show how individual predicates implement this general meaning in their own specific ecologies. This chapter complements the results obtained in 3 three by investigating the surprisingly systematic fine-grained associations that develop between the construction itself and six of the most frequently attested predicates. Three case studies of *exister* 'exist', *rester* 'remain', and *manquer* 'lack' reveal that these predicates almost obligatorily occur with simple impersonals in one of their senses, even though alternative constructions are potentially available. The usage of the less-frequent *arriver* 'arrive', *venir* 'come', and *passer* 'pass' is so heavily constrained that it is essentially formulaic. The predicate-specific analyses developed in this chapter address a different dimension of simple impersonal usage than the construction-specific approach presented in the previous chapter because they assess the specific place of the predicate's impersonal variant within the context of its overall use. The results obtained across these two dimensions reinforce the view of language defended in the usage-based model (Langacker 2000; Bybee 2001) in which meaning directly results from usage and can be located in a large number of associations at various levels of generality. The chapter is structured in the following manner. Section 2 briefly considers some relevant aspects of usage-based linguistics. Section 3 analyzes the impersonal variants of *exister*, *rester*, and *manquer*. Section 4 is devoted to the most frequently attested impersonal *il y a* 'there is'. Section 5 briefly investigates the more peripheral *arriver* 'arrive', *venir* 'come', and *passer* 'pass'. Section 6 recapitulates the results and concludes the chapter.

2.   Usage and grammar

Cognitive Grammar is traditionally known as a usage-based model (Langacker 1988, 2000; Barlow and Kemmer 2000; Bybee 2001). The basic idea behind the term is that usage shapes grammar or, more precisely, issues of frequency, collocations, and semantic prosody lie at the heart of our mental representation of linguistic forms. Perhaps the most central claim is that the grammatical system originates in situ, and therefore includes the linguistic and social context that surrounds the utterance. In order to transmit their conceptualization to others, speakers need to select the appropriate linguistic expression among a large number of conventionalized alternatives. The solution to that task takes the form of a "usage event", namely "a symbolic expression assembled by the speaker in a particular context for a particular purpose" (Langacker 1987: 66). Linguistic units are extracted from language events by the processes of schematization and categorization. More specifically, "semantic units are abstracted from the contextual understanding of occurring expressions", and they "emerge via the progressive entrenchment of configurations that recur in a sufficient number of events to be established as cognitive routines" (Langacker 2008: 220). In this manner, "usage events are the source of all linguistic units" because they provide the ecological soil from which individual units arise (Langacker 2008: 220). These individual units can in turn be used to describe future conceptualizations, and can thus be considered "schematic relative to both the source events and the further events in which they figure" (Langacker 2008: 220). It is important to note that a usage event is "an actual instance of language use, in all its complexity and specificity" (Langacker 2008: 220), and that the context-dependent variant of a lexical item is in a way more fundamental than the context-neutral schematization one finds in a dictionary's lexical entry. For example, the meaning of *send* in isolation can only be extracted from the commonalities observed between the three variants of the verb, namely 'John sent Mary the book', 'John sent the book to Mary', and 'John sent for Mary', which respectively participate in the three separate constructions [send$_1$ NP NP], [send$_2$ NP to NP], and [send$_3$ for NP] (Langacker 2000). These three variants represent three contextual meanings of *send* in the particular ecology of the construction in which it appears. In order to find out the meaning of a context-free *send*, one would need to abstract away from the particular variants observed in specific constructions to see what they have in common. Closer to the concerns of this chapter, the semantic import of the predicates (*exister*, *rester*, or *manquer*, for instance) cannot be established independently of their participation in the impersonal construction because instances of impersonal *exister*, *rester*, or *manquer* necessarily figure among the vast number of instances of every construction that defines those verbs' "behavioral profile" (Gries and Divjak 2009).

2.1   Usage and idioms

The fundamental character of usage events is crucial to determining the semantic matchup of the various components of a construction. That matchup is often considered in terms of "semantic compatibility" (Achard 1998; Yoon 2012) if the various elements are semantically congruent, or "coercion" (Pustejovsky 1989, 1995; Michaelis 2004, 2005, among many others) if the constructional meaning supersedes that of individual components. The necessary fit between its components represents a key aspect of constructional meaning, but obviously it can only be invoked when a construction places specific constraints on its individual components. In Chapter 5, for instance, the semantic compatibility of different classes of predicates with infinitival, subjunctive, or indicative clauses explains the distribution of postverbal expressions in the complex impersonal construction. However, simple impersonals do not impose similar constraints on the nominal that follows the predicate (except with *exister*, to be considered in Section 3.1), but individual predicates nonetheless exhibit sometimes highly idiosyncratic distribution patterns. While *exister*, *rester*, and *manquer* were shown to be compatible with the simple impersonal construction in the previous chapter, this chapter investigates the precise ways in which speakers make use of *il existe*, *il reste*, and *il manque* in order to express their conceptualizations.

   In the usage-based model, expressions at various levels of abstraction can cluster together in a quasi-idiomatic manner. This view stands in sharp contrast with what Sinclair (1991) calls the "open choice principle" and describes in the following manner: "This is probably the normal way of seeing and describing language. It is often called 'slot-and-filler' model, envisaging texts as a series of slots that have to be filled from a lexicon that satisfies local restraints. At each slot, virtually any word can occur" (Sinclair 1991:109). Total freedom, however, does not appropriately describe linguistic usage: "It is difficult to speak spontaneously without lapsing into idiomatic usage. Try it with a foreigner, and you will see that you are often aware of using an idiom only after the event. Even in explaining an idiom, you can find to your expense that you are using another" (Johnson-Laird 1993: ix). It therefore seems that the absolute freedom of choice that the slot-and-filler model provides is largely illusory, and that words tend to combine according to limited sets of choices. Consequently, language production is much more a matter of collocations than previously thought, which has been obscured by an undue emphasis on structural organization: "Words enter into meaningful relation with other words around them, and yet all our current descriptions marginalize this massive contribution to meaning. The main reason for the marginalization is that grammars are always given priority, and grammars barricade themselves against the individual patterns of words" (Sinclair 1996: 76). A more appropriate idiom principle can therefore be proposed to replace the slot-and-filler model: "The idiom principle … is based on the view that the language user has available to her or him a number of semi-preconstructed chunks which constitute single choices are generally used as such or with slight modification" (Gavioli 2005: 43). In this model, "units of meaning" (Sinclair 1996) may be separate from units of grammar. Several techniques have been developed over the recent years to capture these semi-constructed chunks. For example, the semantic affinity between different terms has recently been analyzed in terms of their collocational strength (Stefanowitsch and Gries 2003; Gries and Stefanowitsch 2006). Gries and Divjak (2009) provide ways of evaluating the behavioral profile of specific expressions, that is, of investigating what specific constructions they most readily associate with. The usage-based model is fully congruent with the idiom principle because it incorporates a very large array of structures at different levels of abstraction: "The grammar is held responsible for a speaker's knowledge of the full range of linguistic conventions, regardless of whether these conventions can be subsumed under more general statements. [It is a] nonreductive approach to linguistic structure that employs fully articulated schematic networks and emphasizes the importance of low-level schemas" (Langacker 1987: 494). The resulting system is therefore "one of massive networks in which structures of varying degree of entrenchment, and representing different levels of abstraction, are linked together in relationships of categorization, composition, and symbolization" (Langacker 2000: 5).

The conception of language the usage-based model defends is critical to the themes developed in this chapter because it directly pertains to the relation between the individual predicates and the construction itself. The previous chapter characterized that relation in terms of semantic overlap between the construction and entire classes of predicates, but this chapter investigates the usage of individual predicates. It shows that *il existe* 'there exists', *il reste* 'there remains', and *il manque* 'there lacks' constitute the kind of semi-assembled chunks described in this section because they specialize in coding very specific situations. As such, each one of these assemblies constitutes a meaning unit and takes its place among the vast array of symbolic structures that French speakers have at their disposal to express the content of their conceptualizations. In order to unveil these complex units, we cannot rely on the same data set used in Chapter 3 for two reasons. First, the search was conducted using the construction as the prompt (recall *il* was the item searched, and impersonal tokens were manually extracted), and some of the predicates are too infrequently attested to yield the relevant generalizations. Second, since only the impersonal variant of each predicate was examined, no conclusion can be reached relative to the place of the impersonal construction in its overall behavioral profile. Consequently, in the following sections all the texts that compose the post-1950 section of the FRANTEXT database were searched by individual predicates so that all their variants could be examined. The specifics are described at the beginning of each section. The results show that the impersonal variants of *exister* (*il existe*), *rester* (*il reste*), and *manquer* (*il manque*) are virtually necessary, i.e. attested in the overwhelming majority of the cases, in highly specific situations. Consequently, the association between the predicate and the impersonal construction is best analyzed as the complex symbolic structure French speakers use to conceptualize that situation.

2.2   The core and periphery of simple impersonal usage

As a starting point, the usage and distribution of the individual predicates in the construction allow us to distinguish the core of the simple impersonal category from its periphery. First, it seems reasonable to posit that more frequent predicates define its semantic core (Langacker 2008: 220; see also Bybee 2001), but the level of syntactic and lexical constraints that different predicates exhibit in the construction also factors in their position within the category. One should therefore expect more central predicates to be less severely constrained in their semantic and syntactic distribution than their more peripheral counterparts. In order to evaluate these claims, Table 4.1 compares the frequency of the impersonal variants of *exister*, *rester*, *manquer*, *arriver*, *venir*, and *passer* to their overall frequency in the post-1950 section of the FRANTEXT database. The two numbers in the percentage column refer to the different proportions of simple impersonals and impersonals overall (including complex and zero forms) in the overall distribution of the predicate:

Table 4.1 Impersonal and overall usage of six predicates

Predicate	Impersonals				Overall	Percentage	
	Simple	Complex	Zero	Total		Simple	Overall
Exister	168	N/A	N/A	168	841	19.97	19.97
Rester	245	126	20	391	2664	9.19	14.67
Manquer	120	8	3	131	960	12.5	13.64
Arriver[1]	53	112	N/A	165	2295	2.30	7.18
Venir	17	N/A	N/A	17	4669	0.36	0.36
Passer	3	N/A	N/A	3	4013	0.07	0.07

Table 4.1 interestingly correlates with the numbers presented in the previous chapter that described the frequency of the different predicates in the simple impersonal construction. The most frequent optional predicates in the construction, namely *exister, rester*, and *manquer*, are also those for which the percentage of impersonals in their syntactic profile is the highest. Taken together, the total number of occurrences of a specific predicate in the impersonal construction and the relative importance of that construction in the predicate's syntactic ecology provide an argument in favor of the level of semantic affinity that exists between the two. The numbers are striking in this respect because they clearly isolate two different groups of predicates. The first is composed of *exister, rester*, and *manquer*, for which impersonal usage constitutes between approximately 13 to 20 percent of their overall syntactic context. The second group contains the other predicates, among which *arriver* possesses the highest percentage of impersonal usage with only 2.30 percent of simple constructions (and 7.18 percent including complex forms).

A quick glance at the individual examples confirms the clear distinction between the two groups of predicates. While *exister, rester*, and *manquer* are relatively unconstrained in the semantic nature of their postverbal expression (more on this issue in Section 3), *arriver* exhibits a predominantly idiomatic impersonal usage. Its fifty-three simple tokens are composed of thirty-two instances of the expression *quoiqu'il arrive* 'whatever happens'; ten occurrences of an indefinite NP including the noun *chose* 'thing' (*quelque chose* 'something', *de drôles de choses* 'strange things', and so on); six expressions including a time expression (*moment* 'moment', *heure* 'hour', *âge* 'age', and so on); and three noun phrases that generally describe an event (*evènement* 'event', *conséquence* 'consequence', *coup dûr* 'hard blow'). Only two noun phrases do not fall within these well-delineated categories, namely *un serpent à sept têtes* 'a snake with seven heads' (from a poetic text), and *de nouvelles bêtes* 'new heads of cattle'. In addition to being far less frequent than *exister, rester*,

---

1.   The data include sixteen instances where impersonal *il* is used as an indefinite demonstrative, in the usage discussed in Chapter 3, Section 3.2. These examples were not included in the analysis.

and *manquer*, the impersonal usage of the other predicates is therefore also heavily semantically constrained to the point of being essentially formulaic.

The data presented in Table 4.1 are slightly misleading because they leave out the most frequent impersonal predicates such as *avoir* 'be' (*il y a* 'there is') and *falloir* (*il faut*) 'be necessary'. *Il faut* will be considered in Chapter 5 since it is followed by a nominal or a clausal postverbal expression, but *il y a* certainly needs to figure among the core simple predicates and its inclusion raises the interesting issue of the precise characterization of the construction. The connection between impersonals and existentials is well established in the literature (Carnie and Harley 2005 and Afonso 2008 constitute two recent examples). With respect to French, I have argued in previous work (Achard 1998) that impersonals are primarily existential, but in retrospect this claim is difficult to sustain because both existence and location represent potential candidates. There is no arguing that these two domains are distinct, and can be considered independently. This is illustrated in (4.1)–(4.4) where (4.1) and (4.2) are existentials and thus solely concerned with the presence of the organization and the books in reality, while (4.3) and (4.4) do not question the existence of gold, socks, or shirts, but assess their location within a specific "domain of search" (Langacker 2009: 99).

(4.1)   *On n'a pas supprimé la misère ni l'injustice. Mais tu n'es plus seul. Tu ne peux pas toujours faire respecter tes droits; mais **il y a** une grande organisation qui les reconnaît, qui les proclame, qui peut élever la voix et qui se fait entendre.*
(Weil, S. *La condition ouvrière*: 256)
'We have eliminated neither poverty nor injustice. But you are not alone any longer. You are still not in a position to make people respect your rights, but there is a powerful organization that recognizes them, that proclaims them, and that can raise its voice and make itself heard'.

(4.2)   *– Pourquoi n'écrivez-vous pas? Dit Scriassine. – **Il y a** bien assez de livres.*
(Beauvoir, S. de. *Les mandarins*: 37)
'– Why don't you write? Scriassine asked? – There are more than enough books'.

(4.3)   *Ce genre de réflexion rétablit l'esprit dans son centre, et fait comprendre que bien penser n'est pas plier le genou devant l'expérience, mais au contraire penser l'expérience selon les règles du bien penser. Cela ne signifie pas que la pensée pure nous dira s'**il y a** de l'or dans les montagnes d'Éthiopie; non; cela c'est l'expérience qui nous le dira.*   (Alain. *Propos sur des philosophes*: 10)
'This kind of reflection puts the mind in its proper place, and lets us understand that proper thought does not mean bowing to experience, but, to the contrary, reflecting experience according to the rules of proper thought. This doesn't mean that pure thought will tell us if there is gold in the mountains of Ethiopia, experience will tell us that'.

(4.4)   *Lorsqu'il est arrivé ici avec <u>un trousseau où</u> **il y avait** <u>des chaussettes trouées et</u>*
        <u>*des chemises décousues*</u>, *qui s'est occupé de les faire repriser?*
                        (Montherlant, H. de. *La ville dont le prince est un enfant*: 930)
        'When he arrived here with torn socks in his luggage and shirts coming apart
        at the seams, who saw to it that they were mended?'

Although clearly distinct, the locationals in (4.3) and (4.4) only differ from the
existentials in (4.1) and (4.2) by the presence of a specific search domain (also
underlined in the examples) within which the postverbal entity can be located
(Langacker 2009: 98–99). In the absence of such domain, or if the latter is indistinguishable from reality itself, existence and location cannot be distinguished as in
(4.5) where *il y avait* 'there was' describes at the same time a particular location and
the latter's existence, since the narrative purpose of the sentence precisely seeks to
confirm the existence of a single location that meets the character's highly specific
requirements. In this case, the presence of the search domain (*au monde* 'in the
world') does not permit the distinction between an existential and a locational case
since it is coextensive with reality itself:

(4.5)   *Nul doute que pendant quelques jours il n'ait été un peu heureux. **Il y avait** <u>un</u>*
        <u>*lieu au monde*</u> *aménagé selon ses idées et ses goûts.*
                        (Guéhenno, J. Jean-Jacques. *T. 3*: 329)
        'No doubt that for a few days he was somewhat happy. There was a place in
        the world arranged according to his ideas and tastes'.

Examples such as (4.5) underscore the similar structure of existence and location,
and thus the difficulty of choosing between the two in selecting a primary domain
for the semantic function of simple impersonals. The understanding of existence
in terms of metaphorical location in our models of reality discussed in Chapter 5
serves to further integrate the two domains; we speak of a theory as having "no
basis in reality", for example, which reflects our construal of reality as a physical
domain. Obviously reality can only be construed in this manner because existence
and location are extremely difficult to separate logically. The existence of an entity
can only be evidenced at a particular location (this includes metaphorical locations
for abstract entities such as ideas), and the presence of an entity at any location necessarily entails its existence. As we have seen in examples (4.1)–(4.4), the existential
or locational value of the relevant domain of inquiry is most often made available
by linguistic resources outside the impersonal construction per se – a prepositional
phrase in (4.3) and the head of a relative clause in (4.4). However, even the presence
or absence of a search domain does not serve as a reliable diagnostic for reliably
identifying impersonals as locational and existential respectively because its relevance to the location of the postverbal entity can be recovered pragmatically. For

instance, *il y a de la bière sans alcool* 'there is alcohol-free beer' can be a locational despite the absence of an explicit search domain if the kinds of beverages available in the refrigerator constitute the topic of discussion. Conversely, as we saw in (4.5), the presence of a search domain does not prevent an existential reading.[2]

Given the fact that (1) existence and location are so difficult to disentangle, and (2) the resources to distinguish them come exclusively from outside the impersonal construction, there is no need to specifically name either one as the primary domain of impersonals. The presentational nature of the construction alluded to in Chapter 3 can now be made more specific. As a slight variation of the analysis I proposed earlier (Achard 1998: 279), I suggest that French impersonals are unspecified for a specific domain, and that their existential or locational value is provided by the main verb or elements external to the construction, including pragmatic conditions pertaining to the speech situation at large. This analysis treats French impersonals as a kind of "reference point construction" (Langacker 1993, 2009) where the generalized conceptualizer makes contact with her target (the postverbal entity) through the field (profiled by *il*) used as a reference point. The specific domain within which the target can be located is specified by the main predicate (as with *exister*, for instance, discussed in Section 3.1), linguistic expressions from the immediate discourse, or pragmatic considerations. This very general access strategy through the field (described earlier as presentational) constitutes the semantic import of the impersonal construction.

The representation of the aspects of the simple impersonal construction investigated in this chapter is given in Figure 4.1, in which the predicates in parentheses represent examples of the sense listed in the box above them. It is not exhaustive of the category. For example, it makes no mention of the consequence or sensory predicates such as *s'ensuivre* 'follow' and *régner* 'reign' respectively attested in the data presented in Chapter 3. It should merely be used as a heuristic guide designed to track the relative position of the individual predicates introduced in the following sections.

Two related aspects of Figure 4.1 require some explanation. First, the arrows between the different boxes merely represent the semantic connections that exist between the different senses of the category, in other words, the semantic properties these senses share. They should not be taken as a serious representation of the

---

2. This existential reading can even be available when the search domain is not coextensive with reality, as in (i) for instance, where *il y a* should be considered an existential despite the presence of *dans ces villes* 'in these cities':

(i) #*Il y a <u>dans ces villes des enfants qui n'ont jamais vu la mer</u>*
     'In those cities, there are children who have never seen the sea'

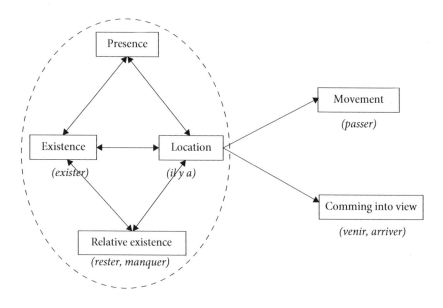

Figure 4.1 The semantic structure of the simple impersonal category

category's conceptual organization. Second, the area within the dashed oblong shape represents the core of the category. As mentioned earlier, the difference between the core and the periphery reflects the frequency variations in the data presented in Chapter 3 and the previous section, but this chapter also shows that it also pertains to the level of idiomaticity of the resulting construction. In the core area, *exister, rester, manquer* are systematically used in their impersonal sense to code a highly specific type of situation, but they impose no constraint on their postverbal expression (intrinsic *il y a* is even more permissive). In the peripheric area, however, the impersonal usage of *arriver, venir,* and *passer* is both very sparse and essentially formulaic, with a very limited semantic range. Within the core, the box labeled "presence" represents the unspecified reference point aspect of the construction. It includes no specific predicate since this general reference point access strategy is implemented within the existential or locational domain.

The individual focus on each of the predicates listed in Figure 4.1 complements the overview of the construction presented in Chapter 3, where the construction itself was being searched, in several ways. First, it affords the consideration of a much larger number of tokens per individual verbs, which allows the relevant generalizations to emerge more clearly. Second, the specific affinity that different predicates exhibit for the impersonal construction determines the overall profile of the construction that Chapter 3 described. In fact, it would be ιpossible to characterize the overall range of the construction presented in

Chapter 3 between each predicate and the impersonal environment without the previous formation of different kinds of semi-assembled chunks of the sort introduced in this section. In other words, *exister* can be claimed to be compatible with the impersonal construction only because *il existe* was analyzed as a meaning unit in a large enough number of different contexts. The predicate-centered account developed in this chapter is thus inherent in the construction-centered analysis of the previous chapter. The following sections simply make it explicit. Finally, placing the focus on individual predicates allows us to assess the nature of the field that the pronoun codes in each instance with greater precision. This is quite welcome because this notion has so far proven rather elusive and difficult to precisely delineate. While assessing the knowledge base that individual conceptualizers apply to the task of identifying specific entities seems impossible, or at the very least too arbitrary and unpredictable to prominently figure in a serious semantic analysis, we need to bear in mind that in order to communicate their conceptualizations speakers need to conform to a much greater degree of conventionalization. Linguistic construal greatly relies on conventionalized patterns at different levels of generality, and consequently individual conceptual construal potential is severely influenced and possibly constrained by the established means by which they can be linguistically shared. To be more specific, because the meaning of each individual predicate is highly conventionalized, the kinds of mental resources drawn upon for its conceptualization are also largely conventional. This conventionalization constitutes the very essence of language, and the CG model recognizes its power throughout the entire linguistic process. The analyses presented in the upcoming sections investigate one of its facets by showing that the different configurations of the field are heavily constrained by the lexical semantic structure of the specific predicate used in the construction, and hence also exhibit high levels of conventionalization.

3.   The core: Existential predicates

The previous section suggested that French impersonal constructions are presentational in nature because they pertain to the location of an entity in some domain. The nature of that domain (reality or a specific location) determines the construction's existential or locational reading. The predicate most often (but not always, as we shall see in this chapter with *il y a* 'there is') contributes to that aspect of the construction's overall meaning. For example, the relative contributions of the predicate and impersonal construction are straightforward in the example in (4.6), repeated from Chapters 1 and 3:

(4.6)   *Gêné par la pensée qu'il* **existe** *un livre appelé le pécheur justifié. Je ne l'ai pas*
        encore lu. J'ai cru que cela me troublerait, mais j'en connais le thème.

        (Green, J. *Journal. T. 5. 1946–1950*: 232)

        'Disturbed by the thought that there is [exists] a book called the justified sinner.
        I haven't read it yet, I thought it would disturb me, but I know what it is about'.

Consistent with the hypothesis presented earlier, the impersonal construction presents the location of the book *le pécheur justifié* 'the justified sinner' in some domain.
The predicate *exister* 'exist' makes that domain specific by identifying it as some conceptualizer's conception of reality (Langacker 1991; Achard 1998; see also Chapter 5).
This conception of reality is not made specific, but as a default case immediate reality
constitutes the obvious candidate. Note that the specific location where the book is to
be found is not specified either. In fact, the passage presented in (4.6) contains no reference to any physical contact between the author and the book (he admits he hasn't
read it); it merely focuses on the latter's presence in reality. The pronoun *il* profiles
the field within which the existence of the book can be ascertained, or in other words
the knowledge base that the generalized conceptualizer uses as a reference point to
locate it. The three major components therefore exhibit the level of semantic overlap
one legitimately expects of a well-entrenched construction. The previous chapter
recognized the participating predicates as those that necessarily invoke their setting
in their scope of predication. Their shared semantic overlap with the simple impersonal construction can therefore also be identified as the elements of that setting
that necessarily factor in the mental range that the conceptualizer uses to locate her
target. This section shows that this semantic overlap between the predicate and the
construction is responsible for the formation of three semi-assembled chunks where
exister, rester, and *manquer* combine with the impersonal construction to code one
of the predicates' specific sense. In this view, *il existe, il reste,* and *il manque* constitute
quasi-idiomatic complex units that serve highly specific semantic purposes.

3.1   *Exister*

The data set used for the examination of *exister*'s impersonal usage includes the
841 instances of the verb in all its different combinations of person, tense, aspect,
and mood extracted from the post-1950 section of the FRANTEXT database (see
Table 4.1).[3] *Exister* participates in two syntactic contexts, namely the intransitive
[NP + *exister*] and the simple impersonal construction. The intransitive structure is
by far the most frequent, with 673 tokens illustrated in (4.7)–(4.10):

---

3. This number of occurrences is not equivalent to the number of tokens presented in the
previous chapter because the data samples are different. Recall that the data in Chapter 3 were
searched by construction; the searches in this chapter are conducted by predicate.

(4.7)   *oh Dieu, **si vous existez**, faites quelque chose!*

> (Green, J. *Journal. T. 5. 1946–1950*: 53)

'Oh God, if you exist, do something!'

(4.8)   *Tes yeux sont toujours tristes, Dora. Il faut être gaie, il faut être fière. **La beauté existe, la joie existe**!*   (Camus, A. *Les justes*: 316)

'Your eyes are always sad, Dora. You must be happy, you must be proud. Beauty exists, joy exists!'

(4.9)   *Elle s'appelait Goldie à cause de ses cheveux et, elle aussi, laissait voir sa gorge, mais jamais il n'avait pensé à elle: lorsqu'il la voyait de loin, il traversait la rue, simplement, et **elle n'existait pas pour lui**.*   (Green, J. *Moïra: roman*: 220)

'Her name was Goldie because of her hair and, she also showed her throat, but he had never thought about her: when he saw her from afar, he would simply cross the street, and she did not exist for him'.

(4.10)   *Je n'approuve pas ce parti de la libération, qui serait créé sur l'initiative anglaise, qui ne se confondrait pas avec la France libre et qui mettrait dans les mains anglaises des fils qui ne doivent être que dans les nôtres. **Le parti français de la libération existe** depuis le 18 juin 1940. C'est la France libre. Il n'y a aucune raison d'en créer un autre.*   (Gaulle, C. de. *Mémoires de guerre, l'appel*: 614)

'I do not approve of this liberation party, which would be created following an English idea that would not coincide with Free France, and would place into English hands some threads that should only be in ours. The liberation party has been in existence [existed] since June 18 1940. It is called Free France. There is no reason to create another one'.

The impersonal construction already presented in (4.6) but further illustrated in (4.11)–(4.14) comes in a distant second with 168 tokens:

(4.11)   *entre nous, je te le rappelle puisque tu m'y forces, **il n'existe pas** de lien de parenté connu. personne ne peut dire d'où tu viens. Si je t'ai recueillie, c'est par bonté de cœur...*   (Green, J. *Moïra: roman*: 35)

'between us, let me remind you since you force me to do so, there is [exists] no known kinship relation. No one can say where you come from. I only welcomed you out of the kindness of my heart'.

(4.12)   *On peut dire qu'en une semaine le destin était scellé. Sur la pente fatale où une erreur démesurée nous avait, de longtemps, engagés, l'armée, l'état, la France, roulaient, maintenant, à un rythme vertigineux. **Il existait**, pourtant, 3000 chars français modernes et 800 automitrailleuses. Les allemands n'en avaient pas plus.*

> (Gaulle, C. de. *Mémoires de guerre, l'appel*: 29)

'We can say that within a week, fate was sealed. France was now falling at breakneck speed down the fatal slope where a monumental mistake had propelled us a long time ago. We had [there existed], nonetheless 3000 modern tanks and 800 mounted guns. The Germans didn't have any more'.

(4.13)   *L'homme qui, avec tant de grandeur, tenait pour infamie de déposer les armes tant qu'il existerait quelque part, un maître et un esclave, est le même qui devait accepter de garder la constitution de 1793 en suspens et d'exercer l'arbitraire.*
(Camus, A. *L'homme révolté*: 161)
'The man who, with such grandeur, considered it an infamy to give up the fight as long as a master and a slave would still exist somewhere in the world [there would still exist a master and a slave in the world] is the same man who would accept suspending the 1793 constitution, and act as a dictator'

(4.14)   *Je t'ai parlé, il y a quelque temps, d'une édition expurgée du théâtre de Shakespeare. Car tu n'es pas le seul que des vers comme ceux auxquels tu fais allusion aient heurté. Aussi existe-t-il une édition de Shakespeare d'où sont exclus les passages de ce genre.*
(Green, J. *Moïra: roman*: 189)
'A while ago, I mentioned to you an expunged edition of Shakespeare's theater. Because other people are also disturbed by lines such as the ones you describe. So there is [exists] an edition of Shakespeare's theater from which such passages have been deleted'.

Although impersonal usage constitutes a healthy 19.97 percent of *exister*'s general distribution, that number alone is not sufficient to indicate any specific affinity between the predicate and the construction. However, a closer examination of the data in (4.7)–(4.10) on the one hand and (4.11)–(4.14) on the other reveals that *exister* has two related but different senses, and that one of these senses is almost exclusively coded by the impersonal construction. Because the assembly that the predicate and the impersonal construction form constitutes the only resource available to French speakers to code a specific situation, we can legitimately say that in this situation the predicate and the impersonal constitute a preassembled meaningful unit.

The examples in (4.7)–(4.10) illustrate what we may call *exister*'s "ontological confirmation" sense because even though the entity coded by the subject is well known and easily identifiable, its ontological status with respect to a specific domain somehow needs to be reaffirmed. This is particularly clear in the example in (4.7). God is a constant presence in human affairs. The centrality of the quest for a supreme being explains his prominence throughout human literary and artistic production. In that sense, God certainly represents a central entity in the artistic, cultural, and spiritual domains, but his empirical existence outside of those domains is not easily established. Consequently the apparent paradox in example in (4.7) in which the speaker directly invokes God and immediately questions his existence is perfectly explainable. God's constant presence in human endeavors makes him a legitimate interlocutor, but his ontological status in everyday reality (a matter of objective fact) nonetheless remains open to question. The use of *exister* in (4.7) is therefore best understood as the ontological confirmation of an entity whose spiritual and artistic existence is beyond debate. The situation is a little different in (4.8) because beauty and joy are well-established conceptual categories, and therefore impossible to question ontologically. What needs to be reaffirmed, however, is their relevance to Dora's mental state. In this context, the kind of existence that the predicate profiles does not strictly refer to the established presence of beauty and joy in reality, but extends to their social function or, more precisely, to Dora's recognition of their possible role in her life. The meaning of *exister* extends even further in (4.9), where the context prevents its literal interpretation. The male character is obviously aware of Goldie's presence in reality (he knows her name), but she presents no particular interest for him. *Elle n'existait pas pour lui* 'she didn't exist for him' can thus be interpreted not as the refusal of Goldie's ontological status, but as the denial of her possible role as the object of his attentions. This extension to the meaning of *exister* takes the predicate into a semantic territory where its literal interpretation is impossible, as illustrated in (4.10) where the creation of the liberation party is being opposed on the grounds that it already exists under a different name. In this case, existence can only be interpreted in terms of functional identity. Since the entity that exists already performs the tasks the new one is designed to accomplish, the latter can be said to already be part of reality even though it makes little literal sense. Despite the semantic nuances that the examples in (4.7)–(4.10) reveal, the 673 examples that share this first sense of *exister* nonetheless exhibit great consistency. In every case, the predicate does not seek to establish its subject's presence in reality but to reaffirm its importance or relevance to a specific domain of experience. The entity the subject codes is thus generally highly accessible cognitively, but its status with respect to a specific domain, ontological or otherwise, is in need of (re)affirmation.

The second or "discovery" sense of *exister* illustrated in (4.11)–(4.14) strongly contrasts with the predicate's ontological confirmation sense because it establishes the presence (or absence) of a specific entity in reality. In (4.11), for instance, the speaker denies the existence of a kinship connection to his protagonist in order to underscore the altruistic nature of his act. In (4.12) the whole passage describes the introduction to the reader of the existence of enough military equipment for the French army to offer more resistance to the German invasion at the beginning of WWII. One can easily infer that the readers were not aware of the existence of these weapons, given France's quick demise. In (4.13) the two entities *un maître* 'a master' and *un esclave* 'a slave' are also presented relative to their existence, but they refer to virtual referents conjured up for the specific purposes of illustrating the current discourse rather than actual characters (Langacker 2008: 289). The strategy of using virtual referents strengthens the author's message because it makes existence alone, rather than possible identification with specific persons, the motivation for continued action. These three examples all share the similar focus of presenting (or denying) the presence in reality of the entity coded by the postverbal expression. It is important to note that even though that entity may not be new in the discourse space, it is nonetheless always presented as such. This is clearly illustrated in (4.14), where the passage elaborates on a former conversation. In a previous turn (*il y a quelque temps* 'some time ago'), the hearer had indicated reservations about the moral content of some of Shakespeare's verse. The speaker had mentioned an edition of Shakespeare's works where those questionable lines had been deleted (*une édition expurgée du théâtre de Shakespeare* 'an expunged edition of Shakespeare's theatre'). In this turn, this expunged edition is brought up again but as a new entity, whose mere presence in reality is invoked as evidence that the hearer's concerns about the morality of some of Shakespeare's words have been shared by other people over the years.

The difference in meaning between *exister* in (4.7)–(4.10) on the one hand and (4.11)–(4.14) on the other should be clear. In its discovery sense, the predicate introduces the presence of a new entity in reality. In its confirmation sense, *exister* confirms the ontological status of a known entity (if that status is the object of debate), or assesses its importance relative to a specific task (if its ontological status is commonly accepted). The most striking difference between the two senses concerns the status of the predicate's theme (the postverbal expression). It is presented as a new entity in the first sense and thus generally coded by an indefinite NP, and as a known entity in the second one in which case the subject NP is definite. This distinction is particularly clear in (4.15):

(4.15)   *Au cours de l'une des séances de la commission, un sénateur ayant demandé à Oppenheimer **s'il existait** un instrument permettant de déceler une bombe atomique cachée dans une ville, le grand physicien répondit: "oui, **cet instrument existe**, c'est un tournevis avec lequel il faudrait ouvrir chaque coffre, chaque armoire, chaque piano de chaque maison de la ville.*
(Goldschmidt, B. *L'aventure atomique: ses aspects politiques et techniques*: 63)
'During one of the commission's meetings, a senator asked Oppenheimer if there was [existed] an instrument capable of detecting a nuclear bomb hidden in a large city. The great physicist answered: "Yes, this instrument exists, it is a screwdriver with which we should open every safe, every dresser, every piano in every house in the city'.

The example in (4.15) contains two instances of *exister*. In the first (impersonal) construction, the object of the senator's question concerns the mere presence of a specific tool in reality. Since the speaker is questioning the tool's possible existence, the instance used is a virtual one, specifically conjured up to express his hopes and fears. In the second (intransitive) construction, the notion of a tool has already been introduced in the discourse (obviously not in reality), and it is thus treated as a known entity whose ontological status is being confirmed. In this example the banal nature of the only tool potentially capable of fending off the nuclear threat serves to further enhance that threat.

For the purposes of this chapter, it is crucial to note that the two separate senses of *exister* are systematically coded by different constructions. The discovery sense is exclusively attested with the impersonal, whereas the confirmation sense is always expressed by the intransitive construction. As expected, the information status of the entity whose existence is being assessed (respectively coded as the subject and postverbal expression in the intransitive and impersonal constructions respectively) is in perfect line with the constructions themselves. Of the 673 intransitive examples, 667 predicates have a definite NP as their subject, while 162 out of 168 impersonal constructions have an indefinite NP in their postverbal expression.[4] This tendency is so strong that in certain possibly ambiguous contexts the presence of a specific determiner is sufficient to decide whether or not the construction should be interpreted as personal or impersonal, as illustrated in (4.16):

---

4. This claim is often made for all impersonals, but, as we will see in the next section, it is overstated. Among the six postverbal expressions that include a definite NP, three only do so from a formal standpoint because the definite article *le/la* is part of the negative expression *pas le/la moindre* 'not the slightest', which should be treated as an indefinite. The other three examples are:

   (i)   *D'un autre côté les choses peuvent empirer, **il existe** ce danger*. (Beckett, S. *Comédie*: 22).
         'On the other hand, things can get worse, this danger exists [there exists this danger]'.

   (ii) *Quelquefois je regarde nos bâtiments, les arbres, les gazons, nos soeurs ou les femmes de charge qui vont et viennent, et j'ai les yeux ouverts et je me dis: "rien de tout cela n'existe. **Il n'existe** au monde que Dieu et moi"*.   (Montherlant, H. *Port-Royal*: 996)
         'Sometimes I look at our buildings, the trees, the grass, our sisters or the servants going back and forth. My eyes are open and I say to myself: "none of that exists. There exists in the world only God and me"'.

   (iii) *Il ajoute qu'il existe en Allemagne tous les éléments d'un nouveau fascisme, que beaucoup d'allemands sont tout prêts à suivre un nouveau Führer*.
                                                (Green, J. *Journal. T. 5. 1946–1950*: 343)
         'He adds that there are [exists] in Germany all the elements of a new fascism, that many Germans are ready to follow a new Führer'.

The example in (ii) is actually part of the restrictive construction *ne…que* 'only', and should be dealt with independently. The other two examples show that the connection between the impersonal construction and the indefinite marking on the postverbal nominal is not automatic, and truly determined by the semantic overlap that exists between the predicate and the construction.

(4.16)   *Le poète psychologue-ou le psychologue poète, s'il en existe-ne peut se tromper en marquant d'un cri animal les différents types d'agression.*

(Bachelard, G. La poétique de l'espace: 56)

'The psychologist poet or the poet psychologist, if there exists any, cannot be mistaken by coding the different types of aggression with animal screams'.

Because in French the impersonal pronoun has the same form as the third-person singular subject pronoun, the sentence in (4.16) is potentially ambiguous. *Il* could possibly refer to *le poète psychologue*, or it could be the impersonal form. The presence of the pronoun *en* alone prevents us from interpreting it as a personal pronoun because it represents a pronominalized noun phrase that contains an indefinite article (*des poètes*).

It should be clear, however, that the introduction of a given entity with respect to its presence in reality (discovery sense), or as a familiar presence whose status demands confirmation (confirmation sense) is often solely determined by the author's rhetorical strategy. This is illustrated in the pair (4.17) and (4.18) where despite their comparable ontological status, Homer and Aristotle receive different linguistic treatments:

(4.17)   *Contre quoi travaillent les historiens, qui en viennent tous à dire qu'**Homère n'a pas existé**; mais aucun Homère n'a existé; aucun mort ne fut digne de ses œuvres...*   (Alain. *Propos sur des philosophes*: 97)

'[this is] what all historians are working against, who all agree that Homer didn't exist; but no Homer ever existed; no dead author was ever worthy of his works'.

(4.18)   *Qu'il soit permis ici de rappeler par quelques formules qu'il **exista** <u>un Aristote</u>, digne encore de nous instruire.*   (Alain. *Propos sur des philosophes*: 49)

'May I be allowed to remind you here by a few formulae that there was someone called Aristotle [there existed an Aristotle], still worthy of educating us'.

The literary figures of Homer and Aristotle enjoy a fairly comparable status in Western culture; both are popular figures who require no introduction. In (4.17) the assertion of existence is restricted to the physical presence in reality at a given time in history of a single character called Homer, who would be responsible for all the works that bear his name. The use of the intransitive construction is expected and totally unproblematic. However, the impersonal in (4.18) is more surprising because as definite nominals proper nouns are usually not a good match in this construction. Because Aristotle is a well-known philosopher and hence readily available cognitively for his readers, the author could have easily resorted to the choice he exercised in (4.17), and used the alternative #*Aristote a existé* 'Aristotle existed'. Nevertheless, the choice of the impersonal construction can be defended on rhetorical grounds. First, the construction's overwhelming preference for an indefinite NP allows the transformation of a proper name into a more general type that the proper name metonymically stands for. This provides more strength to the argument that lessons from the past can still be valuable because it extends the exemplary value of a single individual to all others whose impact was equally important. Furthermore, the explicit mention of the field, i.e. the abstract region composed of the arguments that may justify the choice of Aristotle, provides a search domain within which possible alternatives can be explored and thus strengthens the final choice by anchoring its selection in careful consideration.

The data presented in this section clearly show that the favored (quasi-exclusive) resource available to French speakers to introduce an entity in reality is composed of the cluster Predicate (*exister* here but also *il y a* in certain situations considered in Section 4) + Impersonal + indefinite NP. Importantly, these entities are not cobbled together for structural reasons (we saw that a definite NP was possible if highly disfavored); they combine because their respective semantics overlap to the point of creating a semi-assembled chunk that best meets the requirements of its semantic function.

3.2   Relative existence: *Rester* and *manquer*

The other two predicates examined in this section, *rester* 'remain', and *manquer* 'lack', exhibit some departure from the strict existence *exister* codes because they profile the difference that exists between the conceptualized entity and its initial or ideal form. This is illustrated with *rester* in (4.19), where the predicate profiles the portion of the potatoes that remains uneaten:

(4.19)   *dans la casserole **il restait** environ <u>la moitié des pommes de terre</u>.*
                                                                                (Robbe-Grillet, A. *Le Voyeur*: 144)
            'Approximately half of the potatoes remained in the pan [there remained approximately half of the potatoes]'.

It is worth noting that *rester* does not profile the existence of the potatoes since they have already been identified at a specific location, nor does it profile that location either. What it profiles is the discrepancy between the original amount of food in the pan and what was left over once the meal was finished. In this sense, *rester* (and the next section will show this is also true for *manquer*) profiles what we might call relative existence since only a subpart of a complete entity (what remains for *rester*, what is missing for *manquer*) is being assessed.

3.2.1   *Rester*

Rester possesses two senses respectively translated in English as 'stay' and 'remain'. Only the 'remain' sense is relevant to the concerns of this section because the 'stay' sense does not occur with the impersonal construction. Within the 'remain' sense, however, two situations obtain. In the predicate adjective and nominal constructions illustrated in (4.20)–(4.22), the predicate codes the enduring situation that its subject undergoes.

(4.20)   *La France "considère que **le problème très grave suscité par le programme nucléaire nord-coréen reste entier** et qu'il convient donc de maintenir une position très ferme", a dit le porte-parole, précisant que Paris "poursuit avec ses partenaires à New York des consultations sur l'adoption de sanctions".*   (AFP)
'France "considers that the very serious problem posed by the Korean nuclear program remains unchanged and that a very firm position needs to be maintained", the representative said, adding that Paris "is pursuing discussions over possible sanctions with its partners in New York"'.

(4.21)   *"Simon est mort," se répétait-il comme pour se forcer à croire à cette phrase. Il avait beau faire, cependant, il n'arrivait pas à s'émouvoir. Volontiers il se fût attendri, mais **ses yeux restaient secs** et, la première surprise passée, son cœur s'était remis à battre comme à l'ordinaire.*   (Green, J. *Moïra: roman*: 134)
'"Simon is dead," he repeated to himself, as if to force himself to believe this sentence. Try as he may, however, he could not be moved. He would have loved to become emotional, but his eyes remained dry, and once the effect of surprise wore off, his heart started beating as usual'.

(4.22)   *Cet homme aux cheveux gris garde la tête sur les épaules. "**Une prison restera** toujours **une prison**, mais cette fois elle servira pour les criminels de droits commun", ajoute-t-il.*   (AFP)
'This gray haired man remains realistic. "A jail will always remain a jail, but this time, it will be used for common law criminals", he adds'.

The other sense of the predicate describes the result of a change of state. In (4.19), *rester* quantifies the remainder of the initial potatoes at the end of the meal. Similarly, in (4.23) the predicate evaluates the number of people still waiting to be evacuated.

(4.23)   *Quelque 80 citoyens russes et originaires des anciennes républiques soviétiques sont arrivés par avion dimanche à Moscou en provenance du Yémen, a annoncé le ministère russe chargé des Situations d'urgence, cité par l'agence ITAR-TASS. Samedi, environ 200 personnes étaient arrivées à Moscou venant du Yémen et le ministère avait indiqué qu'**il restait** sur place <u>encore environ 70 personnes</u> à être évacuées.*   (AFP)

'Some 80 Russian citizens from the former Soviet republics flew into Moscow from Yemen on Sunday, the Russian secretary in charge of emergency situations announced, as quoted by the ITAR-TASS agency. On Saturday, around 200 people had arrived in Moscow from Yemen, and the secretary had indicated that around 70 people still needed to be evacuated [there remained around 70 people to be evacuated]'.

Some aspects of the syntactic distribution of these two senses are straightforward. The stable situations described in (4.20)–(4.22) where the subject undergoes no change of state can be described only by predicate or adjective constructions but not by impersonals, as illustrated in (4.24)–(4.26) where the examples are manipulated from their attested counterparts in (4.20)–(4.22):

(4.24) #*Il restait le mystère entier
        'There remained the mystery whole'

(4.25) #*Il restait ses yeux secs....
        'There remained his eyes dry...'

(4.26) #*Il restera toujours une prison une prison
        'There will always remain a prison a prison'

As a consequence, the impersonal construction is only possible when *rester* profiles the discrepancy between the transformed postverbal entity and its unaffected original counterpart, but the personal construction may also be used in those cases. The comparison between the examples in (4.19) where the impersonal construction was used to describe the leftover potatoes and the one in (4.27) where the personal construction introduces the remaining 1,500 refugees highlights the similarities between the two constructions:

(4.27) *Ce bilan, provisoire et n'incluant pas les blessés, a été communiqué par des responsables de Al Koud à un représentant du HCR et à un délégué du Comité international de la Croix-Rouge (CICR) qui se sont rendus sur place samedi, a indiqué à l'AFP Ron Redmond, porte-parole du HCR. Selon ces deux organisations humanitaires, **quelque 1.500 personnes seulement restent** dans ce camp au bord de la côte de l'Océan indien sur les 11.600 qui étaient enregistrées par le HCR.* (AFP)
        'This provisional tally that does not include the injured, was communicated by Al Koud members to the HCR representative and a member of the International Red Cross committee (CICR) who traveled to the site on Saturday, Ron Redmond, the HCR spokesperson said. According to these two humanitarian organizations, only some 1,500 people remain in this camp located on the Indian Ocean coast, out of the 11,600 HCR had registered'.

This section investigates *rester*'s impersonal usage. Two corpora were considered for this purpose. First, 2,664 tokens of the verb in all its possible morphological variations were extracted from the post-1950 FRANTEXT database. Second, 292 instances were randomly selected from the AFP corpus that only describe part/ whole situations where personal and impersonal constructions are in competition.

Two observations immediately emerge from the data. The first is the relatively higher frequency of the impersonal construction over the personal one when the two are in competition. In the AFP corpus 151 instances of impersonals were recorded as opposed to thirty-four personal examples.[5] The second is the extreme systematicity of the impersonal usage, particularly obvious in the AFP corpus where the construction codes highly predictable situations. One might argue that this characteristic merely results from the nature of the corpus. In some measure, this objection is absolutely correct. The kinds of stories newspapers report fall into similar categories, and the journalistic genre does possess its own specificities. However, I do not believe that genre specificity seriously challenges the specificity of *rester*'s impersonal usage because the FRANTEXT corpus exhibits the same systematicity, even though the observed patterns are distributed over a wider range of topics. Because the analysis requires the individual examination of each example in the corpus, and because the AFP corpus is smaller and more manageable it provides the bulk of the examples examined in this section. As indicated earlier, the presence of the impersonal codes the part/whole relationship that exists between the postverbal entity and its original or unaffected counterpart, which is not always specifically mentioned in the immediate discourse even though it is always recoverable from the wider context. The most interesting aspect of *rester*'s impersonal usage for our purposes is the extreme systematicity of the usage patterns encountered in the data. The 151 examples neatly divide themselves into a small number of highly specific groupings.

In the first pattern of ninety-three examples, the postverbal entity describes the quantified portion of a larger well-known and easily accessible whole. This group can further be divided in two. The first one consists of thirty-seven instances that describe the unfinished portion of an activity with a clearly available number of steps. Typical situations include the amount of time left in a sporting contest as in (4.28) (or in any situation with a clear time line), the remaining portion of a long bicycle race as in (4.29), the number of matches to be played at a particular level of a soccer tournament in (4.30), or the number of fields that still need clearing in an effort to find all the remaining American prisoners in Vietnam, as illustrated in (4.31):

---

5.   The remaining examples are composed of complex impersonals, zero impersonals that do not include the impersonal pronoun *il*, and relative clauses where *qui* and *qu'il* are in competition and whose usage is extremely unstable (see note 6 for further discussion of the *qui/qu'il* ambiguity).

(4.28)   *Arrigo Sacchi (entraîneur de l'Italie): "J'ai fait sortir Roberto Baggio parce que j'ai beaucoup de respect pour lui et que je ne voulais pas le transformer en travailleur de l'ombre.* **Il restait** <u>40 minutes à jouer</u> *et il était évident à ce point que j'avais besoin de joueurs condamnés à se battre"*   (AFP)
'Arrigo Sacchi (Italian coach)): "I took Roberto Baggio out because I have a lot of respect for him, and didn't want to turn him into a journeyman. We still had 40 minutes to play [there remained 40 minutes to play], and it was obvious that I needed players condemned to fighting"'.

(4.29)   *Mes limites? Je ne les ai pas encore découvertes. On dit que je suis déjà un champion mais je vous rappelle que je n'ai gagné que deux étapes dans ce Giro et qu'il* **reste** <u>encore deux semaines</u>...   (AFP)
'My limits, I haven't discovered them yet. People say that I am already a champion, but let me remind you that I have only won two stages in this Giro, and that we still have two weeks to go [there still remains two weeks]...'

(4.30)   *Avec la qualification de l'Italie, qui a joué à dix après l'expulsion sévère de Gianfranco Zola dont c'était le 28e anniversaire, l'Europe a accentué son emprise sur la phase finale du Mondial. Alors qu'***il ne reste** <u>qu'un seul huitième de finale</u> *à disputer entre le Mexique et la Bulgarie, ultérieurement mardi à New York, les Européens se sont attribués six des sept places des quarts de finale.*   (AFP)
'With the qualification of Italy, who played with 10 men following the harsh sendoff of Gianfranco Zola on his 28th birthday, Europe increased its grip on the World Cup Finals. With only one game to play in the round of 16, [when there remains only one eighth final to play] between Mexico and Bulgaria on Tuesday in New York, Europeans grabbed six of the seven spots of the quarter finals'.

(4.31)   *Les deux parties poursuivent leur coopération sur le terrain pour tenter de régler le dossier des MIA alors que, sur le plan diplomatique, elles ont annoncé le mois dernier l'ouverture de bureau de liaison dans leurs capitales respectives, première étape de la normalisation complète entre les deux anciens ennemis. Il* **reste** *aux experts américains* <u>entre 60 et 70 sites à défricher</u> *au Vietnam, a précisé le colonel-lieutenant John Cray, en charge du bureau des MIA américains à Hanoi.*
(AFP)
'The two parties continue their cooperation on the ground to try to solve the ongoing issue of the soldiers missing in action, whereas, in the diplomatic arena, they announced last month the opening of a liaison office in their respective capitals, the first stage toward completely normal relations between the two former enemies. American experts still have 60 to 70 sites to clear [there remain 60 or 70 sites for American experts to clear] in Vietnam, Lieutenant Colonel John Cray, the person in charge of the American soldiers missing in action in Hanoi said'.

The second subgrouping is composed of forty-seven cases that describe the precise number of entities that remain in a specific situation. This class of examples illustrated in (4.32) and (4.33) typically involves refugees, soldiers, rebels, endangered species, and so on. In addition, a group of nine examples illustrated in (4.34) describes the same kind of situation but does not specify the exact number:

(4.32) *Le contingent d'environ 6.800 Casques bleus français présents dans l'ex-Yougoslavie connaîtra deux mouvements distincts au cours des prochains mois, qui porteront sur un retrait des bataillons stationnés à Glina (Croatie) et à Bihac (Bosnie). A l'issue de ces deux mouvements, **il restera** dans l'ex-Yougoslavie <u>soit quelque 5.000 Français</u>, si le bataillon de Bihac est rapatrié en France, <u>soit environ 6.000</u>, si ce même bataillon est redéployé à Sarajevo.*   (AFP)
'Two distinct movements will affect the contingent of approximately 6,800 French Blue Helmets stationed in former Yugoslavia. They will involve the withdrawal of the battalion located in Glina (Croatia), and Bihac (Bosnia). At the end of these movements, there will remain in former Yugoslavia either 5,000 French soldiers if the Bihac battalion is sent back to France, or 6,000 if this same battalion is redeployed to Sarajevo'.

(4.33) *Selon les spécialistes, un million et demi de baleines ont été tuées dans l'Antartique au cours du siècle, notamment des baleines bleues, dont **il** ne **reste** plus <u>qu'un millier d'exemplaires</u>...*   (AFP)
'According to experts, a million and a half whales have been killed in Antarctica this century, in particular blue whales, of which only one thousand remain [there remain only one thousand]...'

(4.34) *Samedi matin, du côté serbe, il n'y avait plus d'hommes en uniforme de policiers, mais **il restait** toujours "<u>des civils armés</u>", selon le porte-parole.*   (AFP)
'On Saturday morning, on the Serbian side, there were no longer any men in police uniforms, but "armed civilians" remained [there remained "armed civilians"], according to the spokesperson'.

The second pattern consists of thirty-seven examples, illustrated in (4.35)–(4.37), that describe the unquantified aspects of a project that still stand in the way of its successful completion. The postverbal entity typically includes nominals such as *détails* 'details', *problèmes* 'problems', *questions* 'question', *chemin à parcourir* 'road to travel', and so on, and more specifically, ten instances of the idiomatic *beaucoup à faire* 'lots to be done' illustrated in (4.37).

(4.35) *La brève visite de mercredi à Damas lui permettra de transmettre la réaction des dirigeants israéliens à ces propositions. Le Premier ministre israélien Yitzhak Rabin a indiqué mardi, à l'issue d'un entretien avec M. Christopher, que les deux pays avaient encore des divergences sur des "problèmes majeurs" et **qu'il restait** "<u>un long chemin à parcourir</u>".*   (AFP)

'The short visit to Damascus on Wednesday will allow him to convey the reaction of Israeli leaders to these proposals. The Israeli Prime Minister Yitzhak Rabin indicated on Tuesday, following a meeting with Mr. Christopher, that the two countries still diverged on "major problems" and that there was still [there remained] "a long way to go"'.

(4.36)   *"Je n'aurais jamais pensé que je verrais un jour la moitié du Produit intérieur brut de la Russie provenir du secteur privé", a-t-il déclaré. Toutefois, **il reste** selon lui <u>"des progrès à faire"</u> en matière de lutte contre l'inflation...*   (AFP)
"'I would have never thought that I would see the day when half of Russia's gross interior revenue would come from the private sector", he added. However, according to him, there is still [there remains] "progress to be made" in the fight against inflation...'

(4.37)   *Les entretiens à Damas du secrétaire d'Etat américain Warren Christopher ont marqué le "début d'une nouvelle phase sérieuse" mais Israël et la Syrie ne sont "pas proches d'une percée" dans leurs discussions de paix, a indiqué lundi un responsable américain. "**Il reste** <u>beaucoup à faire</u> mais les deux parties sont engagées de manière sérieuse dans ce processus", a ajouté le responsable...*   (AFP)
'The Damascus meetings with American State Secretary Warren Christopher marked the "beginning of a new serious phase", but Israel and Syria are "not close to a breakthrough" in their peace discussions, an American representative said on Monday. "There is still [remains] a lot to do, but the two parties are seriously committed to the process", the representative added...'

The third pattern is composed of three smaller groups that exhibit a strong degree of internal consistency. In the first, which contains six instances illustrated in (4.38), the postverbal entity describes the results of time, weather, or destruction:

(4.38)   *Situé dans le vieux quartier de Mala Strana, sur un mur appartenant à l'ambassade de l'Ordre de Malte, et en face du Palais Buquoy, siège de l'ambassade de France, le portrait en couleur de Lennon s'écaille de plus en plus, envahi par un maquis de graffiti. **Il n'en reste** plus aujourd'hui que <u>les yeux cerclés de lunettes et le haut du visage</u>.*   (AFP)
'Located in the old Mala Strana neighborhood, on a wall that belongs to the Order of Malta's embassy, and across from the Buquoy Palace where the French embassy is located, the color portrait of Lennon is degrading more and more every day, amidst a forest of graffiti. Only the eyes with the glasses and the top of the face are now left [There now only remains the eyes with glasses and the top of the face]'.

The second group in (4.39) (four tokens) describes the remaining portion of a program or administrative procedure, and the complete entity emerges from the entire context. In (4.39) that context describes the international student exchange agreements in which Guinea participates. Within these agreements, a specific number of slots are reserved for Guinean students to study specific topics in different countries. The leftover slots to study cinema in Cuba are therefore rightfully understood as a fraction of that exchange program.

(4.39)   *"Je devais aller apprendre la médecine en Union soviétique. Avec la guerre, j'ai mis un mois à arriver, à pied, à Conakry. L'avion était parti depuis une semaine. **Il restait des bourses** pour aller à Cuba, étudier le cinéma. Je n'avais jamais vu un film de ma vie mais j'y suis allé", raconte-t-il.*   (AFP)
"I was supposed to go to the Soviet Union to study medicine. It took me a month to walk to Conakry because of the war. The plane had left the week before. There were fellowships left [there remained fellowships] to study cinema in Cuba. I had never seen a movie in my life but I went", he says'.

Finally, the third group of six instances illustrated in (4.40) describes the emotional traces of a traumatic event:

(4.40)   *Le bataillon de casques bleus espagnols de la Force de Protection des Nations unies (FORPRONU) stationné en ville travaille à la restauration des réseaux électriques et d'eau potable de la ville. "**Il reste** encore beaucoup de haine entre les populations.*
'The battalion of the Spanish Blue Helmets of the United Nations Protection Force (FORPRONU) stationed in town is working to restore the city's electrical and drinking water structures. "There is still a lot of hatred [there remains a lot of hatred] among the population"'.

Only the five examples given in (4.41)–(4.45) do not comfortably fit the categories described above:

(4.41)   *Chez Gaultier, tout est question d'accessoires. Si l'on enlève les audaces, **il reste de vrais vêtements**, œuvres d'un excellent tailleur…*   (AFP)
'Gaultier is all about accessories. If you remove the daring style, real clothes remain [there remains real clothes], worthy of a great tailor…'

(4.42)   *"Le quartier de Khormaksar est situé près de l'aéroport, ceux de Maalla et Tawahi près du port, et à Crater, il y a des casernes, "**il ne nous reste** plus que la mer", s'exclame Mohammad Hamed, un jeune mécanicien dont le garage a été incendié jeudi.*   (AFP)
"The Khormaksar neighborhood is located near the airport, those of Maalla and Tawahi near the harbor, and there are barracks in Crater, "the sea is all we have left" [there only remains the sea to us] says Mohammad Hamed, a young mechanic whose garage burned on Thursday'.

(4.43) *L'intérêt des Argentins pour la Coupe du monde a permis aux revendeurs de postes de télévision de Buenos Aires de réaliser d'excellentes affaires depuis un mois. Selon le directeur d'une grande chaine de distribution, l'augmentation des ventes a été de 50%. Mais on est loin de la fièvre de 1990, quand **il ne restait plus** un récepteur à vendre dans tout Buenos Aires avant le coup d'envoi du Mondiale italien.* (AFP) 'The interest of the Argentines for the World Cup allowed the television retailers in Buenos Aires to do good business in the past month. According to the director of a major distribution chain, sales increased by 50%. But we are still far from the fever of 1990, when there was not one set available for sale in Buenos Aires before the Italian World Cup'.

(4.44) *Pour leur première sortie, les Brésiliens ont donc assuré l'essentiel, mais **il leur reste** certainement d'autres choses à montrer et des finitions à soigner.* (AFP) 'For their first game, the Brazilians have accomplished what mattered most, but they certainly have much more to show, and scoring opportunities to capitalize on [there remains to them much more to show, and scoring opportunities to capitalize on]'.

(4.45) *La bière et les préservatifs ne font pas bon ménage: les brasseries canadiennes Molson l'ont appris à leur dépens et ont dû mettre fin à une campagne publicitaire associant les deux après avoir reçu de nombreuses plaintes de consommateurs. "Non seulement vous avez acheté de la bière pour sa soirée baseball, mais **il vous restait** assez d'argent pour acheter un préservatif", proclamait ainsi La publicité pour la Carling Ice, une bière bon marché.* (AFP) 'The Molson brewery learned at their expense that beer and preservatives don't mix, when the large number of customer complaints forced them to terminate an advertising campaign that associated the two. "Not only have you bought beer for his baseball evening, but you still have enough money [there remained enough money for you] to buy a preservative" the advertisement for Carling Ice, a cheap beer, said'.

The way in which the postverbal expression participates in a part/whole relationship with an original or complete entity in the examples (4.41) and (4.42) deserves some explanation. In the evaluation of Gaultier's fashion line in (4.41), the author claims that the originality of the clothes comes mainly from the bold addition of accessories to classically well-designed garments. In this analysis, the accessories are superimposed on the garments that nonetheless stand on their own merits when they are stripped of their fashionable additions. These bare garments can thus be viewed as a reduced part of the fashion artifacts that models wear on the runway. The example in (4.42) describes the desolation that multiple attacks have brought to a neighborhood. In this manner, it is very close to the "destruction" examples illustrated in (4.38), but was not included in that category because its more immediate focus is placed on the feeling of desperation that destruction brings about.

The original entity encompasses more than buildings and structures to include the surroundings, human elements, economic activities, and possible prosperity that made it a desirable area. The waterfront is thus a legitimate part of a more abstract entity composed of all the area's positive features, and the speaker's focus on its sole remaining presence serves to underscore the loss of all its other assets.

Unlike *exister* in its discovery sense, the relationship between the part/whole sense of *rester* and the impersonal construction is not exclusive because it is coded with a personal construction where the predicate's theme (the postverbal expression in the impersonal construction) is coded as subject in thirty-four instances. The usage of the personal construction seems considerably more restricted than that of the impersonal variant, perhaps – but not exclusively – as a result of its lesser frequency. For example, no example has been found in the corpus in which the postverbal expression represents the time remaining in a sporting contest, and very few examples are attested that describe the precise number of people left at a location. These cases do occur unambiguously, as illustrated in (4.46), but it is not always easy to decide with certainty if the predicate has its 'remain' sense considered here, or if it should be analyzed as 'stay' as the examples in (4.47) and (4.48) illustrate.

(4.46)   *Les trois hommes, des Caucasiens, selon la radio, avaient stoppé plus tôt un autocar avec une quarantaine de passagers à bord, avant d'en libérer plusieurs. Six personnes ont pu quitter l'autocar, a indiqué l'agence ITAR-TASS, qui avait auparavant fait état de seize personnes libérées. **Une trentaine de personnes resteraient** donc au total sous la menace des ravisseurs, et non une vingtaine comme indiqué jusque-là par l'agence russe.*   (AFP)
'Earlier, the three men, Caucasians according to the radio, had stopped a bus with approximately forty people on board, before letting several of them go. Six people were able to leave the bus, ITAR-TASS agency said, who had previously stated that sixteen people had been freed. Approximately thirty people would thus remain under the threat of the kidnappers, not around twenty as the Russian agency had been claiming up to now'.

(4.47)   *"Les bombes pleuvaient tout autour de l'hôtel", a déclaré un prêtre, l'un des derniers réfugiés de l'hôtel des Mille Collines où ne **restent** plus que **quelques dizaines de personnes**.*   (AFP)
'Bombs were raining all around the hotel, a priest declared, one of the last refugees of the Thousand Hills hotel where only a few dozen people remain'.

(4.48)   *Selon le porte-parole du département d'Etat, Mme Christine Shelly, cette mesure devrait toucher "environ 120 personnes" des quelque 200 membres du personnel que compte l'ambassade. "**Un nombre suffisant de personnes** devrait **rester sur place** pour continuer à s'occuper de nos opérations essentielles", a-t-elle ajouté, en soulignant que le chiffre exact restait encore à définir.*   (AFP)

'According to Mrs. Christine Shelly, the State Department's spokesperson, this measure should concern "approximately 120 people" out of the 200 members of the embassy staff. "A sufficient number of people should remain in place to continue our essential operations", she continued, further adding that the exact number still remained to be determined'.

The bulk of the personal examples describes the remaining stages of a complex event as in (4.49), and the aspects of a project that still prevent its successful completion as in (4.50):

(4.49)   *Le SZDSZ, dont la tête de liste et prétendant au poste de Premier ministre est l'économiste Gabor Kuncze, 43 ans, est prêt à participer au futur gouvernement aux côtés des socialistes. Il craint toutefois qu'en cas de majorité absolue du MSZP, il n'ait pas assez de poids dans une future coalition pour faire passer ses priorités. 259 sur 386 sièges restent à pourvoir au second tour...*   (AFP)
'The SZDSZ, whose leader and candidate for the Prime Minister position is the economist Gabor Kunze, 43 years old, is ready to take part in the next government alongside socialists. It fears, however, that if the MSZP reaches absolute majority, it may not carry enough weight in the future coalition to impose its priorities. 259 seats out of 386 remain to be filled in the second round...'

(4.50)   *Il a rappelé que Washington avait promis 500 millions de dollars sur cinq ans pour aider à appliquer l'accord sur l'autonomie palestinienne à Jéricho et Gaza, signé le 4 mai au Caire par Israël et l'OLP. Les Etats-Unis, a-t-il précisé, vont notamment reconstruire une clinique pour enfants et équiper en véhicules la police palestinienne. Tout en reconnaissant que "beaucoup reste à faire" pour appliquer pleinement cet accord, il s'est déclaré "très impressionné par l'efficacité" dont ont fait preuve jusqu'à maintenant les Palestiniens en prenant en mains l'autonomie.*   (AFP)
'He confirmed that Washington had promised 500 million dollars over five years to help implement the agreement on Palestinian autonomy in Jericho and Gaza, signed by Israel and the PLO on May 4th in Cairo. In particular, he added, the Americans will build a children hospital and provide cars for the Palestinian police. While agreeing that "a lot remains to be done" to fully implement this agreement, he declared he was "very impressed by the efficiency" the Palestinians have shown in managing their autonomy'.

Several factors seem to favor the personal construction over its impersonal counterpart when both are in competition. First, in twenty-one of the thirty-four personal examples (63.63 percent of the cases), the subject of the predicate is followed by an infinitival complement introduced by *à* (*à faire* 'to do', *à venir* to come', and so on). Conversely, these constructions only occur in twenty-one cases out of 151 with impersonals (21.85 percent). Second, the presence of a superlative in the postverbal expression seems to exclusively favor the personal construction. The thirty-four examples contain ten superlatives illustrated in (4.51), and that number includes eight instances of the strongly idiomatic *le plus dur reste à faire* illustrated in (4.52) and (4.53). Although it is grammatically possible to incorporate superlatives into the impersonal form (*il reste le plus dur à faire*), no such form is attested in the corpus.

(4.51)   *Le pire reste à venir pour les personnels sacrifiés envoyés à Tchernobyl.* (AFP)
         'The worst is yet to come for the sacrificed workers sent to Chernobyl'.

(4.52)   *"La remise en route de l'eau, du gaz et de l'électricité représentera environ 30%"*
         de la somme qui doit être trouvée, estime le numéro deux de l'ICBO. Mais pour ce
         dernier, le plus dur reste à faire: convaincre les pays de s'engager financièrement
         dans la reconstruction de Sarajevo....   (AFP)
         '"The repairs to water, gas, and electricity will represent approximately 30%
         of the money that needs to be raised, the ICBO number two estimates. But
         according to the latter, the hardest part remains: to convince people to commit
         financially to the reconstruction of Sarajevo...'

(4.53)   *La principale innovation vient de l'engagement américain et russe à en soutenir*
         les termes, qui prévoient notamment un partage territorial accordant 51% de la
         Bosnie aux Musulmans et Croates, et 49% aux Serbes. Le plus dur reste donc à
         faire pour les négociateurs du Groupe de contact qui vont devoir convaincre les
         belligérants de respecter un arrêt général des hostilités durant au moins quatre
         mois pour faciliter la reprise des discussions territoriales.   (AFP)
         'The main novelty comes from the American and Russian commitment to
         support the terms, which in particular require a land-sharing program that
         gives 51% of Bosnia to Muslims and Croats, and 49% to the Serbs. The hard-
         est part remains to be done for the negotiators of the contact group who will
         have to convince the combatants to respect a cease fire of at least four months
         to facilitate the land-sharing discussions'.

The distribution between the personal and impersonal constructions following *rester* is thus quite systematic and straightforward. The impersonal variant is not only strongly favored to code most instances of a part/whole relationship, but the kinds of situations encountered in the data reveal a very high level of systematicity that cannot be solely imputed to journalistic prose. The instances of the part/whole relationship that are coded with the personal construction either include a strong idiomatic component (presence of a superlative, expressions such as *le plus dur reste à faire*), or contain a strongly topical entity, and thus present a large amount of new information about that entity. In particular, this is the case in (4.50) and (4.51), where the communicative purpose of the sentence goes beyond a rough assessment of the part of a project that remains to be accomplished to include the detail of the steps that lead to the assessment.[6]

3.2.2   *Manquer*

Semantically, *manquer* is highly polysemous. The senses considered in this section all center around the general idea of the deficiency that some entity exhibits in a specific domain.[7] The predicate's lexical semantic structure makes it strikingly similar to *rester*. First, speakers enjoy the same alternative of selecting a personal construction with the predicate's theme (the lacking quality) entity as the subject, or an impersonal construction, as illustrated respectively in (4.54) and (4.55):[8]

---

6. Some historical factors also serve to confuse the selection of the impersonal construction with *rester*. In the context of a relative clause, the compound-form object pronoun plus impersonal pronoun *qu'il* is so close to the subject relative *qui* that a measure was taken to regulate the matter (Brunot 1936). These two forms remain in competition in contemporary French, as the examples in (i) and (ii) illustrate:

(i)   *Andreas Moeller et Juergen Klinsmann, les attaquants de la Juventus de Turin et de l'AS Monaco, savent ce **qu'il leur reste à faire**.*   (AFP)
'Andreas Moeller and Jurgen Klingsmann, the Juventus Turin and AS Monaco forwards, know what they need to do [what there remains for them to do]'.

(ii) *Me voilà là, à ne plus pouvoir remuer bras ni jambes; crois-tu que c'est la maladie, Aldo? Il n'y a pas quinze jours que j'ai encore forcé un lièvre. Mais j'ai trop fait pour ce **qui me reste à faire**, voilà ce qui est.*   (Gracq, J. Le rivage des Syrtes: 207)
'Here I am, I can't move my arms or legs; do you think I am sick, Aldo? I killed a hare not even two weeks ago. But I have done too much for what I still have to do [that which remains for me to do], that's what it is'.

The examples in (i) and (ii) have a similar structure, and they differ only by the nature of the pronoun and the person of the dative pronoun. These ambiguous examples are not included in the analysis.

7. The verb also has other senses that are not considered here. The first, best translated by 'miss', indicates failure to reach an objective (#*il a manqué la cible* 'he missed the target'). The second describes the emotional vacuum a missing entity leaves (#*son ami lui manque* 'he misses his friend'). In the third sense, the predicates functions as a sort of auxiliary (#*elle a manqué de le renverser* 'she almost ran him over').

8. Just like *rester*, *manquer* also appears in a construction that can be interpreted either as a dislocated construction or a Ø impersonal, since the theme is in the third-person singular and therefore does not allow verbal agreement to distinguish the two alternatives. This is illustrated in (i):

(i)   *Depuis qu'il ne copiait plus, il avait cette peur qu'ont souvent les vieillards, peur que leur **manque le pain des derniers jours**...*   (Guéhenno, J. Jean-Jacques. T. 3:328)
'Since he was no longer writing, he had this fear old people often have, the fear that they will not have enough for their remaining days [to them lacks the bread of their last days]...'

(4.54) *L'Assemblée nationale, forte du soutien de l'énorme majorité de la population, a adopté vendredi la législation la plus controversée de sa brève existence à la quasi unanimité: **une seule voix** des 98 députés **a manqué.*** (AFP)
'On Friday, the national assembly, with the support of a large majority of the population, adopted the most controversial law of its short existence almost unanimously: a single vote was missing among the 98 representatives'.

(4.55) *La coalition de droite qui a remporté les élections législatives de mars dernier peut théoriquement compter sur 156 sénateurs parmi les 326 que compte le Sénat. **Il manque** donc à Silvio Berlusconi **8 voix** pour parvenir à la majorité absolue de 164 sénateurs.* (AFP)
'The right wing coalition that won the legislative elections last March can theoretically count on 156 senators among the 326 in the Senate. Silvio Berlusconi therefore lacks [there lacks to Silvio Berlusconi] 8 votes to reach the absolute majority of 164 senators'.

Second, as was already observed for *rester*, each construction appears in predictable situations. This section shows that the impersonal variant of the predicate not only systematically codes a highly specific kind of situation, but that the individual patterns that instantiate that situation are also remarkably few in number, semantically consistent, and thus very deeply entrenched. The AFP and FRANTEXT corpora on which the analysis is based respectively yield 316 and 481 instances of *manquer* in cases where the impersonal and personal senses are in potential competition. The other senses of the predicate were left out (see note 7).

As the previous section showed for *rester*, the impersonal variant of *manquer* codes the specific way in which a given entity deviates from its optimal value. The example in (4.56) that describes a magazine's comparison of the contestants in a beauty pageant provides a perfect illustration for the impersonal meaning:

(4.56) *La "chirurgie plastique" revient cependant comme un leitmotiv dans la presse et le magazine Chromos, par exemple, qui passe au microscope chaque millimètre d'anatomie des candidates propose sans pitié trois rubriques: "1: Elle a... 2: **Il lui manque**... et 3: sa personnalité...* (AFP)
'"Plastic surgery", however, comes back as a leitmotiv in the press and the Chromos magazine, for example, that inspects each millimeter of the contestants' anatomy under a microscope mercilessly suggest three categories: "1: She has...2: She lacks [there lacks her]... and 3: her personality...'

The list in (4.56) includes the competitors' assets in column 1, as well as the ways in which they deviate from an ideal form of beauty in column 2. This virtual ideal is not specifically mentioned, but it nonetheless constitutes the benchmark relative to which each contestant's chances are evaluated. The presence of the impersonal construction in this example is reminiscent of the situation previously considered with *rester*, and indicative of the overwhelming majority of the *manquer* examples.

The impersonal construction systematically codes situations in which the deficiency of a given entity with respect to its ideal counterpart is quantified or evaluated. The emphasis on the difference between the incomplete entity and its ideal counterpart, even if the latter is not specifically mentioned, represents the construction's most important characteristic. This is the case in both corpora, but here again, due to the nature of journalistic interests; it is particularly clear in the AFP corpus.

Among the ninety-seven instances of impersonal constructions, forty-eight involve a situation where the postverbal entity describes the precisely quantified missing portion that a given entity needs to reach its optional state. This category can be further subdivided. Seven examples illustrated in (4.57) evaluate the number of people required to reach an ideal amount.

(4.57) *Pour sa part, le nouveau technicien du Real, l'Argentin Jorge Valdano, qui entraî-*
nait Tenerife cette saison, a affirmé que Redondo "faisait partie de son projet
initial" et qu'il lui **manquait** *trois autres joueurs afin de compléter l'équipe pour*
le championnat 94–95.   (AFP)
'For his part, Real's new coach, Argentine Jorge Valdano, the Tenerife coach last season, claimed that Redondo "was part of his initial plans" and that he was missing [there lacked to him] three other players to complete the team for the 1994–1995 championship'.

The other forty-one cases illustrated in (4.55) and also further in (4.58)–(4.60) describe the precise amount of time, money, or distance, or the precise number of votes or any other entity to reach an optimal state:

(4.58) *Le total de buts qui était de 1443 à la fin du Mondiale italien en 1990 est passé*
à 1494 après les 51 buts inscrits au terme des 20 premiers matches du Mondial
américain. Il ne **manque** *donc plus que 6 buts pour atteindre le total de 1500*
depuis l'origine de la Coupe du monde (1930).   (AFP)
'The goal total jumped from 1443 at the end of the Italian cup in 1990 to 1494 after the 51 goals scored during the first 20 games of the American cup. We are therefore only short [there only lacks] 6 goals to reach the total of 1500 since the first World Cup (1930)'.

(4.59) *Le journal a dû faire face à trois types de difficultés, a précisé Philippe Tesson*
à l'AFP. "La recapitalisation n'a pas été suffisante, a-t-il précisé. Elle aurait dû
s'élever à 95 millions de FF (17,2 millions de dollars) francs or je n'ai réussi qu'à
obtenir 73 millions de FF (13,2 millions de dollars). Il me **manquait** *donc encore*
22 millions de FF", a expliqué le PDG.   (AFP)
'The paper had to face three kinds of difficulties, Philippe Tesson told AFP. "The raised capital was not sufficient, he said. It should have reached 95 million francs (17.2 million dollars), but I could only raise 73 million francs (13.2 million dollars). I was thus short 22 million francs [there still lacked 22 million francs to me]", the director explained'.

(4.60) *Pour fournir les 75 millilitres d'urine requis pour le contrôle antidopage, le*
        Norvégien Jonas Thern a ingurgité 7,5 litres d'eau (100 fois plus que demandé!)
        *après le match contre la Russie. Mais, même avec une telle quantité, **il manquait***
        encore <u>5 millilitres</u> après deux heures d'attente.   (AFP)
        'To provide the 75 milliliters of urine required for the doping test, Norwegian
        Jonas Thern drank 7.5 liters of water (100 times more than required!) after
        the game against Russia. Despite that quantity, however, he was still short 5
        milliliters [there still lacked 5 milliliters] after two hours'.

In the examples in (4.58)–(4.60) the goal to be attained, and thus the deficit at any
point toward that goal, is quantified with mathematical precision. *Manquer* profiles
the deficit itself, to be further elaborated by the postverbal expression.

    In the second group of forty examples the ideal to be attained takes the form
of a complete entity of eclectic nature. Thirteen of these instances, illustrated in
(4.62) and (4.63), involve the elements missing from an administrative procedure
such as a treaty or legal document:

(4.62) *L'ambassadeur angolais a indiqué que "techniquement les documents étaient*
        prêts" pour que l'UNITA et le gouvernement de Luanda signent en juin les
        *accords de Lusaka et qu'il ne **manquait** plus que <u>la garantie de l'UNITA</u> d'une*
        acceptation des termes de ces accords.   (AFP)
        'The Angolan ambassador indicated that "technically the documents are ready"
        for UNITA and the Luanda government to sign the Lusaka agreements, and
        that the only thing missing was [there only lacked] UNITA's guarantee that
        they would accept their terms'.

(4.63) *Le ministre portugais des Affaires étrangères, M. Jose Manuel Durao Barroso,*
        a indiqué mardi que le paraphe à Lusaka de l'accord de paix angolais par les
        *deux protagonistes de la guerre civile était "un moment important" mais qu'**il***
        ***manquait** encore "<u>la signature définitive</u>" du document.*   (AFP)
        'The Portuguese secretary of Foreign Affairs, Mr. Jose Durao Barroso, indicated
        on Tuesday that the signature in Lusaka of the Angolan peace agreement by
        the two protagonists of the civil war was "an important moment" but that "the
        final signature" of the document was still missing [there still lacked the final
        signature of the document]'.

Even though the individual steps that make up the agreements in (4.62) or the
document in (4.63) official are not specifically itemized in the context, they can
clearly be recovered from existing documents. The use of the impersonal construction makes it clear that the entity that the postverbal expression codes constitutes
the only element missing for a successful procedure.

    The other twenty-seven examples of this category, illustrated in (4.64)–(4.67),
describe an entity that is missing an important part of its internal structure. This

entity can be a concrete object as in (4.64), or a more abstract one as in (4.65)–(4.67), which respectively describe an aspiring top-ten tennis player, a true "great man", and a successful World Cup:

(4.64)   *A la préfecture voisine, dévastée par les pillards, **il manque** comme à la poste, le bâtiment d'à côté, <u>le toit, les portes et les fenêtres</u>.*   (AFP)
'The neighboring administrative building pillaged by looters lost its roof, doors, and windows, just like the post office, the building next door [there lacks just like to the post office the building next door the roof, the door, and the windows]'.

(4.65)   *Tandis que Rios ne pouvait dominer totalement son émotion à ces instants cruciaux, Sampras tenait bon et le N.1 mondial avait finalement le dernier mot. "C'est un très bon joueur à qui **il** ne **manque** que <u>l'expérience</u>. Il m'a donné beaucoup de problèmes", confessait le vainqueur à l'issue d'une rencontre de haut niveau.*   (AFP)
'While Rios couldn't completely control his emotion at the crucial moments, Sampras held on tight and the world number 1 finally had the last word. "He is a very good player who only lacks [to whom there only lacks] experience. He gave me a lot of problems," the world number 1 confessed following a contest played at a high level'.

(4.66)   *Churchill, descendant des ducs de Malborough, a aussi du sang américain: sa mère était la fille du propriétaire du New York Times. Pour lui la "relation spéciale" – qu'il appelait "l'union majestueuse" – n'était pas un vain mot. Roosevelt lui apportera son plein concours dès le début 41, avec la loi dite de "prêt-bail". **Il ne lui aura** <u>rien</u> **manqué**, pas même l'ingratitude sans laquelle la vie d'un grand homme est incomplète.*   (AFP)
'Churchill, a descendant of the Dukes of Marlborough, also has American blood: his mother was the daughter of the *New York Times* owner. For him, the "special" relation – which he called the "majestic union" – was no vain word. Roosevelt helped him greatly as early as the beginning of '41 with the so-called "Lend-Lease Act". He lacked nothing [there to him will have lacked nothing], not even the ingratitude without which the life of a great man is incomplete'.

(4.67)   *Après plus d'une semaine de compétition, le Mondial ne donne toujours pas l'impression de vivre. **Il lui manque** <u>l'ambiance</u>, cette douce folie collective née de la passion de tout un peuple, dans laquelle ont baigné toutes les précédentes éditions, en Italie, en Espagne ou au Mexique.*   (AFP)
'After a whole week of matches, the World Cup still does not seem to be alive. It lacks [there to it lacks] the atmosphere, this sweet collective craziness born from the passion of a people, which permeated all previous editions in Italy, in Spain, or in Mexico'.

Finally, six examples illustrated in (4.68) and (4.69) describe the postverbal entity as the missing piece of a well-known schema that represents familiar social organization. This grouping is perhaps less semantically consistent than the previous ones because the entities it contains are more abstract, but these entities nonetheless also miss only the element coded in the postverbal expression to be structurally complete. In (4.68) the parents represent the missing element of the social structure that would best allow refugees to cope with their predicament. In (4.69) the sole presence of the army in China's streets would complete the parallel between the current situation and what previously occurred at the same location under martial law. [9]

---

9. The three examples in (i)–(iii) are the only ones that do not exactly fit in the groupings presented in this section:

(i) *A 10 h du soir, à l'heure du couvre-feu, commence la ronde de puissantes voitures étrangères le plus souvent sans plaques d'immatriculation, des rafales d'armes automatiques déchirent la nuit. "Il ne **manque** pas de gens riches qui veulent s'amuser, pour eux le couvre-feu n'est pas un problème", explique une serveuse d'un des rares bars de la ville où plusieurs clients arborent ostensiblement des pistolets.* (AFP)
'At 10 o'clock at night, the time of the curfew, the parade of powerful foreign cars more often without registration numbers begins, and shots from automatic rifles erupt in the night. "There is no shortage [there doesn't lack] of rich people who want to have fun, for them, the curfew is not a problem", a waitress at one of the only bars in town where the patrons wear their gun openly explains'.

(ii) *Dans un entretien publié jeudi par le Jerusalem Post, M. Peres a indiqué qu'un canal secret de discussions existait avec la Syrie mais s'est refusé à fournir des détails. "Il est toujours en place, mais sans résultats", a-t-il simplement dit. Interrogé pour savoir si Israël utilisait des tierces parties, tels les ministres européens des Affaires étrangères, M. Peres a répondu: "quiconque se montre prêt à agir, nous l'encourageons". "Il ne **manque** pas de canaux secrets, mais ce qui n'existe pas c'est la disposition syrienne à négocier ... a dit M. Peres.* (AFP)
'In an interview published on Thursday by the *Jerusalem Post*, M. Peres indicated that a secret channel of discussions existed with Syria but he refused to provide further detail. "It is always in place, but without results", he said simply. To the question whether Israel used third parties, such as the European Secretaries of Foreign Affairs, M. Peres answered: "We encourage anyone ready to act". "There is no shortage of [there doesn't lack] secret channels, but what doesn't exist is the Syrian desire to negotiate ... M. Peres said.'

(iii) *Déjà très critiqué par la presse après les trois premiers matches de l'Italie, Roberto Baggio a même été "lâché" par sa mère. La Signora Biaggo a estimé en effet qu'elle avait de la peine à reconnaître son fils en raison de sa discrétion sur le terrain. "Il ne **manquait** plus que cela, maintenant je fais honte même à ma famille", a dit le joueur de la Juventus de Turin.* (AFP)
'Already very criticized in the press following Italy's first three games, Roberto Baggio was even "betrayed" by his mother. Signora Baggio said that she had trouble recognizing her son because he is barely visible on the field. "That tops all [there only lacked that], now even my family is ashamed of me", the Juventus Turin player said'.

(4.68)   *Les bonnes volontés ne manquent pas à N'Dosho, mais les moyens, si. Les scouts*
zaïrois prennent en charge les distributions de repas pour les plus grands. "On
aide depuis quatre jours. On fait aussi l'entretien des tentes, des bâches et des
*toilettes", raconte Clément, 19 ans. "Mais il **manque** les parents. Ici, nous avions*
une structure très familiale", sourit le directeur.   (AFP)
'Goodwill is not lacking in N'Dosho, but financial means are. Scouts from
Zaire are distributing meals for the older children. "We have been helping for
four days", says Clement 19. "But we miss [there lacks] the parents. Family
was very important for us here, the director smiles"'.

(4.69)   *Universités bien gardées, place Tiananmen encerclée par la police, vie nocturne*
réduite, dissidents muselés, télévision censurée: ce n'était certes pas l'état d'urgence
vendredi à Pékin mais cela y ressemblait fort par certains aspects. "Cela n'a jamais
*été comme cela depuis cinq ans. Il ne **manque** plus que l'armée dans la rue et*
ce sera comme en 1989 et 1990 sous la loi martiale", a estimé un diplomate
occidental.   (AFP)
'Universities are under heavy guard, Tiananmen Square is surrounded by the
police, nightlife is reduced, dissidents are silenced, television is censored: The
state of emergency had not been declared on Friday in Beijing, but it almost
looked as if it had. "It hasn't been like this in five years. The only thing missing is [there only lacks] the army in the streets, and it will be like in 1989 and
1990 under martial law", a Western diplomat said'.

Personal constructions involving *manquer* are more frequent than their impersonal counterparts; 219 instances were encountered in the corpus. Their meanings
are also markedly different: of these cases, 134 describe an entity's deficiency in a
specific area. The overwhelming majority of these examples conform to a specific
syntactic pattern in which the subject codes the deficient entity and the postverbal
expression, preceded by the preposition *de*, the area in which it is deficient. This
configuration is illustrated in (4.70)–(4.72):

The first two examples are interesting because they stand out both semantically and structurally.
Semantically there is no readily available complete entity to which the one under evaluation can
be compared, outside of the overall context of the events described. Structurally they are the only
two examples in which the impersonal construction also includes the preposition *de*, in a way
reminiscent of the personal construction described later in this section. These examples may
belong to a separate pattern, but the matter will not be considered further at this point. The third
example involves the idiomatic expression *il ne manquait plus que ça* even though semantically
it conforms to the analysis developed in this section. One can easily imagine that his mother's
disapproval represents the final element that makes Baggio's shame complete.

(4.70)   *Il est impossible de continuer ainsi. Avec Berger, nous avions les mains tétanisées à la fin de la course à cause des difficultés à conduire la voiture. Nos techniciens ne donnent pas leur maximum, **ils manquent de volonté** et peut-être aussi **d'orgueil.***   (AFP)

'It is impossible to go on like this. With Berger, our hands were stiff by the end of the race, because of the difficulties driving the car. Our technicians do not give their best. They lack desire, and maybe also pride'.

(4.71)   *La défense, jadis le point fort de l'équipe avec le tandem Baresi-Costacurta en charnière centrale, n'a pas donné toutes les garanties. Si elle reste une valeur sûre, **elle** a paru parfois **manquer de vitesse d'intervention**, commettant certaines erreurs de placement.*   (AFP)

'The defense, usually the strong point of the team with the duo Baresi-Costacurta in the middle, wasn't entirely reliable. Although it remains an asset, it sometimes seemed to be lacking speed, and made some positioning mistakes'.

(4.72)   *"Les gens sont ici parce qu'ils ont fui des combats, ils ne vont pas aller là où il y en a d'autres", a-t-il ajouté. "On est bien ici, **on manque de nourriture, d'eau et de bois de chauffage**, mais en ce qui concerne la sécurité, ça va", a poursuivi Cyriaque...*   (AFP)

'"People are here because they fled the fighting, they don't want to go where there is more fighting", he added. "We are doing well here, we lack food, water, and firewood, but as far as safety is concerned, we are OK," Cyriaque continued...'

Note that this semantic configuration is quite different from the one expressed by the impersonal construction. The deficiency is not expressed with respect to a complete entity but to its effect on the subject. There is no direct sense of what would make that entity complete, just which areas are cruelly lacking. This distinction between the two constructions is subtle but significant. In order to appreciate it, consider the example in (4.73) where the original from (4.67) has been manipulated to include the personal *manquer de* construction:

(4.73)   #*Après plus d'une semaine de compétition, le Mondial ne donne toujours pas l'impression de vivre. **Il manque d'ambiance**, de cette douce folie collective née de la passion de tout un peuple, dans laquelle ont baigné toutes les précédentes éditions, en Italie, en Espagne ou au Mexique.*

'And yet ... after a whole week of matches, the World Cup still does not seem to be alive. It lacks atmosphere, this sweet collective craziness born from the passion of a people, which permeated all previous editions in Italy, in Spain, or in Mexico'.

The two examples are obviously quite similar but certainly not identical. The presence of the impersonal *il* allows for the explicit comparison between the American World Cup and its ideal form, while the personal variant merely specifies what it is lacking. The personal construction does not include the idea that the atmosphere constitutes the only missing element from the American event.

The second set of examples in the AFP corpus describes situations where an entity coded as subject is diminishing to the point of possibly being extinct. This semantic configuration includes sixty-seven examples illustrated in (4.74) and (4.75):

(4.74)   *Le déplacement est pourtant nécessaire, car, si **la nourriture et l'eau ne manquent pas** pour l'instant, "nous risquons d'épuiser très rapidement nos sources d'approvisionnement en eau à Benaco", a conclu le porte-parole.*   (AFP)
'Moving is necessary however, because if food and water are not lacking yet, "we run the risk of using up our water reserves very rapidly in Benaco, the spokesperson concluded"'

(4.75)   *Déjà, le HCR parle de "catastrophe humanitaire imminente". **Les vivres manquent**. Seuls 25.000 réfugiés ont pu être installés dans des camps.*   (AFP)
'The HCR is already talking about "imminent humanitarian disaster". Supplies are lacking. Only 25.000 refugees could be accommodated in the camps'.

Idiomatic expressions illustrated in (4.76) and (4.77), such as *manquer à l'appel* 'miss at the call', *manquer au tableau* 'missing in the picture', *manquer d'arguments* 'missing assets', or *manquer d'atouts* 'missing qualities' constitute seventeen of these examples:

(4.76)   *Seuls deux des finalistes de 1990 contre l'Argentine **manquent à l'appel**: Augenthaler (36 ans) et Littbarski (34 ans).*   (AFP)
'Only two of the 1990 finalists against Argentina are missing: Augenthaler (36 years old) and Littbarski (34 years old)'.

(4.77)   *Face aux avocats presque aussi célèbres que leur client –Johnnie Cochran défend en même temps Michael Jackson–, qui avancent la thèse du deuxième meurtrier, le procureur, Marcia Clark, et son équipe ne manqueront pas de révéler le détail des tests ADN compromettant, des témoignages troublants. **L'arme du crime manque au tableau** et il n'y a pas eu de témoin visuel.*   (AFP)
'Facing lawyers almost as famous as their client –Johnnie Cochran is defending Michael Jackson at the same time – who are putting forward the theory of a second murderer, prosecutor Marcia Clark, and her team will no doubt reveal details about compromising DNA test results, and suspicious testimonies. The murder weapon is missing and there are no eyewitnesses'.

Finally, in twenty-eight of the sixty-seven examples illustrated in (4.78), the predicate is included in a relative clause, a context that is only attested with the personal construction in the data set:

(4.78) *Le président allemand, élu par un collège de grands électeurs, est quasiment dénué de tout pouvoir. Mais M. von Weizsaecker a justement su tirer profit de cette liberté pour donner à sa fonction un rôle de "conscience morale" et devenir l'un de ces symboles nationaux **qui manquent à son pays**.*   (AFP)
'The German president, elected by an Electoral College, is practically devoid of any kind of power. However, Mr. von Weizsaecker could precisely take advantage of this freedom to give his function the role of "moral consciousness", and become one of these national symbols his country is lacking'.

When these specific uses of the impersonal and personal forms are taken in consideration, the two constructions enter in true semantic competition in only the eighteen cases where the personal construction also describes the discrepancy that exists between an entity and its ideal form. In ten of these cases, illustrated in (4.79) and (4.81), the subject codes a strongly topical entity. In (4.79) *du plutonium* is repeated verbatim from the immediate context. In (4.80) *le mondial* and *le championnat du monde* constitute different lexical versions of the same event. Even though these examples instantiate the semantic part/whole configuration that predominantly favors the impersonal construction, their overall information structure motivates their alternative selection. The immediate context in (4.79) and (4.80) is essentially about the missing plutonium (not some entity missing plutonium to be complete) and the world championships (as opposed to what race the cyclist's career record is missing), two situations that strongly favor a personal variant of *manquer* that codes the strongly topical element as subject.

(4.79) *"Nous n'avons aucune preuve que __du plutonium__ ait été volé et nous savons pourquoi nos comptes ne collent pas", a déclaré Victor Reis, secrétaire à l'Energie adjoint chargé des programmes de Défense. M. Reis a été contraint de faire cette mise au point après que le New York Times eut affirmé vendredi que **du plutonium manquait** au centre de production nucléaire de Hanford (Etat de Washington).*   (AFP)
"'We have no proof that some plutonium was stolen and we know why our records are off", declared Victor Reis, the Vice Secretary of Energy in charge of defense programs. Mr. Reis had to make this statement after the *New York Times* claimed on Friday that some plutonium was missing from the nuclear plant in Hanford (Washington State)'.

(4.80) *J'aimerais bien ne pas changer mon programme où sont inscrits le championnat de Zurich et le Mondial mais la décision appartient à mon directeur sportif. **Le Championnat du monde manque à mon palmarès**. ... Ce serait fantastique de le gagner.*   (AFP)

'I would love to not change my schedule that includes the Zurich championship and the World Championship, but the decision is up to my manager. The World Championships are missing from my record. … It would be fantastic to win them'.

In two other instances the entity that the subject of *manquer* codes is not topical, but its importance to the overall informational content of the passage does not come from its part/whole relation to its ideal or complete counterpart. In (4.81), for instance, the missing gear and backpacks are only relevant as potential clues that could lead to the missing soldiers; their status as a necessary part of a soldier's necessary equipment is only indirectly relevant. This motivates the choice of the personal construction where the gear and backpacks are treated as clues and thus follow another clue in subject position:

(4.81)   *Les deux hommes qui faisaient partie du 2ème RIMA (Régiment d'Infanterie de Marine) ont disparu dans la nuit de jeudi à vendredi, alors qu'ils se trouvaient dans un poste d'observation de l'ONU situé dans une caserne de Serbes bosniaques à Rajlovac, sur la ligne de front, à l'ouest de Sarajevo. Un trou avait été découvert dans l'enceinte de la caserne et **une partie du paquetage des soldats ainsi que leurs sacs à dos manquaient**, selon la même source.*   (AFP)
'The two men who were part of the 2nd RIMA (Regiment of Marine Infantry) disappeared on Thursday night from their UN observation post located in Bosnian Serb barracks in Rajlovac, on the frontline, west of Sarajevo. A hole had been discovered in the fence and some of the soldiers' gear as well as their backpacks were missing, according to the same source'.

The choice between the personal and impersonal construction following *manquer* is therefore very seldom random when language use is considered in its full complexity. In the 219 instances of the personal construction considered in this section, only six can only be imputed to the author's desire to express her conceptualization in this specific manner. One was previously presented in (4.54); another is given in (4.82):

(4.82)   *Mais la maladresse de Timothy Clifford, directeur des National Galleries d'Ecosse, a failli tout faire capoter. Il a avancé en public l'hypothèse que l'offre du milliardaire américain qui vit en Angleterre était due à sa mésentente avec son père, disparu en 1976. Les choses sont rentrées dans l'ordre après des excuses publiques de M. Clifford et John-Paul Getty a maintenu sa proposition. **Ne manquaient plus que 800.000 livres.***   (AFP)
'However, the clumsiness of Timothy Clifford, the Director of Scotland National Galleries, nearly caused everything to collapse. He publicly announced that the offer from the American billionaire who lives in England was due to his disagreement with his father, who died in 1976. Things got smoothed out following M. Clifford's public apology, and John-Paul Getty maintained his proposal. Only 800.000 pounds were missing [were missing only 800.000 pounds]'.

3.3   Recapitulation

This section described the usage patterns of three of the core existential predicates, namely *exister*, *rester*, and *manquer*. *Exister* was shown to describe strict existence, while *rester* and *manquer* profile relative existence in the sense that they evaluate the departure that the entity coded by the postverbal expression exhibits relative to its initial or ideal version. In the three instances, the semantic affinity between the predicates and the impersonal construction explains the formation of semi-assembled chunks that reliably code specific situations. For instance, *il existe* was shown to almost exclusively code the discovery sense of *exister*. In a similar manner, the senses of *rester* and *manquer* where the entity in the postverbal expression is compared to its ideal counterpart are most frequently coded by the predicate's impersonal variant. The specific use of the impersonal variant to describe a part/whole relationship can be explained by the centrality of the unaffected entity to the sentence's overall semantic purpose. If the field represents the mental reach relative to which the postverbal entity can be assessed, the original or unaffected entity necessarily represents a highly salient part of it because it constitutes the benchmark to which the deficient entity needs to be compared. The selection of the impersonal construction that selects the field as its subject therefore provides a privileged way of accessing that original entity, and thus of embedding the postverbal entity within its proper context.

4.   *Il y a*: Existence and location[10]

Il y a poses a strong challenge to the kind of analysis developed in this chapter for several reasons. First, it represents the ultimate "unit of meaning" (Sinclair 1996), and its extremely large range of usage and high frequency require much more space than this chapter can provide. Second, since the expression is intrinsically impersonal the evaluation of the semantic overlap between the predicate and the impersonal construction itself is obviously pointless. Unfortunately, however, these

---

10. *Il y a* 'there is' can be decomposed further into three individual elements, namely impersonal *il*, the locational pronoun *y*, and the predicate *avoir* 'have'. The impersonal form (*il y a un livre sur la table* 'there is a book on the table') is structurally and semantically close to the possessive construction (*j'ai un livre* 'I have a book). Langacker (2009: Chapter 4) points out the two constructions' reference point structure, the most obvious difference between them being the specific nature of the reference point. As this chapter showed, impersonals use the field as the entity relative to which the target is located, while possessives use the possessor to fulfill that role. The internal organization of *il y a* is not considered further in this chapter.

two reasons also make *il y a* impossible to ignore in a chapter devoted to the usage patterns of simple impersonals, especially since the expression constitutes the most frequently attested way of expressing location. Since the questions pertaining to *il y a*'s semantic and syntactic behavior are too numerous to be exhaustively discussed here, this section focuses on two issues of common interest between the expression and the predicates examined in the previous sections. The first is the semantic range that the predicate covers, and how it can be distinguished from possible alternatives (most notably *exister*) in comparable contexts. The second concerns the precise nature of the field that impersonal *il* profiles in different configurations, in other words the mental structures that the field includes in well-delineated environments. Importantly, if the postverbal entity is completely unconstrained (any kind of nominal entity can follow *il y a*), the nature of the field with respect to which that entity is located is much more systematic. A search for the predicate in the post-1950 texts of the FRANTEXT database yielded 3,400 tokens, but because a thorough examination of each example is important for the kind of analysis presented in this section a sample of 500 randomly selected examples provide the data on which the analysis is based.

4.1   Existence

As was mentioned earlier in the chapter, *il y a*, just like *exister*, possesses a discovery sense in which it locates the entity that the postverbal expression codes in reality, as illustrated in (4.83)–(4.88):

(4.83)   *C'était trop ou trop peu. Trop, si l'on demeurait à l'intérieur de la musique tradi-
tionnelle, où le timbre n'est pas un paramètre, ne sert, après tout, qu'à distinguer
les voix de la polyphonie. Il y a <u>suffisamment d'instruments</u> pour cela, et ils ont
l'avantage d'être classiques.*
(Schaeffer, P. *A la recherche d'une musique concrète*: 181)
'It was too much or too little. Too much if one remained inside traditional
music, where tone is not a parameter, merely serves, after all, to distinguish
voices from polyphony. There are enough instruments to do that, and they
offer the advantage to be classical'.

(4.84)   *Jacques de son côté avait ses caprices. Il me décochait des sourires enjôleurs; il
disait: "il y a <u>des êtres irremplaçables</u>" en m'enveloppant d'un regard ému....*
(Beauvoir, S. de. *Mémoires d'une jeune fille rangée*: 231)
'For his part, Jacques was moody. He would cast seductive smiles at me; he
would say "there are people who cannot be replaced" while gazing at me with
emotion...'

(4.85)   *c'est malsain de s'entêter dans le passé; pourtant, on n'est pas très fier de soi*
quand on constate qu'on l'a plus ou moins renié. C'est pour ça qu'ils ont inventé
ce compromis: commémorer; hier du sang, aujourd'hui du vin rouge discrètement
*salé de larmes; **il y a** <u>beaucoup de gens que ça tranquillise</u>. À d'autres, ça doit*
paraître odieux.   (Beauvoir, S. de. *Les mandarins*: 230)
'It is unhealthy to linger in the past; and yet, we are not too proud of ourselves
when we realize we more or less betrayed it. This is why they invented this
compromise: celebrate; yesterday's blood is today's red wine discreetly salted
with tears; there are many people who find this reassuring. Others must find
it repulsive'.

(4.86)   *"Il a beau imaginer un mécanicien qui puisse pulvériser l'univers, il sait que,*
dans la poussière des globes, la vie continuera. L'attentat contre la création est
*impossible. On ne peut tout détruire, **il y a** toujours <u>un reste</u>."*
(Camus, A. *L'homme révolté*: 64)[11]
'"Try as he might to imagine an engineer who could pulverize the universe, he
knows that, in the dust of the spheres, life will go on. The murder of creation is
impossible. You cannot destroy everything. Something always remains [there
is always something that remains]."'

(4.87)   *Dans TOUTE opération mathématique, **il y a** <u>deux choses à distinguer</u>:*
(Weil, S. *La condition ouvrière*: 199)
'In EVERY mathematical operation, two things need [there are two things] to
be distinguished'.

(4.88)   *Tenez, savez-vous pourquoi on l'a crucifié, l'autre, celui auquel vous pensez en ce*
*moment, peut-être? Bon, il y avait des quantités de raisons à cela. **Il y a** toujours*
<u>des raisons</u> au meurtre d'un homme.   (Camus, A. *La chute*: 1530)
'Do you know why he was crucified, the other one, the one about whom you
are thinking about right now perhaps? Well, there were many reasons for it.
There are always reasons to murder someone'.

It is important to note that even though *il existe* and *il y a*, in the sense illustrated in
(4.83)–(4.88), both introduce the postverbal entity as an element of reality, the two
expressions are not interchangeable. While *il y a* can always replace *il existe* with
minimal semantic consequences, the reverse often produces questionable results,

---

11. This example perfectly illustrates the flexibility of construal and the semantic proximity
between *il y a* and the other predicates investigated here because the sentence can easily be
paraphrased as #*Il reste toujours <u>quelque chose</u>* 'there always remains something'. The choice
between these two alternatives depends on what aspect of the conceptualization is ascribed to
the nominal or verbal element.

as in (4.85) where the alternative *#il existe beaucoup de gens que ça tranquillise* seems quite awkward. More generally, the use of *il existe* in each of the examples in (4.83)–(4.88) may feel forced and unnatural to different degrees.[12] This asymmetry in the use of the two expressions can be explained by the combined effect of the construction itself and the predicate in each situation. As suggested in Chapter 3, the semantic import of the construction is to present the location of the postverbal entity in some domain. A predicate such as *exister* specifically names the relevant domain as reality. As a more schematic predicate *avoir* remains neutral, and the relevant domain (reality or a specific location) is pragmatically inferred. One could suggest that *il existe* in (4.83)–(4.88) would feel unnatural because the explicit mention of reality as the relevant location for the postverbal entity would be redundant. Semantically, these examples illustrate two specific patterns of existence where *il y a*'s more general meaning makes it a more appropriate fit. In (4.83)–(4.85), the ontological status of the class of entities considered (musical instruments and human beings) is uncontroversial, but the existence of a more specific subset of them needs to be pointed out. These subsets may result from a particular function the entities serve together (4.83), their intrinsic qualities (4.84), or the shared presence of a physical or mental characteristic (4.85), but in every instance *il y a* points out their existence. The second pattern illustrated in (4.86)–(4.88) groups together situations abstract and common enough to be considered universal truths generally available to anyone, as evidenced by the universal quantifier *toujours* 'always' and *toute* 'every' in the three instances. Here again, the ontological status of the postverbal entity is not up for debate because many instances of the same type need to be examined in order for the general conclusion to be reached, and the examination of multiple instances reinforces the awareness of each one of them. Consequently, one could suggest that in these cases the preference for *il y a* as opposed to *exister* results from the unquestionably uncontroversial status of the postverbal entity, as if it were redundant to explicitly name reality as the domain where a subset of those entities is located when the class they belong to is well established. The impersonal construction provides the mental access necessary to locate the entity, but the predicate does not unnecessarily overstate the relevant domain as reality by explicitly naming it.

---

12. Semantic value judgments are notoriously unreliable, and the felicity of each example can be evaluated differently by different speakers or even by the same speaker at different times.

4.2 Location

In addition to its existential sense, *il y a* also represents the most common and highly grammaticalized way of indicating the presence of an entity at a particular location. This strictly locational sense is illustrated in (4.89)–(4.92):

(4.89) – *C'est ici, dit Praileau en s'arrêtant. Ce mur qu'on aperçoit est le mur du cime-tière. Derrière nous, **il y a** l'étang où les garçons viennent se baigner. Nous serons tranquilles.*   (Green, J. *Moïra: roman*: 28)

   'Here we are, Praileau said stopping. The wall you see here is the cemetery wall. Behind us [there] is the pond where the boys come to swim. We won't be disturbed'.

(4.90) *mais le sommeil ne veut pas venir!* ***Il y a*** cette petite intrigante *qui mijote Dieu sait quoi, contre le repos des familles et des liaisons honorables là-haut, dans sa mansarde tout au bout de l'aile gauche...*

                            (Anouilh, J. *La répétition: ou, l'amour puni*: 108)

   'But sleep wouldn't come! There is this little schemer plotting God knows what, against the tranquility of families and honorable relationships up there, in her room on the other side of the left wing'.

(4.91) *Je suis montée avec elle et pendant qu'elle était dans le cabinet de toilette, j'ai ouvert le sac à fermeture éclair: au fond **il y avait** une petite fiole brunâtre que j'ai enfouie dans ma poche.*   (Beauvoir, S. de. *Les mandarins*: 420)

   'I went up with her, and while she was in the bathroom, I opened the bag with the zipper: at the bottom there was a little brownish bottle I put in my pocket'.

(4.92) Eusébio – ***il y a*** quelqu'un *derrière ce buisson. Qui est-là?*
                            (Camus, A. *La dévotion à la croix*: 574)

   Eusebio – There is someone behind this bush. Who's there?'

As the clearest cases of location, the examples in (4.89)–(4.92) share two important characteristics. First, the located object is concrete. Second, they include the specific mention of a search domain, or more precisely a spatial area within which the entity is contained. This domain is often (but not always) coded by a prepositional phrase (*derrière nous* 'behind us' [4.89], *dans sa mansarde tout au bout de l'aile gauche* 'in her room on the other side of the left wing' [4.90], *au fond* 'at the bottom' [4.91], *der-rière ce Buisson* 'behind this bush' [4.92]). Importantly, as was mentioned at several points of the analysis and will be made more specific at the end of this chapter, this search domain should be kept separate from the field that the impersonal pronoun codes. The location specified by the prepositional phrase is purely physical, while the field is much more abstract and diffuse and profiles the mental scope neces-sary for the conception of the postverbal entity. In cases such as (4.89)–(4.92), the scanning of the area where it can be located certainly figures prominently in the mental effort required to conceptualize the postverbal entity, but it is not exhaustive of it. Among other things, it also at the very least contains the faculty to recognize the object and keep it distinct from other potentially similar ones.

Il y a's existential sense illustrated in (4.83)–(4.88) and its locational sense illustrated in (4.89)–(4.92) represent the two opposite ends that define the predicate's semantic range. However, it is difficult to provide precise linguistic guidelines for reliably identifying these two senses. Numerous cases share important characteristics of both existence and location, and hence provide an argument in favor of the presentational analysis of the construction's meaning. This is illustrated in (4.93):

(4.93)   Kaliayev *je rectifie. Je suis un prisonnier de guerre, non un accusé.* Skouratov *si vous voulez. Cependant, **il y a eu** <u>des dégâts</u>, n'est-ce pas?*
                                                                    (Camus, A. *Les justes*: 366)
         'Kaliayev let me correct you. I am a prisoner of war, not a defendant. Skouratov if you want. However, there was damage wasn't there?

In some respects, the example in (4.93) seems similar to those in (4.89)–(4.92) because it also contains a search domain relative to which the postverbal entity can be located (the incident occurred at a well-known location previously mentioned in the text). However, if the postverbal entity necessarily entails a precise physical location, the predicate is less obviously concerned with this location than with the events that occurred within it (a matter of reality). As a corollary, the entity itself is also more complex because it reifies the mental operations of scanning a scene and comparing the results to an earlier version of the same scene. This comparative evaluation is inherent to the lexical semantics of the noun *dégâts*, and brings to the fore the conceptual manipulations involved in assessing the location/existence of the entity it describes. Importantly for our purposes, the field that the pronoun *il* codes necessarily incorporates the knowledge of the previous situation, as well as the comparative mental efforts required to arrive at the conclusion that the labeling of the current scene as *dégâts* entails. The conceptual interpretation of an observed entity illustrated in (4.93) represents a frequent use of *il y a*, as the examples in (4.94)–(4.97) further attest. Note that in these cases the presence of a search domain does not suffice to produce an unambiguously locational reading.

(4.94)   *Quel approfondissement de la psychologie si l'on pouvait donner la psychologie de chaque muscle!* <u>*Quelle somme d'êtres animaux*</u> ***il y a*** *dans l'être de l'homme!*
                                                           (Bachelard, G. *La poétique de l'espace*: 93)
         'What an advance for psychology if we could explain the psychology of every muscle! What a combination of animals there is in human beings!'

(4.95)   *Ou peut-être est-ce par un sentiment de pudeur qu'on évite de parler de ce qui tient trop au coeur; ou bien **il y a** là une pointe de snobisme, le besoin – comme chez ce personnage de babbit qui disait aimer surtout Rome pour ces délicieux fettucine qu'on peut trouver dans une petite trattoria de la via della scrofa – de se montrer averti et blasé.*

(Sarraute, N. *L'ère du soupçon: essais sur le roman*: 129)

'Or we avoid talking about what really matters to us out of modesty; or it could reveal [there is there] a hint of snobbery, the need – as in the babbit character who said he loved Rome mostly for the delicious fetuccine you can find in a little trattoria on via della scrofa – to appear knowledgeable and blasé'.

(4.96)   *Malgré le détachement bourru qu'il affectait, **il y avait** dans sa voix une interrogation inquiète.*   (Gracq, J. *Le rivage des Syrtes*: 142)

'Despite the gruff aloofness he put on, there was a worried questioning tone in his voice'.

(4.97)   *Les hommes reconnaissaient d'ordinaire à Louis de la séduction intellectuelle, mais il n'avait jamais su plaire aux femmes. **Il y avait** une impatience avare dans le sourire qu'il offrait à Marie-Ange…*   (Beauvoir, S. de. *Les mandarins*: 366)

'Men usually recognized that Louis had intellectual seduction, but he could never make himself attractive to women. There was a miserly impatience in the smile he gave to Marie Ange…'

Despite the presence of the search domain within which the postverbal entity can be located, such as *dans l'être de l'homme* in (4.94), a purely locational reading of the predicate seems difficult to defend because in each case the abstract object the postverbal expression codes results from the speaker's interpretation of reality. One example will suffice. The miserly impatience that the narrator in (4.97) attributes to Louis's smile has no independently attested existence because it only exists through her own conceptual analysis, and other conceptualizers may arrive at different conclusions. Because the purported location of the examined entity cannot be objectively verified, a strictly locational reading is impossible.

Note finally that the concrete or abstract value of an entity is not always clear outside of context, as the example in (4.98) illustrates:

(4.98)   *Jamais on ne l'avait caressé. Jamais on n'avait eu avec lui la patience de la caresse, quand lui-même, toute sa vie, avait été "dévoré du besoin d'aimer". Il est vrai, **il y avait** Thérèse. Elle était là, derrière la porte, qui lavait si consciencieusement les casseroles et les sondes.*   (Guéhenno, J. *Jean-Jacques. T. 2*: 153)

'He had never been cajoled. No one had ever been patient enough to caress him, when he himself had spent his entire life "devoured by the need to love". It is true, there was Therese. She was there, behind the door, cleaning the pots and the probes ever so carefully'.

The situation in (4.98) only superficially resembles the kind of locational described in (4.92). Despite the explicit presence of a search domain expressed by *derrière la porte* 'behind the door', Therese is being assessed with respect to reality as a possible counterexample to Jean-Jacques' position that no one ever loved him, in a way reminiscent of the confirmation sense of *exister*. The scene that follows possesses the appearance of physical location, but each participant (Therese, the door, the instruments) are virtual, specifically conjured up to metaphorically represent Jean-Jacques' emotional space. In that space Therese's physical location and activities signal her emotional irrelevance to Jean Jacques, who fails to recognize love in her zeal and devotion.

4.3   The field

The definition of the field as the mental reach that allows the conceptualization of the entity coded by the postverbal expression may appear problematic because of its highly general character, and the difficulty in predicting with confidence what specific constructs it might include in specific situations. If the field were idiosyncratic to each conceptualized expression its lack of systematicity would not only make it hard for the user to access because of the need to process new structures on line constantly, but also be of limited interest to the analyst. Fortunately, in practice the different configurations that constitute the field exhibit a level of systematicity and conventionalization that make them linguistically usable and analytically relevant. For instance, the previous sections have shown that the lexical semantics of individual predicates often go a long way toward determining the nature of the field. With *rester* and *manquer* in particular, this abstract entity was shown to mostly include the conceptual manipulations that allow the conceptualized entity to be compared to its initial or ideal counterpart.

In a way reminiscent of *exister*, *il y a* provides a stronger challenge because the semantics of *avoir* impose no specific constraints on the postverbal expression, and thus on the mental structures necessary for accessing it. However, this section shows that the kind of field the expression invokes exhibits structure and regularity, and that this regularity comes from the individual patterns that each semantic configuration evokes because each configuration requires different kinds of cognitive structures in order to adequately isolate the postverbal entity. Consequently, just as linguistic expressions conventionally describe specific facets of our experience, the conceptual routines that subtend them are also subject to systematicity and conventionalization, which makes them easier to use and relevant to analyze.

Some configurations are conceptually relatively simple because they primarily involve processing some input and interpreting the results in different domains. In the locational sense illustrated in (4.92) and repeated here, the mental constructs that enable Eusébio to suspect a human presence behind the bush primarily involve the perception of some input (most likely visual or auditory), and the interpretation of that input as indicative of human presence. The specifics obviously vary, but the strictly locational sense of the predicate usually relies strongly on direct sensory perception or memory.

(4.92)   Eusébio – *il y a quelqu'un derrière ce buisson. Qui est-là?*
                                    (Camus, A. *La dévotion à la croix*: 574)
         'Eusebio – There is someone behind this bush. Who's there?'

The input that constitutes the mental reach within which the postverbal expression is assessed also comes from other domains, as in (4.99) and (4.100) where the author calculates the length of time elapsed between different events, and the field therefore primarily includes the temporal stretch revealed in that calculation.

(4.99)   – *Hier, Hélène V. Me raconte l'histoire suivante qui m'a frappé. Il y a quelques*
         années, elle se trouvait en montagne avec un groupe de jeunes gens et faisait avec
         eux l'ascension de je ne sais plus quel pic de La Chartreuse.
                                    (Green, J. *Journal. T. 5. 1946–1950*: 137)
         'Yesterday Helen V. told me the following story that made an impression on
         me. A few years ago [there is a few years], she was in the mountains with a
         group of young people and was climbing some peak in the Chartreuse whose
         name I can't remember'.

(4.100) *Il y a deux mois que la guerre d'Europe s'est terminée par la victoire.*
                                    (Gaulle, C. de. *Mémoires de guerre, le salut*: 584)
         'It has been [there is] two months since the European war ended in victory'.

Similarly, in (4.101) and (4.102) where the postverbal expression describes a section of a written passage, the field primarily includes the perceptual input that comes from the complete entity from which the section is isolated:

(4.101) 8 Février … *Relu une partie de mon malfaiteur avec le grand regret de ne l'avoir*
         jamais publié; il y a dans ce livre un chapitre qui me paraît encore bon.
                                    (Green, J. *Journal. T. 5. 1946–1950*: 23)
         'February 8 … Reread a part of my evil doer with the great regret that I never
         published it; there is a chapter I still find good in this book'.

(4.102) *Le texte est un complexe de sentiments, il associe la politesse et l'espièglerie,*
         l'humilité et l'action. Et puis, il y a le grand mot qui ouvre la page: "j'étais
         magnifiquement seul! "   (Bachelard, G. *La poétique de l'espace*: 76)
         'The text evokes complex feelings. It brings together politeness, mischievous-
         ness, humility and action. And then, there is the great word that opens the
         page: "I was gloriously alone!"'

Other configurations are more complex because they require several types of conceptual manipulations to successfully access the entity in the postverbal expression because the latter results from the analysis and interpretation of a specific scene. In addition to the processing of perceptual stimulus, these manipulations may involve a comparison between two entities as in (4.93), where *des dégâts* implies comparing the observed scene to its earlier state that preceded the traumatic events.

We have already seen that successful access of the target may also require the interpretation of the perceived stimulus as in (4.97), where the mental stretch that subtends *une impatience avare* 'a miserly impatience' contains at the very least the perception of Louis's smile as well as an overall appreciation of his personality, and some expectation of his behavior toward women. Unlike the configuration in (4.93), the author's assessment in (4.97) is purely internal and cannot be independently confirmed.

Finally, the conceptualizer may also have to group together and compare specific types of entities to access her target as in (4.103) and (4.104), where the analysis of their shared properties allows her to identify similar entities within the continuous flow of time and group them together:[13]

---

13. *Il y a* also systematically occurs within the confines of specific syntactic environments. These environments also place consistent requirements on the knowledge structures required to conceptualize the postverbal entity, and hence contribute to the conventionalization of different kinds of fields. For example, in twenty-four examples illustrated in (i) and (ii), the postverbal expression is the demonstrative *ce* 'this' followed by a restrictive relative clause, which creates a nonspecific category composed of the various entities that satisfy the conditions specified by the relative clause:

(i) *Est-ce vraiment autour de ce qu'il y a de moins spirituel en moi que se rassembleront mes*
     ultimes pensées?   (Gide, A. *Ainsi soit-il*: 1223)
     'Is it really around the least spiritual part of me [what there is of less spiritual in me] that
     my ultimate thoughts will gather?'

(ii) *Tout ce qu'il y a de plus riche dans le pays s'entasse sur la plate-forme.*
                                               (T'Serstevens, A. *L'itinéraire espagnol*: 205)
     'The richest people [all that is of most rich] in the area cluster on the platform'.

This second construction is particularly interesting because it places two precise demands on the field. First, a specific quality needs to be isolated, and thus the field has to include the circumstances that allow that discovery to be made. Second, that entity needs to be compared to other possible candidates along the value determined by the adjective that the relative clause contains. Although the content of the field is obviously widely different in the two examples, they nonetheless share a similar investigative strategy. In that sense, the syntactic construction provides a reliable frame within which the mental search leading to the identification of the desired entity can be conducted.

(4.103) *En été, il fait très chaud sur les sables de Maremma.* **Il y a** <u>des journées</u> *où l'air se fait si calme, si lourd qu'il en devient irrespirable.*

(Gracq, J. *Le rivage des Syrtes*: 112)

'In the summer, it is very hot on the sands of Maremma. There are days when the air becomes so still, so heavy, that one can barely breathe'.

(4.104) *Ils allèrent donc au bar d'en face. Assis au comptoir ils devisèrent de choses et d'autres, à bâtons rompus, suivant leur habitude. Ils parlaient, se taisaient, s'écoutaient, ne s'écoutaient plus, chacun à son gré, et suivant son rythme à soi.* **Il y avait** <u>des moments, des minutes entières</u>, *où Camier n'avait pas la force de porter son verre à sa bouche.* (Beckett, S. *Mercier et Camier*: 33)

'So they went to the bar across the street. At the counter, they chatted about some thing or other, as they usually did. They would talk, be quiet, listen to each other, stop listening to each other, as they pleased, each at his own pace. There were moments, whole minutes, when Camier didn't have the strength to raise his glass to his mouth'.

This brief overview does not pretend to exhaust the large number of possibilities, but it suffices to show that the conceptual underpinnings that provide the necessary background for the apprehension of the postverbal entity present some systematicity. This result is completely congruent with the Cognitive Linguistic view of linguistic production. One of the movement's most interesting contributions to the study of the mind was to show that linguistic expressions emerge from the rich and structured soil of "backstage cognition" (Fauconnier and Turner 2002). Language representations group together different conceptualized scenes, and these groupings in turn also share important facets of the conceptual strategies that produce them. There is nothing mysterious in this process. If language can be described as a set of conventionalized units, it stands to reason that the conceptual routines that provide the background for those conventions are also at least partially conventionalized themselves since they are consistently and reliably invoked in predictable circumstances.

5. The periphery: *Arriver, venir, passer*

The peripheral status of the verbs *arriver* 'arrive', *venir* 'come', and *passer* 'pass' in the simple impersonal category is reflected in their lower frequency (see Table 4.1), and also in the constrained nature of the postverbal expression. The latter is either part of a highly specific semantic domain or almost formulaic, with very little flexibility. Because of the scarcity of these predicates in the post-1950 section of the FRANTEXT database, the search was opened to the entire twentieth-century FRANTEXT collection.

5.1   *Arriver*

As was the case earlier for *rester* and *manquer*, speakers may select the impersonal construction to express their conceptualization. In another variant, the theme of the predicate can be found in subject position. These two variants are respectively illustrated in (4.105) and (4.106):

(4.105)   *Bref, il me répéta qu'il ne croyait à la possibilité d'un nouvel attentat qu'à cause de cette extraordinaire coïncidence qu'il avait remarquée et que le juge d'instruction, du reste, lui avait fait remarquer. "S'il arrivait* <u>quelque chose</u> *à Mlle Stangerson, dit-il, ce serait terrible et pour elle et pour moi".*

(Leroux, G. Le mystère de la chambre jaune: 101)

'In short, he repeated that he did not believe in the possibility of another attack only because of this extraordinary coincidence he had noticed and that the judge had also pointed out. "If something happened [arrived] to Ms. Stangerson", he said, "it would be terrible for her and for me"'.

(4.106)   *De nouveau le long appel blanc: trois sifflements se tendent, s'étirent, s'effondrent.* **Quelque chose est arrivé.**   (Sartre, JP. *La mort dans l'âme: roman*: 248)

'Again the long call: three whistles soar, stretch out, collapse. Something happened [arrived]'.

Arriver's analysis is based on a set of 348 impersonal examples. The predicate's impersonal usage is severely constrained in the sense that it is almost exclusively reserved for two semantic categories. The first, which includes 233 instances, describes the natural course of events, or in other words the structure of the evolutionary momentum that constitutes our daily experience (Langacker 1991; Achard 1998; see also Chapter 5). The various subclasses of this large semantic area reflect the different ways in which we segment and interpret time and the events that unfold within it. The first group of thirty-six instances illustrated in (4.107)–(4.109) recognizes that the passage of time is not exclusively linear but also cumulative, and involves special moments when specific events happen. The postverbal nominals typically describe these turning points as a conventionalized loosely construed time unit such as *moment*, *temps*, *âge*, most of which can be translated by English 'time':

(4.107)   *Comme toutes les pensées conduisent à la mort,* **il arriverait** <u>un certain moment</u> *où il ne verrait plus qu'elle avec lui dans son cinéma.*

(Céline, LF. Voyage au bout de la nuit: 404)

'Since all thoughts lead to death, there would come [arrive] a time when it would be the only thing left with him in his movie'.

(4.108) *Il arrivera* <u>un jour</u> *où les poètes seront seuls à comprendre mon œuvre.*
(Barrès, M. *Mes cahiers, T. 10 1913–1914*: 56)
'There will come [arrive] a day when the poets will be the only ones to understand my works'.

(4.109) *En sortant de table, il prit le jeune homme à part et lui dit: – il arrive* <u>un temps</u> *où la mort des autres commence presque à vous faire plaisir…*
(Druon, M. *Les grandes familles*: 157)
'After the meal, he took the young man aside and told him: – There comes [arrives] a time when the death of others almost begins to please us…'

The second subgroup codes the unknown nature of the precise path reality might take, and the way in which humans need to prepare for a wide range of contingencies. Among the thirty-four instances in this subgroup illustrated in (4.110) and (4.111), thirty-three contain the set expression *quoi qu'il arrive* 'whatever happens', the other member being the other idiomatic expression *quoi qu'il en soit* 'whatever the case may be':

(4.110) *Cette histoire n'est pas finie.* Sevrais **quoi qu'il arrive**, *je prends toutes les responsabilités.* (Montherlant, H. de. *La ville dont le prince est un enfant*: 904)
'This issue is not over. *Sevrais* whatever happens [there arrives], I take full responsibility'.

(4.111) *Une question domine tout: les pouvoirs publics sauront-ils,* **quoi qu'il arrive**, *mettre l'état hors d'atteinte, conserver l'indépendance et sauvegarder l'avenir?*
(Gaulle, C. de. *Mémoires de guerre, l'appel*: 39)
'One issue dominates all others: will the administration be able to, whatever happens [whatever there arrives], place the state out of danger, preserve its independence, and salvage its future?'

The third subgroup of 233 tokens describes some conceptualizer's interpretation of the events that compose reality. In 121 instances this interpretation expresses fear about a negative outcome. In some cases, as illustrated in (4.105), the dreaded outcome is coded by its vaguest possible expression *quelque chose* 'something', which receives its negative interpretation pragmatically. The coding can also be more specific, as illustrated in (4.112)–(4.114), where the postverbal expression contains an array of lexical items that describe unfortunate happenings such as *malheur* 'misfortune', *accident* 'accident', *catastrophe* 'catastrophe', or *coup dur* 'hard blow':

(4.112) *Soyez sûrs que je ferai bien attention. Je sais ce que c'est que la situation d'un ouvrier dans une usine. Je ne voudrais pour rien au monde que par ma faute il* **arrive** <u>un coup dur</u> *à l'un de vous.*   (Weil, S. *La condition ouvrière*: 212)
'Rest assured I will be very careful. I know what it's like to be a worker in a factory. I could never accept it that due to a mistake of mine, some misfortune would occur [there arrives a hard blow] to one of you'.

(4.113) *Chez les Dieri, quand **il arrive** <u>un accident</u> à un enfant, ses proches se donnent des coups sur la tête soit avec un bâton soit avec un boomerang, jusqu'à ce que le sang coule sur leur visage.*

> (Durkheim, E. *Les formes élémentaires de la vie religieuse*: 50)
> 'Among the Dieri, when an accident happens [there arrives an accident] to a child, his family hit themselves on the head with a stick or a boomerang, until blood flows on their face'.

(4.114) *Au matin donc le tramway emporte sa foule se faire comprimer dans le métro. On dirait à les voir tous s'enfuir de ce côté-là, qu'**il leur est arrivé** <u>une catastrophe</u> du côté d'Argenteuil, que c'est leur pays qui brûle.*

> (Céline, LF. *Voyage au bout de la nuit*: 298)
> 'So in the morning the tramway brings its crowd of people to the subway to be compressed. One would think, upon seeing them flee in that direction, that some disaster happened to them [there to them arrived a disaster] near Argenteuil, that their country is on fire'.

The conceptualizer can also remain more emotionally neutral with respect to the occurring event. In these sixty-five cases illustrated in (4.115)–(4.117), postverbal expressions such as *aventure* 'adventure', *histoire* 'story', *évènement* 'event', and so on merely serve to reify entire narrative episodes into a single concept:

(4.115) *Et il n'y a que chez elle **qu'il arrive** <u>des histoires comme ça.</u>*

> (Bernard, T. *Monsieur Codomat*: 145)
> 'It is only at her house that things like this happen [there arrives things like this]'.

(4.116) ***Il arrive** <u>une singulière aventure</u> à Ramsay Mac Donald avec la Palestine.*

> (Baniville, J. *L'Angleterre et l'empire.britannique*: 134)
> 'A strange adventure happens [there arrives a strange adventure] to Ramsay McDonald with Palestine'

(4.117) *Dans le monde mythique, bien que les conditions du milieu fussent les mêmes, **il arrivait** <u>toutes sortes d'événements qui ne se produisent plus de nos jours</u>.*

> (Levy-Bruhl, L. *La mythologie primitive*: 3)
> 'In the mythical world, although the environmental conditions were similar, all kinds of events happened [there arrived all kinds of events] that no longer occur'.

When the conceptualizer does not understand the events unfolding before her well enough to evaluate them in any manner, the postverbal expression often contains the noun *chose* 'thing', as illustrated in (4.118) and (4.119):

(4.118) *Il regarda autour de lui en souriant: "depuis que j'habite ici, **il arrive** <u>de drôles de choses</u>*   (Beauvoir, S. de. *Les mandarins*: 326)
> 'He looked around and smiled: "since I have lived here, some strange things have been happening [there arrive strange things]"'.

(4.119) *Par exemple, dans le récit que la femme Orulo fait de sa propre vie, elle raconte l'épisode suivant: "Quelque temps après, **il arriva** une chose étrange. Ma mère avait fait cuire des côtes de morse, et elle était assise, en train de les manger, quand l'os qu'elle tenait à la main se mit à rendre un son".*

        (Levy-Bruhl, L. *Le surnaturel et la nature dans la mentalité primitive*: 36)

    'For example, in the story of her life an Orulo woman tells the following story: "Sometime later, a strange thing happened [there arrived a strange thing]. My mother had cooked walrus chops, and she had sat down to eat them, when the bone she was holding started to emit a sound"'.

In a small group of ten examples illustrated in (4.120) and (4.121), the recapitulative nominal specifically codes the logical relation that exists between different aspects of reality, i.e. other events, expectations, and so on:

(4.120) *Il y a une sagesse des faibles, qui veut que chacun se développe selon les autres, tous imitant et imités. Chacun alors, selon ce qu'il a de vertu, sacrifie sa propre nature au devoir de ressembler à tous, ce qui est d'avance obéir à tous. Or, de cette morale bien parlante, **il arrive** deux conséquences remarquables.*

        (Alain. *Propos sur des philosophes*: 71)

    'There is a wisdom of the weak, which requires everyone to develop according to others, everyone imitating everyone. Every individual then, depending on his level of virtue, sacrifices his own nature to the duty to resemble others, which means to obey everyone. From this very highly representative morality, two remarkable consequences follow [there arrives two remarkable consequences]'.

(4.121) *la Constituante posa devant le monde des principes pacifistes. L'Europe féodale s'arma pour vaincre ces pacifistes, ces internationalistes, ces humanitaires; elle croyait que ce serait chose facile que de venir à bout de gens censément démoralisés, dévirilisés par la philosophie. **Il arriva** tout le contraire: ces Français philosophes préférèrent mourir plutôt que de renoncer à leurs idées…*

        (Aulard, A. *Polémique et histoire*: 78)

    'The constitutive assembly proposed pacifist principles to the world. Feudal Europe took up arms to defeat these pacifists, these internationalists, these humanists; it believed that it would be easy to vanquish these dispirited people, weakened by philosophy. Quite the opposite happened [there arrived just the opposite]: those French philosophers chose to die rather than renounce their ideas…'

Finally, in thirty-seven instances illustrated in (4.122) and (4.123), the postverbal expression is the indefinite pronoun *ceci* or *ce que/ce dont*. In this case, the conceptualizer does not interpret the event but she describes it in its complexity, and the pronoun represents a mental space to be further elaborated in the following context (see Chapter 6):

(4.122)   *De son côté, Michel put penser que Natacha n'aurait d'autre mari que lui. Mais*
           *son affaire n'était point d'épouser une fille pauvre. Et, fatalement, **il arriva** <u>ceci</u>:*
           que Natacha, dans cette infernale intrigue, traitait pour la vie de son père...
                                                                 (Leroux, G. *Rouletabille chez le tsar*: 171)
           'For his part, Michel could think that Natacha would have no other husband
           than him. But it wasn't in his plans to marry a poor girl. And of course, this
           happened [there arrived this]: Natacha, in this devilish intrigue was dealing for
           her father's life...'

(4.123)   *On bâilla sa vie autrement qu'un livre à la main, l'on se passionna pour des jeux*
           *auxquels l'intelligence avait une part moins directe. **Il arriva** <u>ce dont M. Anatole</u>*
           <u>France s'est malignement réjoui dans une page de son histoire contemporaine</u>.
                                                       (Maurras, C. *L'avenir de l'intelligence*: 49)
           'We lived our lives differently than with a book in our hands; we started enjoying
           games where intelligence was less directly involved. What happened is [there
           arrived] what Mr. Anatole France cleverly enjoyed in a page of his contemporary
           history'.

The second semantic class of examples (forty-three instances) illustrated in (4.124)–
(4.130) describes the emergence of an entity onto a scene. The entity can be animate,
as illustrated in (4.124)–(4.126) (twenty-six instances); inanimate, as shown in (4.127)
(thirteen tokens); or it can pertain to the atmospheric conditions that surround the
scene, namely the light, temperature, or wind that infuses it, as (4.128)–(4.130) illustrate (four instances). It is important to note that when the post verbal expression
describes an animate, the situation overwhelmingly pertains to a recapitulation or
a summary of different individual events. This habitual construal is reflected by the
presence of a set of abverbials (*quelquefois, à toute heure, sans cesse*), which underscore
the repetitive nature of the individual arrivals and thus the recapitulative nature of the
construal that the impersonal codes. This type of construal is perfectly congruent with
the analysis given in Chapter 3 because the repeated instances of the process diminish the intrinsic salience of the entity that the postverbal expression codes, and thus
explains the presence of the impersonal construction (see Chapter 3, Section 4.3).

(4.124)   *Quelquefois **il arrivait** <u>des visites</u>, le plus souvent c'était Mme R... avec sa fille,*
           Marie.   (Gautier, J. *Le Collier des jours*: 68)
           'Sometimes visitors came by [there arrived visitors], most often it was Mrs. R
           with her daughter Marie'.

(4.125)   *Des gens s'en revinrent. D'autres, avec des branches de pin allumées en guise de flam-*
           *beau, continuaient de chercher. À tout moment **il arrivait** <u>quelqu'un</u> aux Escures.*
           (Pourrat, H. *Les vaillances, farces et gentillesses de Gaspard des montagnes*: 120)
           'Some people came back. Others, using flaming pine branches as torches, kept
           searching. At any moment someone would arrive [there would arrive someone]
           at Escures'.

(4.126)   *Le marché est important. **Il arrive** sans cesse <u>de nouvelles bêtes</u>.*
                              (T'Serstevens, A. *L'itinéraire espagnol*: 189)
          'The market is large. New animals constantly arrive [there constantly arrives new animals]'.

(4.127)   *Depuis la mort de Nourry **il était arrivé** <u>deux lettres</u> à son nom.*
                              (Dorgelès, R. *Les croix de bois*: 142)
          'Since Nourry had died, two letters in his name had arrived [there had arrived two letters in his name]'.

(4.128)   *Au quai, l'eau poussait dur sur les péniches bien rassemblées contre la crue. De la plaine de Gennevilliers **il arrivait** encore <u>plein de froid</u> par bouffées tendues sur les remous du fleuve à le faire reluire entre les arches.*
                              (Céline, LF. *Voyage au bout de la nuit*: 617)
          'By the pier, the water was pushing hard against the barges clustered together against the raising water. From the plain of Genevilliers, gusts of cold still arrived [there still arrived gusts of cold] hanging tight against the raging water that glistened between the arches'.

(4.129)   *– Ah! Mesdames, j'avais écrit vos commissions sur des petits papiers, pour m'y reconnaître. Sitôt à Lyon, j'ai rangé ces papiers sur le parapet du grand pont, en posant l'argent dessus, quand on me l'avait remis. Ma foi, **il est arrivé** <u>un coup de vent</u>. Tout ce qui n'avait pas été financé est allé dans le Rhône.*
          (Pourrat, H. *Les vaillances, farces et gentillesses de Gaspard des montagnes*: 31)
          'Ah! Ladies, I had written your groceries on little pieces of paper to remember them. As soon as I got to Lyon, I sorted these notes on the parapet of a large bridge, putting the money on top of them when it had been given to me. Well, a gust of wind came [there arrived a gust of wind]. Everything that had not been paid for ended up in the Rhone'.

(4.130)   *Le couloir, qui ne laissait le passage qu'à une personne, était sombre. Pourtant **il arrivait** <u>une petite lumière</u> d'une lucarne ovale qu'on découvrait dans un renfoncement à gauche.*   (Romains, J. *Les hommes de bonne volonté*: 245)
          'The hallway where only one person could walk was dark. However, a pale light was shining [there arrived a small light] from an oval skylight you could see in a recessed corner to the left'.

Here again, the presence of the impersonal construction is not surprising. In order to access her target, the conceptualizer necessarily invokes the whole scene within which it is located.[14]

---

14. Only two examples do not fit the categories described here. They are given in (i) and (ii):
     (i)   *Malheureusement **il arriva** dans ce temps-là <u>des élections législatives</u>.*
                              (Péguy, C. *L'argent*: 1247)
           'Unfortunately, during that time there were [arrived] elections'.

5.2   *Venir*

The lexical semantic structure of *venir* 'come', investigated in 158 instances from the entire twentieth-century text bank of the FRANTEXT database, is very similar to that of *arriver*. Just like with *arriver*, forty-four instances illustrated in (4.131)–(4.133) include a specific temporal section of the evolutionary momentum of reality in the postverbal expression:

(4.131)   *Par exemple, l'habitude de spéculer abstraitement sur des concepts, qui nous vient des Grecs, est un des legs les plus précieux que ce peuple admirable nous ait laissés. Sans lui, nous n'aurions eu ni notre philosophie, ni sans doute nos sciences. Mais **il vient** <u>un moment</u> où la dialectique abstraite, opérant sur des concepts, loin de servir au progrès de la science, lui est au contraire un obstacle:*
(Levy-Bruhl, L. *La morale et la science des moeurs*: 172)
'For example, the habit of speculating abstractly over concepts, which comes to us from the Greeks, is one of the most precious gifts this admirable culture has left us. Without it, we would have had no philosophy, nor certainly science. But there comes a time when abstract dialectics, which operates on concepts, becomes an obstacle to science rather than an asset'.

(4.132)   *Pendant que l'humeur se débat ainsi contre elle-même, **il vient** toujours <u>un temps</u> où, par la maladie et l'âge ensemble, l'être aimé se déforme et se diminue au-delà de ses craintes*   (Alain *Les idées et les âges*: 72)
'While our moods fight against themselves in this manner, there always comes a time when the combination of age and disease deform and diminish the loved one beyond their fears'.

(4.133)   *Certes, ce que vous demandez est difficile, ô mon Dieu, et vos exigences sont bien lourdes. Et il y en a beaucoup qui ne demandent pas mieux que de vous suivre et qui sont tout prêts à vous faire des concessions. Mais enfin c'en est trop: **il vient** <u>une heure</u> où la raison se révolte...*   (Psichari, E. *Le voyage du centurion*: 205)
'Of course what you request is difficult, my God, and your demands are quite heavy. And there are many people who are quite happy to follow you and give a lot to you. But in the end that's too much: there comes a time [an hour] when reason rebels...'

(ii)   *Je vous rappellerai les Mémoires de deux jeunes Mariées de Balzac, où il est évident que chaque lettre se développe en liberté, d'après la fougue naturelle à celle qui écrit. D'où **il arrive** <u>un dépassement continuel</u>.*   (Alain. *Lettres à Sergio Solmi*: 9)
'Let me remind you of Memories of two newlywed brides from Balzac, where it is obvious that each letter develops freely, following the author's natural passion. From there follows [there arrives] a constant increase in passion'.

In a way strongly reminiscent of *arriver*, impersonal *venir* also codes the ways in which the emergence of an outside element modifies the content of a given scene. This outside element can be animate (seventy-one instances) as in (4.134) and (4.135); inanimate (seven tokens) as in (4.136); or a new sensation (noise, wind, or rain, for instance), which the participants at a specific location are beginning to experience (nineteen examples illustrated in [4.137] and [4.138]):

(4.134)   *Augustine dit encore: – Je me suis dépêchée parce que je sais qu'il **vient** beaucoup de bonnes se présenter chez vous...*   (Renard, J. *Journal*: 1190)
'Augustine added: I came quickly because I know that many maids come [there comes many maids] to you looking for a job...'

(4.135)   *Je sème des mies de pain. **Il vient** quelquefois un oiseau...*
(Bousquet, J. *Traduit du silence*: 219)
'I leave bread crumbs. Sometimes, a bird comes [there sometimes comes a bird]'.

(4.136)   *à ce propos, continua-t-elle en dépliant le quotidien, **il est venu** en même temps une lettre pour vous, Thimotée; elle est là, sur la cheminée.*
(Châteaubriant, FR. M. *des Lourdines*: 59)
'talking about that, she continued unfolding the paper, a letter came [there came a letter] for you as well, Timothy; it is here, on the chimney'.

(4.137)   *Ah! dites-donc, pendant que j'y pense, c'est au propriétaire que je m'adresse, cette salle où nous nous tenons toujours est très agréable, mais, là, quand on est près de ce mur, il **vient** une humidité!...*   (Feydeau, G. *Le circuit*)
'Ah, while I am thinking about it, it is to the landlord that I am speaking now, this room where we always are is very nice, but when you stand next to this wall, you can feel [there comes] such humidity!'

(4.138)   *Depuis un moment, il a recommencé à vivre, mais il a gardé les yeux fermés. **Il est venu** un grand bruit doux et une fraîcheur: plusieurs voix d'arbres qui parlaient ensemble.*   (Giono, J. *Regain*: 121)
'He came back to life a while ago, but he kept his eyes shut. There came a great soft noise and a cool breeze: several tree voices speaking together'.

Despite their similarity, *arriver* and *venir* essentially exhibit four major differences. The first pertains to *arriver*'s greater overall frequency and use with complex impersonals, as the next chapter shows. The second difference concerns the lack of highly conventionalized expression with *venir*. Third, while the interpretation of events (in particular the fear of a negative outcome) constitutes a major part of *arriver*'s impersonal profile, one of the only two (negative) instance attested in the *venir* corpus is given in (4.139):

(4.139) *Le premier malheur est passé. Voici **il vient** encore <u>deux malheurs</u> après cela.*
(*Bible, Apocalypse*: 9)
'The first disaster has passed. Two more disasters come [there still comes two disasters] after that'.

Finally, unlike *arriver*, *venir*'s usage includes a group of nine examples, illustrated in (4.140)–(4.142), where the postverbal expression is an abstract entity:[15]

(4.140) *il suffit de penser à cette agitation ridicule qui nous prend lorsque notre pied ne rencontre pas la marche qu'il attendait. Cette espèce de chute étonne le plus résolu; et, par réaction, **il vient** encore <u>une sorte de colère</u>, car il y a offense.*
(Alain. *Les idées et les âges*: 2)
'We only need to think about the ridiculous agitation we experience when our foot does not meet the step it expected. This kind of fall surprises the most resolute among us; and, as a reaction, we also feel [there also comes] some sort of anger, because we feel some offense has been committed'.

(4.141) *Voilà le contremaître. Qu'est-ce qu'il va me dire? "Arrêtez." J'arrête. Qu'est-ce qu'on me veut? Me renvoyer? J'attends un ordre. Au lieu d'un ordre, **il vient** <u>une sèche réprimande</u>...* (Weil, S. *La condition ouvrière*: 249)
'Here is the foreman. What is he going to tell me? "Stop". I stop. What does he want with me? Fire me? I am waiting for an order. Instead of an order, a sharp reprimand comes [there comes a sharp reprimand]...'

(4.142) ***Il venait** fort rarement à un Athénien <u>l'idée de douter des dieux de la cité</u>.*
(Le Bon, G. *Psychologie de l'éducation*: 124)
'Athenian rarely ever doubted [there rarely came to an Athenian the idea of doubting] the Gods of the city'.

5.3   *Passer*

Passer is the least frequent of the predicates considered in detail in this section, with only forty-five instances recorded in the twentieth-century FRANTEXT data. The predicate is predominantly concerned with the translational motion of

---

15. Six examples that do not fit comfortably in the categories are presented in this section. The six postverbal nominals include *ceci* 'this', *ce qui était venu* 'what came', *autre chose* 'something else' (two tokens), *hoquet* 'hickup', and *une mauvaise grippe* 'a bad flu'. These examples do not, however, challenge the analysis presented in this section. *Ceci* and *autre chose* have already been observed with *arriver* and *hoquet*, and *une mauvaise grippe* may be analyzed as a sensation. The last example: *il était venu ce qui était venu* 'whatever came came' (Giono, J. *Un de Baumugnes*: 69) occurs in a passage imitating rural Southern dialects, and may be treated as a regional expression.

animates (twenty-four tokens), inanimate objects (seven instances), or natural elements such as water, or electricity (five examples). These categories are respectively illustrated in (4.143), (4.144), and (4.145):

(4.143)   *Rue des Pyrénées, **il passe** du beau monde.*
                                             (Frapié, L. *La maternelle: roman*: 126)
          'On Pyrenees street, you see a lot of rich people [there passes some rich people]'.

(4.144)   *De temps en temps **il passait** un avion, peu rapidement il me semblait.*
                                  (Beckett, S. *Nouvelles et textes pour rien*: 101)
          'From time to time a plane flew by [there passed a plane], rather slowly it seemed'.

(4.145)   *Le fait brut c'est: je vois le spot se déplacer sur l'échelle, et le fait scientifique c'est:*
          ***il passe** un courant dans le circuit.*   (Poincaré, H. *La valeur de la science*: 223)
          'The observable fact is: I see the spot move on the scale, and the scientific fact is: some current is passing [there passes some current] through the circuit'.

As we have seen for *arriver* and *venir*, five impersonal instances of *passer* also code the emergence of meteorological changes in the scene considered, as illustrated in (4.146) and (4.147):

(4.146)   *Elle murmure: – il y avait du sang sur la porte; on a cru à un malheur et on a couru. … **il passe** sur le silence un grand coup de vent plein de l'odeur des aubé-*
          pines.   (Giono, J. *Regain*: 128)
          'She whispers: There was blood on the door; we thought something terrible had happened and we ran. … A strong gust of wind fragrant with hawthorn breaks the silence [there passes over the silence a strong gust of wind fragrant with hawthorn]'.

(4.147)   *dans la petite rue bien resserrée, **il passait** un zéphyr glacial…*
                                              (Céline, L.F. *Mort à crédit*: 263)
          'In the narrow lane, an icy wind was coming through [there passed an icy wind]'.

Finally, and once again in a way reminiscent of *venir*, four cases illustrated in (4.148) include an abstract entity in their postverbal expression:

(4.148)   ***il passe** parmi les inventeurs des bouffées terribles, des impulsions qu'ils ne*
          connaissent plus…   (Céline, L.F. *Mort à crédit*: 534)
          'Terrible flashes, impulses they no longer recognize, pass among inventors [there passes among inventors terrible flashes, impulses that they no longer recognize…'

The most interesting aspect of the periphery of the simple impersonal construction is the combination of semantic overlap and idiosyncrasy that the three predicates exhibit. On the one hand, their semantic similarity is reflected in their distribution, as they all describe pictures of organized memories in which inanimate or animate entities come onto a scene at varying frequencies, as well as meteorological changes to the environment. On the other hand, each predicate presents its own particularities. *Arriver* and *venir* alone are suitable to evoke a turning point in time (*un moment, un temps, une période*), but *arriver* represents the overwhelming choice to describe the negative turn of events (*quelque chose, un malheur, une catastrophe*, and so on). Furthermore, *arriver* is the only predicate that frequently combines with indefinites to produce strongly idiomatic expressions (*quelque chose, quoiqu'il arrive*). *Arriver*'s idiosyncratic distribution cannot be attributed to its own meaning, since very close equivalents to those idioms are attested with other semantically related predicates (*quoiqu'il advienne* 'whatever happens', *il s'est passé quelque chose* 'something happened', which interestingly occurs with *se passer* and not *passer*). This situation is representative of Sinclair's "idiom principle" presented in Section 2. In order to express their conceptualizations in the semantic domains covered in this section, French speakers have developed a large inventory of semi-preconstructed chunks that offer various degrees of flexibility. Some are completely idiomatic (*quoiqu'il arrive* 'whatever happens', *il s'est passé quelque chose* 'something happened'); some provide some but not total flexibility at the predicate and postverbal slots (*il arrive/vient/*passe un moment/une heure* 'there comes a time/an hour'); and some provide three alternatives (*il est venu/ passé/arrivé beaucoup de gens* 'there came/arrived/passed many people'). Far from being problematic, this semi-idiomatic grammatical organization is the norm in a usage-based model where "idioms and schemas that sanction the use of regular expressions constitute the opposite endpoints of a massive array of symbolic structures at different levels of abstraction" (Achard 2007: 12).

6. Recapitulation: Simple impersonals

Chapters 3 and 4 described simple impersonals where the postverbal expression is a nominal. Even though these two chapters were separated for clarity's sake, they should clearly be considered together for a clearer understanding of the construction. Simple impersonals were shown to be presentational constructions, i.e. structures that identify or locate an entity in some domain. The relevant domain (most frequently existence or location) is either elaborated by the predicate or inferred pragmatically. Within that construction, the pronoun *il* profiles the field, namely the mental constructs that enable the general conceptualizer to locate her target. The field was shown to exhibit some degree of conventionalization, which makes it both linguistically and analytically useful. For one thing, it is partially determined by the semantic structure of the predicate that clearly indicates what mental resources contribute to the successful apprehension of the postverbal entity. With *rester* 'remain' and *manquer* 'lack', for instance, the field necessarily incorporates the conception of the ideal or initial entity, as well as the necessary resources to compare it to its deficient counterpart coded in the postverbal expression. Even when the predicate imposes no such constraints, as in the case of *il y a*, each semantic configuration evoked by the predicate provides the level of mental systematicity required to reliably identify the right target, and hence provide stability to the field.

The semantic range of the construction, i.e. the kinds of predicates that participate in it, is partially determined by the semantic overlap that exists between the construction itself and the individual predicates. More precisely, predicates that critically invoke their setting in their scope of predication provide the best fit in the impersonal construction because the setting figures prominently among the mental resources drawn on to locate the conceptualized target. However, the impersonal construction is heavily unbalanced between the core of the category and its periphery, characterized at the same time by the frequency of the predicates and the degree of semantic constraints on the postverbal expression. In addition to the intrinsic *il y a*, *exister*, *rester*, and *manquer* impose no restrictions on their postverbal expression, but the more peripheral *arriver*, *venir*, and *passer* exhibit much less variation since their impersonal usage is much more restricted to the conventionalized expression of specific domains, often down to almost idiomatic expressions.

However, the semantic overlap between the predicate and the construction is not solely responsible for the distribution of simple impersonals because it would be very hard (and not particularly insightful) to show that core predicates are more compatible with the construction than their peripheral neighbors. In fact, the notions of core and periphery are created by the emergence of lower-level individual patterns at different degrees of generality and abstraction. In this manner the general analysis of the construction presented in Chapter 3 and the predicate-specific investigations of Chapter 4 truly represent two sides of the same coin.

One final issue deserves some brief mention, namely the discrepancy mentioned in the introduction between morphological and functional impersonals. The semantic investigation of the semantics of the morphological category developed in Chapters 3 and 4 allows us to claim with confidence that the overwhelming majority of simple *il* constructions describe generally available situations, and that they are also therefore functionally impersonal. This is true in particular for the core of the category as it was described in Section 2.1. The predicates *exister*, *rester*, *manquer*, and *avoir* (*il y a*) describe the state of a given scene, and their conclusions are available to anyone in a position to observe it. Although the individual elements of each scene may vary in granularity, the scene itself is always presented as generally available.

The issue is slightly more complex at the periphery of the category because the attested predicates are more dynamic, in the sense that they involve the presence of a participant in the scene they describe. Despite this participant, peripheric *il* constructions are also predominantly functionally impersonal because the presence of that participant does little to diminish the focus on the overall quality of the described scene. This focus can be retained in several different ways. First, the participant may be difficult to distinguish from the scene itself because it represents an inherent part of it. It can describe an atmospheric element as in the examples in (4.137) and (4.138), or an indeterminate (negative) interpretation of what happened as in (4.105). All examples in this section are partially repeated for convenience:

(4.137) *quand on est près de ce mur, **il vient** <u>une humidité</u>!...* (Feydeau, G. *Le circuit*)
'when you stand next to this wall, you can feel [there comes] such humidity!'

(4.138) ***Il est venu** <u>un grand bruit doux</u> et une fraîcheur...*   (Giono, J. *Regain*: 121)
'There came a great soft noise and a cool breeze'

(4.105) *S'**il arrivait** <u>quelque chose</u> à Mlle Stangerson, dit-il...*
(Leroux, G. *Le mystère de la chambre jaune*: 101)
'If something happened [arrived] to Ms. Stangerson, he said...'

Even when the participant itself is not so obviously part of the scene as in (4.126) and (4.135), its habitual nature makes it more generally available because it is expected to occur with some regularity, and thus become available to anyone who can observe it (see Chapter 7 for further development). The construction's functional impersonal status can therefore be retained:

(4.126) *Le marché est important. **Il arrive** sans cesse <u>de nouvelles bêtes</u>.*
(T'Serstevens, A. *L'itinéraire espagnol*: 189)
'The market is large. New animals constantly arrive [there constantly arrives new animals]'.

(4.135) *Je sème des mies de pain. **Il vient** quelquefois <u>un oiseau</u>...*
(Bousquet, J. *Traduit du silence*: 219)
'I leave bread crumbs. Sometimes, a bird comes [there sometimes comes a bird]'.

The discrepancy between morphological and functional impersonals arises when the situation described in the construction obviously occurs only once, at a precise moment, and is therefore only available to its immediate witnesses. This is the type of situation described in the introduction (1.36), repeated in (4.149), and also in (4.129):

(4.149) *Tu attendras encore, une heure s'il le faut.* **Il passera** <u>une voiture</u> *qui ralentira*
         et s'arrêtera à la hauteur du ravin pour te laisser monter.
                                                                    (Green, J. *Moïra: roman*: 244)
         'You will wait again, one hour if you have to. A car will come [there will pass
         a car]. It will slow down and stop by the ravine to let you in'.

(4.129) – *Sitôt à Lyon, j'ai rangé ces papiers sur le parapet du grand pont, en posant*
         l'argent dessus, quand on me l'avait remis. Ma foi, **il est arrivé** <u>un coup de vent</u>.
         Tout ce qui n'avait pas été financé est allé dans le Rhône.
         (Pourrat, H. *Les vaillances, farces et gentillesses de Gaspard des montagnes*: 31)
         'As soon as I got to Lyon, I sorted these notes on the parapet of a large bridge,
         putting the money on top of them when it had been given to me. Well, a gust
         of wind came [there arrived a gust of wind]. Everything that had not been
         paid for ended up in the Rhone'.

The constructions illustrated in (4.149) and (4.129) do not meet the level of generality functionally required of impersonal constructions. They do not, however, challenge the analysis developed in this monograph because, as we saw in this chapter,
they constitute a small minority of fringe simple *il* constructions. To the contrary,
their presence is representative of the way in which language users manipulate
grammatical constructions. Once they recognize their functional potential they
commonly extend it to different kinds of scenes, if some of their characteristics
best serve their communicative purpose. Many reasons can be given to explain the
selection of morphological impersonals in such contexts. Some can be relatively
systematic. For instance, one might suggest that *il*'s presence in (4.149) results
from the desire to place *une voiture* 'a car' after the predicate, in a position best
suited to new information. However, in other instances such as the one in (4.129),
the selection of an impersonal construction merely reflects the user's preference.

CHAPTER 5

Complex impersonals

This chapter investigates complex impersonals, namely constructions where the postverbal expression is an infinitival or finite complement. The analysis shows that the presentational analysis proposed for simple impersonals in the two previous chapters naturally extends to these complex constructions once the specificities of the postverbal expression have been recognized. It also shows that the distribution of complement constructions reflects the semantic overlap between the infinitive, subjunctive, and indicative inflections and the individual predicates.

1. Introduction. Complex impersonals: Forms and functions

In Chapters 3 and 4, impersonal constructions were claimed to be presentational in nature, because they introduce the concrete or abstract entity coded in the postverbal expression within a specific domain. This definition is relatively straightforward for simple impersonals because these constructions mainly involve the reference, or mental access, of the entity that the postverbal entity codes. The reference of an entity essentially pertains to its possible identification, and the selection of a definite or indefinite nominal depends on the speaker's evaluation of the cognitive status of the entity she wants to introduce into her interlocutor's mind in the discourse. Interestingly, the simple impersonal construction itself and the predicates that participate in it impose few constraints on the selection of definite or indefinite nominals. Outside highly specific circumstances, such as the overwhelming frequency of indefinites in the discovery sense of *exister* (Chapter 4), more general semantic and pragmatic principles determine the selection of definite or indefinite nominals.

The presentational hypothesis does not readily extend to complex impersonals because the shift from a nominal complement to a clausal one involves some important formal and conceptual changes that need to be carefully examined before complex impersonals can also be argued to be presentational constructions. First, since simple impersonals always include a nominal as their postverbal expression, they consistently profile a concrete or abstract "thing" (Langacker 2008: 23). The situation is not as clear cut with complex impersonals because the post verbal expression may take the form of an infinitival clause, as in (5.1) and (5.3), a finite clause in the indicative as in (5.2), or in the subjunctive as in (5.4). Furthermore, the infinitival forms are preceded by prepositions – *à* and *de* in (5.1) and (5.3) respectively – but their indicative and subjunctive counterparts are always preceded by the complementizer *que* 'that'.[1] Given the eclectic nature of the complements in (5.1)–(5.4), it is difficult to immediately see what each form specifically codes and, in a related manner, what the postverbal expression more generally profiles.

(5.1)   *Même Rai, décevant en début de stage, semble revenu à son meilleur niveau et il ne subsiste que deux légères incertitudes dans l'esprit du sélectionneur: l'arrière gauche Branco est en balance avec Leonardo et **il reste** à attribuer le brassard de capitaine, vraisemblablement entre Ricardo Rocha, Dunga et Jorginho.* (AFP)
'Even Rai, disappointing at the beginning of camp, seems to have returned to form, and only two slight uncertainties remain in the coach's mind: at left back, where Blanco and Leonardo are in competition, and he still needs to designate the captain [there remains to give the captain's armband], most likely between Ricardo Rocha, Dunga and Jorginho'.

(5.2)   *Mais, s'il est vrai que des élections générales constituent la seule voie par où doive, un jour, s'exprimer la souveraineté du peuple, **il reste** que le pays, quoique écrasé et bâillonné, manifeste par mille signes évidents quels sont ses sentiments profonds.*   (Gaulle, C. de. *Mémoires de guerre: l'unité*: 542)
'But, if it is true that general elections constitute the only way in which the people's sovereignty can be expressed, it remains that the country, crushed and silenced as it is, nonetheless demonstrates its true feelings through thousands of obvious signs'.

(5.3)   *– Je sais que Dubreuilh croit à la paix et aux chances d'une Europe", dit Scriassine; il sourit avec indulgence: "**il arrive** même aux grands esprits de se tromper.*
(Beauvoir, S. de. *Les mandarins*: 36)
'I know that Dubreuilh believes in peace and a European destiny, said Scriassine; he smiled indulgently: even great minds [it even happens to great minds to] make mistakes'.

(5.4)   *Mais il est clair que cette entente est encore loin d'être parfaite. Jerrie Hulme, confirme, sans vouloir donner de chiffres, ce que d'autres responsables étrangers admettent avec plus ou moins de réticence: **il arrive** encore que des Musulmans soient expulsés des quartiers à prédominance croate.*   (AFP)
'But it is clear that this agreement is far from being perfect. While refusing to provide figures, Jerrie Hulme confirms what other foreign officials admit more or less reluctantly: Muslims are still [it still happens that Muslims are] expelled from predominantly Croatian neighborhoods'.

---

1.   With some predicates such as *falloir* (*il faut*) 'to be necessary' investigated in Section 4, the postverbal expression is a bare infinitive.

Second, complex impersonals impose tight constraints on their postverbal expression, which yields a very specific distribution between individual predicates and complement forms. This distribution is considered in detail throughout this chapter; at this introductory stage it suffices to note that certain predicates, such as *falloir* (*il faut*) 'be necessary', can only be followed by bare infinitival or subjunctive complements, while others such as *il se peut* 'it is possible' can only be followed by a subjunctive clause. Consequently, while the formal matchup between the predicate and the postverbal expression was of little interest to the investigation of simple impersonals, it figures prominently in the analysis of complex constructions. Perhaps the best way to address these two issues and be more specific about the nature of complex impersonals is to first examine their obvious similarities with their simple counterparts, and then focus on their idiosyncrasies. The predicate *rester* provides an ideal starting point since its simple variant was analyzed in detail in Chapter 4, and its complex impersonal forms were illustrated in (5.1) and (5.2).[2]

Recall from Chapter 4 that *rester*'s simple impersonal variant profiles the discrepancy that exists between the entity that the postverbal expression codes and its initial or ideal form. For instance, in *dans la casserole il restait environ la moitié des pommes de terre* 'in the pan, there remained approximately half of the patatoes', an example presented in (4.19) in the previous chapter, the postverbal expression describes the difference that exists between the conceptualized entity (the observed scene), and the contents of the pan before the meal. The complex cases illustrated in (5.1) and (5.2) both present a very similar situation but their different forms force us to pay individual attention to each example. The communicative purpose of the passage in (5.1) is to describe what the Brazilian coach needs to do to ensure that his team is ready for the World Cup. The function of a coach is make a number of decisions to implement a strategic vision, select individual players, organize the team in a specific way, and so on. Every decision triggers the occurrence of a specific event – a player is selected, the captain is chosen, and so on. The passage in (5.1) assesses what event still needs to occur in order for the Brazilian team to reach the ideal stage where everything is set. The situation in (5.1) therefore only differs from the simple impersonal cases in that the postverbal expression describes an event that is yet to occur. The passage in (5.2) describes the situation in France at the end of World War Two. The adjectives *écrasé* 'crushed' and *bâillonné* 'silenced' clearly indicate the desperation of the time. The postverbal expression represents the note that dissents from the ambient negativity. In this sense, the complex impersonal construction conforms to its previously expressed meaning. The "ideal" state of complete desperation is only prevented by the content

---

2.   A similar analysis could be conducted for *arriver* 'arrive' illustrated in (5.3) and (5.4).

of the indicative clause. Unlike in (5.1), however, the postverbal expression does not describe an event but an established facet of reality or "proposition" (to be explained in Section 2).

This quick examination of the simple and complex variants of the same predicate yields a very simple difference. The function of simple impersonals is to identify things, but that of complex impersonals is to evaluate the likelihood of occurrence of events. This difference has profound conceptual ramifications because clausal grounding essentially pertains to epistemic evaluation. The remainder of this chapter shows that the infinitival, subjunctive, or indicative clauses attested in complex impersonals represent different levels of epistemic assessment of the conceptualized event. More specifically, infinitives profile events while finite complements profile propositions. The distinction between indicative and subjunctive complements pertains to the nature of the grounding of the complement predicate, and essentially corresponds to the definite/indefinite distinction for nominals. Consequently, the nature of the complex expressions' grounding, i.e. the psychological operation by which the conceptualizer makes contact with the entity that they code, crucially distinguishes them from their simple counterparts.

The remainder of this chapter shows that once these distinctions in the nature of the postverbal expression are recognized, complex impersonals conform to the original definition and can thus be described as presentational constructions. The following sections are organized in the following fashion. Section 2 investigates the conceptual correlates of complex complements in detail, with particular focus on the concept of epistemic control. Section 3 introduces the data set used throughout the chapter and presents an overview of the complex impersonal domain. Section 4 analyzes the conceptual import of the infinitival, subjunctive, and indicative complements. Section 5 presents the semantic overlap between these complement forms and the different classes of predicates. Section 6 is devoted to the particular case of impersonal passives that has generated a large amount of controversy in the syntactic literature. Section 7 recapitulates the results and concludes the chapter.

2.   Epistemic evaluation: Reality, events, and propositions

Several factors combine to establish the parallel between simple and complex impersonals. First, the pervasive metaphor IDEAS ARE OBJECTS (Lakoff 1987) provides a way for French speakers to treat any position they subscribe to or believe in as a physical object, and manipulate it as such. The content of any infinitive or finite clause can therefore be introduced, located, assessed, and evaluated in a quasi-physical manner. Second, nominals and finite clauses, the linguistic devices best suited to coding objects and propositions, exhibit similar semantic functions. Langacker (1991: 33) clearly expresses this parallel in the following manner: "The semantic relationship between a simple noun and a full nominal (e.g. between *bear* and *the bear*) is held to be precisely analogous to that between a verb stem and a finite clause (e.g. *taunt* and *Harry taunted the bear*)". More specifically, a nominal and a clause both profile "a *grounded instance* of a thing or process *type*" (Langacker 2008: 264, emphasis in the original).

At the conceptual core of a nominal and a finite clause, the lexical head (noun or verb) names the specific class or type of entities under consideration, while the full nominal or finite clause "directs attention to a particular thing or process accorded a certain epistemic status in relation to the ground", and thus serves a "referential" function (Langacker 2008: 264). The separate component functions of type specification, instantiation, quantification, and grounding are internally layered in similar ways, even though they occur in different domains.[3] In order to be grounded, a lexical type first needs to be instantiated, i.e. considered at a level where the different members of the type can be distinguished from each other. Objects are typically distinguished from each other by the specific locations in space that they inhabit. For instance, since two pencils cannot exist at the same location, space represents the domain where they are distinguished. Space therefore constitutes the domain of instantiation for nouns. By contrast, because two instances of the same process type cannot cohabitate at the same temporal address, processes are primarily distinguished in time. Time therefore represents their domain of instantiation. Finally, grounding "singles out a particular instance as the intended referent" (Langacker 2008: 265), and therefore allows the hearer to direct her attention toward precisely the one entity the speaker has in mind. Determiners provide that function for nominals. For instance, a speaker's use of the phrase *this book* to express her conceptualization narrows down the choice of possible referents to the very instance of the book type she is pointing to. For clauses, grounding predications include the tense, person, and modality markers that relate the clause content to the speech situation.[4]

The respective natures of nominal and clausal grounding reflect our primary cognitive interaction with objects and events. Our everyday life includes a very large number of certain types of objects (books, cars, cups, or plates) that constitute highly stable features of our environment. Objects are stable, and we do not routinely question their existence. Consequently, "the primary epistemic concern

---

3. Quantification will not be discussed in detail. While the concept is self-explanatory for nominals, aspect and voice markers provide this function for finite clauses.

4. For the justification of the French person markers on the verb as grounding expressions, see Achard (1998: 51–52).

is not existence but identification" (Langacker 2008: 296), and "nominal grounding centers on the problem of directing attention to a particular referent from a pool of eligible candidates" (Langacker 2008: 296). By contrast, when we talk about an event what we need to ascertain is "whether it happens, not which one it is" (Langacker 2008: 296). Because "existence, rather than identification is primarily at issue", "clausal grounding is mainly concerned with the status of events with respect to their actual or potential occurrence" (Langacker 2008: 296).

The clausal grounding system reflects our partial knowledge of the things that happen around us. We acquire most of our knowledge indirectly through other people's worldview, our own inferences, anticipation of future events, projection into the past or future, and other similar conceptual manipulations. The only areas to which we enjoy direct access, albeit in a fragmentary fashion, are the immediate present and recent past events that we personally witnessed. However, our insatiable curiosity is unfazed by our cognitive limitations, and we "nevertheless think and talk about the entire sweep of history and the endless reach of the future, knowledge of which ranges from insecure to wholly speculative" (Langacker 2009: 297). The clausal grounding system expresses the discrepancy between what we know and what we feel the need to describe linguistically: "For each situation we describe, there is a need to indicate its epistemic status – where it stands in relation to what we currently know and what we are trying to ascertain" (Langacker 2009: 297). The processes by which we establish the epistemic status of events are numerous, complex, and difficult to articulate in an all-encompassing model. For illustrative purposes it is therefore preferable to concentrate on several independent aspects of our view of reality, without undue emphasis on their possible integration and structural unity.

"We experience the world sequentially, one moment at a time" (Langacker 2008: 300), and the succession of occurrences of these events "either accompanies or constitutes the passage of time" (Langacker 2008: 301). Basically, reality is thus defined by the unidirectional flow of these occurrences through time, and metaphorically represented by a cylinder perpetually growing to incorporate new occurrences, as illustrated in Figure 5.1 (from Langacker 2008: 301).

The model one might call basic reality (elaborated epistemic model in Langacker 1991: 244; see also Achard 1998: 224) in Figure 5.1 emphasizes at the same time the constantly evolving nature of reality and its individual character. The leading face of the cylinder, i.e. current reality, captures the events and situations that are currently occurring or are in progress. Those that the cylinder leaves behind in its constant growth, namely the earlier stages of current reality, compose reality per se, which in this view is best characterized as the "history of what has occurred up through the present moment" (Langacker 2008: 297). Obviously no

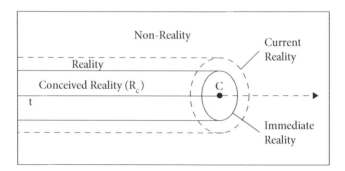

Figure 5.1 A model basic reality (from Langacker 2008: 301)

one can ever hope to know everything that happens in the world, so each of us develops our own personal view of reality (conceived reality in the model), whose internal structure mirrors reality. Immediate reality stands for the aspect of the individual's conception where growth is currently occurring. The dashed lines that surround conceived and immediate reality indicate that C has no access to the events that occur within this area, but that they may figure among other conceptualizers' conceived reality.

However, a more complete version of reality needs to reach much further. Our knowledge and experience is not limited to the past and present but stretches into the future with different degrees of confidence. Consequently, a more elaborated model of reality needs to emphasize its dynamic nature, which allows us to predict different events at various levels of certainty. This epistemic stance is rendered possible by the perpetual forward growth of reality that constrains its "evolutionary momentum" (Langacker 1991: 276) in predictable directions. Evolutionary momentum refers to reality's tendency "to continue its evolution along certain paths in preference to others" (Langacker 2008: 277) once it has reached its current state. This dynamic property connects past, present, and future because it allows all of us to use our experience and knowledge of history to predict future events at different degrees. In the model of elaborated reality (dynamic evolutionary model in Langacker 1991: 277; see also Langacker 2008: 306) illustrated in Figure 5.2, the double dashed arrow represents evolutionary momentum, which carries reality along certain paths to the detriment of others. The possible paths (i.e. the ones that reality is not completely prevented from taking), collectively define the area of potential reality. Within potential reality, certain paths seem particularly likely to be followed given the current orientation of evolutionary momentum. Those paths are so predictable that C would be surprised if they were not followed. Collectively, they define the area of projected reality where things can be predicted with confidence despite their future character.

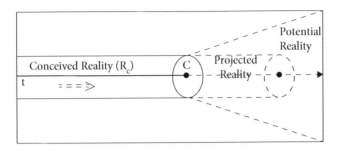

Figure 5.2 A model of elaborated reality (from Langacker 2008: 306)

Even though basic and elaborated reality ultimately represent two facets of the same model (the figures in 5.1 and 5.2 represent two different views of the same integrated conception), they nonetheless illustrate two different ways in which humans interact with the world around them, each one based on a different set of cognitive abilities. Recall that basic reality was described as the "history of what has occurred up through the present moment" (Langacker 2008: 297). At this level of conceptual organization, the elements that compose it are events or situations that a conceptualizer accepts as real. Cognitively, our apprehension of events involves at the very least our ability to construe a process, to view it as immediate or past, real, or imagined (Langacker 2004: 545). Basic reality is thus primarily "effective" (Langacker 2009: 291) because it is concerned with the way in which reality itself evolves. To give just one example, Langacker (2009: 291) notes that "with a root modal (e.g. You must see this movie!), it is aimed at influencing the course of reality itself (R)".

By comparison, elaborated reality involves a higher level of conceptual organization because it is primarily concerned with the epistemic stance that the conceptualizer adopts toward the conceived event. Cognitively, this epistemic stance involves not only the abilities already discussed for basic reality but also the explicit assessment of the location of the event with respect to reality, that is, among others, the set of comparative, evaluative, and inference making abilities involved in assessing it as likely, possible, probable, or certain. The elements of basic reality therefore need to be distinguished from their counterparts in elaborated reality. While basic reality is effective and composed of events, elaborated reality is the level of "epistemic" relations that "hold at the level of *knowledge*, and thus involve *conceptions* of reality" (Langacker 2009: 291, emphasis in the original). For instance, "with an epistemic modal (e.g. 'He might retire early'), it pertains to the evaluation of C's reality conception RC" (Langacker 2009: 291). Elaborated reality is thus composed of "propositions" (Langacker 1991, 2001, 2004: 546). This distinction is of crucial importance for the purposes of this chapter; since propositions are considered with respect to their position in reality they require a putative address in reality, and hence the full grounding that a finite clause in the indicative provides (to be explained in detail in Section 5). By contrast, events are not considered epistemically, that is for the expressed purpose of assessing their position in reality, and hence not fully grounded. Section 5 shows that the French pattern of complex impersonal complements in the infinitive, subjunctive, or indicative mood largely results from the event/proposition distinction.

In addition to its internal structure, another part of our model of reality captures the relation between specific conceptualizers and reality per se. We are, of course, aware that the limitations of human experience and reality's all-encompassing character makes it impossible for anyone to access it in its entirety (see the difference between reality and conceived reality in Figure 5.1). Nonetheless, there is a sense in which reality per se transcends personal knowledge, and remains out of the reach of individual conceptualizers whose knowledge is fragmentary, incomplete, and in constant need of being reevaluated. The very nature of our epistemic quest consists precisely in getting our own view of the world to resemble reality per se as closely as possible. This pursuit may take different forms, from taking classes to extensive reading, but comparing our own view of reality (R_C) to that of other speakers whose experiences differ is equally important to its enrichment.

The ways in which human beings learn, confirm, reject, or envisage new facts are important to consider because they clearly delineate the different facets of our epistemic pursuits. Epistemic evaluation relies on fundamental domains of experience such as the conception of a bounded entity, the perception of continuity, change, and cyclic patterns, as well as the understanding of the kinesthetic notions of tension, force, and release, and so on (Langacker 2008). The control cycle presented in Chapter 2 and repeated here for convenience represents the articulation of these concepts in a highly abstract cognitive model that can be applied to a wide range of situations.

The four phases of the model – initial stasis, tension, force, and release (return to stasis) – have already been presented in Chapter 2, but this chapter is more concerned with their specific adaptation to the epistemic domain, and more specifically to the "acquisition of propositional knowledge" (Langacker 2004: 538). The basic idea partially relies on the IDEAS ARE OBJECTS metaphor (Lakoff and Johnson 1980). In our search for knowledge the different elements that compose elaborated reality, namely propositions, can be acquired, controlled, exchanged, and lost just like physical objects. Each conceptualizer's conception of elaborated reality (R_c) can therefore be considered an "epistemic dominion" (Langacker 2001: 542), in which propositions can be added, confirmed, or eliminated in various ways. The control cycle analogically describes the addition of a proposition to some conceptualizer's dominion.

Just like the perception of a potential prey can arouse a predator out of its state of stasis into tension, action (exercise of force), and release following the strike, the integration of a particular facet of the world into a conceptualizer's epistemic dominion also involves the four phases of initial knowledge (prior to the consideration of the new potential addition); potential (while the candidate for incorporation is being formulated, assessed, and evaluated); action (the actual epistemic decision to accept the newly entertained notion as an established proposition); and result (the conception of reality that includes the result of the manipulative cycle). These different phases of the epistemic control cycle are illustrated in Figure 5.3 (adapted from Langacker 2004:540) in which a French personal verb illustrates each stage of the cycle. The impersonal predicates are considered in detail in Sections 4 and 5.

Once complex postverbal expressions are considered in this manner, their parallel with their simple counterparts is obvious, and the presentational analysis of the French impersonals suggested in the previous chapters can be maintained. As an illustration, let us reconsider the example in (5.2) repeated here:

(5.2)   *Mais, s'**il est vrai** que des élections générales constituent la seule voie par où doive, un jour, s'exprimer la souveraineté du peuple, **il reste** que le pays, quoique écrasé et bâillonné, manifeste par mille signes évidents quels sont ses sentiments profonds.*   (Gaulle, C. de. *Mémoires de Guerre: l'unité*: 542)
'But, if it is true that general elections constitute the only way in which the people's sovereignty can be expressed, it remains that the country, crushed and silenced as it is, nonetheless demonstrates its true feelings through thousands of obvious signs'.

The argument developed in (5.2) about the social, economic, and political situation in France following the end of World War Two is relatively complex. The earlier context brings up the notion that the nation's sovereignty can only be determined by people voting in general elections. The narrator considers that position, and decides to adopt it as true. In other words, he accepts the corresponding proposition *des élections générales constituent la seule voie par où doive, un jour, s'exprimer la souveraineté du peuple* as part of his conception of reality. The selection of the predicate *être vrai* 'be true', as well as the indicative inflection that locates the conceived proposition in (current) reality, reflect his epistemic evaluation. The incorporation of the proposition in the narrator's view of reality therefore provides a metaphorical equivalent to the locational cases following *il y a* introduced in Chapter 4. The acceptance of the proposition as real entails that no behavior outside of general elections should be observed that allows French people to express their sovereignty. However, the second sentence suggests that France has found an alternative way of manifesting its feelings and desires that the narrator also accepts

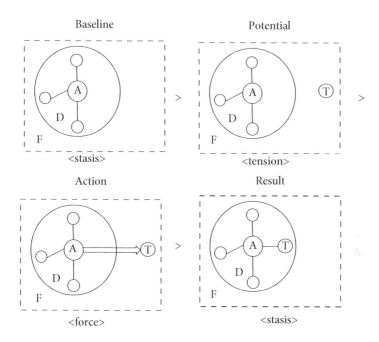

Figure 5.3 The control cycle (from Langacker 2001: 536)

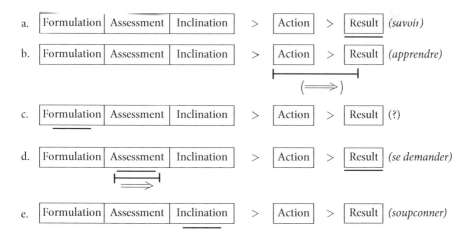

Figure 5.4 Epistemic control cycle [adapted from Langacker (2004: 540)]

as true, as evidenced by his selection of the indicative mood on the complement verb to locate the corresponding proposition in current reality (considered more specifically in Section 4.1). The simultaneous presence of both propositions in the narrator's conception of reality at the same time produces some form of dissonance, which is made specific by the selection of the predicate. The choice of *rester* shows that while it does not provide a strong enough argument to challenge the initial epistemic judgment expressed by *il est vrai*, the recognition of the second proposition as true nonetheless tempers its original strength by leaving something unexplained. In this light, the use of *rester* with a complex postverbal expression precisely parallels the predicate's simple uses. Just like simple *rester* profiles the discrepancy between the conceived entity and its initial or ideal counterpart, the complex variant of the predicate in (5.2) profiles the section of reality that still remains to be explained once the position expressed in the first proposition has been accepted. Importantly, in both cases complex constructions conform to the general analysis of impersonals because the proposition is presented as a general property of reality. The narrator is undeniably responsible for the evaluation of the conceived proposition, but the latter's specific location is depicted as a property of reality itself. Here again, impersonal *il* profiles the field, in this case the circumstances that provide the narrator with the necessary material for his epistemic evaluation.

The notions briefly considered in this section merely serve to introduce complex impersonals and show that they too can be analyzed as presentational constructions. The following sections respectively address the semantic range of the construction and the syntactic nature of the postverbal expression.

3.   The complex impersonal domain

Complex impersonals provide a commentary about the likelihood of occurrence of an event or the epistemic evaluation of a proposition. Impersonal *il* profiles the mental stretch that allows the conceptualizer to state her position, and the predicate specifies the position of the content of the postverbal expression with respect to reality. This represents a wide semantic domain, covered by a large number of predicates that naturally divide into a small number of morphosyntactically and semantically consistent classes. In order to survey the complex impersonal category at a glance, 1,010 predicates were randomly selected from the corpus (511 from FRANTEXT, 499 from AFP) and analyzed. This sample is certainly too small to be considered exhaustive, but it offers the advantage of being amenable to in-depth analysis. This section examines the syntactic and semantic groupings of participating predicates; the following section concentrates on the distribution of clausal complements that follow different predicates.

The first observation that emerges from the investigation of the sample is the overall consistency of the two corpora. The attested predicates are largely identical, and their relative frequencies are also very similar. Some relatively small differences do exist, and they will be introduced at the relevant points of the analysis, but they occur in places where variation is expected and can easily be explained by the range of topics respectively presented in journalistic and literary prose. Overall, the consistency of the predicates inspires confidence that the sample selected is representative of the complex impersonal category despite its small size. The second observation concerns the severe frequency discrepancy among the participating predicates. In both corpora a relatively small number of predicates accounts for a large proportion of the instances, while a very large number of others only provide one or two tokens. Finally, the predicates of both corpora can easily be divided into the same consistent semantic and morphological/syntactic classes. Morphosyntactically, complex impersonals include both single predicates (such as *il semble* 'it seem', or *il faut* 'it is necessary'), and copular predicates that contain a form of the *être* 'be' copula followed by an adjective such as *il est nécessaire* 'it is necessary', or *il est certain* 'it is certain'.[5] This distinction is important for the purposes of this chapter as well as for the analysis of demonstrative impersonals developed in Chapter 6.

Several reasons justify keeping the two classes of predicates separate and analyzing them individually. First, the two kinds of predicates differ widely in their relative frequencies. While single predicates are far less numerous, they include the most frequently attested forms. Conversely, the copular predicate class is so open that it is virtually impossible to provide an exhaustive list. In the corpus the group of single predicates includes twenty-four members for a total of 669 tokens, or 66.23 percent of the total number of examples. Among the twenty-four verbs, *falloir* alone (*il faut*) represents the lion's share of the occurrences with 409, or almost 40.5 percent of the overall instances (45.20 percent in FRANTEXT, 37.5 percent in AFP). Although not quite as frequent as *falloir*, *sembler* nonetheless provides ninety-seven instances or 9.6 percent of the data. These two predicates are part of a group of twelve attested in both corpora, the other ten being *convenir* 'be necessary' (seven), *se pouvoir* 'be possible' (nine), *vaut mieux* 'be preferable' (twenty-two), *s'agir* (*il s'agit*) 'be about' (twenty-six), *apparaître* 'appears' (five), *rester* 'remain' (eighteen), *suffire* 'suffice' (twenty-four), *arriver* 'happen' (twelve), *paraître* 'rumor is/appears' (nineteen), and *empêcher* (*il n'empêche*) 'not prevent' (one). In addition, *ressortir* 'stands out' (one), *incomber* 'behoove' (four), *faire un doute* 'be doubtful' (one), *servir à rien* 'be useless' (one), and *appartenir* 'belong' (one) are attested only in the AFP corpus. Finally,

---

5. Predicates that include passive morphology such as *il a été décidé* 'it was decided' or *il a été prouvé* 'it was proven' were excluded from the sample because impersonal passives are analyzed separately in Section 6.

seven predicates are solely observed in the FRANTEXT corpus, namely *manquer* 'lack' (one), *tarder* 'long' (one), *tenir* (*il tient à vous*) 'it is up to you' (one), *se passer* 'occur' (one), *se faire* 'turn out' (three), *plaîre* (*il me plaît*) 'like' (one), and *suivre* 'follow' (one). By contrast, the 341 instances of copular predicates are divided among a large class of eighty-nine verbs, only eighteen of which are common between the two corpora. Within this class, the relative frequency is much more evenly distributed than among the single class. Although *être possible* 'be possible' is the most frequently attested with forty-one overall occurrences (thirty-two in AFP and nine in FRANTEXT), several other predicates can also be found in a similar frequency range, namely *être probable* 'be probable' (twelve), *être vrai* 'be true' (fifteen), *être nécessaire* (fourteen), *être clair* (eighteen), *être impossible* 'be impossible' (seventeen), *être difficile* 'be difficult' (twenty-two), *être temps* 'be time' (fourteen), and *être question* 'be question' (twenty-five). All the other predicates contribute fewer than five occurrences, with the large majority contributing only one example.

Second, the single and copular predicates behave differently syntactically. Generally speaking (some exceptions are considered in the course of the analysis), single predicates do not allow the postverbal expression to appear in subject position. This is illustrated in (5.5)–(5.10), where the examples in (5.6), (5.8), and (5.10) are created on the basis of the attested forms in (5.5), (5.7), and (5.9) respectively:

(5.5)   *Ma chère, j'ai horreur des romans policiers. … Quand **il m'arrive** d'en ouvrir un, … je m'endors toujours avant la découverte du coupable.*
                                        (Anouilh, J. *La répétition: ou, l'amour puni*: 79)
        'My dear, I hate detective novels. … When I occasionally [when it happens to me to] open one, … I always fall asleep before the culprit is discovered'.

(5.6)   **Quand d'en ouvrir un m'arrive*
        'But when opening one happens to me'

(5.7)   *Positivement: si je ne l'aimais pas tendrement comme je l'aime, cela m'agacerait. Mais **il se trouve** que je l'aime …*
                                        (Anouilh, J. *La répétition: ou, l'amour puni*: 96)
        'In truth: if I didn't love him as much as I do, it would annoy me! But it so happens that I love him …'

(5.8)   **Mais que je l'aime se trouve*
        'but that I love him turns out'

(5.9)   *Oui, j'ai honte. J'ai visé trop haut. **Il faut** que je travaille à ma place. Une toute petite place.*   (Camus, A. *Les justes*: 346)
        'Yes, I am ashamed. I aimed too high. I have to [it is necessary that I] work at keeping my place. A very small place'.

(5.10) **Que je travaille à ma place faut*
        'That I work on keeping my place must'

On the other hand, copular impersonals almost invariably allow the postverbal expression to occur in subject position, as illustrated in (5.11)–(5.16) where the examples in (5.12), (5.14), and (5.16) are obtained by modifying the attested examples in (5.11), (5.13), and (5.15):

(5.11) '"*La Turquie a conservé sa neutralité vis-à-vis des affrontements entre le PDK et l'UPK, mais en cas de coopération d'un de ces mouvements avec l'organisation séparatiste (PKK),* **il ne sera plus possible** *pour elle* de poursuivre cette neutralité", avait averti le porte-parole de la diplomatie turque, M. Ferhat Ataman.* (AFP) '"Turkey preserved its neutrality with respect to the conflict between the PDK and the UPK, but if one of these movements cooperates with the separatist organization (PKK), it will no longer be possible for it to remain neutral", the spokesperson of Turkish diplomacy, Ferhat Ataman, warned'.

(5.12) #Poursuivre cette neutralité **ne sera plus possible** 'To remain neutral will no longer be possible'.

(5.13) 27 *Octobre. – Plaisir de relire.* Salammbô. *Les phrases du début sont d'une résonance merveilleuse.* **Il est amusant** de retrouver de vieilles connaissances. (Green, J. *Journal. T. 5. 1946–1950*:216) 'October 27. Reread Salammbô with pleasure. The sentences at the beginning resonate wonderfully. It is amusing to encounter familiar characters again'.

(5.14) #Retrouver de vieilles connaissances **est amusant** 'To encounter familiar characters again is amusing'

(5.15) *Souvent il a raison, mais* **il me** **semble** *un peu* **facile** d'avoir raison de cette manière, *je veux dire en faisant voir l'inanité des plaisirs du monde.* (Green, J. *Journal. T. 5. 1946–1950*:229) 'He is often right, but it seems to me that it is a little too easy to be right in this manner, I mean by pointing out the silliness of the pleasures of the world'.

(5.16) #*Souvent il a raison, mais* avoir raison de cette manière me **semble** *un peu* **facile** 'He is often right, but to be right in this way seems a little too easy to me'

Finally, while single predicates can generally only be preceded by *il*, copular predicates often occur with a form of the neuter demonstrative *ce, ça, c',* or *cela* as illustrated in (5.17)–(5.20). The example in (5.18) is modified from the one in (5.17). Examples (5.19) and (5.20) are repeated from Chapter 1.[6]

---

6. The single predicates *arriver* 'happen' and *se trouver* 'turns out', as well as the weather verbs illustrated in (i) can also be preceded by *ça* in certain contexts. These cases are considered in Chapter 6 when the distribution of *il* and *ça* impersonals is investigated:

(i) *Oui* **ça** *pleuvait Oui* **ça** *pleuvait Comme à Ostende* (Ferré, L. *Comme à Ostende*) 'Yes it [that] was raining Yes it [that] was raining Like in Ostend'

(5.17)   *Il semble* toutefois *qu'après les événements tragiques d'Imola, le Prince Rainier lui-même pourrait décider que le Grand Prix de Monaco n'ait pas lieu.* (AFP)
'It seems, however, that after the tragic events of Imola, Prince Rainier himself might decide that the Monte Carlo Grand Prix may not be held'.

(5.18)   **Ça semble* toutefois *qu'après les événements tragiques d'Imola, le Prince Rainier lui-même pourrait décider que le Grand Prix de Monaco n'ait pas lieu*
'This seems, however, that after the tragic events of Imola, Prince Rainier himself might decide that the Monte Carlo Grand Prix may not be held'

(5.19)   *Pour la première fois je sentais qu'il était possible que ma mère vécût sans moi*
(Proust, M. *A l'ombre des jeunes filles en fleurs*: 648)
'For the first time I felt it was possible for my mother to live [that my mother live] without me'

(5.20)   *bien sûr que la journée ne se passera pas sans pluie. Ce n'était pas possible que ça reste comme ça,* il faisait trop chaud
(Proust, M. *Du côté de chez Swann*: 101)
'Of course the day will not finish without rain. It [this] was simply not possible that it [this] would stay like this, it was too hot'

Finally, from a semantic point of view, although single and copular predicates overlap in a small number of areas, each class of predicates largely specializes in specific domains. Single predicates essentially describe the simple occurrence of events as well as deontic situations in which the occurrence of the event in the complement is deemed necessary, while copular predicates predominantly describe the epistemic evaluation of the proposition coded in the complement, or a reaction (emotional or evaluative) to the complement content. The remainder of this section provides a brief overview of the semantic classes that constitute the complex impersonal domain, including the small areas of overlap between the single and copular predicates.

The first class strictly contains single predicates that describe the occurrence of an event. It includes the following forms illustrated in (5.21) and (5.22): *sembler* 'seem', *paraître* 'appear', *apparaître* 'appear', *s'agir (il s'agit)* 'it is about', *arriver* 'arrive', *se faire* 'turns out', *se trouver* 'happens', *rester* 'remain', *se passer* 'happen', *suivre* 'follow', *empêcher* 'prevent', *manquer* 'lack', and *ressortir* 'come out'.[7] The complement of this class of predicates is usually in the indicative, as (5.21) and (5.22) show.[8]

---

7.   *S'agir (Il s'agit)* 'this means' presents specific problems that require more detailed investigation. This predicate is analyzed independently in Section 4.

8.   The situation with this class of predicates is simplified. If the predicate is in the negative form or if the sentence is interrogative, the subjunctive can be selected, as (i) illustrates. Furthermore, some verbs such as *rester* 'remain' also occur with an infinitive with a deontic sense. Finally,

(5.21)   *Dans les circonstances présentes, **il apparaît** <u>que la nécessité du haut-commissa-</u>*
          <u>*riat ne s'impose plus*</u>*, en raison de la création du comité national et de la situation*
          actuelle des territoires de l'Afrique française libre.

                        (Gaulle, C. de. *Mémoires de guerre, l'appel*: 670)
          'In the current circumstances, it appears that the necessity for a high command
          is no longer felt, because of the creation of the national committee and the
          current situation of the territories of free French Africa'.

(5.22)   *Les détails de l'accident restaient obscurs, mais **il semble** <u>qu'une voiture était</u>*
          <u>*impliquée*</u> *et au moins une personne a été tuée, selon le capitaine de police Bill*
          Alexander.   (AFP)
          'The details of the accident are not clear, but it seems that a car was involved and
          at least one person was killed, according to the police captain Bill Alexander'.

The second group consists of deontic predicates. It includes the single predicates
falloir (*il faut*) 'must', *convenir* 'be necessary', *suffire* (*il suffit*) 'it suffices', *incomber*
'behoove', *tenir* (*il tient à vous*) 'it is up to you', *appartenir* 'belong', but also a small
number of far less frequent copular predicates such as *être nécessaire* 'be necessary',
être indispensable 'be indispensable', *être crucial* 'be crucial', *être vital* 'be vital', *être*
interdit 'be forbidden'. The single and copular deontic predicates are respectively
illustrated in (5.23) and (5.24), and (5.25) and (5.26). The complement of both
single and complex constructions is in the infinitive as in (5.23) and (5.24), or in
the subjunctive as in (5.25) and (5.26):

(5.23)   *"**Il incombe à la police palestinienne** <u>d'empêcher l'arrivée d'éléments armés aux</u>*
          <u>*points de passage avec Israël"*</u>.   (AFP)
          '"It is up to the Palestinian police to prevent the arrival of armed people to the
          entry points into Israel"'.

(5.24)   *Pour lui, l'élargissement de cette dimension sociale alourdit le "fardeau des entre-*
          *prises" et explique un chômage élevé dans l'Union. **Il convient donc**, estime-t-il*
          <u>*d' "inverser cette situation"*</u>.   (AFP)
          'For him, the increase of social cost imposes a heavy "burden on companies"
          and explains the Union's high unemployment rate. It is thus necessary, he
          argues, to "turn this situation around"'.

---

arriver 'arrive' is usually followed by a subjunctive complement. All these cases are considered
in the course of the analysis.

 (i)   *Comment **se fait**-il <u>qu'un acte déterminé ou explicable après coup soit toujours imprévisible</u>*
        <u>*avant le fait*</u>?   (Jankélévitch,V. *Le je-ne-sais-quoi et le presque-rien*: 201)
        'How is it that a determined act or one that we can explain afterward is always unpredict-
        able beforehand?'

(5.25)   *Pour qu'il y ait art, **il faut** que <u>la forme, de même que le contenu, atteigne une</u>*
         <u>*qualité propre à lui donner un prix aux yeux des autres*</u>.

                                    (Huyghe, R. *Dialogue avec le visible*: 101)
         'In order for something to be called art, its form, as well as its content need to
         reach a quality that makes it valuable in other people's eyes'.

(5.26)   *Le petit volume que j'ai là contient des résumés et des extraits des tragédies les*
         *plus célèbres: Hamlet, Othello, Antoine et Cléopâtre. **Il est indispensable** <u>que tu</u>*
         <u>*les connaisses au moins de cette manière-là*</u>.   (Green, J. *Moïra: roman*: 189)
         'This small volume I am holding contains summaries and excerpts from the
         most famous tragedies Hamlet, Othello, Anthony and Cleopatra. It is impera-
         tive that you know them at least in this manner'.

The third group is composed of epistemic predicates that assess the presence in
reality of the event or proposition that the postverbal expression codes. This class
is predominantly composed of a large number of copular predicates illustrated in
(5.27)–(5.30) that include *être faux* 'be false', *être sûr* 'be sure', *être clair* 'be clear',
être vrai 'be true', *être vraisemblable* 'be likely', *être certain* 'be certain', *être incertain*
'be incertain', *être probable* 'be probable', and so on.[9] The predicates in this class
cannot be followed by infinitival complements. The postverbal expression is either
a clause in the indicative mood as in (5.27) and (5.28), or in the subjunctive as
in (5.29) and (5.30):

---

9. *Se pouvoir* (*il se peut*) 'it is possible' and *faire pas de doute* 'makes no doubt', the only two
single predicates attested in this category, are illustrated in (i) and (ii):

   (i)   *Selon un diplomate occidental, le prolongement du séjour de M. Christopher témoigne des*
         efforts intensifs déployés par les Etats-Unis pour aider les parties syrienne et israélienne
         *à se rapprocher. "**Il ne fait pas de doute** <u>que la Syrie accueille favorablement les efforts</u>*
         <u>*américains*</u> *et espère que la mission du secrétaire d'Etat débouchera sur un progrès réel et*
         constructif", a affirmé pour sa part le commentateur de la radio officielle syrienne. (AFP)
         'According to a Western diplomat, M. Christopher's extended stay reflects intensive ef-
         forts by the United States to help the Syrian and Israeli sides to get closer to each other.
         "It makes no doubt that Syria very favorably welcomes the American efforts, and hopes
         that the State Secretary's mission will lead to real and constructive progress", the com-
         mentator for the official Syrian radio said'.

   (ii) *Si nombreux que soient encore les chrétiens dans le monde, si étroite leur union mystique,*
         ***il ne se peut** <u>qu'à un moment ou l'autre ils n'aient le sentiment d'une terrible solitude</u>...*
                                    (Green, J. *Journal. T. 5. 1946–1950*: 107)
         'As many Christians as there may still be in the world, as tight as their spiritual con-
         nection may be, it is impossible that at some time or other, they do not experience the
         feeling of terrible solitude...'

(5.27)   *Comment pouvait-il se faire qu'un homme tuât la femme qu'il aimait? On ne*
         tuait que ses ennemis. **Il est vrai** <u>que cela se passait dans un livre</u>: *c'était une*
         histoire inventée, un mensonge.   (Green, J. *Moïra: roman*: 195)
         'How could a man kill [it happen that a man killed] the woman he loved? One
         only kills one's enemies. It is true that it happened in a book: the story was a
         fabrication, a lie'.

(5.28)   *Nuançant néanmoins son propos, M. Carlot a tenu à préciser que cela ne signifiait*
         pas pour autant qu'il se rangeait derrière des organisations comme Greenpeace.
         *"***Il est certain*** <u>que le monde libre a besoin du nucléaire</u>, mais Vanuatu ne signera*
         pas le traité de non-prolifération".   (AFP)
         'Adopting a somewhat softer position, M. Carlot clarified that this didn't mean
         he was siding with organizations such as Greenpeace. "It is certain that the free
         world needs nuclear power, but Vanuatu will not sign the non-proliferation
         treaty"'.

(5.29)   *"Même au quart du prix actuel,* **il n'est pas sûr** <u>que les téléviseurs russes fassent</u>
         <u>un tabac à l'étranger</u>*", commente un entrepreneur.*   (AFP)
         'Even at a quarter of their current price, it is not certain that Russian televisions
         will be very popular abroad", one businessman comments.

(5.30)   *– mon enfant, il* **n'est pas certain** <u>que Dieu veuille vous retirer déjà de ce monde</u>.
                                                               (Gide, A. *Robert*: 1339)
         '– my child, it is not certain that God already wants to withdraw you from this
         world'.

Finally, the last class of predicates presents a given conceptualizer's evaluative stance
with respect to the event or proposition described in the postverbal expression. It
contains only three single predicates, namely *plaire* 'please' illustrated in (31), *tarder*
'long', and *sert à rien* 'be useless'.

(5.31)   *Je me sens pris, en lisant ces pages, d'un regain d'amour pour Keats. ...* **Il me**
         plaît <u>que ce jeune homme</u>, *qui était loin d'être une mauviette ...* <u>ait écrit à la</u>
         <u>femme qu'il aimait</u>: *"le monde est trop brutal pour moi–je suis heureux que la*
         tombe existe".   (Green, J. *Journal. T. 5. 1946–1950*: 156)
         'When I read these lines, I feel renewed love for Keats. ... It pleases me that
         this young man, who was far from being a weakling ... wrote to his beloved
         wife: "the world is too rough for me – I am glad the grave exists"'.

In addition, this class contains a very large class of copular predicates illustrated
in (5.32)–(5.35), which includes among others *être possible* 'be possible', *être*
impossible 'be impossible', *être regrettable* 'be regrettable', *être plaisant* 'be pleasant',
être agréable 'be agreable', *être amusant* 'be amusing', *être honteux* 'be shameful',

être décevant 'be disappointing', *être scandaleux* 'be scandalous', and so on. This class of predicates can select infinitival complements as in (5.32) and (5.33), or a subjunctive clause as in (5.34) and (5.35).[10]

(5.32)　*Je dois dire que je viens de trouver Sevrais très compréhensif. Je redoutais un éclat. Comme **il est agréable** de se trouver devant quelqu'un d'intelligent!*
　　　　　　　　　(Montherlant, H. de. *La ville dont le prince est un enfant*: 919)
　　　　'I must say that I found Servais very understanding. I was dreading an outburst. How nice it is [it is nice] to be dealing with an intelligent person!'

(5.33)　**Il est bien plaisant** de voir deux disputeurs de grammaire ou de métaphysique montrer de la colère.　　　　　　　　　　　(Alain. *Propos*: 1230)
　　　　'It is really pleasant to see two people discussing grammar or metaphysics show anger'.

(5.34)　*"Il n'y a pas de changement dans le déploiement des troupes", a dit lundi le porte-parole de la FORPRONU à Sarajevo, le commandant Rob Annink. "**Il est décevant** que les forces serbes de Bosnie n'aient pas réagi conformément à l'accord", a-t-il ajouté.*　　　　　　　　　　　　　(AFP)
　　　　'"There is no change in the deployment of troops", the spokesman for FORPRONU in Sarajevo, Commander Rob Annink, said. "It is disappointing that the Serbian forces in Bosnia did not act according to the agreement", he added'.

(5.35)　*Mme Lévy a indiqué qu'un grand nombre de colons de Naama, au nord de la zone de Jéricho, étaient en route pour le Bureau de coordination du district de Jéricho (DCO), situé à l'entrée de Jéricho. "Cette histoire va faire beaucoup de bruit. **Il est scandaleux** que nous ne puissions pénétrer librement à Jéricho où tout le monde nous connaît et où nous n'avons jamais eu de problèmes", a-t-elle poursuivi.*　　　　　　　　　　　　　　　(AFP)
　　　　'Mrs. Levy indicated that a large number of settlers in Naama, North of the Jericho area were on their way to the Coordination Office for the Jericho district (DCO), situated at the entrance of Jericho. "This affair will make a lot of noise. It is scandalous that we cannot freely enter Jericho where everyone knows us and we have never had any problems", she continued'.

A subclass of the verbs of emotional stance pertains to the evaluation of the degree of difficulty of the event coded by the postverbal expression. This subclass, illustrated in (5.36) and (5.37), is exclusively composed of copular predicates and includes *être facile* 'be easy', *être aisé* 'be easy', *être difficile* 'be difficult', *être bon* 'be good', and *être mauvais* 'be bad':

---

10. The inclusion of *possible* and *impossible* among the evaluative rather than the epistemic class of predicates is based on their complement selection, and is explained in Section 5.3.

(5.36) *Je sentis alors, écrit-il, qu'**il n'est pas** toujours aussi **aisé** qu'on se l'imagine <u>d'être</u>*
        <u>*pauvre et indépendant.*</u>   (Guéhenno, J. Jean-Jacques. T. 2:23)
        'I felt then, he wrote, that it is not always as easy as one imagines, to be poor
        and independent'.

(5.37) *Le sésame est délivré par le quartier général du Deuxième Corps, responsable*
        du secteur nord-est. Tout le monde, femmes et enfants compris, doit en posséder
        *un mais **il est** particulièrement **difficile**, dit-on, à un homme entre 17 et 55 ans*
        <u>*de l'obtenir.*</u>   (AFP)
        'The pass is issued by the general headquarters of the Second Corps, in charge
        of the northeast section. Everyone, including women and children, needs to
        have one but people say that it is particularly difficult for men between the
        ages of 17 and 55 to obtain one'.

A brief glance at the examples in (5.21)–(5.37) reveals the very specific complement distribution in the four complex impersonal semantic classes. The occurrence predicates overwhelmingly only select a finite indicative clause, while the
deontics and emotion reaction predicates select either infinitival or subjunctive
complements. Finally, the epistemics select either indicative or subjunctive forms.
This distribution is recapitulated in Table 5.1 where the number indicates the
number of the example in the previous text, and is analyzed in detail in the next
section.

Table 5.1 Distribution of complements following complex impersonals

Predicates	Infinitives	Indicative	Subjunctive
Occurrence		*il semble qu'une voiture était impliquée* (5.23)	
Deontic	*Il convient donc, estime-t-il d' "inverser cette situation"* (5.24)		*Il est indispensable que tu les connaisses au moins de cette manière-là* (5.26)
Epistemic		*Il est vrai que cela se passait dans un livre* (5.27)	*il n'est pas certain que Dieu veuille vous retirer déjà de ce monde* (5.30)
Evaluative	*il est agréable de se trouver devant quelqu'un d'intelligent!* (5.32)		*Il est scandaleux que nous ne puissions pénétrer librement à Jéricho* (5.35)

4.   Complement forms: Events and proposition

By now the conceptual dynamics of complex impersonals is clear. These constructions assess the position with respect to reality of the event or the proposition
coded in the postverbal entity. This assessment is obviously accomplished by a
specific conceptualizer, the default case being the speaker, but it is not presented
as such. Rather, the complement status is coded as a property of reality itself.
Impersonal *il* profiles the field, and thus represents the starting viewing platform
from which any observer is able to zoom in and evaluate the element under consideration. The main (impersonal) predicate and the tense/modality markers on the
complement verb combine to provide the result of the assessment, and therefore
exhibit a significant amount of semantic overlap. The main predicate specifies "the
status of occurrences with respect to a conception of reality" (Langacker 2009: 309).
For instance, in the positive form *il est certain* 'it is certain' situates the following
proposition in reality, while *il est possible* 'it is possible' indicates doubt that the
event considered actually happened. The grounding elements (markers of person,
tense, mood) perform a rather similar function by providing the entity coded in
the complement with a possible address vis-à-vis reality. The connection between
the main predicate and the grounding predication on the subordinate verb is thus
obvious, and a great deal of semantic overlap is expected between the two. For
instance, in *il est vrai que cela se passait dans un livre* 'it is true that it happened
in a book' in (5.27), *il est vrai* situates the proposition in reality and the imperfect
marker on the subordinate verb more specifically locates it in past reality.

This section explores the relation between the main and subordinate predicates. The hypothesis is that the type of grounding on the subordinate verb reflects the split previously considered between events and propositions. More
specifically, infinitive and subjunctive complements profile elements of basic
reality or events, while their indicative counterparts profile propositions, or in
other words entities that compose elaborated reality. The remainder of this section examines the conceptual import of these three complement structures in
further detail. The next section evaluates their semantic matchup with the different classes of predicates.

Whether one seeks to describe reality or influence it, the task begins with the
selection of a process as the target. At that point, that process merely includes
information relative to a specific type. In *il convient donc … d'inverser cette situation* 'it is thus necessary…to turn this situation around' in (5.24), for instance, the
infinitival form *inverser* names a process type. The mere fact of invoking that type
in the particular context of the narrative situation indicates that a specific instance
is being considered as a possible solution. The infinitive, however, includes no

further information. In particular, it says nothing about potential participants, and it includes no potential address in reality. In fact, the instance of the type that the infinitive represents is virtually created in order to express the author's narrative needs. Infinitival complements therefore constitute the most basic level of event elaboration where everything besides type specification is left unspecified.

When the participants are specified, the event in the complement is described by a subjunctive form, as illustrated in (5.38) where the subject *ceux qui ont cette experience locale* 'those who have this local experience' is followed by the subjunctive form of the copular *être* (*soient*):

(5.38) *L'incendie est d'abord un problème local. Il faut que ceux qui ont cette expérience locale soient consultés dans une concertation qui était jadis quasi naturelle.*
(AFP)
'Wildfires are primarily local problems. It is necessary that those who have this local experience be consulted in a discussion that used to be almost natural'.

The only difference between the event in (5.38) and the one in (5.24) that is coded by an infinitival complement is that the participants are specified as subject; everything else remains the same. The content of the subjunctive clause in (5.38) is not considered vis-à-vis reality, it is also merely conjured up to illustrate the speaker's point. The person marking on the subordinate verb can be considered a grounding predication because it relates the participants to the speech situation, but it does not provide any information about the reality of the event in the complement (Achard 1998: Chapter 6). In this sense, because it profiles a virtual instance of a process type the subjunctive inflection represents the clausal equivalent of the indefinite article for nominal grounding (Achard 1998, 2002; Langacker 2009: Chapter 6).

A finite clause in the indicative represents the clausal equivalent of a definite nominal. The indicative inflection profiles a grounded instance of a process type, complete with a potential address in reality. In (5.27), for instance, *Il est vrai que cela se passait dans un livre* 'It is true that it happened in a book', the third person/ imparfait/indicative inflections combine to present the event in the complement as a valid element of past reality. Because it is presented as part of the narrator's epistemic dominion, which includes "a set of propositions, not just the history of occurrences" (Langacker 2009: 309), it is considered at the level of elaborated reality.

At this point, an important observation needs to be made. If an indicative form is sufficient for providing a proposition with an address in reality, it must follow that all indicative clauses describe propositions accepted as real. This obviously cannot be maintained because the presence of a negative form (*Il n'est pas vrai que cela se passait dans un livre* 'it is not true that it happened in a book') denies the reality of the proposition, but the predicate nonetheless remains in the indicative. While the presence of negation on the main predicate often influences the mood of the subordinate process in French, it does not always do so, and the semantic function of the indicative inflection thus needs to be further investigated. The key point to consider is that the formulation of a proposition, i.e. its conception as a possible candidate for insertion into R_C, is different from its assertion as a valid member of one's epistemic dominion, and that the two operations require two separate conceptual strategies. First, internally, a finite clause profiles a process and specifies its epistemic status relative to some conceptualizer C (its grounding). At this stage the clause does not evoke a specific conceptualizer but conjures up a virtual one for the mere purposes of the formulation. In other words, C is a virtual conceptualizer. The acceptance of the proposition as valid requires the further analytical step of assessing how it fits into the speaker's worldview. Acceptance of the proposition as valid is accomplished by the speaker and main conceptualizer C_0's (a generalized conceptualizer in the case of impersonals) "strong identification" with the virtual ground (Langacker 2004: 549). Through the identification process the virtual ground internal to the proposition and the real one, i.e. the epistemic act of establishing its reality, are essentially merged.

The example in (5.27) provides a clear illustration of the different levels of conceptual organization inherent in complement constructions. The complement clause *cela se passait dans un livre* 'it happened in a book' profiles the process *passait* 'take place' as well as the latter's location in reality, namely past reality, as indicated by the past marking on the verb. Internally, because that clause includes the epistemic stance of some conceptualizer C toward its reality, it thus describes a proposition. However, that conceptualizer C is only virtual, conjured up in order to formulate the proposition for evaluation. At the sentence level the complement clause is embedded in a broader configuration that includes the main predicate *être vrai* 'be true'. With impersonals this broader unit is presented as the conceptualization of a generalized conceptualizer, often representing the speaker's views. The semantics of the main predicate *être vrai* indicate that this generalized conceptualizer endorses the proposition as true by strongly identifying with its own internal virtual ground. The endorsement can be "weak" (Langacker 2004: 549) if the generalized conceptualizer does not fully agree with the proposition-internal virtual assessment. In *Il n'est pas vrai que cela se passait dans un livre* 'It is not true that it happened in a book', the generalized conceptualizer refuses to include the proposition in reality, and therefore merely (weakly) acknowledges the internal virtual grounding of the proposition. French also offers the alternative option of denying the suggested reality of the proposition by merely referring to it as an event whose epistemic location is not even debatable. The use of the subjunctive (*Il n'est pas vrai que cela se soit passé dans un livre* 'It is not true that it happened in a book') reflects that refusal. Similar cases are considered in the following section.[11]

This analysis captures at the same time the large amount of semantic overlap that exists between the main predicates and the grounding expressions, and the basic distinction between the infinitival and subjunctive complements on the one hand and the indicative ones on the other. The next section makes these two characteristics more explicit by further examining the distribution of the three complement forms with the different predicate classes.

5. Predicates, events, and propositions

The preceding section emphasized the role that the main predicate and the grounding expressions on the subordinate predicate play in evaluating the event/proposition in the complement with respect to reality. This section considers each of the four semantic classes of predicates individually to show that complement distribution reflects their natural overlap with the different complement structures.

5.1 Deontic predicates

The deontic predicates constitute perhaps the most straightforward case of the semantic motivation of complement forms because their sole felicity with infinitival and subjunctive complements reflects their incompatibility with a proposition. These

---

11. The situation becomes more complicated with personal verbs in sentential complement constructions (Achard 1998). Consider the example in (i):

(i) *La colère flamba dans ses prunelles. – Je sais à quoi tu penses, fit-il.* **On croit** *que je ne comprends pas.* (Green, J. *Moïra: roman*: 110)
'His eyes lit up in anger. – I know what you are thinking, he said. People think that I don't understand'.

As was mentioned with impersonals, the clause *je ne comprends pas* 'I don't understand' is internally virtually grounded. It is also strongly endorsed by its immediate conceptualizer C_1, namely the main clause subject *on* 'people' (Achard 1998). However, there is another conceptualizer in the sentence, the speaker who acts as the conceptualizer (C_0) of the whole sentence *on croit que je ne comprends pas*. That sentence also describes a more inclusive proposition with its own virtual ground conjured up to formulate it and propose it for inclusion into C_0's conception of reality. The semantics of *croire* also indicate that C_0 believes C_1's conception is mistaken and therefore refuses to consider the proposition as part of reality. His identification with its internal virtual ground is thus weak in the sense that the two entities merge only for the purposes of formulating the proposition.

predicates are not concerned with an epistemic assessment of their complement, but with the changes that need to occur in order for the world to conform to a stated or implicit ideal. This characteristic is shared by all the predicates in the class, but it is only illustrated with *falloir* (*il faut*) in this chapter because the predicate was not described in the previous chapter, and its high frequency deserves specific treatment.

The "effective" emphasis (Langacker 2009:291) of deontic predicates is independent of the nature of the postverbal expression. Consistent with the analysis developed in the previous chapter, simple *il faut* describes the requirements that, if they materialized, would allow the conceived entity to conform to its ideal form. In (5.39), that ideal form is the perfect fruit, and the predicate profiles the various elements required for its successful development. Each underlined nominal describes a component without which the fruit will not reach its mature stage:

(5.39)   *Ce fruit, il y faut le sol et ses sucs, l'arbre qui les drainera pour en faire la sève; il*
         y faut le climat où il se gonfle; mais il y faut surtout un noyau qui le constitue,
         qui ne soit qu'à lui, autour duquel puissent lentement s'accumuler la pulpe, la
         chair, la peau qui consacre cet isolement, cette gravitation autour d'un centre.
                                   (Huyghe, R. *Dialogue avec le visible*: 211)
         'This fruit, it needs [there must be in it] the soil and its juices, the tree that will
         drain them to create sap; it needs [there must be in it] the climate where it ripens;
         but it mostly needs [there must mostly be in it] a stone that gives it its shape,
         which exclusively belongs to it, around that the pulp, the flesh, the skin which
         glorifies this isolation, this gravitation around a center can slowly gather'.

The entity that describes the requirements can be concrete as in (5.40), or abstract as in (5.41):

(5.40)   *Si vous vendiez cette bicoque à courants d'air où il y a plus de place qu'il n'en*
         ***faut** pour cinquante personnes, nous pourrions enfin respirer.*
                                   (Aymé, M. *Clérambard*: 19)
         'If you sold this drafty old house where there is more room than fifty people
         need [it is necessary for fifty people], we could breathe a little better'.

(5.41)   *Il est inadmissible et en dernière analyse impossible qu'une catégorie sociale*
         irresponsable impose ses désirs par la force et que les chefs, seuls responsables,
         *soient contraints de céder. **Il faut** ou un certain partage des responsabilités, ou*
         un rétablissement brutal de la hiérarchie ...
                                   (Weil, S. *La condition ouvrière*: 262)
         'It is inadmissible, and in the final analysis impossible, that an irresponsible
         social class could impose its wishes by strength, and that the leaders, the only
         ones with responsibilities, would have to yield to them. It requires either a
         certain sharing of responsibilities, or the forceful reestablishment of social
         hierarchy ...'

The examples in (5.39), (5.40), and (5.41) show that the notions of ideal entity and necessity cover the widest possible range of domains and situations. In (5.39) the conditions that govern the fruit's successful development are objectively imposed by the laws of physics, but they are much more subjective in (5.40) where the optimal amount of space per person in a house very much depends on personal preference, or in (5.41) where the properties of the ideal state of justice as well as the nature of the requirements to conform to it are solely determined by the author's analytical capacities and her sense of social order. In yet other situations the ideal entity may be completely disconnected from reality, and reside solely in some conceptualizer's desire.

The meaning of *il faut* remains virtually unchanged in the complex impersonal construction, as illustrated in (5.42) and (5.43) where the complement clause respectively takes the form of an infinitive and subjunctive clause:

(5.42)   – *Nous sommes en 1920, Jo. Vos idées sont d'un autre temps.* **Il faut** <u>vous réveiller, sortir de vous-même, écouter ce qui se dit autour de vous.</u>

（Green, J. *Moïra: roman*: 173）

'– We are in 1920, Jo. Your ideas belong to another time. You have [it is necessary] to wake up, get out of yourself, listen to what people around you are saying'.

(5.43)   *"C'est un premier pas. Mais si on ne nous écoute pas,* **il faudra** <u>que quelque chose se passe</u>*", a simplement précisé l'Italien Michele Alboreto à la sortie de la réunion.*   (AFP)

'"It's a first step. But if they don't listen to us, something will have to happen [it is necessary that something happen]", Italian Michele Alboreto simply said, following the meeting.

In a way reminiscent of simple impersonals, the sentence in (5.42) profiles the improvements that the speaker's interlocutor needs to make in his personality in order to conform to the ideal of a twentieth-century man. The three infinitival clauses *vous réveiller* 'wake up', *sortir de vous même* 'get out of yourself', and *écouter ce qui se dit autour de vous* 'listen to what people are saying around you' specify which precise events need to take place in order for the hearer to be in tune with the concerns of his time. The infinitival processes are ungrounded, and thus not evaluated with respect to their location in reality. The author's focus is placed on the necessary occurrence of those events, not on the evaluation of their epistemic position. Despite the inflection on the subordinate predicate, the example in (5.43) functions in essentially the same manner. The passage summarizes the position of a participant who expresses the desire for action following a meeting. The complement clause profiles the change required to avoid open conflict. The subjunctive inflection on the subordinate verb indicates that the process is partially grounded in the sense that the very general participant *quelque chose* 'something' is explicitly mentioned as subject, but it does not profile a proposition because it provides no possible location in reality. As indicated earlier, French subjunctive indicates the virtual quality of the clausal content without any requirement for that content to be located in relation to reality (Achard 1998). While this virtuality does not per se distinguish the subjunctive inflection from its indicative counterpart internally (recall that clause internal grounding is also virtual), it nonetheless makes it impossible for the speaker C_0 to endorse it, since no putative address in reality is provided. The important point here is that regardless of whether the complement clause is in the infinitive or subjunctive, the events that the postverbal expression of deontic verbs profile can only be conceived at the level of basic reality where their mere future existence is at issue. The future and effective (as opposed to epistemic) orientation of *falloir* (*il faut*) in particular, and all deontics more generally, makes those predicates incompatible with a proposition, and therefore motivates their infelicity with the indicative inflection.

5.2   Evaluative predicates

Evaluative predicates are predominantly copular, that is, they are composed of the form [*il* + *être* + ADJECTIVE + (finite or infinitival) COMPLEMENT CLAUSE]. This specific form represents a good starting point into the investigation of its own semantic import. The field within which the subordinate process can be assessed constitutes the focal figure in the profiled relation, and thus coded as subject. The copula provides the predicate with its stable, imperfective value, and the adjective contributes the specific nature of the assessment. The copular construction therefore profiles the evaluation of the subordinate process as possessing a stable quality. That evaluation is obviously performed by a specific conceptualizer, but it is not presented as such. In the construction it is performed by a generalized conceptualizer who may or may not become associated with a particular discourse participant in any given context. This generalized conceptualizer ensures that any individual person in the same situation looking at the same facts would invariably reach the same conclusion.

The evaluative class of predicates exhibits a very consistent complement distribution pattern, with both infinitival and subjunctive complements attested with all participating members. Semantically, the extremely diverse class includes "experiential" (*surprenant* 'surprising', *charmant* 'charming'); "evaluative" (*bon* 'good', *remarquable* 'remarkable'); and "normative" (*étrange* 'strange', *bizarre* 'bizarre') adjectives (Langacker 2009: 321). These are illustrated in (5.44) and (5.45). However, it would be impossible and rather pointless to attempt to provide an exhaustive list or airtight classification because virtually any adjective that can be used to describe the reaction to an event can be used in the construction. This is illustrated in (5.46) and (5.47) where the two adjectives *mesquin* 'petty' and *culoté* 'gutsy' are more commonly used to describe people or people's behaviors. They are extremely infrequent in their impersonal use where they evaluate events (each only occurs once in the two corpora combined), but they are nonetheless perfectly grammatical.

(5.44) *Et sans doute **il est charmant** <u>que Werther s'éprenne de Charlotte</u> au moment où celle- ci beurre gentiment les tartines des enfants …*

(DuBos C. Journal T. 3:199)

'And without a doubt, it is charming that Werther fell in love with Charlotte when she was sweetly spreading butter on the children's bread …'

(5.45) ***Il est remarquable** <u>que l'espèce ait pu se maintenir jusqu' à nos jours</u> dans des conditions aussi défavorables à son développement.*

(Maeterlinck, M. La vie des abeilles: 45)

'It is remarkable that the species survived until today in conditions so adverse to its development'.

(5.46) *Le gouvernement britannique avait annoncé jeudi soir que la volonté des habi- tants d'Ulster sur l'avenir politique de la province s'exprimera par un référendum, dans un communiqué publié après avoir répondu aux questions du Sinn Fein. Londres ne précisait pas la question qui sera posée à ce référendum, ni le moment auquel il se tiendra. "**Il serait mesquin** <u>de ne pas reconnaître que le fait que le gouvernement a répondu à chacune de nos 20 questions est en soi un signe positif</u>…"*

(AFP)

'The British government had announced on Thursday night, in a press release published after answering Sinn Fein's questions, that the will of the Ulster inhabitants concerning the future of the province would be expressed in a referendum. London didn't specify the question that will be asked in this referendum, nor when it will take place. "It would be petty not to recognize that the fact that the government answered each of our twenty questions is by itself a positive sign …"'

(5.47) ***Il serait culoté** de notre part, après notre expérience de 27 ans à Gaza, <u>de reprocher le chaos ou l'échec de l'accord à la police palestinienne</u>, deux ou trois jours après son entrée dans des conditions extrêmement difficiles et sans argent.*   (AFP)

'After our 27 year experience in Gaza, it would be gutsy on our part, to blame the Palestinian police for the chaos and the failure of the agreement, two or three days following its beginning in extremely difficult conditions and without financial resources'.

The presence of the infinitival and subjunctive inflections following the evaluative predicates is not as straightforward as with their deontic counterparts. Evaluatives are certainly not incompatible with a finite clause because the event coded in the complement clause really did occur, and therefore can easily be construed as a proposition. Other languages such as Spanish or English and even Old French select that option, and the equivalent predicates are followed by indicative complements. One could suggest that in contemporary French the presence of the subjunctive indicates the reaction to the event described in the complement, rather than its epistemic value. We react to events without consciously assessing their location in reality; the content of the complement clause acts as a stimulus that prompts the evaluative reaction that the main predicate expresses. In other words, the presence of the subjunctive inflection in French underscores the effective nature of evaluation.

5.3   Epistemic predicates

Epistemic predicates are also overwhelmingly copular constructions. They code the level of confidence that the conceived proposition is real and should therefore be included in reality. Here again, due to their impersonal nature the judgment is presented as that of a generalized conceptualizer who evaluates reality at large as opposed to the specific conception of the person making the epistemic assessment. Copular predicates predominantly profile the "inclination" and "result" stages of the epistemic control cycle (see Figure 5.3). Inclination predicates illustrated in (5.48) and (5.49) include *il est probable* 'it is probable', and *il est vraisemblable* 'it is likely'. These predicates indicate that the conceptualizer is reasonably confident of the reality of the proposition under consideration, and that she is almost ready to consider it an established part of reality.

(5.48)   *Après trois semaines d'Athènes, on se dit: **Il est probable** que je suis devant la perfection, mais tout de même, je suis bien à l'aise.*
                                        (Barrès, M. *Le voyage de Sparte*: 49)
          'After three weeks in Athens, one says to oneself: It is likely that I am in front of perfection, but nonetheless, I feel quite comfortable'.

(5.49)   *Concernant Maradona, **il est vraisemblable** que le match disputé contre le Nigeria, aura été le dernier d'une carrière controversée au cours de laquelle il a connu de nombreux démêlés avec la drogue.*   (AFP)
          'Concerning Maradona, it is likely that the game against Nigeria was the last one of a controversial career during which he had a lot of problems with substance abuse'.

Result predicates include *il est sûr* 'it is sure', *il est vrai* 'it is true', *il est certain* 'it is certain', *il est clair* 'it is clear', *il est indéniable* 'it is undeniable', and so on. They are illustrated in (5.50)–(5.52):

(5.50) *D'après des rapports indiscutables, les allemands ont perdu déjà, dans cette lutte incessante, depuis le début de juin, au moins 8000 morts, plus de 2000 prison-niers et une quantité très grande de matériel. **Il est certain** que les effectifs que les allemands sont contraints d'employer à lutter contre nos troupes sur le sol métropolitain atteint la valeur de 7 ou 8 divisions au moins.*
(Gaulle, C. de. *Mémoires de Guerre: l'unité*: 582)
'According to reliable reports, since June, the Germans have already lost in this continuous fight 8,000 dead, more than 2,000 prisoners, and an important quantity of equipment. It is certain that the amount of personnel the Germans have to use to fight our troops on the French soil has reached the level of at least 7 or 8 divisions'.

(5.51) *À voir cela, il me semble que la révolte est plus loin de nous que je ne croyais d'abord. **Il est vrai** que je suis avec des montagnards, écartés des centres industriels et très fatalistes.* (Alain-Fournier, H. *Correspondance avec J. Rivière*: XX)
'When I see this, it seems to me that the rebellion is further from us than I first thought. It is true that I am with mountain men, remote from the industrial areas, and very fatalistic'.

(5.52) *En l'an 2000, le secteur agricole ne devrait plus représenter que 20% de la valeur de la production de la province contre 40% pour les secteurs secondaires et tertiaires. "**Il est clair** que nous devons modifier notre politique …", indique M. Wang.*
(AFP)
'In 2000, agriculture should only represent 20% of the production of the province against 40% for the secondary and tertiary areas. "It is clear that we need to modify our strategy …", Mr. Wong said'.

The impersonal meaning of these predicates is somewhat different from their personal counterparts. While personal *certain* (*je suis certain* 'I am certain') is distinguished from *je sais* 'I know' by the individual nature of the assertion that may not be shared by other persons, this restriction obviously does not apply to the impersonal predicate due to the general character of the construction. In (5.50) for instance, the author's statement is not restricted to his own beliefs but is presented as true for everyone. *Vrai* 'true' also presents the proposition in the complement as independently verifiable, and thus threatens to completely overlap with *être certain*, but its specialized discursive function allows it to retain its distinctiveness. In (5.51) the author confirms the presence in reality of a proposition that had already been presented as a viable candidate. The main discursive function of that confirmation, however, is to temper a previously made statement by presenting a piece of information that challenges its force (Achard 2010). The author obviously knows the local crowd well, but its specificity needs to be reaffirmed and brought into focus in order to amend his position concerning the violence in the area. In this case the speaker's epistemic effort does not primarily involve evaluating a fact with respect to reality, but activating a relevant facet of reality in order to use it for communicative purposes. This specialized usage of *il est vrai* is considered in detail in Chapter 6.

The presence of the indicative inflection with inclination and result predicates is straightforward. Since the result predicates profile the final stage of the epistemic control cycle where the conceptualizer accepts the conceived proposition as part of reality, it naturally follows that it includes the precise address where it can be located. With inclination predicates the process in the complement is not yet accepted as real, but the conceptualizer's level of confidence toward its presence in reality is such that it is nonetheless presented as such, namely as a proposition with a putative address in reality. However, as was mentioned earlier, and illustrated in (5.30), any doubt in the outcome of the complement clause may result in the use of the subjunctive. This is further illustrated in (5.53), which can be compared to (5.48) where the same predicate is followed by an indicative complement. Here again the complement content is not presented as a proposition, but as an event whose occurrence is highly doubtful.[12]

(5.53) *En attendant,* **il est peu probable** *que le Crédit Lyonnais fasse procéder à la vente des meubles de M. Tapie, car une telle vente, qui nécessite notamment la préparation d'un catalogue, et une certaine publicité, ne paraît pas réalisable avant plusieurs mois.*   (AFP)
'In the meantime, it is hardly likely that the Credit Lyonnais will organize the sale of Mr. Tapie's furniture, because such a sale, which among other things requires establishing a catalogue, and a certain amount of publicity, doesn't seem feasible before several months'.

---

12. Mood selection truly rests on a person's selection of the best possible way of expressing her conceptualization, as opposed to structural properties of the language itself. Although the verb classes presented in this section are rather consistent in their complement distributions, some attested examples reflect unconventional choices. In (i), for example, *il est vraisemblable* 'it is likely' is followed by a subjunctive complement, while its negative counterpart in (ii) selects an indicative clause.

  (i) *Après 24 heures au contact des gaz denses qui entourent Vénus à basse altitude,* **il est vraisemblable** *que Magellan brûle, ou perde toute autonomie énergétique.*   (AFP)
       'After 24 hours in contact with the dense gases which surround Venus at lower elevation, it is likely that Magellan will burn, or lose all energetic autonomy'.

  (ii) *"Nous serions très surpris si ce budget changeait radicalement des précédents", a déclaré Tony Twine, un des analystes économiques d'Econometrix. "Il est peu probable que ce budget portera la marque de la nouvelle politique gouvernementale", a-t-il ajouté.*   (AFP)
       '"We would be very surprised if this budget were radically different from the previous ones", Tony Wine, one of the economic analysts with Econometrix, said. "It is hardly likely that this budget will bear the mark of the government's new policy", he added'.

One might wonder if the evaluative and epistemic classes are truly as separate as they have been presented in this section. On the one hand, labels are not very important and the majority of predicates considered in this chapter could probably be grouped in a variety of overlapping categories. On the other hand, the two classes were shown to have highly distinctive syntactic behaviors, principally with respect to their complement distribution. As was already pointed out, evaluatives select either infinitival or subjunctive complements, while epistemics only select indicative ones. In that light, the behavior of *il est clair* 'it is clear' illustrated in (5.52) is straightforward. Semantically, the predicate could be considered either evaluative or epistemic, but its syntactic behavior, i.e. the fact that it can only be followed by an indicative complement, clearly indicates that it is an epistemic.[13]

Il est possible/impossible 'it is possible/impossible' can be analyzed in a similar manner. Semantically, these predicates undeniably describe an assessment of the complement content with respect to reality, but they merely involve the recognition that the considered event may indeed occur, not the stronger manipulation to assert the location in reality where its corresponding position may be located. In that sense, one might consider the conceptualizer's assessment as merely evaluative information, much in the manner of *facile* 'easy' or *difficile* 'difficult'. Syntactically, they clearly behave as evaluatives since they can be followed by an infinitival complement as in (5.54) and a subjunctive one as in (5.55). For these reasons, they are classified, perhaps surprisingly, as evaluative in this analysis. It would be entirely possible, on the other hand, for other languages to categorize them differently.

---

13. The distribution of complements is not always so straightforward. For instance, *il est douteux* 'it is doubtful' is followed by a subjunctive complement as illustrated in (i), but not by an infinitival complement.

(i) *Leur passage soulevait les clameurs des gamins ..., mais **il était douteux** que ce fût aux enfants seulement que les masques eussent souhaité faire peur*. (Gracq, J. *Le rivage des Syrtes*: 186)
'Children screamed as they passed ..., but it was doubtful that it was only the children that these masks intended to scare'.

Interestingly, when the negative *douteux* 'doubtful' is itself negated, the resulting positively evaluated complement can be in the indicative, as (ii) illustrates:

(ii) *Il est naturel que Blanqui se plaçant sur des positions petites-bourgeoises, au sujet de la nature de l'exploitation capitaliste, ne soit pas en mesure de comprendre la structure de classe de la société capitaliste. **Il n'est pas douteux** que sa conception petite-bourgeoise de l'exploitation capitaliste est liée à ce fait qu'il assimile le prolétariat à tout l'ensemble des groupes sociaux vivant de leur travail sans exploiter le travail d'autrui.*
(Blanqui, L. *Auguste Blanqui, textes choisis*: 24)
'It is natural that on the matter of the nature of capitalistic exploitation, Blanqui's bourgeois conceptions prevent him from understanding the class structure of capitalistic society. It makes no doubt [is not doubtful] that his bourgeois conception of capitalistic exploitation is due to the fact that for him, the proletariat includes all the social groups who live off their labor without exploiting the labor of others'.

(5.54)   *"Avec l'avènement de la démocratie en Ukraine, **il sera possible** <u>de défendre les</u>*
         <u>*citoyens et leurs droits*</u> *par la loi, et les forces du crime seront vaincues", a déclaré*
         M. Freeh avant son départ de Kiev pour Moscou, où il est arrivé samedi soir pour
         une visite de trois jours.   (AFP)
         '"With the rise of democracy in Ukraine, it will be possible to defend citizens
         and their rights by law, and the criminal forces will be defeated", Mr. Freeh
         declared before leaving Kiev for Moscow, where he arrived on Saturday night
         for a three-day visit'.

(5.55)   *Meignerais, je suis obligé de vous demander, si pénible que cela puisse vous être*
         à tous égards, de le voir et de nous donner ensuite les renseignements que vous
         *pourriez posséder sur lui. Remarquez, continua le directeur, **il est fort possible***
         <u>*que vous ne le connaissiez absolument pas*</u>.
                                                (Druon, M. *Les grandes familles*: 239)
         'Meignerais, I have to ask you, as painful as it may be for you on all levels,
         to see him, and then to give us all the information you may have about him.
         But you know, the director continued, it is quite possible that you don't know
         him at all'.

5.4   Occurrence predicates

The occurrence predicates describe an existing facet of reality. They are distinguished from the epistemic class because they profile no explicit assessment on
the conceptualizer's part. The content of the complement clause is described as
if it were emanating from the world itself as it presents itself to the conceptualizer, without any specific effort on her part. Most predicates of this class such as
paraître/apparaître 'appear', *arriver* 'arrive', *s'agir* 'to be about', *se passer* 'happen',
and *rester* 'remain' are also attested in the simple construction. Unlike deontic
falloir (*il faut*) presented in Section 5.2, which exhibited remarkable similarity
in its simple and complex uses, the occurrence predicates show more variation.
Even the most consistent ones such as *s'agir* (*il s'agit*), which was not presented
in the previous chapter due to its intrinsic character, reveal some discrepancies
worth investigating.

When *il s'agit* is followed by a nominal postverbal expression it profiles the
elaboration of a previously mentioned entity, as in (5.56) where it clarifies the
content of the phrase *avoir de l'expression* 'to be expressive'. More precisely, the
postverbal expression conveys the additional characteristic required to understand exactly what the author intends to convey. The example in (5.57) translates
a series of symptoms into a diagnostic, and the one in (5.58) provides another
form of diagnostic, namely the most likely interpretation of a woman's complaints. In a more general context the predicate can also profile the similarity
that connects two domains as in (5.59), where the hypothesis formulated for the

animal domain can only be extended to humans with the consequences elaborated in the following discourse.[14]

(5.56) *Quand nous parlons d'une beauté et même d'une laideur expressives, quand nous disons qu'un visage a de l'expression, **il s'agit** d'une expression stable peut-être, mais que nous devinons mobile.*

                        (Bergson, H. *Le rire. Essais sur la signification du comique*: 14)

    'When we talk about an expressive beauty or even ugliness, when we say that a face is expressive, we make reference to [it is about] a stable expression perhaps, but we know it may vary'.

(5.57) *Je suis au lit, depuis quatre jours. ... **Il s'agit** d'un point pleurétique. Fâcheux. Le médecin est venu trois fois.*   (Duhamel, G. *Journal de Salavin*: 62)

    'I have been in bed for four days. ... It is pleurisy. Annoying. The doctor came three times'.

(5.58) *Aucune femme parmi nos anciennes malades n'a eu lieu, à ma connaissance, de se plaindre de nos soins. ... **Il s'agit** sans doute encore d'une pauvre égarée...*

                         (Céline, LF. *Voyage au bout de la nuit*: 577)

    'No woman among our former patients has had, to my knowledge, any reason to complain about our treatment. ... She [it] is probably another poor lost soul...'

---

14. The elaborative function of the French predicate is reflected in the English choices in translation illustrated by the examples in (i) (iii), taken from the parallel corpus of EEU parliament deliberations:

    (i)   **Il s'agit** d'une décision de l'Assemblée
    (i′) This **is** the decision of Parliament
    (ii) **Il s'agit** de présenter les priorités de la Commission
    (ii′) This **means** putting forward the Commission's priorities
    (iii) En ce qui nous concerne, il n'est donc pas nécessaire que soit indiqué sur la face antérieure des emballages de chocolat un texte de mise en garde en lettres fluorescentes qui clignotent. **Il ne s' agit pas de cigarettes.**
    (iii′) As far as we are concerned, there is no need for warnings in flashing neon letters on the front of chocolate packaging. **After all, chocolate is not exactly a product like cigarettes.**

The selection of the demonstrative expressions 'this is' in (i′) and 'this means' in (ii′) is perfectly congruent with *il*'s profiling of the field. The close relation between *il* and demonstratives is described more thoroughly in Chapter 6. The examples in (iii) and (iii′) clearly illustrate *il s'agit*'s wide scope. The example presents a possible transfer between the domains of cigarettes and chocolate, and the legislation that governs their respective packaging. Note that *il s'agit* provides an immediate shift between the two domains where the referred entity (chocolate) is not specifically mentioned. In English, the lack of equivalence between the two products is explicitly mentioned by the phrase 'a product like'. Solutions closer to the French usage are sometimes selected in such contexts. For example, a translation such as 'we are not talking about cigarettes here' could have been selected. 'We are (not) talking about...' constitutes an attested translation of *il s'agit* in other more informal contexts.

(5.59) *je propose de dire que, sous l'aiguillon de la douleur, l'esprit invente des manières de vivre susceptibles de procurer du plaisir, qui recouvrent assez la douleur pour que celle-ci semble seulement un incident dont nous pourrions débarrasser l'ordre naturel. Quand **il s'agit** des animaux, l'instinct et l'éducation présentent à la volonté des systèmes tout faits qui laissent une bien faible latitude au libre choix...* (Sorel, G. *Introduction à l'économie moderne*: 200)

'I suggest to say that under the sting of pain, the mind invents ways of living capable of providing pleasure, which cover pain enough so that the latter only seems like an accident, of which we could rid the natural order. For [when it is about] animals, instinct and education provide their will with already made systems that leave a very small part to free choice...'

The predicate predominantly retains its elaborative meaning in its complex impersonal usage where it is often used to correct a mistaken impression, as in (5.60) where the author provides the correct interpretation of a political treaty in response to erroneous fears, and (5.61) where a general explains the intention behind the decision to close a section of Cisjordania to visitors as the desire to keep trouble-makers away:

(5.60) *Il n'est pas question, a expliqué Bernard de Montferrand, conseiller diplomatique de M. Balladur, de remettre en cause le tracé des frontières, mais **il s'agit** d'apporter une "garantie politique" de la communauté internationale aux accords de bon voisinage déjà signés et à ceux devant encore être négociés.* (AFP)

'It is out of the question, Bernard de Montferrand, a diplomatic advisor to Mr. Balladur explained, to reconsider borders, but the goal is [it is about] to provide a "political guarantee" by the international community to the good neighborhood agreements that have been signed already, as well as to those still to be negotiated'.

(5.61) *Le commandant militaire de la Cisjordanie, le général Ilan Biran, a maintenu Jéricho "zone militaire fermée", une mesure qui interdit aux non-résidents de s'y rendre. Selon lui, **il s'agit** "d'empêcher les Israéliens hostiles au processus de paix de créer des troubles, car cette ville est devenue le symbole de l'autonomie en Cisjordanie".* (AFP)

'The military commander of Cisjordania, General Ilan Biran, maintained Jericho as a "closed military area", a measure that prevents any visitor from entering the city. According to him, the measure aims to [it is about] "prevent[ing] the Israelis who oppose the peace process from creating trouble, because this city has become the symbol of autonomy in Cisjordania"'.

As was previously observed with *il faut*, the infinitive clause following *il s'agit* codes an event, but in this case it is presented as an established element of basic reality. Its reality is being offered as the explanation for otherwise ambiguous behavior.

In certain contexts, however, the predicate takes on a deontic meaning, as illustrated in (5.62) and (5.63) where the complement process does not provide the explanation for a previously misconceived act but introduces the necessary course of action in the future. The presence of *maintenant* 'now' in the majority of the cases clearly indicates the separation between the situation described in the earlier context and the desired outcome. These deontic cases are closer to *il faut* than to those illustrated in (5.60) and (5.61). These cases serve to remind us that meaning is highly dependent on context, and that some highly specific senses can arise in particular environments.

(5.62)   *Le cabinet Hata était largement considéré comme éphémère puisqu'il était minoritaire dans les deux chambres du parlement. Sa chute ouvre une nouvelle période d'incertitudes. **Il s'agit** maintenant <u>de voir si la coalition pourra finalement s'entendre avec le parti socialiste sur un retour éventuel de cette formation politique pour retrouver une majorité au parlement</u>.*   (AFP)
'The Hata government was generally considered temporary since it was in the minority in the two houses in parliament. Its fall leads to a time of uncertainty. We now need to [It is about] see[ing] if the coalition will finally agree with the socialist party about their possible return to regain the majority in parliament'.

(5.63)   *L'hôpital du Comité International de la Croix-Rouge (CICR) à Kigali est tombé aux mains des rebelles du Front patriotique rwandais (FPR), a annoncé lundi à Genève un porte-parole de l'organisation. "Tout s'est passé ce matin dans le calme", a précisé M. Tony Burgener. ... "**Il s'agit** maintenant <u>d'acheminer du matériel médical et de prévoir une évacuation partielle de cet hôpital surpeuplé qui accueille 400 blessés dont une centaine d'enfants</u>", a-t-il précisé.*   (AFP)
'The hospital of the International Red Cross Committee (IRCC) in Kigali fell to the rebels of the Rwanda Patriotic Front (RPF), a spokesperson for the organization announced in Geneva on Monday. "It happened this morning without violence", Mr. Tony Burgener continued. ... "We now need [it is now about] to transport[ing] medical equipment and plan[ning] the partial evacuation of this overcrowded hospital with its 400 patients, including approximately one hundred children"'.

The complement distribution pattern of occurrence predicates is also far less consistent than with the other classes, and several individual verbs require particular scrutiny. First, predicates such as *il se trouve* 'it so happens', *il ressort* 'it comes out', and *il reste* 'it remains' follow their epistemic counterpart in taking indicative complements and not accepting infinitival ones, as illustrated in (5.64) and (5.7) repeated here.

(5.64)   *De ces différents témoignages, **il ressort** <u>que le fauve est soit un puma, soit une</u>*
<u>*panthère*</u>. *Les spécialistes sont formels: les traces qu'il a laissées sont celles d'un*
félin adulte.   (AFP)
'All these testimonies indicate [from all these testimonies, it comes out] that
the beast is either a puma or a panther. The specialists are positive: the tracks
it left behind belong to an adult feline'.

(5.7)   *Positivement: si je ne l'aimais pas tendrement comme je l'aime, cela m'agacerait.*
*Mais **il se trouve** <u>que je l'aime</u>…*
(Anouilh, J. *La répétition: ou, l'amour puni*: 96)
'In truth: if I didn't love him as much as I love him, it would annoy me! But it
so happens that I love him…'

The examples in (5.64) and (5.7) clearly reveal how the conceptualizer came to
know the location in reality of the proposition in the complement. In (5.64), absolute knowledge is provided by analyzing the evidence that the animal left behind.
While this certainly requires conceptual effort, that effort is not epistemic per se.
No energy was spent considering whether a specific event actually occurred; the
truth revealed itself in the observed tracks. In (5.7) the speaker is well acquainted
with her own emotional landscape, and her love for the character under discussion
has already been discovered. The utterance in (5.7) merely amounts to a statement
of a well-established fact. The presence of the indicative with occurrence predicates
is unproblematic. Just like their epistemic counterparts, they profile the result stage
of the epistemic control cycle even though they differ in the kind of action that
produced that result. Since the indicative inflection codes the presence in reality
of the proposition described in the complement clause as opposed to the epistemic
effort to assert its presence there, these occurrence predicates are just as compatible
with it as the result epistemic predicates.[15]

Other verbs in the same class exhibit a very different complement distribution.
In particular, this is the case with *arriver* 'arrive', which selects either an infinitive
or a subjunctive clause in the complement clause. This was already illustrated in
(5.3) and (5.4) repeated here, and also in (5.65):

---

15. The complement clause can be in the conditional as well, as illustrated in (i) where it indicates
that its reality depends on the satisfaction of specific conditions (Achard 2002):

(i)   *J'offre d'être, pour vous, l'ouvrier d'une œuvre très belle, et **il se trouve** <u>que votre consente-</u>*
<u>*ment me sauverait des tourments les plus horribles*</u>.   (Bloy, L. *Journal T. 1*: 48)
'I offer to be for you the craftsman of a very beautiful work of art, and it so happens that
your agreement would rescue me from the most horrible troubles'.

(5.3)   – *Je sais que Dubreuilh croit à la paix et aux chances d'une Europe, dit Scriassine;*
il sourit avec indulgence: **il arrive** *même aux grands esprits <u>de se tromper</u>.*
(Beauvoir, S. de. *Les mandarins*: 36)
'I know that Dubreuilh believes in peace and a European destiny, said Scriassine;
he smiled indulgently: it even happens to great minds to make mistakes'.

(5.4)   *Mais il est clair que cette entente est encore loin d'être parfaite. Jerrie Hulme,*
confirme, sans vouloir donner de chiffres, ce que d'autres responsables étrangers
admettent avec plus ou moins de réticence: **il arrive** *encore <u>que des Musulmans</u>*
<u>soient expulsés des quartiers à prédominance croate</u>.   (AFP)
'But it is clear that this agreement is far from being perfect. Jerrie Hulme
confirms without willing to provide figures what other foreign officials admit
with more or less reluctance: it still happens that Muslims are expelled from
predominantly Croatian neighborhoods'.

(5.65) *Selon une association parisienne, Halte-Aide aux femmes battues, les femmes*
évoquent dans plus de 10% des cas lors de leurs appels téléphoniques à l'asso-
ciation les retransmissions de matches de football. ... **Il arrive** *<u>qu'un homme</u>*
<u>regardant un match "ne se sente plus du tout dans le domicile conjugal</u>, mais
sur le terrain avec les joueurs", explique-t-on à Halte-Aide aux femmes battues.
(AFP)
'According to a Parisian organization Stop-Help to battered women, in more
than 10% of their telephone calls to the center, women mention soccer games
on television. ... Often, when watching a game, [it happens that] a man "doesn't
feel like he is at home with his wife any more, but on the field with the players",
workers at Stop-Help to battered women explain'.

This distribution of complements may appear surprising because semantically
arriver resembles *se trouver* or *ressortir* in profiling an observed facet of reality.
However, unlike those predicates, it primarily focuses not on currently observed
phenomena but habitual scenes grouped together through many repeated occurrences. This characteristic is particularly clear in (5.65), where the situation described in the complement represents over 10 percent of the situations in which
battered women seek the organization's help. This focus on the habitual nature of
the event described in the complement naturally motivates the presence of the
infinitive and subjunctive inflection; both marks of the effective nature of reality
because it makes it impossible to provides the address in reality of each specific
instance in the group. The infinitive and subjunctive inflection following *arriver*
represent a motivated choice because the predicate profiles a series of events, clus-
tered together due to their similarity even though they each occurred at different
locations, and different points in time, and involved different participants.

If the form of the complement clause can obviously be semantically motivated, one should, however, resist the temptation to overestimate that motivation to the detriment of usage or conventional issues. For instance, *Il se fait* 'it turns out' might be expected to follow the same pattern as *il ressort* and *il se trouve* on semantic grounds alone, and yet its usage is entirely different. *Il se fait que* in its positive form is not attested in either corpus, and all occurrences are in the form of direct or indirect questions with subjunctive inflection in the complement clause.[16] The presence of the subjunctive does not per se constitute a challenge to the analysis proposed here. The conceptualizer can certainly construe the complement content as a mere event (a part of effective reality), even though its presence in reality has been historically established, as illustrated in (5.66) where the presence of the subjunctive inflection reflects the conceptualizer's strict concern with what happened rather than the assessment of its epistemic reality:

(5.66)   *Je lui demande, puisqu'il n'est pas nazi et qu'il n'aime pas du tout Hitler, comment il se fait que l'Allemagne ait pu suivre un homme de cette sorte.*
(Green, J. *Journal. T. 5. 1946–1950*: 343)
'I ask him, since he is not a Nazi and he does not like Hitler at all, how it happened [it makes itself] that Germany could follow a man in that manner'.

The example in (5.66) perfectly illustrates the flexibility of the narrator's construal, who selects a construction that underscores the very process of Germans following Hitler rather than the historical fact that they did. The interesting point from the perspective investigated in this monograph is that *il se fait*, or often *se fait-il*, has been recruited almost exclusively to describe similar kinds of events. This underscores the point that semantic motivation alone is not sufficient to account for the shape of grammar, but that considerations of usage and convention play a crucial part.

Reality does not always reveal itself with full clarity. *Sembler* 'seem', for instance, profiles the impression a conceptualizer has that things have evolved in a certain manner. This impression may be expressed as a proposition that she is considering for inclusion in her conception of reality (inclination phase) as illustrated in (5.67), or as an event whose effective reality is being considered as in (5.68):[17]

---

16. The complement clause is in the indicative in one instance illustrated in (i), but it should be noted that the impersonal pronoun is not *il* but *ça*. The difference between the two pronouns is considered in detail in Chapter 6.

(i)   *Comment ça se fait que tu n'es pas au journal, à cette heure-ci? Demanda Lambert.*
(Beauvoir, S. de. *Les mandarins*: 242)
'How is it [it makes itself] that you are not at the paper at this time? Lambert asked'.

17. An added particularity of *sembler* is that it also has a "raised" sense (Achard 2000; Langacker 1995) where the subject of the complement clause is coded as the main subject. These cases are not considered here.

(5.67) *Les détails de l'accident restaient obscurs, mais **il semble** <u>qu'une voiture était</u>*
<u>*impliquée*</u> *et au moins une personne a été tuée, selon le capitaine de police Bill*
Alexander. (AFP)
'The details of the accident are not clear, but it seems that a car was involved
and at least one person was killed, according to police captain Bill Alexander'.

(5.68) *– La lecture d'une notice sur le pêcheur justifié (il s'agit du roman de Hogg) m'a*
*tant soit peu inquiété, car **il semble** bien **que** dans ce livre comme dans le mien*
<u>*il y ait une certaine ressemblance sous le rapport de la psychologie.*</u>
(Green, J. *Journal. T. 5. 1946–1950*:199)
'Reading a report about the justified sinner (it is Hogg's novel) worried me
somewhat, because it seems that in this book, like in mine, there is a certain
resemblance regarding the role of psychology'.

As previously observed for epistemics, the mood in the complement verb directly
correlates with the conceptualizer's level of confidence in the reality of the complement content. More specifically still, the subjunctive represents the preferred
choice when she is aware that she is experiencing an illusion and the reality of the
scene is therefore not at issue. In these cases, illustrated in (5.69) and (5.70), the
subjunctive is particularly well suited to describing the event itself, rather than the
epistemic reality of a proposition that the speaker knows to be illusory.[18]

(5.69) *Et puis, cet Harpagon est répugnant de vieillesse et de saleté: **il semble** <u>qu'on</u>*
<u>*puisse le sentir.*</u> (Green, J. *Journal. T. 5. 1946–1950*:132)
'And this Harpagon is repulsively old and dirty: It seems that you can smell
him'.

(5.70) *– J'ai un petit appartement dans la Sankt Annae Gade. Il y a une terrasse d'où je*
*vois le clocher de l'église dite de notre-sauveur; j'en suis même si près qu'**il semble***
<u>*qu'en allongeant le bras on puisse le toucher du doigt.*</u>
(Green, J. *Journal. T. 5. 1946–1950*:283)
'– I have a little apartment in Sankt Annae Gade. There is a balcony from which
I can see the steeple of the so-called our savior's church; I am so close that it
seems that if you extend your arm you can touch it with your finger'.

---

18. The indicative is also possible in this context, as illustrated in (i):

   (i) *Il me parle de ce livre de telle sorte que je me demande s'il ne le connaît pas mieux que*
   *moi. … **Il m'a semblé** <u>qu'il parlait du livre d'un autre</u>.*
   (Green, J. *Journal. T. 5. 1946–1950*:135)
   'He talks to me about this book in such a way that I wonder if he doesn't know it better
   than I do. … It seemed to me that he was talking about someone else's book'.

Finally, *rester* 'remain' presents an idiosyncratic complement distribution because it can be followed by either an infinitival clause as in (5.1) repeated here and (5.71), or by a finite clause in the indicative as in (5.2) and (5.72):

(5.1)   *Même Rai, décevant en début de stage, semble revenu à son meilleur niveau et il ne subsiste que deux légères incertitudes dans l'esprit du sélectionneur: l'arrière gauche Branco est en balance avec Leonardo et **il reste** à attribuer le brassard de capitaine, vraisemblablement entre Ricardo Rocha, Dunga et Jorginho.*   (AFP)
'Even Rai, disappointing at the beginning of camp, seems to have returned to form, and only two slight uncertainties remain in the coach's mind: at left back, where Blanco and Leonardo are in competition, and he still needs to designate the captain [there remains to give the captain's armband], most likely between Ricardo Rocha, Dunga and Jorginho'.

(5.71)   *Outre les 9 circonscriptions qui doivent revoter dimanche 19 juin (17 à 18.000 inscrits), **il reste** à décompter les votes des quelque 20.000 (bien 20.000) Portugais à l'étranger ayant voté par correspondance…*   (AFP)
'In addition to the 9 districts that need to vote again on Sunday June 19th (17 to 18,000 voters), [there remains to count] the absentee ballots of approximately 20,000 (yes 20,000) Portuguese living abroad still need to be counted…'

(5.2)   *Mais, s'il est vrai que des élections générales constituent la seule voie par où doive, un jour, s'exprimer la souveraineté du peuple, **il reste** que le pays, quoique écrasé et bâillonné, manifeste par mille signes évidents quels sont ses sentiments profonds.*   (Gaulle, C. de. *Mémoires de Guerre: l'unité*: 542)
'But, if it is true that general elections constitute the only way in which the people's sovereignty can be expressed, it remains that the country, crushed and silenced as it is, nonetheless demonstrates its true feelings through thousands of obvious signs'.

(5.72)   *Si l'intérêt sportif de ce combat paraît des plus discutables, **il reste** que "Big" George est actuellement le seul faire frémir le public américain…*   (AFP)
'If the sporting interest of this fight seems dubious at best, "Big" George nonetheless currently remains [it remains that "Big" George is] the only one to raise the interest of the American public…'

The complement structures illustrated in these four examples are only surprising because the combination indicative/infinitive is seldom attested, but *rester*'s distribution is perfectly congruent with the analysis proposed in this chapter. It was said in the introduction that the events described in (5.1) and (5.71) as well as the propositions depicted in (5.2) and (5.72) represent the pieces missing from an ideal or complete entity, and therefore closely resemble the predicate's simple usage described in Chapter 4. This is undeniably true for the infinitival complements in

(5.1) and (5.71), which simply name the processes still to be performed to complete the overall task. The indicative cases, however, are more difficult to analyze in this manner because the discourse value of the construction goes beyond the part/whole relationship that exists between the complement content and the ideal entity. What (5.2) and (5.72) indicate is that despite the reality of the broader statement that should not allow it, the content of the complement clause is also real. In (5.72) a fight that presents no sporting interest should not be exciting to the public. Furthermore, this element that runs counter to the broader trend constitutes the important part of the message that drives future behavior, i.e. the fight in (5.72) will indeed take place. Rather than completing the situation covered in the broader statement, the complement content therefore stands in opposition to it, and is used as such rhetorically. This meaning, however, arises solely in the context of the *rester que* construction.

Upon closer examination even the infinitival complements are not as straightforward as the examples in (5.1) and (5.71) would lead us to believe. Of the thirty-eight examples of *rester à* in the AFP corpus, fifteen involve the verbs *voir* 'see' or *savoir* 'know' as the subordinate predicate, as illustrated in (5.73)–(5.75). These cases diverge from the infinitival pattern described earlier because the complement content cannot be interpreted as a missing step toward the completion that the immediate context describes:

(5.73) *Le président du PS, Tomiichi Murayama, a quant à lui dit que les socialistes étaient prêts à former une alliance avec le PLD dont le président Yohei Kono s'est déclaré ouvert à une telle formule. **Il reste** à voir si ces deux partis, ennemis jurés tout au long du règne du PLD, peuvent s'entendre.* (AFP)
'Former socialist party president, Tomiichi Murayama, said that the socialists were ready to form an alliance with the PLD whose president Yohei Kono said was open to such a move. It remains to be seen if these two parties, sworn enemies while the PLD was in power, can get along'.

(5.74) *Mais Lewis, dont l'intelligence est désormais plus rapide que les jambes, a son explication. "Je n'étais pas affûté. Je ne suis pas parti aussi bien que ces derniers temps. Une bonne course pour moi car elle m'a appris beaucoup". **Il reste** à savoir si les organisateurs – qui paient – se satisferont longtemps de ces excuses de plus en plus fréquentes.* (AFP)
'But Lewis, whose intelligence is now faster than his legs, had his own explanation. "I wasn't sharp. My start wasn't as good as it had been lately. A good race for me because it taught me a lot". It remains to be seen how long the organizers – who foot the bill – will be satisfied with these increasingly frequent excuses'.

(5.75)   *La publication très attendue vendredi du chiffre de la croissance américaine*
          au 3ème trimestre a apporté un vent d'optimisme sur l'ensemble des marchés
          *financiers et renforcé le dollar, mais **il reste** à savoir si cette envolée sera durable*
          ou si la déprime qui sévit depuis neuf mois reprendra le dessus.   (AFP)
          'The eagerly expected publication of the American third-quarter growth rate on
          Friday brought a wave of optimism to the financial markets and strengthened
          the dollar, but it remains to be seen if this rise will last, or if the depression of
          the past nine months will resurface'.

In the infinitival constructions illustrated in (5.1) and (5.71), the agent of the overall process is also exclusively in charge of the missing part that the content of
the infinitival clause represents. The Brazilian coach in (5.1) is in charge of the
team's preparation, and the selection of captain also falls within his job description.
Similarly, in (5.71) counting absentee ballots and organizing the second election
in the relevant precincts also falls within the duties of the election officials who
oversee the entire procedure. The examples in (5.73)–(5.75) are organized differently. First, it is not entirely clear that the complement content represents the last
stage of a complex process. It may be possible, although not particularly insightful,
to view the reaction to a process as its ultimate stage, but even under this generous
interpretation these situations still distinguish themselves by their agentive structures. Unlike other infinitival constructions, the agent of the broader procedure,
if it can be identified, is not exclusively responsible for the content of the infinitive
clause. Rather, the construal of that content prominently involves the interpretation of another conceptualizer, often the speaker representing the public at large.
The *il reste à savoir* construction is thus best analyzed as the speaker's doubtful
evaluation of the event described in the passage rather than the description of the
last step toward its completion.[19] Any doubt that these constructions do not involve
the part/whole relation representative of the other infinitival constructions should
be erased by the example in (5.76), where the content of the infinitival clause represents a commentary on the entire procedure:

---

19. Another variant of *rester* occurs without impersonal *il*, as illustrated in (i). The difference
between the *il* and these zero impersonals is not considered here.

(i)   *Une première série de discussions ONU-OTAN le 17 octobre, également à New York, n'avait*
       *abouti à aucun changement dans les procédures. **Reste** à savoir comment les Russes, tra-*
       ditionnellement sensibles aux intérêts des Serbes, réagiront aux procédures agréées jeudi.
                                                                                   (AFP)
       'A first series of talks UN-NATO on October 17th, also in New York, had led to no change
       in procedures. It [ø] remains to be known how the Russians, traditionally responsive to
       Serbian interests, will react to the procedures agreed upon on Thursday'.

(5.76) *Après avoir longtemps rejeté une telle possibilité, les Etats-Unis ont admis qu'ils*
étaient prêts à discuter de la création d'une telle confédération, si les belligérants
venaient à se mettre d'accord sur les arrangements constitutionnels du futur état
*bosniaque. Une telle confédération "demeure notre objectif ultime, mais **il reste***
<u>à savoir comment on pourra la réaliser</u>", note Radmilo Bogdanovic, proche
collaborateur du président serbe.   (AFP)
'After rejecting such a possibility for a long time, the United States admitted
that they were ready to discuss the creation of such a confederation, if the protagonists could agree on the constitutional organization of the future Bosnian
state. Such a confederation "remains our ultimate goal, but it remains to be
known how we can achieve it", Radmilo Bogdanovic, a close collaborator of
the Serbian president said'.

5.5 Recapitulation

This section considered the complement distribution of the four classes of predicates. Infinitival, subjunctive, and indicative clauses were shown to be semantically
motivated. Expectedly, given the analysis provided in this chapter, infinitival and
subjunctive complements occur together following deontic and evaluative predicates because these predicates are more directly concerned with effective reality
than the epistemic evaluation of the complement clause content. In a similar vein,
epistemic predicates were shown to be solely compatible with the indicative inflection because they profile the inclination or result stages of the epistemic control
cycle where the conceptualizer either considers or accepts the conceived proposition as real. If the epistemic evaluation leads the conceptualizer to doubt or refuse
the reality of the complement content, the latter can be considered as an event and
be marked in the subjunctive. Occurrence predicates were shown to diverge somewhat from those configurations, and individual predicates were shown to possess
their own idiosyncratic patterns. Importantly, as the previous chapter presented
for simple impersonals, less abstract, lower-level clusters were observed where the
resulting construction takes on a specific meaning. These cases once again remind
us that semantic motivation alone cannot fully account for the form of grammar,
and that considerations of usage and convention also need to be factored in.

6. Impersonal passives

Only impersonals with active morphology have been considered so far. In the
syntactic literature, however, passives have generated more interest because impersonalization and passivization are generally being considered as two separate

structural operations, and their interaction has been investigated in detail. For example, in the Relational Grammar framework (Perlmutter and Postal 1984; Legendre 1990 among others; see also Blevins 2003, and Carney and Harley 2008 for treatments in other frameworks), passive predicates are characterized by the demotion of their subject to an oblique. Consequently, the subject position remains available for the dummy to be inserted. The distribution of predicates in the impersonal passive construction is therefore argued to follow strict structural criteria. Any predicate that can be passivized (in the case of French this includes transitive and some unergative predicates) should be acceptable in the impersonal passive construction. This position is summarized by Legendre (1990: 82) who notes that "ICs with passive morphology typically involve transitive predicates", even though certain unergative predicates are also attested in the construction. Her examples of impersonal passives include those in (5.77) and (5.78) (from Legendre 1990: 98):

(5.77) *Il a été arrêté beaucoup de terroristes en Italie*
'Many terrorists were arrested [there were arrested many terrorists] in Italy'

(5.78) *Il a été bu trop d'alcool samedi soir chez les Dupont*
'People drank too much alcohol [there was too much alcohol drunk] at the Duponts on Saturday night'

Conceptually, the particularity of the impersonal passive construction is the extremely low focus it places on the participants in the profiled relation. The combination of the passive and impersonal aspects allows it to defocus both the agent and the patient at the same time. The passive construction by itself has already been presented as an agent defocusing construction (Shibatani 1985; Langacker 1982, 2008), but in isolation it performs this function by selecting another participant, namely the patient as the focal figure. When it combines with the impersonal construction, however, no character is given special prominence since the field is selected as the focal entity. Consequently, the impersonal passive construction defocuses all the participants in the profiled relation by selecting the field as the focal figure, and therefore focuses primarily on the event that the predicate codes. Impersonal passives are thus similar to their active counterparts in that they present a property of the scene considered. Consistent with the approach developed throughout this monograph, this section shows that the usage of impersonal passives does not conform to structural constraints. Rather, as has been witnessed in several instances with active impersonals, the bulk of the attested examples clusters around a relatively small group of semantically consistent predicates that describe very specific social situations in which participants themselves are not given any level of prominence. Consequently, the best way to analyze passive impersonal usage is to recognize the semantic import of the construction itself and to highlight the semantic characteristics it shares with the individual predicates that participate in it.

In order to investigate the construction's usage, 168 examples of impersonal passives were manually extracted from the AFP (eighty-one examples) and FRANTEXT (eighty-seven examples) corpora. These data reveal that (1) the most frequently attested predicates are not transitive, and (2) the overwhelming majority of instances naturally arrange themselves into well-delineated semantic categories. The impersonal passive construction therefore does not constitute a structural possibility of which all transitive verbs can equally avail themselves but prototypically codes a certain type of events, and can exceptionally be extended to cover other kinds of events if the context requires. With respect to the first point, of the fifty-three predicates that appear in the data, ten are transitive and eleven unergative in the sense that they occur with a nominal postverbal expression (zero marked for the transitive predicates and marked as an oblique for the unergative ones). However, these predicates only yield a total of forty instances altogether (fourteen for transitives and twenty-six for unergatives). Transitive predicates are illustrated in (5.79)–(5.81), where the postverbal expression (or part of it, in some cases) is underlined:

(5.79)   *Seulement la caisse d'assurances de Renault ... est en grève, mais sans drapeaux à la porte, et affiche deux exemplaires d'un papier démentant la dissolution du syndicat, annonçant qu'il compte 3.500 adhérents, qu'il en a été constitué d'autres semblables chez Citroën, Fiat, etc., et qu'il va immédiatement se mettre à recruter parmi les ouvriers.*   (Weil, S. *La condition ouvrière*: 261)
'Only Renault's insurance division ... is on strike, but without banners on the door. It exhibits two copies of a leaflet denying the union's dissolution, claiming that it has 3,500 members, that several similar ones were created [there were created several similar ones] at Citroën, Fiat, etc., and that it will start recruiting among workers immediately'.

(5.80)   *Parmi les français qui ont, par le meurtre ou par la délation, causé la mort de combattants de la résistance, il en aura été tué, sans procès régulier, 10842, dont 6675 pendant les combats des maquis avant la libération, le reste après, au cours de représailles. D'autre part, 779 auront été exécutés en vertu de jugements normalement rendus par les cours de justice et les tribunaux militaires.*
(Gaulle, C. de. *Mémoires de guerre, le salut*: 38)
'Among the French people who, by murder or denunciation, caused the death of resistance fighters, 10,842 were killed without trial [there will have been killed, without trial 10,842], including 6,675 in fights before the liberation, the rest afterward, during reprisals. Besides, 779 will have been executed following the decision of juries or military tribunals'.

(5.81)   *Il a été gagné, dans cet ouvrage, un temps précieux, un espace précieux, qui sans cela eussent été perdus, par l'omission systématique, après le verbe dire, du pléthorique pronom réfléchi.*   (Beckett, S. *Watt*: 8)
'Precious time and space that would otherwise have been lost were saved in this book [there was saved in this work precious time and precious space, which otherwise would have been lost], by the systematic omission, following the verb dire, of the plethoric reflexive pronoun'.

Intransitive (unergative) predicates are illustrated in (5.82)–(5.84):

(5.82)   *S'il a été beaucoup parlé de force, de pouvoir et de contrainte à l'occasion des problèmes économiques…*   (Perroux, F. *L'économie du XXe siècle*: 25)
'If force, power, and constraint have very much been talked about [it has been talked a lot about force, power, and constraint] during troubled economic times…'

(5.83)   *Le modèle dont il a été fait usage reste ouvert…*
                                            (Perroux, F. *L'économie du XXe siècle*: 208)
'The model that has been used [there has been made use of] remains open…'

(5.84)   *Quant aux embryons surnuméraires, il sera mis fin à la conservation de ceux qui ont été congelés depuis 5 ans à la date de promulgation de la loi.*   (AFP)
'As to the leftover embryos, those that had been frozen for five years at the time the law passes will not be preserved [it will be put an end to those that had been frozen for five years at the time the law passed]'.

The predicates *parler* 'speak', *faire usage* 'make use', and *mettre fin* 'put an end to' select for an oblique complement preceded by the preposition (*de* or *à).* As such, they cannot be considered transitive, but nonetheless select for a nominal post-verbal expression.

However, the majority of the instances attested in the impersonal passive construction (127, or approximately 76 percent of the data) occur with a sentential (infinitival or finite) complement. These structures are illustrated in (5.85)–(5.89), where the preposition or complementizer that introduces the complement is bold and underlined:

(5.85)   *Enfin, en 1958, il fut décidé de créer un quatrième établissement nucléaire…*
                (Goldschmidt, B. *L'aventure atomique: ses aspects politiques et techniques*: 146)
'Finally, in 1958, it was decided to create a fourth nuclear site'

(5.86)   *Il ne sera pas dit que rien au monde nous est plus cher que la vie du peuple espagnol.*   (Weil, S. *Écrits historiques et politiques*: 19)
'It will not be said that anything in the world is more important to us than the life of the Spanish people'.

(5.87)   *"Il a été très sérieusement **envisagé** que ce projet puisse ne pas être concrétisé",*
         a-t-il ajouté.   (AFP)
         '"It was considered very seriously that this project may not be terminated", he
         added'.

(5.88)   *"Il a été également **établi** que ces activités ont reçu le soutien tacite d'une certaine*
         représentation diplomatique étrangère à Lagos", a souligné le communiqué.
                                                                                   (AFP)
         '"It has also been established that these activities have received the unspoken
         support of a certain foreign diplomatic mission in Lagos", the statement said'.

(5.89)   *"Il a été **confirmé** au-delà de tout soupçon que les explosions ont été causées par*
         la foudre.   (AFP)
         '"It has been confirmed beyond all suspicion that the explosions have been
         caused by lightning"'.

Most interestingly from the standpoint of the analysis presented in this chapter,
the predicates attested in impersonal passives are not only restricted in number
but also semantically consistent. The overwhelming majority of them have as their
base a complex model of social interaction where a given group, formally (court,
government, and so on) or informally (friends or family, for example), comes together in order to reach a decision. Although this process is not usually smooth,
the difficulties that often precede a consensus have been solved, and the decision
is presented as mutually agreed upon with equal input and support by each member, so that the decision can be presented as being endorsed by the whole group.
Individual predicates profile different aspects of this decision-making process.
Expectedly, the most frequently attested is the most generically recapitulative of
the global process, namely *décider* 'decide'. This predicate alone is responsible for
fifty examples, or over 29.75 percent of the total instances. The other predicates
in the construction profile the different possible nuances or stages of a complex
deliberation. The most obvious of these stages are grouped into the closely related
verb classes illustrated in (5.90)–(5.92), where a representative example follows
the relevant group of predicates. The number of tokens for each class is indicated
in bold numbers; the number of tokens for each predicate follows that predicate
in parentheses:

(5.90)   **Description of the deliberative aspect of the process (twenty-four):** *parler*
         (three), *tenir compte* 'take into account' (three), *discuter* 'discuss' (one), *pré-*
         ciser 'precise' (two), *proclamer* 'proclaim' (two), *dire* 'say' (nine), *exprimer*
         'express' (one), *announcer* 'announce' (one), *notifier* 'notify' (one), *rappeler*
         remind' (one).

(5.90′) *Ils sont revenus sur leur menace de boycottage afin de faire valoir leurs arguments lors de cette réunion, où **il sera discuté** <u>de la procédure que devront suivre les députés lors de leurs futurs travaux</u>...* (AFP)

'They came back on their boycott threat in order to present their arguments during this meeting where the procedure that representatives will have to follow during their future tasks will be discussed [it will be discussed of the procedure that representatives will have to follow during their tasks]...'

(5.91) **Description of the overall result of the deliberative process (ninety-one):** *décider* 'decide' (fifty), *convenir* 'agree' (thirteen), *entendre* 'agree' (nine), *prouver* 'prove' (seven), *établir* 'establish' (six), *juger* 'judge' (two), *conclure* 'conclude' (two), *déterminer* 'determine' (one), *démontrer* 'demonstrate' (one), *reconnaître* 'recognize' (one).

(5.91′) *Il avait été entendu <u>que cette année enfin je passerais trois semaines avec Zaza au pays basque</u> et j'avais hâte d'être près d'elle.*
(Beauvoir, S. de. *Mémoires d'une jeune fille rangée*: 248)
'It had finally been agreed that this year I would spend three weeks with Zaza in the Basque country, and I was looking forward to being with her'.

(5.92) **Description of the outcome of the deliberation (thirteen):** *conseiller* 'advise' (one), *permettre* 'allow' (one), *promettre* 'promise' (two), *proposer* 'propose' (two), *recommander* 'recommend' (one), *demander* 'demand' (six), *reprocher* 'reproach' (one).

(5.92′) *Il a été demandé aux services du gouvernement <u>de préparer des listes de projets susceptibles d'être financés sur fonds privés</u>, qui seront publiées prochainement.* (AFP)

'Government services were asked [it was demanded of the government services] to prepare lists of projects susceptible to be financed by private funds, which will be published soon'.

Note that this list is largely independent from the structure of the predicate since it straightforwardly includes several transitive and unergative predicates such as *parler* 'speak' (see example [5.82]), *convenir* 'agree', *discuter* 'discuss', *dire* 'say', *promettre* 'promise', *exprimer* 'express', and *prouver* 'prove'. Furthermore, two additional transitive predicates, namely *faire* 'do' and *lancer* 'throw', can also be added to the list since in the context of the corpus the expressions *faire des objections* 'make objections' (two instances) and *lancer des nouvelles* 'throw news' also pertain to the model of communication and decision making the above-mentioned predicates profile a part of.

Note that as it stands at this point the analysis does not provide a convincing account of the examples presented in (5.83) and (5.84) repeated here, as well as other predicates illustrated in (5.93):

(5.83) *Le modèle* <u>*dont*</u> ***il a été fait usage*** *reste ouvert…*

(Perroux, F. *L'économie du XXe siècle*: 208)

'The model that has been used [there has been made use of] remains open…'

(5.84) *Quant aux embryons surnuméraires,* ***il sera mis fin*** <u>*à la conservation de ceux qui*</u>
<u>*ont été congelés depuis 5 ans à la date de promulgation de la loi.*</u>   (AFP)

'As to the leftover embryos, those that had been frozen for five years at the time the law passes will not be preserved [it will be put an end to those that had been frozen for five years at the time the law passed]'.

(5.93) ***Il a été procédé*** <u>*à un large tour d'horizon*</u> *des différents aspects du Mondial-98…*

(AFP)

A broad overview of the different aspects of the '98 World Cup was performed [there was performed a broad overview of the different aspects of the '98 World Cup]…'

Here again, however, these predicates present a consistent semantic class where each individual member profiles a specific aspect of a commonly managed action or project. Specific predicates include *faire usage* 'make use of' (1), *procéder* 'procede' (6), *mettre fin* 'put an end to' (4), *prévoir* 'plan' (1), *constituer* 'constitute' (1), *recourir* 'resolve' (1), *pourvoir* provide' (1). Given (1) the consistency of this semantic grouping, and (2) its close connection to the model of decision making presented above, it seems reasonable to suggest an extension to this model so that it also includes a collectively managed project or initiative in addition to a collectively made decision. Note that in certain cases the line between decision and action is impossible to draw, as illustrated in (5.94):

(5.94) *Ce groupe comprendra également le délégué technique Formule Un de la FIA,*
Charly Whinting, le délégué Sécurité de la FIA, Roland Bruynseraede, ainsi que
l'ingénieur Harvey Postlethwaite et le pilote autrichien Gerhard Berger. ***Il sera***
fait d'autre part appel <u>*à des experts extérieurs.*</u>   (AFP)

'This group will also include the FIA technical representative for F1 Charly Whinting, the safety officer for FIA, Roland Bruynseraede, as well as the engineer Harvey Postlethwaite and the Austrian pilot Gerhard Berger. Outside specialists will also be called [there will also be called outside specialists]'.

In (5.95) the predicate *faire appel* 'call' (three instances in the corpus) can be viewed as profiling either a decision or an action. There is no particular need to decide between the two possibilities, but these intermediate cases provide an argument in favor of an analysis in which collectively made decisions and collectively managed projects are treated together.

With this updated model only the two examples presented in (5.80) and (5.81) repeated here remain to importantly remind us that profiling is a matter of construal, and that a conceptualizer's decision to present her conceptualization in a particular fashion remains her prerogative. In Chapter 9, the issue of the selection of a particular construction when several are possible, such as the impersonal passive and the passive constructions respectively attested in different parts of the example in (5.80) and both indicated in bold print, will be considered specifically.

(5.80)   *Parmi les français qui ont, par le meurtre ou par la délation, causé la mort de combattants de la résistance, **il** en **aura été tué**, sans procès régulier, 10842, dont 6675 pendant les combats des maquis avant la libération, le reste après, au cours de représailles. D'autre part, **779 auront été exécutés** en vertu de jugements normalement rendus par les cours de justice et les tribunaux militaires.*
(Gaulle, C. de. *Mémoires de guerre, le salut*: 38)
'Among the French people who, by murder or denunciation, caused the death of resistance fighters, 10,842, were killed without trial [there will have been killed, without trial 10,842], including 6,675 in fights before the liberation, the rest afterward, during reprisals. Besides, 779 will have been executed following the decision of juries or military tribunals'.

(5.81)   **Il a été gagné**, *dans cet ouvrage, un temps précieux, un espace précieux, qui sans cela eussent été perdus, par l'omission systématique, après le verbe dire, du pléthorique pronom réfléchi.*   (Beckett, S. *Watt*: 8)
'Precious time and space that would otherwise have been lost were saved in this book [there was saved in this work precious time and precious space, which otherwise would have been lost], by the systematic omission, following the verb dire, of the plethoric reflexive pronoun'.

For now, I merely point out that although the two predicates in (5.80) and (5.81) are indeed transitive they occur in rather low transitive environments (Hopper and Thompson 1980). This is especially true in (5.80). First, the patient of the predicate is presented separately, as in the sentence topic introduced by *parmi* 'among'. In the clause under examination it occurs as the pronominalized form *en* 'of'. Furthermore, the killing event does not stand for a well-delineated act between clearly outlined agents and patients, but for the higher-level reification of several thousand acts under the same category. This higher-level construal removes some of the inherent salience of the participants and allows the field, i.e. circumstances in general, to be construed as the focal figure in the profiled relation.

The data examined in this section show that impersonal passives in French are overwhelmingly used to code a complex social situation involving a collectively taken decision or a collectively managed project. Each component part of the construction serves a particular purpose. *Il* profiles the field, which in this case can be equated with the set of circumstances that yields the outcome of the negotiation or action. The predicate profiles the relevant facet of the complex social event, as the different semantic categories presented in (5.90)–(5.92) illustrate. Finally, the postverbal event, most often coded by the infinitival or the finite complement, profiles the result of the deliberation or action. The discursive consequence of the selection of the construction is that the origin of the decision or action is not directly available. It is diffuse and subsumed into the overall circumstances that the impersonal pronoun profiles. It is interesting to briefly examine why passive impersonals can represent a good choice for coding this kind of event. We can first note that the kind of event most likely to be coded in the impersonal passive does not give much prominence to participants. The agent, as we saw, is diffuse and mostly represents a collective entity. The other participant in the profiled relation is often not a participant per se but an event or a proposition. The conceptualizer's choice of designating the field as the focal figure of the profiled relation can thus be explained by the lack of obvious other candidates. It does not, however, explain why this strategy may be favored as opposed to other strategies that also minimize the emphasis placed on participants, but this will be left for further research.

The data presented in this section also make it clear that, in a way similar as was presented for active impersonals, the structure of the predicates does not represent the most important factor in their distribution in impersonal passives. Despite the structural possibility of coding any transitive situation with an impersonal passive, transitive predicates tend to not be used in this construction unless the conceptualizer can imagine a scenario in which the inherent salience of the participants can naturally be overlooked. In this case, their interaction can be presented as a part of the scene in which it occurs.

7.   Recapitulation and conclusion

This chapter showed that once the specificity of verbal complements is considered, complex impersonals are also presentational constructions that pertain to the existence of events and the epistemic evaluation of propositions. The distribution of infinitive, subjunctive, and indicative complements reflects the semantic overlap between the individual predicates and the inflections themselves. The effective character of deontic predicates makes them incompatible with an indicative clause because they do not provide any assessment of the event in the complement with respect to reality. Their infinitive or subjunctive complements reflect that incompatibility. As factive predicates (Kiparsky and Kiparsky 1970; Karttunnen 1971), evaluatives are potentially compatible with indicative complements, but we tend to react to events, not propositions, and consequently these predicates follow the effective pattern characteristic of deontics. Epistemic predicates are compatible with an indicative clause because they profile the inclination and result phases of the epistemic control cycle, and thus profile the acceptance of the proposition in the complement in reality. Finally, the occurrence predicates demonstrated a much higher level of idiosyncrasy in their distribution. Some, such as *se faire* 'happens', follow the epistemic pattern in describing a facet of reality and thus taking indicative complements, while others like *arriver* 'arrive' follow the deontic pattern, their infinitival or subjunctive complements reflecting their construal of events that happen regularly.

Although simple and complex impersonals were shown to fulfill similar semantic functions, the relationship between the individual predicates and the postverbal expression is quite different in both instances. In Chapter 4 simple predicates were shown to impose few constraints on the entity that follows the predicate, but form some low-level semi-preassembled chunks that specialize in profiling specific situations. Even though the complex predicates impose stricter constraints on the form of the complement clause they are not completely regular, and some idiosyncrasies observed in the meaning of specific constructions serve to remind us that usage remains a key contributor to grammatical form.

CHAPTER 6

Demonstrative impersonals

This chapter shows that in the context of the copular complement construction [*c' + être* + ADJECTIVE + COMPLEMENT CLAUSE], the demonstrative *ça/ce* functions as an impersonal pronoun. While *il* profiles the field, *ça* profiles the abstract setting, namely the section of current discourse from which the postverbal expression is extracted for expressive purposes. The semantic characteristics of impersonal *ça* are directly inherited from the pronoun's other uses. The distribution of *il* and *ça* impersonals reflects both pronouns' semantic proximity.

1. Introduction: *Il* and *ça* impersonals

We are now in a position to consider more specifically the claim made in Chapter 1 that demonstrative *ça* should be considered impersonal in the contexts illustrated in (6.1) and (6.2):

(6.1) *Pour la première fois je sentais qu'***il était possible*** que ma mère vécût sans moi*
           (Proust, M. *A l'ombre des jeunes filles en fleurs*: 648)
           'For the first time I felt it was possible for my mother to live without me'

(6.2) *bien sûr que la journée ne se passera pas sans pluie. **Ce n'était pas possible** que ça reste comme ça, il faisait trop chaud*
           (Proust, M. *Du côté de chez Swann*: 101)
           'Of course the day will not finish without rain. It [this] was not possible that it [this] would stay that way, it was too hot'

Recall from Chapter 1 that in order to consider *il* in (6.1) and *ça* in (6.2) as structurally similar, and hence part of the same impersonal category, we need to show that (1) *il* is not a meaningless placeholder, and (2) *ça* does not straightforwardly refer forward to the postverbal expression. With respect to (1), the first five chapters of this monograph have shown that *il* is meaningful because it profiles the conceptualizer's scope of awareness that allows the entity in the postverbal expression (thing, event, or proposition) to be identified. This chapter addresses the second part of the argument, namely the claim that *ça* does not directly refer forward to the upcoming entity. The basic idea, developed throughout the following sections, is that the demonstrative profiles the abstract setting (see Chapters 1 and 2), or in other words the immediate context from which the postverbal expression is extracted for rhetorical reasons. *Il* and *ça* are thus very close in meaning, the difference between the two essentially pertaining to the salience of the conceptualizer's role in the construal of the entity coded in the postverbal expression. The distribution of the two structures reflects this semantic proximity.

This chapter is organized in the following manner: Section 2 presents a brief overview of the scope of demonstrative usage. Section 3 examines the pronouns' meaning properties and shows that demonstrative impersonals exhibit characteristics similar to those the pronouns exhibit in other constructions. Section 4 analyzes the conditions under which demonstratives meet the impersonal criteria. Section 5 is concerned with the distribution of *il* and *ça* impersonals. Section 6 summarizes the results and concludes the chapter.

2. Semantic function of demonstratives: Identification, categorization, and evaluation

French possesses a series of neuter demonstratives that refer to an often ill-defined idea or previous section of discourse. These forms include *ceci, cela, ça, ce, c'*, which can all be translated in English as 'this/that'. For the purposes of this chapter, *ce, c', ça*, and *cela* will be considered together because of their close diachronic relation. *Cela* is a compound form of *ce* (Guénette 1996), and *ça* is a reduced form of *cela* (Brunot 1936; Wilmet 1997). Furthermore, all four forms are attested in the constructions under investigation even though their distribution is quite specific. *Ce*, (along with *ça* and *cela*) only occurs preceding a consonant initial form of the *être* 'be' copula (*ce/ça/cela serait bien de les revoir* 'it would be nice to see them again'). By contrast, *c'* alone is possible with a vowel initial form of the copula (*c'/*ça/*ce/*cela est bien de les revoir* 'it is nice to see them again'). With all other verbs, *ça* and *cela* are often claimed to indicate register differences, *ça* being more colloquial. It therefore seems clear that if the four demonstratives cannot be said to be semantically equivalent in the constructions considered in this chapter, they nonetheless exhibit a common semantic core that justifies their being treated together. Because the investigation of the more fine-grained distinctions would necessarily include the examination of sociolinguistic considerations that lie well beyond the scope of this chapter, the matter will be left for further research.[1]

---

1. For an analysis that distinguishes *ce* and *ça* see Moignet (1974). For an overview of the French demonstrative system see Guénette (1996).

Ça's primary function is to identify, categorize, or evaluate an entity. When used alone as a nominal and generally accompanied with a gesture, the pronoun profiles a precategorized mass, as illustrated in the manufactured example in (6.3):

(6.3) #*Je voudrais ça s'il vous plait*
'I would like this please'

In (6.3) the referent of the pronoun is indicated by visually pointing to it. It is not lexically categorized as a specific type. In the identification copular construction *ça*, most frequently under the *c'* form, identifies a previously uncategorized entity as a member of a specific type, as illustrated in (6.4) where the entity responsible for the event profiled in the following clause is identified:

(6.4) *Nous avons reçu les résultats de l'autopsie de Senna qui nous permettent main-tenant de dire que c'est **une pièce de suspension** qui a percé son casque et occa-sionné la blessure mortelle, a déclaré Max Mosley.*   (AFP)
'We have received the results of Senna's autopsy, which now allow us to say that it [this] is a piece of the suspension system that went through his helmet and caused the mortal wound, Max Mosley declared'.

In other instances the demonstrative identifies a specific time or place as in (6.5), confirms the type of an entity as in (6.6), or corrects it if necessary as in (6.7):

(6.5) #*C'est l'automne/l'hiver/l'heure/l'endroit que je cherchais*
'It [this] is fall/winter/time/the place I was looking for'

(6.6) *Chose ahurissante: le fauteuil voisin de la dame est occupé par un ours. Celui-ci s'absente quelques instants, à l' entr'acte. Le spectateur en profite: "Excusez-moi, dois-je croire mes yeux? **C'est un ours** qui vous accompagne? "*
(Gide, A. *Ainsi soit-il*: 1188)
'Incredible thing: the seat next to the lady is occupied by a bear. During the intermission, the latter steps outside for a moment. The spectator takes advan-tage: "Excuse me, can I believe my eyes? It [this] is a bear with you?"'

(6.7) *je ne sais ce que ça donnera: j'ai résolu d'écrire au hasard. Entreprise difficile: la plume (**c'est un stylo**) reste en retard sur la pensée.* (Gide, A. *Ainsi soit-il*: 1163)
'I do not know how it will come out: I decided to write at random. A difficult task: the quill (it [this] is a pen) is slower than the mind'.

The act of categorization is not restricted to the mere identification of a basic type. The examples in (6.8) and (6.9) present entities whose initial categorization, although easily accessible, is deemed insufficient, and whose further identification as members of more specific subcategories is required, thus justifying the use of the indefinite article.

(6.8)   *il serra les doigts à se les broyer et tournant les yeux de l'autre côté, il vit un*
        grand livre ouvert sur la table, près de la pile de vêtements. C'était un volume
        de l'encyclopédie britannique qu'on avait consulté et laissé là.
                                                    (Green, J. *Moira: roman*: 238)
        'he squeezed his fingers together hard enough to break them, and, looking the
        other way, he saw a big book open on the table, next to the pile of clothes. It
        [this] was a volume of Encyclopedia Britannica someone had opened and left
        there'.

(6.9)   *Son pas résonna dans l'antichambre, puis sur la véranda dont la porte grillagée*
        se referma derrière lui avec le bruit sec d'une arme à feu. Simon répondit alors
        à la question que Joseph se retenait de poser: c'est un garçon de la Caroline du
        sud. Je crois qu'il s'appelle Bruce Praileau et c'est sa deuxième année ici.
                                                    (Green, J. *Moira roman*: 12)
        'His steps echoed down the antechamber, then through the veranda, whose
        metallic door slammed shut behind him like a gunshot. Simon then answered
        the question that Joseph refrained from asking: he [this] is a boy from South
        Carolina. I think his name is Bruce Praileau and he is in his second year here'.

The reference in the examples in (6.9) is indefinite, thereby showing that the nominal that follows the copula is not presented as a specific instance of its type, but
as a member of a finer-grained type (Langacker 2008: 268). In contrast, a specific
instance of a given type can also be identified, as illustrated in (6.10) and (6.11)
where the reference is definite:

(6.10) *Papillon! Il est vivant! C'est lui! C'est mon chien!*   (Ayme, M. *Clérambard*: 41)
        'Papillon! He is alive! It [this] is him. It [this] is my dog!'

(6.11) *À propos de Mark Rutherford, il me dit que c'est Bennett qui lui a fait lire ce*
        livre admirable et parfaitement inconnu en France.
                                            (Green, J. *Journal T. 5. 1946–1950*: 39)
        'About Mark Rutherford, he tells me that it [this] is Bennett who got him to
        read this admirable book no one knows in France'.

Finally, the demonstrative specifies the relation of similarity that exists between
two entities, as illustrated in (6.12) and (6.13):

(6.12) *On m'appelle La Langouste parce que j'ai des taches de rousseur sur le ventre.*
        Mon nom, c'est Léonie Vincent.   (Aymé, M. *Clerambard*: 46)
        'They call me the lobster because I have freckles on my belly. My name [this]
        is Léonie Vincent'.

(6.13) *Oublié de dire qu'au déjeuner de l'autre jour, Mme X. à qui je parlais de la chanson*
        tartare entendue à la radio m'a dit que c'était la chanson préférée de Staline!
                                            (Green, J. *Journal T. 5. 1946–1950*: 149)

'Forgot to mention that at lunch the other day, Mrs. X with whom I was discussing the Tartar song I heard on the radio, told me that it [this] was Stalin's favorite song!'

Even though the categories discussed in this section are presented separately for expository purposes, they are often difficult to keep apart. For example, because we routinely use people's behaviors to categorize them into specific groups, identification often leads to further categorization, as in (6.14)–(6.16):

(6.14) *Vous ne pouvez pas être la maîtresse de cet homme! … Il se moque de vous; c'est* **un coureur.**   (Anouilh, J. *La répétition ou l'amour puni*: 60)
'You cannot be this man's mistress! … He is making a fool out of you; he [this] is a womanizer'.

(6.15) *J'ai dévoré son ouvrage presque en entier, l'autre soir, pris d'un regain d'affection pour le vieux bonhomme à qui je dois d'avoir appris beaucoup de choses avec plaisir et facilité.* **C'était un professeur de génie…**
               (Green, J. *Journal T. 5. 1946–1950*: 302)
'I devoured his book almost in its entirety the other night, as I had a surge of affection for the old man who made learning many things easy and fun for me. He [this] was a fantastic teacher…'

(6.16) *Vous ne connaissiez pas ma tante.* **C'était une femme étonnante,** *incapable d'aucune sorte de remords…*   (Anouilh, J. *La répétition ou l'amour puni*: 18)
'You didn't know my aunt. She [this] was a surprising woman, incapable of the slightest kind of remorse…'

The description of the aunt's character in (6.16) is accomplished by an act of categorization that establishes her as an instance of the subcategory of women *femmes étonnantes* 'surprising women'. An alternative strategy is available where a predicative adjective evaluates the character (*elle est étonnante* 'she is surprising'), but in this case, the demonstrative would be impossible (**c'est étonnante*). Interestingly, these two strategies are in competition in most descriptions, as illustrated in (6.17) where *il était petit et blond* 'he was short and blond' represents a possible alternative:

(6.17) *L'image qu'on se forme de ce saint est à peu près celle que nous a laissée Zurbaran: un personnage blême, émacié, aux yeux de braise, aux cheveux d'un noir d'encre. En réalité,* **c'était un petit homme blond.**
               (Green, J. *Journal T. 5. 1946–1950*: 95)
'The image one has of this saint is approximately the one that Zurbaran left us: a pale gaunt character, with fiery eyes and jet black hair. In fact, he [this] was a short blond man'.

Facts, thoughts, beliefs, and opinions can also be categorized as illustrated in (6.18)–(6.20):

(6.18) *Parle du curé de Saint-Nicolas. Le dimanche, il gueule, **c'est son métier**.*
                                                   (Green, J. *Journal T. 5. 1946–1950*: 253)
       'Talk about the Saint-Nicholas priest. On Sunday, he screams. It [this] is his job'.

(6.19) *C'est paresse que de trop étudier, dit Bacon.*
                                                   (Green, J. *Journal T. 5. 1946–1950*: 313)
       'It's [this is] laziness when one studies too much, Bacon said'.

(6.20) *Résumer, c'est dénaturer, c'est trahir.* (Green, J. *Journal T. 5. 1946–1950*: 234)
       'To summarize, [this] is to misrepresent, [this is] to betray'.

The examples in (6.18)–(6.20) categorize (or recategorize) events. In (6.18) the priest's screaming is analyzed as part of the category *métier* 'job'. Similarly, in (6.19) and (6.20) some actions are categorized as part of wider categories, or simply other categories. These events are not always coded by nouns but the entities that represent them can be construed as reified regions that are recognized as elements of the category that follows the demonstrative. For example, in (6.20) any instance of summarizing is categorized as an instance of betrayal.

Finally, any object, event, thought, or belief can be evaluated, as illustrated in (6.21)–(6.29), even if it is not explicitly specified as in (6.24):

(6.21) #*C'est difficile/grand/petit/ombragé*
       'It [this] is hard/big/small/shaded'

(6.22) *Eh bien, j'ai préparé ça à tout hasard; sans doute que tu ne refuseras pas de signer. **Ça serait trop méchant** de ta part.* (Claudel, P. *La J. F. Violaine 2. Version*: 608)
       'Well, I prepared this just in case; you will certainly not refuse to sign. It [this] would be too mean on your part'.

(6.23) *ne me regarde pas ainsi. **Ça m'intimide**.*   (Bataille, H. *Maman Colibri*: 11)
       'do not look at me like this. It [this] intimidates me'.

(6.24) *en voulez- vous encore des cerises? Prenez- les. **Ça me ferait honneur**!*
                                       (Adam, P. *L'Enfant d'Austerlitz*: 317)
       'Do you want any more cherries? Take them. It [this] would honor me'.

(6.25) *Cette question parut embarrasser Joseph, l'éclair d'une seconde. Mais il se remit vite … – je ne sais pas, moi, madame, dit- il, du ton le plus naturel … mais, c'est vrai … les chiens n'ont pas aboyé. Ah! Ça, **c'est curieux**, par exemple!*
                                 (Mirbeau, O. *Journal d'une femme de chambre*: 367)
       'This question seemed to embarrass Joseph for a second. But he quickly recovered … – I don't know, madam, he said in his most natural tone … but, it's true … the dogs didn't bark. Oh! Yes, it's [this is] truly curious!'

(6.26)   *On me regarde beaucoup, **ça ne me déplaît pas.***
                                        (Colette, G. *Claudine à l'école*: 301)
         'A lot of people are looking at me, it is not unpleasant [this doesn't displease me]'.

(6.27)   *Au début, de les voir mourir, **ça me gênait.***
                                    (Barres, M. *Mes cahiers T. 3 1902–1904*: 196)
         'In the beginning, to see them die, it [this] was bothering me'.

(6.28)   *Vraiment, ma pauvre fille, tu es trop simple et lâche, **ça dégoûte** et **ça met en***
         colère, *comme les gens malades!*   (Claudel, P. *La J. F. Violaine 2. Version*: 608)
         'Really, my poor child, you are so simple and cowardly, it [this] is disgusting
         and it [this] makes one mad, like sick people!'

(6.29)   *vous êtes mon parrain, **c'est vrai**. Et vous avez été très bon de vous occuper de*
         moi, mais je ne voulais rien vous devoir.
                                    (Anouilh, J. *La répétition ou l'amour puni*: 57)
         'You are my godfather, that's true. And you were very kind to look after me,
         but I didn't want to owe you anything'.

The examples in (6.21)–(6.29) are very eclectic, but in each case the demonstrative
picks out one entity for the purposes of identifying it, categorizing it, or evaluating
it. However, the very nature of that entity is not always straightforward, and the
next section investigates how exactly *ça* serves its referring function.

3.   Semantic properties of demonstratives

The following quote by Grevisse (1986: 1054, my translation) clearly represents the
consensus French grammarians share in their analysis of demonstratives:

> *Les pronoms démonstratifs désignent un être ou une chose en les situant dans l'es-*
> *pace, éventuellement avec un geste à l'appui (fonction* déictique). *Ils peuvent aussi*
> *renvoyer à un terme qui précède (fonction* anaphorique) *ou qui suit (fonction* cata-
> phorique) *dans le contexte.*

> 'Demonstrative pronouns designate a person or a thing by situating them in space,
> sometimes with an accompanying gesture (*deictic* function). They can also refer to
> a preceding term (*anaphoric* function) or a following term (*cataphoric* function)
> in the context'.

This position may roughly characterize demonstratives in general, but it is incomplete to describe the meaning of *ça* because it fails to mention three additional characteristics that make the pronoun unique in French grammar. The first concerns
the highly flexible nature of the entity to which *ça* refers (henceforth the referred
entity); the second the inherently subjective construal (Langacker 1985, 1990)
the pronoun imposes on its referent; and the third pertains to the impossibility

of clearly distinguishing between the pronoun's anaphoric and cataphoric senses. The description of these characteristics reveals that *ça*'s impersonal usage is deeply rooted in the pronoun's meaning in unambiguously anaphoric contexts.

3.1   *Ça* and flexible reference

It is well documented in the literature (Cadiot 1988; Corblin 1995; Carlier 1996; Achard 2001, among others) that a strictly referential analysis of *ça* is untenable because (1) the pronoun behaves differently from true anaphors syntactically, and (2) the entity to which it refers is often difficult to delineate with precision.

With respect to (1), *ça* differs from true anaphors in that its agreement with the following predicate is always third-person singular and thus independent from the number and gender specifications of its antecedent. This "décalage référentiel" 'referential shift' (Cadiot 1988) distinguishes true anaphors such as the personal pronouns in (6.30a) and (6.31a) from their demonstrative counterparts in (6.30b) and (6.31b). The example in (6.30b) is adapted from Carlier (1996):

(6.30)   a.   #*Les gosses, <u>ils</u> se lèvent tôt le matin*
             'The kids, they get up early in the morning'
         b.   *Les gosses, <u>ça</u> se lève tôt le matin*
             'Kids, they [that] get[s] up early in the morning'

(6.31)   a.   #*Les Français, <u>ils</u> se plaignent tout le temps*
             'The French, they are always complaining'
         b.   #*Les Français, <u>ça</u> se plaint tout le temps*
             'French people, they [that] are [is] always complaining'

In (6.30a) and (6.31a) the personal pronoun *ils* 'they' is strictly anaphoric of its referent because the agreement on the verb matches up with the latter's gender and number. Furthermore, the preferred reading of the utterance is specific, i.e. the predication is made of a particular referent. In (6.30b) and (6.31b), by contrast, the singular subject/verb agreement does not match the referent's number, and the reading of the utterance is necessarily generic, as shown in (6.32) by the restrictions that exist on the determiner allowed in the NP that denotes *ça*'s referent (Carlier 1996).

(6.32)   a.   *Le/mon/les gosses du voisin, ils se lèvent tôt le matin*
             'The/my/the neighbor's kids, they get up early in the morning'
         b.   **Le/mon/les gosses du voisin, ça se lève tôt le matin*
             'The/my/the neighbor's kids, that gets up early in the morning'

With respect to (2), in a large number of instances the pronoun's referent is not immediately identifiable, as illustrated in (6.33) from Achard (2001) where no specific nominal is available in the current discourse to serve as the pronoun's referent:

(6.33)   *J'avais gardé de bons copains du temps de l'Opéra, dont un qui était passé chez*
Cuevas. Il m'a attrappé dans un bar de la rive gauche et m'a conseillé la mode,
m'a envoyé présenter mes dessins. A l'époque, je m'habillais beaucoup, j'étais
presque un personnage avec des avions, des nuages d'or et d'argent découpés sur
le dos de mes blousons. Je ne savais rien, j'ai préparé un dossier, ça a marché.
J'ai appris comme ça, et je n'ai pas arrêté.
'I had kept good friends from the Opéra days, including one who had gone
to Cuevas. He caught me in a bar on the left bank, and advised me to go into
fashion, and told me to show my drawings to people. At the time, I dressed
up a lot, I was almost a character with planes, gold and silver clouds cut outs
on the back of my jackets. I didn't know anything, I prepared a portfolio, it
[this] worked out. I learned like that, and I never stopped'.

In order to account for those referential shifts, I have suggested in previous work
(Achard 2001) that *ça* provides the hearer with the instructions to create a specific
region within the space provided by the immediate discourse. To put it differently,
within the space of the context of the utterance, *ça*'s presence instructs the hearer
to construe a group of entities as interconnected (Langacker 1987b, 1991). The
entities to be considered together are not always made specific, and the pronoun's
presence often requires the hearer to actively manipulate the current discourse in
order to achieve the appropriate construal. In that view, *ça*'s presence enables the
speaker and hearer to interactively sequence and group certain elements of the text
for communicative purposes.

In some cases the elements that constitute the region that the pronoun refers
to are directly available from the immediate discourse. In (6.34), for example,
the context enumerates the qualities top tennis players have shared throughout
history. The pronoun's "loose" referents, namely Nadal and Federer, anchor the
region composed of the abilities they possess along with figures from the past,
such as Sampras or Becker. To put it differently, *c'* refers to the characteristics of
Nadal's and Federer's games that allow them to dominate tennis, which their name
metonymically represents:

(6.34)   *On a l'impression qu'il arrive à se transcender dans l'adversité. Cela m'a toujours*
frappé quand je jouais contre des Sampras ou des Becker. Je sentais que plus
cela devenait difficile, non seulement ils ne rataient pas, mais ils franchissaient
un cran supplémentaire. Dans son match, Jo va chercher les points dans les
moments difficiles, encore plus que d'habitude. C'est ce que font tous les meilleurs
joueurs. Ils sont capables d'élever leur niveau de jeu tout en gardant une marge
de sécurité. Sur différents gros matches que je l'ai vu faire, Jo possède aujourd'hui
cette capacité. Nadal et Federer, c'est encore au-dessus. Mais Jo s'en rapproche.
(Interview Guy Forget. *L'équipe online* March 7, 2009) http://www.lequipe.fr/
Tennis/breves2009/20090307_002345_forget-dans-les-temps.html

'One has the impression that he manages to get better when things get tougher. This always struck me when I played against players such as Sampras or Becker. I had the feeling that the harder things got, not only didn't they miss anything, but they raised their game another notch. In his match, Jo goes after points even more than usual when times get tough. This is what all best players do. They can raise the level of their game while playing safe. Judging from the high-level matches I have seen him play, Jo is capable of doing that today. Nadal, Federer, it [this] is still better. But Jo is getting closer'.

In other instances the connected entities are not made specific because the speaker knows they are easy to recover. In (6.35) from Achard (2001), the proper name *Matignon* refers to the French prime minister's residence, and thus to a position that the politician discussed in the example is seeking. This function importantly includes considerations of money, power, prestige, and influence that the newspaper's French audience is well acquainted with. Although these elements are not explicitly mentioned, they nonetheless constitute the set of entities that the term *Matignon* metonymically stands for and that the pronoun *ça* refers to:[2]

(6.35)   *Tenez, sans aller si loin, il était pas bien mon Jacquot à l'Hotel de Ville? Non, **Matignon**, ça la foutait mieux, c'était plus classe question adresse.*
'There we go, no need to look further. City Hall wasn't good enough for Jacky baby? No, Matignon, that sounded better, that was an address with some class'.

Instead of a person, the abstract region that *ça* evokes can be composed of the circumstances that surround a specific incident, as in (6.36):

(6.36)   *Et puis, un soir de janvier 1989, le téléphone a sonné. C'est Daniel qui a décroché, là-bas près du canapé rose. "Manuela, quoi Manuela? – Elle vivait avec un jeune homme. Ça s'est mal passé entre eux. Il l'a tuée. Venez vite. On vous attend".*
'And then, one evening in January 1989, the telephone rang. Daniel picked up over there by the pink sofa. "Manuela, what about her? – She was living with a young man. It went sour between them. He killed her. Come quickly. We are waiting for you"'.

In (6.36) *ça* evokes the subpart of reality that encompasses the common life of Manuela and her boyfriend. Its contents are available to the hearer as part of her world knowledge of what the life of a young couple might entail. *Ça* instructs the hearer to connect the different facets of what she knows about life as a couple to create a nominal construal of the young lovers' experience. The ensuing event or proposition can then be predicated of that created nominal.

---

2.   All examples in the remainder of this section as well as Section 3.2 are from Achard (2001).

Finally, the scope of the region that *ça* evokes can be wide enough to incorporate all the elements relevant to current reality being what it is, as shown in (6.37):[3]

(6.37) *Une femme est debout dans l'entrée, blonde, les cheveux sur les épaules. Une apparition. "Tu me reconnais?", demande-t-elle. "Oui", répond Suzy. "Mais comment ça se fait que t'es là?"*
'A woman is standing in the hallway, blond, shoulder length hair. An apparition. "Do you recognize me?" she asks. "Yes", Suzy answers. "But how come you are here [how this makes itself that you are here]?"'

The creation of the abstract region to which the pronoun refers often requires the extensive cognitive manipulation (summarizing, abstracting, or inferencing) of information already available in the context or in the hearer's world knowledge, as shown in (6.38) where the pronoun's presence instructs the hearer to summarize the information at her disposal:

(6.38) *Les affaires de Manuela? Elles étaient sous scellés, intouchables. Les seules parcelles de réalité, les seules preuves symboliques de la mort de Manuela, Maité Gourjault les a puisées alors dans ces rares images: un policier dans un souterrain, un avocat à qui elle donne un chèque, deux rendez-vous chez le juge d'instruction, l'incinération d'une caisse de bois anonyme et quelques papiers qu'elle a pu feuilleter. Et puis il y eut les lettres du jeune homme écrites depuis sa prison, "Bonjour Maité, dis moi comment tu vois tout ça vu de l'extérieur. Pour ma part, tout reste inexplicable."*
'Manuela's stuff? It was sealed, out of reach. The only fragments of reality, the only symbolic proofs of Manuela's death, Maité Gourjault dug them out of these rare images: a policeman in a tunnel, a lawyer whom she gave a check to, two appointments with the judge, the incineration of an anonymous wooden box, and a few pieces of papers she could flip through. And then there are the young man's letters from his jail cell. "Hello Maité, tell me how you see all this from the outside. For my part, everything remains inexplicable"'.

The example in (6.38) comes from the same article as the one in (6.36) where Maité's daughter Manuela was killed by her boyfriend. It is quite difficult to precisely identify the abstract region that *ça* evokes, but it clearly involves the summary of all the circumstances leading to and including the current situation. Because the circumstances of Manuela's death are obviously different for her murderer and her mother, the young man's use of *tout ça* 'all that' instructs the mother to summarize her views, beliefs, feelings, and opinions about the whole incident in order to gain insight.

---

3. The passage of time figures prominently among the aspects of reality that *ça*'s presence renders particularly salient, as the example in (i) shows:

(i) – *Mon Jules, quel Jules? Ça va faire deux ans qu'on est plus ensemble.*
'My fellow, what fellow? It will be two years we haven't been together'.

The presence of *ça* often involves other conceptual manipulations in addition to summarizing. Some of them are illustrated in (6.39):

(6.39) *Vous avez vu Radio Days, de Woody Allen, c'était exactement **cela**! Je ne peux pas dire mieux! Cette maison était la mienne, la femme qui ne se marie pas, c'était ma tante! **La rue qui donne sur la mer, les voisins, l'école, les parents, le football, le base-ball**, tout ça était ma vie!*
'You saw Radio Days by Woody Allen, it was exactly that! I can't say it any better! That house was mine, the woman who doesn't marry, it was my aunt! The street that overlooks the sea, the neighbors, the parents, football, baseball, all that was my life!'

In (6.39) the author is attempting to describe his childhood years in the United States. His communicative strategy is to compare it to the kind of life described in the movie Radio Days by Woody Allen. This is accomplished in the first sentence by a parallel structure that establishes the entity evoked by the first *c'* as similar to that of *cela*. The entity that *c'* evokes is the summary of the author's life. At this point it is fairly abstract to the hearer. The entity that *cela* evokes is the summary of the events and situations presented in the film. It is readily available to the hearer, assuming she has seen the movie. The predicate that links the two entities allows the hearer to make the referent of *c'* more concrete by filling it in with elements of the movie. The author later makes his point more specific by establishing similar correspondences between specific elements. The entity that the final *ça* evokes recapitulates and summarizes these elements.

Finally, in other cases the entity evoked by *ça* is only available by an inference created by the presence of specific elements in the immediate context, as illustrated in (6.40):

(6.40) *A Hambourg, mercredi dernier, la ville où les Beatles ont fait leurs classes, McCartney a quand même réussi à conjurer par moments ce malaise étrange. On ne pourra jamais s'empêcher d'être injuste avec McCartney, de lui reprocher de ne plus être ce qu'il a été. Et c'est vrai qu'il est un peu mesquin dans le choix des morceaux: pas une chanson ne porte la patte de John Lennon, ça n'aurait pourtant pas manqué d'élégance, mais c'est peut-être la qualité qui lui fait le plus défaut, comme en témoigne le goût douteux des rares effets scéniques.*
'In Hamburg, last Wednesday, the city where the Beatles played in their early days, McCartney managed at times to overcome this strange discomfort. One won't ever be able to stop being unfair to McCarney, to stop blaming him for no longer being what he once was. And it is true he was a little classless in his choice of pieces: not a single song with John Lennon's signature, even though it [this] would have shown some class, but class is perhaps the quality he lacks the most, as attested the questionable taste of the rare scenic effects attests'.

In (6.40) the pronoun's referent is not directly available in the immediate discourse. The entity that *ça* evokes is a nominal created by inference out of the preceding negative statement. It can roughly be characterized as *une chanson qui porte la patte de John Lennon* 'a song with John Lennon's signature'.[4]

---

4. The flexible organization of context that *ça* allows is a powerful narrative tool, and the previous relatively short examples barely touched on the possible intricacies that the repeated use of the pronoun can introduce in a text. The one presented in this footnote is much longer and will not be analyzed in detail. It will be left as an exercise for the reader to appreciate the difficulty of precisely delineating the region evoked by each occurrence of *ça*, as well as to evaluate the validity of the constructs proposed in this chapter to describe the pronoun's flexible usage.

    (i)   *C'est vraiment des minables, ces pauvres Amerloques. Ce qu'ils peuvent être cons, c'est pas croyable. Ils auraient comme une faille que ça m'étonnerait pas. Ils sont là, ils vaquent à leurs affaires de San-Diego à San-Francisco, le cul entre deux plaques qui risquent à chaque instant de se rentrer dedans en foutant tout en l'air. Et qu'est-ce qu'ils font? Rien. Ils se contentent de construire des gratte-ciel genre culbuto capables de tenir debout quand la terre tremble sous leurs pieds selon des normes parasismiques que leur envie le monde entier. Des nuls, je vous dis, parce que enfin c'est bête comme chou. Suffit de planter deux électrodes je ne sais plus où, pour capter je ne sais plus quoi, et dès que ça commence à s'agiter, à s'emmêler les pinceaux en sous-sol, ça déclenche un signal d'alarme. On vous sonne: Allez, dégagez, poussez-vous de là, il y a du hoquet dans l'air. Si jamais la Terre avait un renvoi, vous vous retrouveriez sous une giclée de gravats. D'où je tiens ça? Ben, tiens, d'Haroun Tazieff. Il nous l'a expliqué hier soir à la télé. Ça se pratique en Grèce, ce truc-là. Et lui, il va l'installer dans l'Isère, où il fait conseiller général. Question faille, c'est infaillible. Alors, qu'est-ce qu'ils attendent pour l'adopter ailleurs, son système D? Vous allez rigoler: ils sont tellement bêtes, tellement obtus, qu'ils refusent d'y croire! Ils prétendent que ça tient pas debout. Et ça, en cas de séisme, évidemment, c'est quand même embêtant.*

                                                        (AFP)

        'They are totally lame, these poor Americans. How stupid can they be, I can't believe it. They would have like a fault that wouldn't surprise me. They mind their own business from San Diego to San Francisco, their ass between two sheets that might collide with each other at any given time and destroy everything, And what do they do? Nothing. They are happy building skyscrapers on stilts capable of standing up when the earth trembles under their feet according to parasismic norms the whole world envies. Dummies, let me tell you, because there's nothing to it. You just have to plant two electrodes I don't remember where, to record I don't remember what, and as soon as it starts to get agitated, to get all mixed up in the basement, that gives out an alarm signal. They ring you: Let's go, move on, get away from here, the place has the hiccups. If the earth had a repeat, you would end up under a pile of rubbles. Where do I get that from? From Haroun Tazieff that's who. He explained it to us last night on TV. That is done is Greece that gadget. And he is going to install it in the Isère where he is a representative. To detect faults, that has no faults. So what are they waiting for to adopt it elsewhere his gismo? You are gonna laugh: they are so stupid, so close-minded that they refuse to believe in it. They pretend that that doesn't stand up. And that, in case of an earthquake, that is quite worrisome'.

3.2   A subjective construal of the referent

The second aspect of the meaning of *ça* that accounts for the pronoun's behavior as an impersonal is the subjective construal it imposes on the entity it evokes. The notion of subjectivity, used here in the sense of Langacker (1985, 1990), refers to the vantage point from which a linguistic expression is conceptualized as well as the viewing arrangement that exists between the conceptualizer and her conceptualization. The analysis of an expression's viewing organization crucially involves the investigation of the conceptual asymmetry in the construal relation between the conceptualizing subject and the object of conceptualization. Different configurations have been shown to have important linguistic correlates (Langacker 1985, 1990; Achard 1998). The subjective construal that *ça* imposes on the entity it evokes is illustrated in (6.41) and (6.42):

(6.41)   *Les Archaos ont investi le Cirque d'Hiver, et* **ça** *fait du vacarme. Ils se déguisent en punks désinvoltes, pratiquent la dérision-déglingue avec une fraicheur revigorante, en bons enfants des Monty Python et du Magic Circus, cependant respectueux des lois du cirque. Simplement, ils les habillent à leur manière.*
'The Archaos have invaded the Cirque d'Hiver, and it [that] makes a lot of noise. They dress up as carefree punks, poke fun of everything with invigorating freshness, the rightful heirs of Monty Python and Magic Circus, who nonetheless respect the rules of the circus. Simply, they dress them up in their own style'.

(6.42)   *Clair de terre n'est pas une pièce rose. Ça se passe dans nos campagnes.*
'Clair de terre is not a light play. It [That] takes place in our countryside'.

The pronoun *ça* has already been shown to differ from true anaphors in terms of its flexible reference, but the distinction between the two forms also extends to their respective viewing arrangements. In order to illustrate this distinction let us replace *ça* in (6.41) with *ils*, which anaphorically refers back to *Les Archaos*, to produce the closely related alternative *Les Archaos ont investi le Cirque d'Hiver, et ils font du vacarme* 'the Archaos have invaded the Cirque d'Hiver, and they are making a lot of noise'. In this alternative, the verb *faire* 'make' profiles the speaker's conceptualization of the relation between the source of the noise (*ils*) and its creation (*le vacarme*). The viewing organization maximizes the asymmetry between the subject and object of conceptualization. The elements that compose the conceptualized scene, namely the source, process, and result of the noisemaking, are profiled separately, well delineated, and placed onstage as mere objects of conception. By comparison, the conceptualizer, namely the speaker, remains offstage and is thus treated as a pure conceptualizing presence. This alternative to (6.41) perfectly illustrates the optimal viewing arrangement (Langacker 1985), where the subject and object of conceptualization are maximally differentiated because they are each confined to their specific role.

The situation is quite different in (6.41). As was mentioned earlier, *ça* does not refer to the source of the noise (*Les Archaos*), but to a more diffuse and abstract location of time and space where it is taking place. Importantly, that abstract location contains at the same time the source of the noise and the speaker who presents the scene from an internal vantage point. The verb *faire* does not individually profile the source of the noise and its outcome, but the ambient sensation that permeates the entire scene that the speaker experiences. The presence of *ça* therefore imposes an egocentric viewing arrangement (Langacker 1985), which blurs the difference between the object of conceptualization (the source and production of the noise) and the conceptualizing subject (the speaker) by making them both an undistinguished part of the profiled scene. The situation is similar in (6.42). The viewing organization that the pronoun imposes on the scene gives the impression that the play is viewed from within by someone actually watching the show. This explains why *ça* is often used to present a scene in a lively manner, which yields an interactive and hence colloquial tone as the example in (6.43) shows:

(6.43)   *Vous avez vu un peu ce qui se passe dans ce pays? C'est la folie! Ça proteste, ça*
         rouscaille, ça rouspète dans tous les coins.
         'Have you seen what's going on in this country! It's crazy! People are protesting [That protests], complaining [that complains], bitching [that bitches] on every street corner'.

The source of social unrest in (6.43) is clearly people in general. A possible alternative could easily be *les gens protestent, rouscaillent, rouspètent* 'people protest, complain, bitch'. However, that source is subjectively construed, implicitly situated within the abstract setting profiled by the subject *ça*. The main verbs do not portray well-defined actions with clearly identifiable sources, but rather the more global atmosphere that results from the subjective construal of the conceptualized scene.[5]

3.3   *Ça* has no strict cataphoric sense

So far we have been concerned strictly with *ça*'s anaphoric sense. However, this chapter is more directly interested in the contexts in which the pronoun is followed by a finite or infinitival clause, which is often analyzed as its referent. The most important issue for our purposes is thus to determine whether *ça* has a cataphoric sense where it unambiguously refers forward to the following clause. This section shows that it is not the case. A comparison with the other demonstrative *ceci* 'this'

---

5.   This subjective construal and thus the internal evaluation of the described scene also explains *ça*'s presence in weather expressions such as #*ça pleuvait fort* 'it was raining hard' (Ruwet 1991). Weather expressions are not considered in this chapter.

reveals that (1) *ça* does not have a strictly cataphoric sense, and (2) the pronoun's characteristics in its anaphoric sense (flexibility, subjectivity) are also attested when the pronoun is followed by a finite or infinitival clause. Consequently, *ça*'s analysis as a cataphoric pronoun is untenable, and a more suitable alternative needs to recognize at the same time the characteristics that the pronoun displays in its anaphoric sense, and the specificity of the contexts where the presence of a clause following the predicate has led researchers to interpret it as the pronoun's referent.

I have argued in previous work (Achard 2010) that a comparison between *ça* and *ceci* clearly reveals the former's lack of strict cataphoric sense.[6] In one of the three types of structurally and semantically well-delineated constructions in which cataphoric *ceci* occurs (110 instances out of 221 in Achard [2010]), the referred entity (underlined in the examples) is set apart from its immediate context by punctuation. It can be presented as directly reported speech and hence introduced by a colon and surrounded by quotation marks, as illustrated in (6.44) and (6.45) repeated from Chapter 1 for convenience:

(6.44)   *La voix du lecteur est si volontairement terne qu'il faut un effort pour le suivre. J'entends **ceci**: "une incroyante me dit un jour: 'si j'avais la foi, votre bréviaire me brûlerait les mains'".*   (Green, J. *Journal*: 11)
'The reader's voice is so deliberately dull that following requires an effort. I hear this: "a non-believer tells me one day: 'If I had faith, your breviary would burn my hands'"'.

(6.45)   *Revenant l'autre soir du théâtre avec Robert, nous passons près d'un groupe d'agents qui causent entre eux à mi-voix, et **ceci** parvient jusqu'à nous dans le grand silence de la rue déserte: "il lui a filé un coup de lame".*
                                                                          (Green, J. *Journal. T. 5. 1946–1950*: 210)
'On our way back from the theater with Robert the other night, we walked past a group of policemen talking to each other in low voices, and this comes to us in the silence of the deserted street: "he cut him with a blade"'.

Even though it is not presented as reported speech, the referred entity can also be set apart from the immediate context by punctuation, namely a colon as in (6.46), or a period as in (6.47):

---

6.   Although it is not considered in this chapter, *ceci* also has an anaphoric sense illustrated in (i), where the pronoun in bold print refers to the underlined entity:

(i)   Stepan: *l'organisation t'avait commandé de tuer le grand-duc. C'est vrai. Mais elle ne m'avait demandé d'assassiner des enfants. Annenkov Yanek a raison. **Ceci** n'était pas prévu.*
                                                                          (Camus, A. *Les justes*: 334)
'Stepan: the organization had ordered you to kill the grand Duke. It is true, but it hadn't asked me to kill children. Annenkov Yanek is right. This was not planned'.

(6.46) (Plus bas, mais fermement:) *frères, je veux vous parler franchement et vous dire au moins **ceci** que pourrait dire le plus simple de nos paysans: <u>tuer des enfants est contraire à l'honneur.</u>*   (Camus, A. *Les justes:* 340)

'(Lower, but in a firm voice:) brothers, I want to speak frankly and tell you at least this that the least educated of our peasants could say: there is no honor in killing children'.

(6.47) Kirilov, se lève et semble réfléchir. *De quoi faudra-t-il me déclarer coupable? Pierre vous le saurez. Kirilov bon. Mais n'oubliez pas **ceci**. <u>Je ne vous aiderai en rien contre Stavroguine.</u>*   (Camus, A. *Les possédés; pièce en trois actes:* 1043)

'Kirilov, stands up and seems to be thinking. What will you have to find me guilty of? Pierre you will find out. Kirilov good. But do not forget this. I will not help you in any way against Stavroguine'.

This construction with *ceci* is particularly important for our purposes because it clearly illustrates the strictly cataphoric use of a demonstrative. In the examples in (6.44)–(6.47), the entity that follows the pronoun and to which the latter refers enjoys a maximal level of independence from its immediate context. In other words, there is nothing in the previous context that announces its semantic content. In (6.45), for instance, nothing in the preceding context semantically anticipates the utterance *il lui a filé un coup de lame* 'he cut him with a blade' beyond the maximally abstract information that an unknown policeman is responsible for it. In this construction the formal separation that the presence of punctuation creates between the pronoun and the referred entity iconically represents the high level of independence that entity enjoys with respect to the surrounding discourse. Another facet of that independence is that *ceci* does not relate to any aspect of the immediate context except to announce the following entity. In this strict cataphoric use, the pronoun unambiguously refers to the following entity because there is nothing in the preceding context it could possibly refer to.[7]

---

7. Cataphoric *ceci* is also attested in two other constructions. In the first, illustrated in (i), the phrase that contains the pronoun is surrounded by two commas and provides a kind of parenthetical commentary. In the second, illustrated in (ii), the pronoun is directly followed by a relative pronoun (overwhelmingly *que*):

(i) *Il me dit encore, et **ceci** me paraît beaucoup plus juste, <u>qu'il craint que tenir un journal ne nuise au romancier, n'ôte au roman son "impulsion".</u>*
                                             (Green, J. *Journal. T. 5. 1946–1950:* 70)

'He also tells me, and this seems much more to the point to me, that he fears keeping a journal may be detrimental to a novelist, that it may take away the novel's "momentum"'.

(ii) *Toutes ses difficultés avec les êtres lui venaient de **ceci**, <u>qu'il ne pouvait leur faire comprendre l'extrême péril de leur situation.</u>*   (Green, J. *Moïra: roman:* 122)

'All his difficulties with people came from this, that he couldn't make them understand how extremely dangerous their situation was'.

In these two constructions the referred entity exhibits a higher level of semantic integration in the overall discourse context than in the strict cataphoric sense. See Achard (2010) for further details.

Ça radically differs from *ceci* because it does not have a strict cataphoric sense. Generally, and contrary to what was observed with *ceci*, the referred entity is closely integrated into the surrounding context. This shared thematic content manifests itself in a variety of ways. In perhaps the most obvious cases, the referred expression repeats a lexical item from the previous discourse, as illustrated in (6.48) and (6.49) where the shared lexical items are underlined. In both instances the referred entity is so well integrated into the surrounding context that it can be viewed as lexically redundant and possibly left out without major semantic modification.

(6.48)   *"Promenons-nous. Amusons-nous tant qu'il nous reste de la chair sur les os." Il haussa les épaules: "tu sais bien que ça n'est pas si facile de s'amuser".*
                                            (Beauvoir, S. de. *Les mandarins*: 93)
         '"Let's go for a walk. Let's have fun while we still have flesh on our bones". He shrugged: "you know that it [this] is not so easy to have fun"'.

(6.49)   *Josette soupira: "Il va falloir que je me montre un peu, pour ma publicité; alors je dois m'habiller. – Ça ne t'ennuie pas de t'habiller?*
                                            (Beauvoir, S. de. *Les mandarins*: 281)
         'Josette sighed: "I will have to show myself a little, for advertising purposes; so I need to dress up. – It [this] doesn't bother you to dress up?"'

In other instances the referred entity expresses a reformulation of the previous context, which often involves reanalysis as in (6.50) where the referred entity, *le péché par omission* 'a sin by omission', constitutes a recapitulation and generalization of the situation described in the previous context:

(6.50)   *quand on pense à tout ce qu'on pourrait faire et qu'on ne fait pas! Toutes les occasions qu'on laisse échapper! On n'a pas l'idée, pas l'élan; au lieu d'être ouvert on est fermé; c'est ça le plus grand péché: le péché par omission.*
                                            (Beauvoir, S. de. *Les mandarins*: 70)
         'when you think about all you could do and don't do! All these opportunities we waste! For lack of imagination, of energy; we are closed instead of being open; this is the greatest sin: a sin by omission'.

Finally, the shared information between the referred entity and the previous context can be provided by the set of inferences made available by well-established schemas or the larger context of the sentence, as the examples in (6.51) and (6.52) respectively illustrate:

(6.51)   *elles avaient toutes des robes noires, des cheveux couleur d'oréal, des talons très hauts, de longs cils et une personnalité, différente pour chacune, mais fabriquée dans les mêmes ateliers. Si j'avais été homme ça m'aurait été impossible d'en préférer aucune...*   (Beauvoir, S. de. *Les mandarins*: 343) 'they were all wearing black dresses, bottle-colored hair, very high heels, long eyelashes and different personalities, nonetheless crafted in the same salons. If I had been a man, it [this] would have been impossible to choose any one of them...'

(6.52) *Robert avait senti que je n'avais guère envie de parler et lui il avait des tas de choses à me raconter: il racontait. Il était beaucoup plus gai qu'avant mon départ: ce n'est pas que la situation internationale lui parût brillante, mais il avait repris goût à sa vie. Ça comptait beaucoup pour lui de s'être réconcilié avec Henri...*

(Beauvoir, S. de. *Les mandarins*: 492)

'Robert had sensed that I didn't feel like talking and he had a lot to tell me about: he was talking. He was much happier than before I left: it isn't because he was happy with the international situation, but he had regained his taste for life. It [this] mattered a lot to him to have reconciled with Henri...'

In (6.51) the connection between the referred entity *d'en préférer aucune* 'to prefer one of them' and the preceding context is made available by the presence of a schema that structures the social interaction and possible seduction between men and women, and the knowledge of the criteria men usually use to select their potential partner. In (6.52) we know from previous context that Robert and Henri have reconciled, and the referred entity echoes their reconciliation. The examples presented in (6.48)–(6.52) underscore the difference between *ceci* and *ça* in the pronouns' cataphoric use. In the overwhelming majority of the *ça* cases and in a manner that radically contradicts the conclusions reached for *ceci*, the referred entity shares a great deal of semantic information with the immediately preceding context. Consequently, unlike *ceci* whose anaphoric and cataphoric senses are sharply delineated, *ça* does not have a strict cataphoric sense.

While *ça* never unambiguously refers forward to the upcoming clause, it is nonetheless followed by a clause, the exact status of which needs to be recognized. We therefore need an analysis of cataphoric pronouns that accounts at the same time for the strict cases illustrated with *ceci* and the more ambiguous cases encountered with *ça*. Smith (2000, 2004) argues that the cataphoric pronouns illustrated in (6.53) and (6.54) in English and German serve a "space designating function" (Smith 2000: 486) by which they "anticipate the mental spaces set up by space builders" by "designating the spaces themselves in the grammar" (Smith 2000: 487; see also Fauconnier 1985).[8]

(6.53) I despise it that John voted for the governor

---

8. The Russian data that Smith also presents is not considered in this chapter.

(6.54)   *Wir bedauern (es) daß Hans so dumm ist*

(respectively [1a] and [1b] in Smith [2000:483])

'We regret [it] that Hans is so stupid'

Smith's analysis is directly applicable to *ceci*'s strict cataphoric sense as the example in (6.45) repeated once again, illustrates:

(6.45)   *Revenant l'autre soir du théâtre avec Robert, nous passons près d'un groupe d'agents qui causent entre eux à mi-voix, et **ceci** parvient jusqu'à nous dans le grand silence de la rue déserte: "il lui a filé un coup de lame."*

(Green, J. *Journal. T. 5. 1946–1950:* 210)

'On our way back from the theater with Robert the other night, we walked past a group of policemen talking to each other in low voices, and this comes to us in the silence of the deserted street: "he cut him with a blade"'.

Consistent with Smith's analysis for other languages, the predicates that precede the pronoun in cases such as (6.45) are unquestionable space builders (Fauconnier 1985). *Ceci* profiles the abstract nominal entity that announces the utterance to follow, and the following quote elaborates this abstract setting.

Strict cataphorics such as *ceci*'s first sense or Smith's examples in (6.53) and (6.54) constitute a limiting case because the mental space that announces the up-coming entity is maximally abstract and devoid of specific contextual content. There are, however, no limits as to the possible internal structure of this space, and it seems reasonable to posit that it may be contextually elaborated at different degrees. I therefore suggest that the cases involving *ça* only differ from the strict cataphorics as to the level of contextual elaboration of the abstract setting that the pronoun designates. Rather than empty and maximally abstract, it can contain a wide range of elements already present in the context or easily inferable from it. At the opposite end of the continuum from the strict cataphorics, this abstract setting may be fully inclusive of the discourse context within which the referred entity is extracted for specific purposes. For instance, in the example in (6.55) this purpose may include the need to synthesize and analyze the diverse elements of a globally construed context in order to present them in a way more suitable for communication:

(6.55)   *il gagnait du terrain en province; et ce qu'il y avait de réconfortant, c'est que les communistes ne l'attaquaient plus: l'espoir d'une union durable se réveillait. C'est à l'unanimité que le comité décida en novembre de soutenir Thorez contre De Gaulle. "**Ça** facilite bien la vie de se sentir en accord avec ses amis, ses alliés, avec soi-même", pensait Henri…*   (Beauvoir, S. de. *Les mandarins:* 231) 'he was gaining ground outside Paris; and what comforted him the most was that the communists weren't attacking him any more: the hope of a lasting alliance was awakening. The committee unanimously decided to support Thorez against De Gaulle in November. "It [this] makes life easier to feel in agreement with one's friends, one's allies, and oneself", Henri thought…'

In a manner already described for *ça*'s anaphoric sense, the mental space that the pronoun profiles in (6.55) is composed of the subjectively construed region that contains the previously mentioned events pertaining to Henri's relations with his allies. Because of its subjective, undifferentiated construal, the different elements that compose this space are not easily isolated and explicitly mentioned individually. The following infinitival clause represents the objectification of some of these elements in a synthetic format that makes them more suitable for communicative expression. The pronoun therefore does not profile the infinitival clause per se, but the undistinguished mass of the abstract contextual setting that contains it. This analysis is perfectly compatible with some interesting observations found in the literature, in particular with what Bally (1932: 197–198, my translation) calls *une anticipation* 'an anticipation' and describes as follows:

> *Le parleur se fondant sur une pensée qu'il n'exprime pas se borne à énoncer ce qui est essential pour lui. … Mais, constatant que l'entendeur ne peut comprendre la raison d'être de ces formules, il y ajoute, dans une seconde phrase, en manière d'explication, le motif de l'énoncé.*

> 'On the basis of an idea that he does not express, the speaker only explicitly mentions what he considers essential. … However, when he notices the hearer cannot understand the motivation for his words, he adds the reason for the utterance in a second sentence, as a means of explanation'.

The shared semantic content between the context that precedes *ça* and the referred entity often makes it difficult (and not particularly insightful) to precisely determine whether the pronoun should be considered anaphoric or cataphoric, as the examples in (6.56) and (6.57) illustrate:

(6.56)   *Une morale de l'universel, on peut tâcher de l'imposer. Mais le sens qu'on donne à sa vie, c'est une autre affaire. Impossible de s'en expliquer en quatre phrases: il faudrait amener Lambert à voir le monde avec mes yeux. Henri soupira. C'est à **ça** que ça sert la littérature: <u>montrer aux autres le monde comme on le voit</u>…*

(Beauvoir, S. de. Les mandarins: 255)

'One can try to impose a universal morality. But the meaning one gives to one's life, it is something else. Impossible to explain this in a few words. You would have to get Lambert to see the world through my eyes. Henri sighed. This is what literature is for [to what it serves, literature]: showing others the world as one sees it.'

(6.57)   *Tu ne te promènes jamais? – Je n'ai pas le temps. – Qu'est-ce que tu fais donc? – Il*
         y a toujours tant à faire; les cours de diction, les courses, le coiffeur: tu n'imagines
         *pas quel temps ça prend, le coiffeur; et puis les thés, les cocktails. – **Ça t'amuse***
         <u>***tout ça?***</u>   (Beauvoir, S. de. *Les mandarins*: 280)
         'You never go for a walk? – I don't have the time.-What do you do with your
         time? – There is always so much to do; diction classes, shopping, hairstyl-
         ist appointments: you cannot imagine how long it [this] takes, a hairstylist
         appointment; then tea parties, cocktail parties. Do you find all of this fun
         [Does this amuse you, all this]?

In (6.56) and (6.57) a strict cataphoric analysis would obscure the pronoun's anaphoric role with respect to the preceding context. Note that if the underlined entities were eliminated from all the examples, each of them would resemble the
cases in the preceding section where anaphoric *ça* summarizes and generalizes the
previous context. This is particularly obvious in (6.56). Since, on the one hand, the
semantic import of *tout ça* 'all that' is to summarize and synthesize the elements
of the previous context, and on the other hand *ça*'s cataphoric role refers to that
entity, the pronoun's anaphoric and cataphoric roles necessarily greatly overlap.

The symbiotic character of the *ça*'s anaphoric and cataphoric values is further
illustrated by a large number of cases illustrated by the pair in (6.58) and (6.59)
where the entities that respectively precede and follow the pronoun can be reversed
without noticeable change in meaning:

(6.58)   *– Comment ça t'est venu, de vouloir écrire? – Oh! Ça remonte loin, dit Henri.*
         Ça remontait loin, mais il ne savait trop quelle importance accorder à ses sou-
         venirs. – Quand j'étais jeune, ça me semblait magique <u>*un livre*</u>*.*
                                                              (Beauvoir, S. de. *Les mandarins*: 92)
         '– How did it come to you to want to write? – Oh! it was a long time ago, Henri
         said. It was a long time ago, be he didn't know how relevant his memories
         were. – When I was young, a book seemed magical to me [this seemed magical
         to me, a book]'.

(6.59)   *"Promenons-nous. Amusons-nous tant qu'il nous reste de la chair sur les os." Il*
         haussa les épaules: "tu sais bien que ça n'est pas si facile de s'amuser. – Essayons.
         <u>*Une grande balade dans les montagnes*</u>*, ça serait bien, non?"*
                                                              (Beauvoir, S. de. *Les mandarins*: 93)
         "'Let's go for a walk. Let's have fun while we still have flesh on our bones". He
         shrugged: "you know it isn't easy to have fun. – Let's try. A long hike in the
         mountains, it [this] would be fun wouldn't it?"'

The direction of the relation between the pronoun and its referent is reversed between the examples in (6.58) and (6.59). In (6.58) *ça* cataphorically refers to *un livre*
'a book', whereas in (6.59) the pronoun anaphorically refers to *une grande balade*

dans les montagnes 'a long hike in the mountains'. In both cases, however, the referential relation could easily be reversed. A possible alternative to (6.58) could be #*un livre, ça me semblait magique* 'a book, it seemed magical to me', and the example in (6.59) could be changed to #*ça serait bien, non, une grande balade dans les montagnes?* 'it would be fun wouldn't it, a long hike in the mountains?' without a noticeable change in meaning. The possibility of these reversed construals clearly illustrates that the information conveyed by the referred entity is at least partially already available from the context, and that the speaker chooses to present it before or after the pronoun for expressive purposes. The semantic import of cataphoric *ça* therefore lies in the narrative benefits of presenting it after the pronoun. Some possible reasons for this choice are considered in the following sections.

Given the semantic similarity between the context that precedes the pronoun and the postverbal expression, we can legitimately wonder if the pronoun should even be considered to have a cataphoric sense at all. With respect to the issues that concern us here and because an exhaustive account of cataphoric pronouns does not constitute a goal of this chapter, the answer is mainly definitional. On the one hand, as this section illustrates, *ça*'s anaphoric and cataphoric senses both conceptually manipulate the preceding context in order to conjure up the region that the pronoun profiles. On the other hand, cataphoric *ça* involves the extra step of singling out and objectifying a specific aspect of that region so that the resulting entity elaborates the abstract setting that the pronoun designates. It is certainly reasonable to claim that this extra step constitutes sufficient motivation to call this specific use of *ça* cataphoric, but it should be clear that this label does not in any form justify the structural distinction between demonstratives and impersonals that most syntactic accounts posit to explain their analyses of the distribution presented in (6.1) and (6.2). In other words, if *ça* is indeed called cataphoric in examples such as (6.2), the next section shows how similar it is to impersonal *il* in the contexts where they are in competition.

4.   Two impersonal constructions in the copular complement construction

We are now in a position to assess *il* and *ça*'s semantic similarities and differences. Recall from the earlier chapters that *il* profiles the field or, in other words, the abstract location that constitutes the mental reach that allows the conceptualizer to locate the entity coded in the postverbal expression. The preceding section has shown that *ça* also profiles an abstract location, namely the region composed of the immediate discourse context from which that entity is extracted. The distinction between *il* and *ça* is thus analogous, albeit more abstract, to that previously introduced in Chapter 1 and repeated in (6.60) and (6.61), which respectively illustrate a field and setting construction.

(6.60)   *It's cold in Chicago*   (adapted from Langacker 2009: 143)

(6.61)   *Chicago is cold*

Recall that both constructions in (6.60) and (6.61) place the emphasis on an abstract location that is somehow presented as responsible for the cold sensation that unfolds within it. In the impersonal construction in (6.60) the trajector is the scope of awareness within which the experience is endured; in (6.61) the spatial setting expressed by Chicago is selected as the focal figure of the main relation. The distinction between these two locations "is a matter of whether the trajector is identified as the experiential field per se or as the spatial setting with which it is largely co-extensive" (Langacker 2009: 144).

The distinction between *il* and *ça* can be analyzed in a similar manner. Just as Chicago provides the boundaries within which the sensation of cold can be experienced, the abstract region that *ça* designates in (6.58), for instance, outlines the section of discourse context (the literature-related memories) from which the following entity (*un livre*) is extracted. The entity in the complement represents the expression of a specific part of that scene singled out for expressive reasons. In this specific discourse context demonstrative impersonals are therefore true abstract setting constructions where the setting, i.e. the abstract region that the pronoun refers to, is composed of interconnected entities from the current discourse context. One of the most important communicative functions of the *ça* construction is to make explicit some aspect of reality that might have been overlooked in a more holistic construal. This aspect of *ça*'s meaning is particularly apparent with verbs such as *consister* 'consist', *impliquer* 'imply', *vouloir dire* 'mean', and *signifier* 'signifies', illustrated in (6.62) and (6.63), which specify an aspect of the previous context that may not be immediately apparent:

(6.62)   *"attention ...", reprit Antoine. Codifier la guerre, vouloir la limiter, l'organiser (l'humaniser, comme on dit!) décréter: "ceci est barbare! Ceci est immoral!" – ça implique <u>qu'il y a une autre manière de faire la guerre</u> ... une manière parfaitement civilisée ... une manière parfaitement morale ...*

                                        (Martin du Gard, R. *Les Thibault. Epilogue*: 872)

"'Be careful ...' Antoine resumed. To codify war, to attempt to limit it, to organize it (to humanize it as one says) to declare "this is barbaric! This is immoral!" It [this] implies that there is another way of fighting wars ... a perfectly civilized way ... a perfectly moral way ...'

(6.63)   *Une nouvelle méditation plissa son front, et il déclara: – et puis, entre nous et eux, il y a le gouffre de l'esprit de corps. – j'aimerais, fis- je, à en connaître votre définition. – bon, dit- il, vous le savez bien: ça consiste <u>à mépriser les autres corps</u>!*   (Mille, P. *Barnavaux et quelques femmes*: 51)

'A new thought furrowed his brow, and he declared: – and then, between us and them, there is the abyss of feeling like a unified body. I would like, I said, to know your definition. All right, he said, you know it: it [this] consists in despising the other bodies'.

In (6.62), for example, the pronoun *ça* profiles a conception of war that aims at codifying different aspects of conflicts because some practices are judged immoral or barbaric. The author further specifies this particular view by pointing out the inference it contains, namely that some practices are moral. Part of the author's argument consists of showing that this inference, coded in the complement clause, is indeed part of the section of discourse that *ça* subsumes, but that it needs to be objectively conceptualized and singled out so that the overall position that includes it can be fairly evaluated. Importantly for our purposes, *il* is not appropriate because the existence or location of the facet of reality described in the complement clause is not debated or assessed. Rather, it is already presented as a part of reality that only needs to be individuated and extracted from its context for better observation.

This analysis captures the subtle distinction between *il* and *ça*, and therefore the compatibility of both forms with English *it* (Achard, in press). *Il* places maximum emphasis on the mental effort necessary to assess the entity in the complement while *ça* is more concerned with the immediate circumstances from which that entity is extracted than the mental act itself. *Il* is therefore somewhat larger in scope because it includes the conceptualizer-centered considerations of assessment and analysis among others, while *ça* is more specifically context bound. The competition between the two pronouns and hence the distribution of *il* and *ça* constructions is considered in detail in Section 5, but the relevance of the conceptualizer's construal effort to pronoun selection is immediately apparent in the examples in (6.64)–(6.67) where even though both *il* and *ça* are potentially possible with *arriver* 'arrive' they are not interchangeable in every situation:

(6.64)   *Vous oubliez que la situation de l'Urss est une situation de guerre; les puissances capitalistes n'attendent que le moment de lui tomber dessus. – Même comme ça, rien ne prouve qu'ils le soient, dit Henri. Personne ne veut le mal pour le mal, et tout de même **ça arrive** souvent <u>qu'on le fasse inutilement</u>.*

(Beauvoir, S. de. *Les mandarins*: 381)

'You are forgetting that the USSR is in a state of war; capitalist powers are only waiting for the right moment to pounce on it. – But even so, nothing proves they are, Henri said. No one wants evil for evil's sake, but nonetheless, it [this] happens that one does it unintentionally'.

(6.65)   *Allons! Reprit Édouard en éteignant sa bougie, je suis heureux de voir se terminer pour le mieux cette histoire, qui paraissait sans autre issue que le désespoir. **Ça arrive** à n'importe qui de faire un faux départ.*

(Gide, A. *Les faux-monnayeurs*: 1106)

'Come on! Edward said snuffing the candle, I am happy to see a happy end to this story, which seemed to be heading straight to desperation. Anyone can [this happens to anyone to] start the wrong way'.

(6.66)   *Les mines sont posées par des rebelles, ou le plus souvent par des bandits qui veulent stopper un convoi pour le dévaliser. **Il arrive** aussi qu'un train saute sur un engin "oublié" le matin par des villageois vivants près de la voie...*   (AFP)

'Mines are set by rebels, or more often by thieves who want to stop a train to rob it. It also happens that a train explodes because of a device some villagers who live near the railroads "forgot" in the morning...'

(6.67)   *10 Janvier. – **Il arrive** qu'on se demande si l'on a bien la vie qu'on voulait avoir. À vingt ans, je rêvais une vie d'écrivain dans un décor de bibliothèque.*

(Green, J. *Journal. T. 5. 1946–1950*: 139)

'January 10. – It happens that one wonders if one truly has the life one wanted to have. At twenty, I was dreaming of the life of a writer in the background of a library'.

Although *il* could replace *ça* in (6.64) and (6.65) without radical change in meaning, the reverse substitution (*ça* for *il*) in (6.66) and (6.67) would yield very awkward results at best. This asymmetry is largely due to the presence or absence of a contextual basis to the pronoun's referent. In (6.64) and (6.65) the complement clause content is introduced as a generalization over the specific experience that the earlier context describes, as attested by the adverbials *souvent* 'often' and *à tout le monde* 'to everyone'. Consistent with the analysis presented in the previous section, it is thus deeply rooted in the immediate context. This is not the case in (6.66) and (6.67) where the situation evoked in the complement clause represents the initial conversation topic in (6.67), or a specific case related but not identical to those described in the immediate context in (6.66). This separation between the complement content and the immediate context is formally represented by the presence of *aussi* 'also' in (6.66), and the construction's sentence-initial position in the journal entry in (6.67). *Ça* would be very awkward in these two contexts because the pronoun requires a higher degree of contextual reference. Note that the reverse is not true. The replacement of *ça* by *il* in (6.64) and (6.65) poses no particular problem because the observation of the immediate context can always be used as a starting point for the epistemic or evaluative effort leading to the conclusion evoked in the complement clause.

The preceding sections have shown that *ça* has the semantic potential to act as an impersonal pronoun, but this does not per se suffice to turn the construction in which it participates into an impersonal, as illustrated in (6.68)–(6.71).

(6.68) *et toi, mauvais gredin, que je t'y reprenne à courir les routes en faisant le conspi-rateur!... ça t'étonne <u>que je t'aie tiré de là, hein?</u>*
(Adam, P. *L'enfant d'Austerlitz*: 280)
'As for you, you good-for-nothing scoundrel, don't let me catch you running around doing mischief! It [this] surprises you that I got you out of this, doesn't it?

(6.69) *– j'ai su ça, vous savez, par les domestiques... – que vous ne vouliez pas louer à des "grues". Codomat. ... ça m'étonnerait <u>d'avoir dit une chose pareille...</u>*
(Bernard, T. *Monsieur Codomat*: 147)
'I heard this from the help – that you didn't want to rent to "whores". Codomat. ... it [this] would surprise me to have said such a thing...'

(6.70) *Je pars demain pour la Suisse. Je vais beaucoup mieux, mais comme tout est beau sauf la Suisse, ça m'ennuie bien <u>de partir.</u>*
(Alain-Fournier, H. *Correspondance avec J. Rivière*: 229)
'I am leaving for Switzerland tomorrow. I am feeling much better, but since everything is beautiful except Switzerland, it [this] really bothers me to be leaving'.

(6.71) *Le lendemain, il ne fut pas question de me rendre l'argent, et je ne voulus pas le réclamer. Ça me faisait plaisir <u>qu'il eût quelque chose de moi...</u>*
(Mirbeau, O. *Journal d'une femme de chambre*: 246)
'The next day, there was no word of giving me my money back, and I didn't want to ask for it. I liked the fact [this was making me happy] that he had something of mine...'

In the examples in (6.68)–(6.71), the demonstrative itself could easily be analyzed as an impersonal pronoun. For instance, in (6.68) where the speaker describes the hearer's surprise at reality having taken a specific way, *ça* profiles the section of current reality that contains the event or proposition described in the complement. Because this global subjective construal does not isolate the precise element that creates the surprise, the latter is later objectified and presented in the complement clause. Importantly, the content of that clause is totally contained in the section of discourse that *ça* subjectively profiles, even before being objectified and singled out as the specific reason for the hearer's surprise. Despite the pronoun's semantic import, however, in the examples in (6.68)–(6.71) the construction as a whole cannot be considered impersonal because the scope of the predicate (i.e. who has potential access to the event or proposition coded in the complement) is restricted to one of its own participants, the second-person singular *t'* referring to the hearer in (6.68). In other words, the construction lacks the degree of generality required to be considered an impersonal.

As was mentioned several times throughout this monograph, it is very difficult and not particularly enlightening to precisely delineate every situation in which a construction is general enough to be considered impersonal because generality is a gradual notion, and it can be obtained in a variety of ways. For instance, the example in (6.72) may well be considered impersonal even though it is very close in meaning to the ones in (6.68)–(6.71) because (1) it does not name a specific person that the scope of the predicate is restricted to, and (2) it possesses a sort of generic value that makes it applicable to a generalized conceptualizer:

(6.72) *Dame, tu comprends, quand on se sent si loin de son pays, au milieu des sauvages,*
      ça fait rudement plaisir <u>de se retrouver</u>*.*
                                      (Moselly, E. *Terres lorraines: roman:* 100)
      'Well, you see, when one feels so far away from home, among savages, it is a great pleasure [this makes great pleasure] to get together'.

Although the inclusion in the impersonal category of constructions such as that in (6.70) would be unproblematic given the analysis presented in this monograph, it would nonetheless require a careful analysis of a large number of predicates, as well as a clear understanding of the conditions under which their level of generality meets the impersonal requirement. Importantly, however, and consistent with the hypothesis introduced in Chapter 1, the copular complement construction [*c'* + *être* + ADJECTIVE + COMPLEMENT CLAUSE] illustrated in (6.73)–(6.75) constitutes a stable environment that can consistently be called impersonal:

(6.73) *même si tu ne touches pas le grand public, ça vaut la peine, dit- il. Tu as ta*
      voix, tes dons à toi. **Ça serait intéressant** <u>d'essayer d'en tirer tout ce que tu peux</u>*.*
                                       (Beauvoir, S. de. *Les mandarins:* 119)
      'Even if you don't become popular, it is worth it, he said. You have your own voice, your own gifts. It [this] would be interesting to try to get as much as you can out of them'.

(6.74) *Sans doute, ce détrousseur de morts avait tout intérêt lui-même à n'attirer point*
      sur soi l'attention; et s'il prétendait malgré tout se servir de sa découpure, ma foi!
      Ça pourrait être assez plaisant <u>d'entrer en composition avec lui</u>*.*
                                      (Gide, A. *Les caves du* Vatican: 847)
      'Without a doubt, this grave robber has no interest in attracting attention to himself; and if he still pretended to use his template, well, it [this] might be quite pleasant to team up with him'.

(6.75) *Les enfants m'ont demandé ce que je lisais toujours. J'ai dit que c'était une lettre de vous. Aurora a regardé le papier, avec commisération, et elle a dit: "comme* **ça doit être ennuyeux** <u>*d'écrire une si longue lettre!*</u>*"*

(Rolland, R. *Jean-Christophe la nouvelle journée*: 1474)

'The children asked me what I was always reading. I said it was a letter from you. Aurora looked at the paper with pity and she said: "how boring it [this] must be to write such a long letter!"'

Unlike the constructions in (6.68)–(6.71), the copular complement constructions do not consider the event/proposition coded in the complement exclusively with respect to its effect on a specific conceptualizer, but relative to the general categories of reality (epistemic modals), necessity (deontic modals), or emotion (evaluative predicates), usually available to anyone. Because any conceptualizer in the right position will invariably experience the surprise caused by the observation of the scene that the complement clause profiles, the constructions illustrated in (6.73)–(6.75) meet the impersonal definition.[9] They are semantically very close to the ones in (6.68)–(6.71), but the presence of the copula provides the additional level of generality required of impersonal constructions. It is within this particular context that *ça* can reliably be considered an impersonal pronoun. It seems reasonable to assume that the generality of access to the event in the complement that the copular complement construction affords is directly responsible for the competition between *il* and *ça*, since it is only in the context of this construction that the two pronouns constitute possible alternatives to each other with the same predicates (recall *il* is impossible in [6.68]–[6.71]), as the examples in (6.76)–(6.78) illustrate:[10]

(6.76) *L'homme a la faculté de ne pas se soumettre aux lois de la nature; et, de savoir s'il a tort ou raison d'user de cette faculté, c'est le point le plus grave et le moins éclairci de sa morale. Mais* **il n'en est pas moins intéressant** <u>*de surprendre la volonté de la nature dans un monde différent.*</u>

(Maeterlinck, M. *La vie des abeilles*: 23)

'Men have the faculty of not yielding to the laws of nature; and, whether or not they are right to use this faculty, constitutes the most critical and obscure aspect of their morality. However, it [this] is no less interesting to surprise the will of nature in a different world'.

---

9. Diessel (1999: 5) recognizes the specificity of the copular environment for French demonstratives.

10. This pattern holds true for most emotion/reaction and epistemic predicates.

(6.77)   *Oh! Qu'**il est plaisant** <u>d'être belle</u>! L'homme qui nous recherche est toujours beau.*
(Bernanos, G. *Sous le soleil de Satan*: 101)
'Oh! How pleasant it is to be beautiful! The man who courts us is always beautiful'.

(6.78)   *Le mal ne doit pas être bien grand, mais si elle n'aime pas les boucles d'oreilles …*
il est ennuyeux <u>*de lui faire percer des trous qui ne se refermeront jamais*</u>.
(Gyp. *Souvenirs d'une petite fille T. 1*: 85)
'The pain cannot be that great, but if she doesn't like earrings … it is a problem to have holes pierced that will never close'.

Although the copular complement construction does not constitute the only environment in which *ça* is an impersonal, it constitutes the most stable and consistent one and will thus constitute the sole focus of the remainder of this chapter. In the copular complement construction French therefore has two kinds of impersonals, respectively introduced by *il* and *ça*. As the preceding sections have indicated, the two pronouns are very close in meaning and their syntactic overlap reflects their semantic proximity. *Il* profiles the field, i.e. the conceptualizer's awareness or mental reach that permits the situation profiled in the complement to be assessed (Achard 1998; Langacker 2009; Smith 2006). Demonstrative impersonals profile the subjectively construed abstract setting, i.e. the immediate circumstances from which the event or proposition coded in the complement clause can be extracted. The complement clause represents the objectification of a specific part of that scene singled out for expressive reasons. In this specific discourse context demonstrative impersonals are therefore true abstract setting constructions where the setting, i.e. the abstract region the pronoun refers to, is composed of interconnected entities from the current discourse context.

The semantic difference between the two pronouns is thus subtle and essentially pertains to *il*'s emphasis placed on the conceptualizer's mental effort to assess the scene in the complement. While *ça* is more specifically concerned with the immediate context itself, *il* is larger in scope because it includes the conceptualizer-centered considerations of assessment and analysis, among others. However, this distinction is particularly tenuous within the confines of the copular complement construction where the mental effort required to locate or evaluate the event/proposition in the complement is largely based on the examination of the circumstances that surround it. In this context *il* and *ça* exhibit such a large amount of conceptual overlap that the competition in their distribution is inevitable. The next section considers this distribution more specifically.

5. Distribution of *il* and *ça* impersonals

The exhaustive description of the distribution of *il* and *ça* in all the contexts where they are in competition is an extremely difficult task because pronoun selection is primarily determined by speaker choice, and thus susceptible to many contextual factors. This section follows Achard (2010) in investigating the pronouns' distribution from three different perspectives. The first assesses the relative frequency of *il* and *ça* in Simone de Beauvoir's *Les mandarins*. Second, this frequency within one single work is compared to the numbers obtained in the 760 twentieth-century texts available in the FRANTEXT database searched by individual predicate. Finally, a more in-depth comparison of *il* and *ça* is presented with the predicate *être vrai* 'be true'. These different sources of data serve complementary purposes. On the one hand, a complete novel provides a unique context from which the author's selections stand out more acutely and each form's narrative function can be exploited more visibly, and it constitutes an integrated entity with respect to which the relative distribution of different classes of predicates can be evaluated. However, because the meaning distinction between *il* and *ça* impersonals is quite subtle, a great deal of author- and genre-specific variation can be expected and the examination of a single work can yield results too idiosyncratic to be safely generalized. Consequently the results obtained from a single text need to be evaluated against the predicate-specific investigations conducted across many texts.[11] Finally, because individual predicates exhibit very different distributions within the same semantic class, *être vrai* is used as an example of the methodology that needs to be applied to every single one to produce an exhaustive account.[12]

5.1 *Il* and *ça* in *Les mandarins*

The observation of *Les mandarins'* data, recapitulated in Table 6.1, reveals that *ça* impersonals outnumber their *il* counterparts by far:

Table 6.1 Overall distribution of copular impersonals in *Les mandarins*

	il				*ça*			
	Deontic	Epistemic	Evaluative	Total	Deontic	Epistemic	Evaluative	Total
Instances	1	8	26	35	Ø	40	167	207

---

11. We should also remember that the conclusions reached in this chapter concerning written French cannot be extended to the spoken language.

12. The analysis developed in the remainder of this section, including all the numbers and tables, is essentially that in Achard (2010).

This distribution calls for some observations. First, even though deontic, epistemic, and evaluative forms are attested, at least for one form, the overwhelming majority of copular impersonal predicates are evaluative. The scarcity of deontics is explained by the quasi-monopoly in French of another impersonal form, namely *il faut* 'it is necessary' (401 instances in *Les mandarins*). Second, epistemic predicates are represented by a very small number of forms, as illustrated in Table 6.2:

Table 6.2 Distribution of epistemic copular impersonals in *Les mandarins*

	il		*ça*		Total	
	Number	%	Number	%	Number	%
Vrai	2	6.06	31	93.94	33	100
Possible	5	62.5	3	37.5	8	100
Impossible	Ø	0	5	100	5	100
Probable	1	100	Ø	0	1	100
Sûr	Ø	0	1	100	1	100

Finally, as was observed in Chapter 5, the category of copular evaluative predicates is extremely large. While the twenty-six *il* instances represent seventeen separate predicates, the 167 *ça* examples distribute themselves among sixty-seven different predicates. The only overlapping predicates are illustrated in Table 6.3:

Table 6.3 Overlapping copular impersonals

	il		*ça*		Total	
	Number	%	Number	%	Number	%
Facile	3	20	12	80	15	100
Urgent	2	40	3	60	5	100
Important	2	33.3	4	66.7	6	100
Absurde	1	16.7	5	83.33	6	100
Inutile	1	25	3	75	4	100
Bon	2	33.3	4	66.7	6	100
Naturel	1	11.1	8	88.9	9	100

The relatively small number of overlapping predicates merely illustrates the great variety and eclecticism of the two constructions. It should not be interpreted as meaning that the nonattested forms are ungrammatical, but simply that they were not selected.[13] The examination of *Les mandarins* provides a snapshot of *il* and *ça*'s

---

13. The few predicates where the attested *ça* cases (1) have no corresponding example with *il* in the larger corpus, and (2) sound highly questionable when an *il* equivalent was manufactured are given in (i)–(iv):

usage in copular complement constructions, but we cannot forget that this snapshot is critically shaped by the author's general narrative and aesthetic purposes. As such, it cannot be considered fully representative of the pronouns' overall distribution in written French. However, this does not question the validity of examining a single text. Any discrepancy between the usage observed in that text and more general tendencies can provide valuable insights into the meaning of the two pronouns if the discrepancies can be shown to correlate with the author's narrative strategies.

A cursory glance at the comparison of the data from individual predicates in *Les mandarins* to larger sets taken from the 760 twentieth-century documents of the FRANTEXT database reveals important differences. For example, Tables 6.4 and 6.5 respectively recapitulate the overall distribution of epistemic and some evaluative predicates in the larger corpus. If we compare them to Tables 6.2 and 6.3, we realize that unlike what was observed in *Les mandarins*, *il* is much more

---

(i) *Quand on réussit, on a un tas de problèmes, mais on en a aussi quand on ne réussit pas. Ça doit être morne de parler et de parler sans jamais éveiller un écho.*
     (Beauvoir, S. de. *Les mandarins*: 507)
     'When you are successful, you always have problems, but you also have problems when you are not successful. It [this] must be gloomy to be talking and talking without ever getting a response'.

(ii) *Il se leva: "venez vous promener. La nuit sent si bon. – Il faut revenir chez ces gens, Lewis. Ils vont remarquer notre absence …: ça ne serait pas gentil de disparaître comme ça".*
     (Beauvoir, S. de. *Les mandarins*: 452)
     'He stood up: "Let's go for a walk. The night smells so good. – We need to go back inside, Lewis. These people will notice we are gone …: it [this] wouldn't be nice to disappear without saying anything"'.

(iii) *– Je voudrais un café. J'ai peur d'avoir trop bu. Il sourit: "une américaine demanderait un autre whisky", dit-il. "Mais vous avez raison: ça serait moche si un de nous deux n'avait plus toute sa tête".* (Beauvoir, S. de. *Les mandarins*: 73)
     'I would like a cup of coffee. I am afraid I drank too much. He smiled: "an American would ask for another whisky", he said. "But you are right: it [this] would be ugly if one of us didn't have her wits about her"'.

(iv) *Je contemplais avec détresse la table chargée de pâtés, de salades, de gâteaux: ça serait long d'en venir à bout!* (Beauvoir, S. de. *Les mandarins*: 522)
     'I looked at the table loaded with pâtés, salads, cakes with despair: it would take a long time [this would be long] to finish all this.'

These adjectives seem very closely tied to the event itself (*long* 'long', *morne* 'gloomy', *moche* 'ugly'), or to the sensation that their occurrence provokes (*gentil* 'nice'). If we compare them to others that are also felicitous with *il* such as *inconcevable* 'unconceivable' or *agréable* 'pleasant', they seem to be less capable of providing the analytical judgment these adjectives convey. This observation is compatible with the analysis presented here, but needs to be confirmed by further research.

frequent than *ça*. The difference is even more striking for individual predicates. For example, *il* occurs in only 6.06 percent of the cases involving *vrai* in *Les mandarins*, but in 77.25 percent of the overall corpus. Similarly, *ça* is attested in 80 percent of the instances with *facile* 'easy' in *Les mandarins*, whereas in the more general corpus it only represents 19.2 percent of the cases. However, the end of this section shows that the discrepancy between the two corpora can be explained by the narrative strategies used in *Les mandarins*, and that the meaning of the two pronouns as it is described in this chapter provides a possible motivation for the author's unconventional selection.

Table 6.4 Distribution of some epistemic predicates in the larger corpus

	il		*ça*		Ø		Total	
	Nb.	%	Nb.	%	Nb.	%	Nb.	%
Vrai	1256	77.25	370	22.75	Ø	0	1626	100
Possible	946	93.67	47	4.65	17	1.68	1010	100
Probable	224	95.32	0	0	11	4.68	235	100

Table 6.5 Relative distribution of four evaluative predicates in the larger corpus

	il		*ça*		Ø		Total	
	Nb.	%	Nb.	%	Nb.	%	Nb.	%
Facile	481	80.1	115	19.2	4	0.7	600	100
Agréable	88	67.7	42	32.3	0	0	130	100
Ennuyeux	2	6.45	29	93.55	0	0	31	100
Dommage	15	10.87	37	26.81	86	62.32	138	100

The data in Table 6.5 also reveal that the distribution of impersonal forms varies greatly depending on the meaning of individual predicates, even within the same general semantic classes. For example, even though the four predicates *être facile* 'be easy', *être agréable* 'be pleasant', *être ennuyeux* 'be annoying', and *être dommage* 'be a pity' are all evaluative, their relative distribution with the three impersonal forms varies considerably. Whereas *facile* 'easy' and *agréable* 'pleasant' favor *il*, *ennuyeux* 'boring' overwhelmingly prefers *ça*, and *dommage* 'pity' is most frequently attested with Ø.[14] The individual idiosyncrasy of each predicate illustrated in Table 6.5 makes it difficult to find global strategies that determine the use of a particular pronoun beyond general observations concerning the more-familiar registers *ça* is assumed to cover. Even the more sophisticated accounts have had problems with the large amount of individual variation that these predicates exhibit. For example,

---

14. It is interesting to note that Ø impersonals constitute the most frequent form with *dommage* 'pity', although they are seldom mentioned in the literature.

Le Bidois and Le Bidois (1938: 116) essentially claim that impersonal demonstratives provide greater force to a statement: "Toutes les fois qu'on veut mettre de la force dans l'énonciation d'un jugement, c'est *ce* qui est aujourd'hui préféré" 'Every time additional force is needed in a judgment, *ce* is preferred nowadays'. Furthermore, "l'énonciation purement objective, rationnelle, se contente très bien de *il*; mais qu'il intervienne un élément subjectif, sentimental, on voit tout de suite paraître *ce*" 'rational, objective statements are perfectly content with *il*, but as soon as a subjective, emotional element occurs, *ce* immediately appears'. These observations are certainly sound and the analysis presented in the remainder of this section is largely compatible with them, but they are meant to apply to the distribution as a whole and cannot therefore adequately distinguish *agréable* from *ennuyeux*, for example, and explain their different distribution. The only way of dealing with this amount of idiosyncrasy within similar semantic classes is to address each predicate individually. The next section therefore considers *il* and *ça*'s (*c'*) distribution with the epistemic copular predicates *est vrai* 'is true'. For an exhaustive analysis of the distribution of the two forms, other individual predicates need to be analyzed in a similar fashion before any general conclusion can be drawn.

5.2   *Vrai*

As an existential expression *il* introduces the postverbal entity with respect to the domain of its existence or reality. As a demonstrative, *ça* pertains to the evaluation of the postverbal entity. Chapter 5 showed that the epistemic expressions profile the conceptualizer's efforts to assess the location of the proposition coded in the complement with respect to the most analytical reality conception R'. In the case of *vrai* 'true', that proposition is accepted as part of some conceptualizer's conception of reality. By contrast, with impersonal demonstratives the proposition previously considered is confirmed, i.e. evaluated as true. The notions of existence and evaluation that suitably describe *il* and *ça* respectively are therefore inherited from both pronouns' more prototypical senses. In the context of the copular complement construction the difference between the two is often too subtle to carry a substantial semantic distinction, as in the example in (6.79) where *c'* could be used as an alternative to the attested *il* with little difference in meaning:

(6.79)   *Il me suffira de rappeler comment M. Klein, dans une question relative aux surfaces de Riemann, a eu recours aux propriétés des courants électriques. **Il est vrai** <u>que les raisonnements de ce genre ne sont pas rigoureux…</u>*

(Poincaré, H. *La valeur de la science*: 154)

'It will be sufficient to remind you how M. Klein, in a question relative to Rieman surfaces, used the properties of electrical currents. It is true that arguments of this kind lack rigor'.

However, existence and evaluation can also be reinterpreted within the domain of discourse coherence where they essentially pertain to the management of argumentation, i.e. the articulation of the different propositions that constitute the overall discursive strategy of a given passage. For instance, *il* is frequently attested if the proposition it introduces serves to temper a previously made statement by presenting a piece of information that challenges its force. This is illustrated in the examples in (6.80) and (6.81):

(6.80)   *À voir cela, il me semble que la révolte est plus loin de nous que je ne croyais d'* *abord.* **Il est vrai** <u>*que je suis avec des montagnards, écartés des centres industriels*</u> <u>*et très fatalistes.*</u>   (Alain-Fournier, H. *Correspondance avec J. Rivière*: 120)
         'When I see this, it seems to me that the rebellion is further from us than I first thought. It is true that I am with mountain men, remote from industrial areas, and very fatalistic'.

(6.81)   *Au reste, vins, bières, ou cidres, il savait rendre justice à tout ce que le seigneur* *a créé d'excellent. Il n'était pas assez malavisé pour laisser sa raison dans son* *verre, et il gardait la mesure.* **Il est vrai** <u>*que cette mesure était copieuse, et que*</u> <u>*dans son verre une raison plus débile se fût noyée.*</u>
                          (Rolland, R. *Jean-Christophe le matin*: 123)
         'Besides, wine, beer, or cider, he knew how to do justice to all the excellent things the Lord created. He didn't have the bad judgment to leave his reason in his glass, and he kept his measure. It is true that this measure was large, and that in his glass, a weaker reason would have drowned'.

In the examples in (6.80) and (6.81) the proposition that *il* introduces presents a piece of information that challenges the generalizing force of the previous statement. In (6.80) the author's earlier position about the state of the rebellion is nuanced by his further consideration of the fatalistic nature of his companions. *Il*'s selection is consistent with its meaning described in the previous section because the mere statement of the existence of a fact that runs counter to the overall argument suffices to weaken the latter's scope and power. Furthermore, the proposition in the complement has not been presented before, and even though the speaker is obviously aware of the events it is reporting, the impersonal construction merely asserts its existence with respect to R'. The presence of *c'* in this context is not impossible, but it would indicate that the proposition in the complement had somehow been previously established and is now being evaluated. In the context of (6.80) and (6.81), each passage would come across as a piece of internal dialogue where the speaker plays the role of a distinct protagonist and answers his own objections as if they came from other discourse participants. This construal is obviously marked since such dialogic practices are more frequently reserved for interactive communication.

Conversely, and also consistent with the pronoun's meaning, *c*'s presence often indicates that the proposition it introduces directly corresponds to some element of the immediate context, as illustrated in (6.82) and (6.83).

(6.82) *Je sais: il a tué un pauvre vieil homme sans défense:* <u>*Farnese était seul,*</u> *– pas un laquais, – et le coup de revolver a été tiré par derrière. Je sais tout ça … mais écoutez un peu:* **ce n'est pas vrai** <u>*que Farnese était seul.*</u>

                                   (Farrère, C. *L'homme qui assassina*: 280)

      'I know: he killed a poor defenseless man: Farnese was alone, – not a servant, – and the shot was fired from behind. I know all that … but listen for a minute: It [this] is not true that Farnese was alone'.

(6.83) *S'il te faut une confiance perpétuelle sache que tu l'as et que c'est elle qui s'inquiétait quand j'écrivais ma dernière lettre. Mais sache aussi que cette confiance est exigeante et demande qu'on la satisfasse.* **C'est vrai** <u>*que je suis "près de mes intérêts".*</u> *Plus je vais, plus je veux acquérir.*

                          (Alain-Fournier, H. *Correspondance avec J. Rivière*: 207)

      'If you require everlasting trust, know that you have it and it was that trust that was getting worried when I wrote my last letter. Be also aware, however, that this trust is demanding and expects to be satisfied. It [this] is true that I am "close to my interests". I want to acquire more and more as time passes'.

In the examples in (6.82) and (6.83) the proposition *c'* introduces express agreement with a statement made in the previous discourse. In (6.82) *Farnese était seul* 'Farnese was alone' repeats a section of the preceding discourse verbatim. In (6.83) the quotes surrounding "*près de mes intérêts*" 'close to my interests' indicate that this very expression was used in a previous letter. The examples in (6.82) and (6.83) are very different from those in (6.80) and (6.81). They describe multicharacter interactions where the impersonal demonstrative is used dialogically to manage the exchange between the participants. The literary register of these examples also suggests that the impersonal demonstratives' dialogic character rather than their confinement to lower linguistic genres is responsible for the often-made statements about their conversational nature. If the content expressed in the complement proposition has already been established in the context and the communicative purpose of the predicate *vrai* is merely to confirm it, *c'* alone is possible. For example, in (6.84) *c'*'s presence is expected because the speaker confirms a rumor about himself. *Il* would be awkward because it would imply the speaker is stating the existence of what is already common knowledge.

(6.84) *Mais je ne prendrai pas un coup, Maria, pas un seul! Il hésita un peu et demanda*
        abruptement, les yeux à terre: – peut- être… vous a- t- on dit quelque chose contre
        moi? – non. – c'est vrai que j'avais coutume de prendre un coup pas mal, quand
        je revenais des chantiers et de la drave; mais c'est fini.

                                                    (Hémon, L. *Maria Chapdelaine*: 93)

        'But I won't have a drink, Maria, not a single one! He hesitated a little and
        asked suddenly, his eyes downcast: maybe someone told you something against
        me? – no. – it [this] is true that I used to drink quite a bit when I came back
        from working or cutting wood; but it's over'.

Because of the interactive value of the demonstrative impersonals and the possibility for the pronoun to present speaker-internal arguments, *c*'s acceptability
greatly relies on the hearer's ability to get independent access to the proposition it
introduces so that she can anticipate the speaker's adjustments as if they were her
own, and hence follow the general trend of discourse. This independent evidence
may come from the context itself or from global world knowledge. Consider the
examples in (6.85) and (6.86):

(6.85) *La reproduction des organismes unicellulaires consiste en cela même, l'être vivant*
        se divise en deux moitiés dont chacune est un individu complet. Il /#c'est vrai
        que, chez les animaux plus complexes, la nature localise dans des cellules dites
        sexuelles, à peu près indépendantes, le pouvoir de produire à nouveau le tout.
                                            (Bergson, H. *L'évolution créatrice*: 12)
        'The reproduction of single cell organisms works in this very manner, the being
        divides itself into two halves, each of which is a complete being. It/this is true
        that, with more complex animals, nature places in the almost independent,
        so-called sexual cells, the power to reproduce the whole again'.

(6.86) *Les systèmes délimités par la science ne durent que parce qu'ils sont indissolu-*
        blement liés au reste de l'univers. Il /#??c'est vrai que, dans l'univers lui- même,
        il faut distinguer, comme nous le dirons plus loin, deux mouvements opposés,
        l'un de "descente", l'autre de "montée".   (Bergson, H. *L'évolution créatrice*: 10)
        'The systems outlined by science only last because they are forever connected
        to the rest of the universe. It/??this is true that in the universe itself, we must
        distinguish, as we will say later, two opposite movements, one "descending",
        the other one "ascending"'.

Both examples in (6.85) and (6.86) illustrate the pattern already presented in
(6.80) and (6.81), where the proposition that follows the predicate tempers the
overall force of the previous utterance. As mentioned earlier, *c*'s presence in these
cases is interpreted as some kind of internal dialogue where the speaker is construed as answering self-evoked, unexpressed dissenting arguments. As indicated
above, the difference in acceptability between (6.85) and (6.86) is imputable to the

speaker's being able to access the proposition coded in the complement independently so that she can follow the speaker's progress through his own arguments. This is certainly the case in (6.85) because people are generally aware of some rudiments of complex cell reproduction, and the proposition that follows the predicate is thus readily available as an objection that the speaker considers (and agrees with) as such. In (6.86), on the other hand, the presence of *comme nous le dirons plus loin* 'as we will say later' indicates that the proposition *il faut distinguer deux mouvements opposés, l'un de "descente", l'autre de "montée"* 'we must distinguish two opposite movements, one "descending", the other one "ascending"' has never been introduced in the discourse before. It is also highly unlikely that the hearer will be acquainted with the concept independently, which makes the interpretation of the proposition as an unmentioned objection that the speaker agrees with difficult to accept given regular discourse conventions, and hence renders *c*'s presence awkward.

The analysis presented in this section is strengthened by the presence of several lexical/syntactic environments that allow a more precise observation of the meaning of the pronouns. Two will be considered here. First, the split between the evaluative and argumentative functions respectively encountered for *il* and *ça* in the previous examples can also be observed when the proposition that the pronoun introduces starts with the hypothetical *si* 'if'. In this context every one of the ten attested instances of *si c'est vrai* 'if it is true' indicates the speaker's attempt to confirm the status of the proposition with respect to reality. The important point for our purposes is that in each case the proposition's epistemic status is not established with certainty, but merely considered potentially true. The motivation for the speaker's desire for epistemic confirmation may be prompted by a rumor as in (6.87), or a suspicion arising from the interpretation of suspicious behavior as in (6.88). In any case, however, the pronoun's import is clearly evaluative because its primary function is to elicit the truth of the proposition coded in the complement.

(6.87)   – *monsieur, dites- moi un peu si c'est vrai que vous faites des vers charmants?
Je l'ai entendu dire en ville.*   (Colette, G. *Claudine à l'école*: 118)
'– sir, please tell me if it [this] is true that you write charming poetry? I heard it in town'.

(6.88)   – *"si c'était vrai que t'es grosse", dit la mère, "la seule chose, c'est de te laisser courir après par les deux Merlavigne".*
(Martin du Gard, R. *Vieille France*: 1096)
'– "if it [this] is true that you are with child", the mother said, "the only thing to do, is to let the two Merlavigne cozy up to you"'.

This evaluative function of confirmation can also be observed with *il* as illustrated in (6.89), but it is only attested in thirteen of the 124 instances of *s'il est vrai*.

(6.89)   *je me souviens que je lui ai demandé **s'il était vrai** que son frère était parti.*
(Simenon, G. *Les vacances de Maigret*: 137)
'I remember that I asked him if it was true that his brother had left'.

In a way congruent with the tendencies observed earlier, the overwhelming majority of the *s'il est vrai* cases pertain to the management of the diverse facets of the speaker's argument, or more specifically to the establishment of specific relations between different propositions to advance that argument in the desired direction. With *il* the *si* clause sets up a proposition as true and considers the ramifications for the rest of the argument. The relations between the proposition introduced by the *si* clause and other propositions that follow are varied. The cases where the *si* clause presents the protasis in a hypothetical construction are the most frequently attested with fifty-seven instances, illustrated in (6.90):

(6.90)   *Ignore-toi toi-même, c'est le premier précepte de la sagesse. **S'il est vrai** que Montaigne composa ses essais pour étudier son propre individu, cette recherche lui dut être plus cruelle que les pierres qui lui déchiraient les reins.*
(France, A. *Le petit Pierre*: 265)
'Ignore thyself is the first rule of wisdom. If it is true that Montaigne wrote his essays to study his own self, this search must have been more painful than the stones that broke his back'.

Other instances present different logical configurations between the different propositions that constitute the overall argument. For example, despite its reality the scope of the *si* clause is reduced by the following proposition in (6.91):

(6.91)   *Mais nous avons pris l'individu à l'état isolé, sans tenir compte de la vie sociale. En réalité, l'homme est un être qui vit en société. **S'il est vrai** que l'intelligence humaine vise à fabriquer, il faut ajouter qu'elle s'associe, pour cela et pour le reste, à d'autres intelligences.* (Bergson, H. *L'évolution créatrice*: 158)
'But we have considered an individual alone, without taking his social life into account. In reality, man is a social being. If it is true that human intelligence aims to build things, it must be added that to do this, as to do anything else, it collaborates with other intelligent beings'.

In (6.92) the *si* clause serves as a given to introduce another proposition of equal status, although it may not be so readily available:

(6.92)   ***S'il est vrai** que la mer ait été autrefois notre milieu vital où il faille replonger notre sang pour retrouver nos forces, il en est de même de l'oubli, du néant mental…* (Proust, M. *A l'ombre des jeunes filles en fleurs*: 820)
'If it is true that the sea once was our life environment where we need to immerse our blood to recover our strength, the same can be said about [it is the same for] oblivion, or mental vacuum…'

The exact nature of the relation between the different propositions, as well as the number of different cases, is difficult to precisely isolate. The important point for our purposes is that in each case the *si* clause constitutes the reference point with respect to which the following clause is considered. This is fully consistent with the pronoun's meaning as it was presented earlier. The statement alone of the proposition (i.e., its existence) and not its evaluation is sufficient for calculating the status of the other proposition with respect to which it is evaluated.

It should be noted that the evaluative and argumentative senses favored respectively by *ça* and *il* are not as separate as this presentation implies for expository purposes. In fact, the situation described in (6.88) conforms to the protasis/apodosis in some way since the course of action that the mother advocates should only be carried out if her daughter's pregnancy is confirmed. However, despite the logical relation that exists between the two elements of the sentence, the pronoun's sense remains predominantly evaluative because the truth of the proposition coded in the *si* clause is still being debated. With *il*, the truth of the proposition does not constitute the speaker's primary focus. For example, in (6.90) we will never know the true reasons that prompted Montaigne to write, but it does not detract from the overall validity of the argument. The emphasis is placed on the resulting consequences should the hypothesis be true, or in other words on the logical relation that exists between the two propositions. In this environment again, the two pronouns behave in a way consistent with their meaning as it was presented in the previous sections.

Finally, in the context of *n'en est pas moins vrai* 'nonetheless remains true' only *il* appears. The sequence *il n'en est pas moins vrai* 'it is nonetheless true' occurs ninety-nine times in the corpus (7.90 percent of the *il est vrai* cases), while no example is attested with *ça*. This construction is illustrated in (6.93) and (6.94):

(6.93) *Un général victorieux et qui apportait de l'argent se rendait indispensable. Et la popularité de Bonaparte grandissait.* **Il n'en est pas moins vrai** que bien des français se demandaient si l'on allait se battre toujours, enrôler toujours, conquérir toujours. (Bainville, J. *Histoire de France*: 196)
'A victorious general who brought in money was making himself indispensable. So Bonaparte's popularity grew. It is nonetheless true that many French people were wondering if they would always be enrolling new soldiers, always be fighting, always be conquering new lands'.

(6.94) *Voici qu'une fois encore un des grands sujets de mon cours le George a été saboté- pas tout à fait par ma faute cette fois- ci à cause et de ma santé et de l'ouragan Keyserling; mais* **il n'en est pas moins vrai** que depuis l'ouverture de ce cours il y a quatre ans, j'enregistre de plus en plus de désastres… (DuBos, C. *Journal T*. 3:63)
'Once again, one of the most important topics in my course, the George has been sabotaged – not by any fault of mine this time, because of my health and the Keyserling hurricane; but it is nonetheless true that since I started this course four years ago, I have been the victim of an increasing number of disasters…'

In the examples in (6.93) and (6.94) the mitigating circumstances that surround the proposition introduced by the impersonal pronoun are not sufficient to obscure its reality. This structure matches up perfectly with the *il* construction that codes the existence of the proposition. This function of the pronoun makes it ideally suited to express this sort of narrative bottom line.

This section has shown that the distribution of *il* and *c'* with the epistemic predicate *est vrai* conforms to specific tendencies, and that these tendencies are congruent with the two pronouns' respective meanings. *C'* is specifically concerned with the evaluation of the proposition coded in the *si* clause as real, while *il* focuses more directly on that proposition's sheer existence or, alternatively, its being treated as real in order to evaluate the ensuing consequences for the reminder of the argument. However, the example in (6.95) serves to remind us that these tendencies are not absolute. Despite the fact that the complement content represents an almost-verbatim repeat of a former statement and that the communicative purpose of the sentence is to confirm the protagonist's statement, *il* is used. Other factors, in particular sociolinguistic ones and ultimately author choice, also bear on the selection of the impersonal pronoun.

(6.95)   *Tu as une grande fièvre. Tu es pétrie de tristesse. Ton âme est pétrie de tristesse.*
        Ton oncle est allé la chercher, hein. Jeannette – **il est vrai** <u>*que mon âme est dans*</u>
        <u>*la tristesse.*</u>   (Péguy, C. *Le mystère de la charité de Jeanne d'Arc*: 16)
        'You have a great fever. You are immersed in sadness. Your soul is immersed
        in sadness. Your uncle went to fetch her, didn't he. Jeanette – it is true that my
        soul is in sadness'.

We can now come back to the discrepancy observed between the distribution of the two pronouns in the larger corpus and that in *Les mandarins*, where *ça* (*c'*) outnumbers *il* by thirty-one to two. The dialogic nature of the novel and the way in which the ideas emerge out of conversations between the protagonists goes a long way toward explaining this frequency difference. Nineteen examples occur in conversation and precisely follow the tendency observed throughout this section, namely the confirmation of the potential for the proposition coded in the *si* clause to be true, as illustrated in (6.96):

(6.96)   *C'est l'ensemble qui est moche: comme ils ménagent les fritz, y compris les nazis,*
        et comment ils traitent les types des camps. – Je voudrais bien savoir si **c'est vrai**
        <u>*qu'ils interdisent les camps à la croix-rouge française,*</u> *dit Henri.*
                         (Beauvoir, S. de. *Les mandarins*: 131)
        'The whole picture is ugly: how they tiptoe around the Krauts, including the
        Nazis, and how they treat people in the camps. – I would like to know if it
        [this] is true that they do not allow the French Red Cross into the camps, Henri
        said'.

Furthermore, twelve of the thirty-one examples of *c'* involve speaker internal dialogue, some of which, illustrated in (6.97), preserves the formal structure of dialogue with the quotation marks:

(6.97)   *Henri s'arrangerait pour l'associer de plus en plus étroitement à la vie du journal;*
         Lambert se formerait politiquement, il se sentirait beaucoup moins perdu dans
         le monde, et une fois tout à fait dans le coup, il ne se demanderait plus que faire
         *de sa peau. "C'est **vrai** <u>que ce n'est pas commode d'être jeune en ce moment</u>", se*
         dit Henri.   (Beauvoir, S. de. *Les mandarins*: 255)
         'Henri was finding ways to integrate him more and more closely to the daily
         life of the paper; Lambert would learn politics, he would feel far less lost in the
         world, and once he was totally comfortable, he would no longer wonder what
         to do with himself. "It [this] is true that it is not easy to be young nowadays",
         Henri said to himself'.

Even when there are no quotation marks the internal dialogue originates from a conversation and the proposition whose truth the character confirms originates as a result of the previous conversation as if the protagonist were continuing the dialogue for herself, as illustrated in (6.98):

(6.98)   *Lewis se mit à rire: – Pauvre petite gauloise! Comme elle a l'air pitoyable dès*
         *qu'on ne fait plus ses quatre volontés! Je rougis. **C'était bien vrai** <u>que Lewis ne</u>*
         <u>pensait jamais qu'à me faire plaisir.</u>   (Beauvoir, S. de. *Les mandarins*: 438)
         'Lewis started laughing: – My poor little Gaulish girl! How pitiful she looks
         when things don't go her way! I blushed. It [this] was really true that Lewis
         was always trying to make me happy'.

It is therefore clear that the difference in frequency between *Les mandarins* and the larger corpus does not present any challenge to the analysis developed in this section. To the contrary, the systematic use of the demonstrative impersonal along with similar discursive strategies designed to highlight the interactive and conversational tone of the novel provides further validation for that pronoun's meaning, as it is presented in this chapter.

Unfortunately, the analysis of *vrai* cannot directly be extended to other predicates because the adaptation of the pronouns' meaning to the discourse context is obviously mediated by the semantic import of the predicate. If the interactive, evaluative, and argumentative functions the pronouns have displayed in this section represent well-motivated adaptations of the pronouns' meaning in other contexts, we should not necessarily expect to see them reproduced with other predicates, especially with predicates from other semantic classes. For this reason, general statements about the overall distribution of *il* and impersonal demonstratives only stand a chance of being correct if they are based on fine-grained analyses of individual predicates.

6.   Recapitulation and conclusion

This chapter explored the semantic import of the neuter demonstrative *ça*. It showed that the pronoun's function is to identify, categorize, or evaluate an entity, and that that entity often needs to be constructed from the immediate discourse context and the inferences it affords. The scene that the pronoun profiles is also construed subjectively, i.e. in a global fashion, which blurs the distinction between the participants in the main relation and includes the conceptualizer (most frequently the speaker) in its scope of predication. These characteristics are common to all senses of *ça*, but they are critical to understanding the pronoun's use in impersonal contexts because they render a strict cataphoric analysis impossible to maintain. When an infinitival or finite clause follows the predicate, *ça* does not solely refer forward to that clause but in equal parts back to the immediate context from which it is extracted and objectified for expressive purposes. The essence of the pronoun's meaning in such contexts is precisely to isolate a section of the previous discourse and single it out for repetition, reformulation, generalization, or other possible cognitive operations that further the speaker's narrative purposes.

Ça is thus very close semantically to *il*, the difference between them pertaining essentially to the conceptualizer's role in evaluating the complement content. When the described situation is general enough to be available to a generalized conceptualizer, French therefore possesses two impersonal pronouns, with *il* profiling the field or scope of awareness for the content of the complement clause, and *ça* describing the abstract setting from which that content is extracted. This competition between the two pronouns consistently and reliably occurs in the copular complement construction where the predicate enjoys the required level of generality to be considered impersonal. Within that context the distribution between the two pronouns depends highly on the author's narrative strategy, as well as on the meaning of individual predicates. In Simone de Beauvoir's novel *Les mandarins*, the quasi-systematic use of *ça* to the detriment of *il* partakes of a general narrative strategy to enhance the novel's interactive and conversational tone where important ideas emerge from character-internal dialogue or from conversations between the protagonists. With individual predicates, the distribution of *il* and *ça* may pertain to the management and organization of the different parts that constitute an overall argument. With *être vrai* 'be true', *il* is used to temper a previously made statement by introducing information that undermines its overall force, while *ça*'s presence generally indicates that the complement content directly corresponds to a section of the immediate context. However, the observations made in this chapter are necessarily fragmentary and incomplete because many more individual predicates need to be investigated before more general conclusions can be drawn.

CHAPTER 7

Middle impersonals

This chapter investigates middle impersonals, in other words constructions where the predicate contains the middle marker *se*. It shows that middle impersonals are structurally similar to other middles, but are distinguished by the presence of specific semantic and pragmatic features. In particular, the responsibility of the affected entity for the occurrence of the profiled process gradually contributes to the latter's generality because it overrides the differences between individual agents. As was already the case with demonstrative impersonals, middle impersonals are reliably identified within two stable constructions where they are consistently impersonals.

1. Introduction

The impersonal constructions investigated in the previous chapters all exhibit radical departure from a prototypical transitive clause in their selection of some abstract location (Achard, in press) as the main figure in the profiled relation. In Chapters 3 to 5 the core *il* impersonals were shown to select the field as the focal figure, while Chapter 6 argued that demonstrative (*ça*) impersonals choose the abstract setting as subject. The middle impersonals analyzed in this chapter defocus the agent of the profiled process by selecting an alternative participant as the focal figure. In the example in (7.1), the agent is the (virtual) unmentioned person using the cane, but the underlined theme *les coups de bâton* 'cane strokes' is selected as the main focal figure and thus marked as subject. Similarly, in (7.2) repeated from Chapter 1, the agent is the potential cook, namely anyone following the recipe, but the dish itself is selected as the primary figure in the profiled relation:

(7.1)   Scapin. – *Oh monsieur, **les coups de bâton ne se donnent pas à des gens comme lui** et ce n'est pas un homme à être traité de la sorte.*

(Claudel, P. Le ravissement de Scapin: 1344)

'Scapin: – Oh sir, cane strokes are not given [do not give themselves] to people like him and he is not a man to be treated in this manner'.

(7.2)   *Il note que le pain sans levain est cuit sur des plaques de tôle et ressemble à de*
la galette ou aux crêpes de carnaval, que le saucisson d'Arles se fait avec de la
viande de mulet.   (Durry, MJ. *Gérard de Nerval et le mythe*: 82)
'He notes that yeast-free bread is cooked on flat metal sheets and resembles
biscuits or the pancakes of carnival time; that the sausage from Arles is made
[makes itself] with mule meat'.

As was mentioned in Chapter 1, the constructions in (7.1) and (7.2) are clearly
impersonal according to the two criteria proposed in this monograph. First, as
the previous paragraph indicated, the agent is defocused by the selection of an
alternative participant as the primary figure in the main relation, and second, the
process that the predicate profiles is available to a generalized conceptualizer since
the proper treatment of important people in (7.1) constitutes a social obligation
from which no one is immune, and the culinary recipe described in (7.2) is independent from any specific cook.

Grammarians and linguists in the French tradition have long recognized the
general character of these constructions traditionally referred to as *constructions*
moyennes (Martinon 1927; Sandfeld 1929; Blinkenberg 1960; Stéfanini 1962; Gross
1968; Ruwet 1972; Zribi-Hertz 1982; Jones 1996). For instance, Ruwet (1972: 95)
observes that: "D'une manière générale, la construction moyenne ne peut pas être
utilisée pour signifier un événement particulier localisé en un point du temps;
elle peut en revanche prendre des valeurs habituelles, normatives, ou génériques
'Generally, the construction moyenne cannot be used to describe a specific event
occurring at a given point in time; it can, however, have a habitual, normative, or
generic value'. In the Generative tradition (Ruwet 1972; Zribi-Hertz 1982; Jones
1996), these *constructions moyennes* are kept separate from the *constructions neu-*
tres illustrated in (7.3) and (7.4):

(7.3)   *Olivier avait un frisson, au milieu de cet univers aveugle et ennemi. Il tressaillait,*
comme un levraut, au bruit d'une pomme de pin qui tombait, ou d'une branche
sèche qui se cassait... (Rolland, R. *Jean-Christophe à Paris: Antoinette*: 837)
'Olivier shivered in this blind and hostile world. He jumped like a young hare
to the sound of a falling pine cone or a dry branch breaking [that was breaking
itself]...'

(7.4)   *À ce moment, on frappa doucement, et comme tiré d'un rêve, Joseph cria: –*
Entrez! **La porte s'ouvrit** *alors pour livrer passage à une vieille négresse vêtue*
de noir...   (Green, J. *Moïra: roman*: 177)
'At this moment, someone knocked softly, and as if awakening from a dream,
Joseph shouted: – Come in! The door then opened [itself] to let in an old black
woman dressed in black...'

Despite their similar surface forms, the *constructions moyennes* in (7.1) and (7.2) are distinguished from their *neutres* counterparts illustrated in (7.3) and (7.4) by the nature of the agent of the process the predicate describes. The constructions *neutres* are ambivalent as to that agent's precise nature. For instance, the breaking of the branch in (7.3) may have resulted from the actions of an animate agent, or be imputable to some other indeterminate source such as water, rain, or sheer structural fatigue, but the identification of that source is not provided by the predicate. Similarly, the agent who opens the door in (7.4) is only revealed later on in the sentence, but the predicate itself remains neutral as to its origin. In the *constructions moyennes*, on the other hand, the lexical semantic structure of the predicate necessarily includes an implicit human agent. In (7.1), for instance, the cane strokes require someone holding the cane, while the making of the sausage in (7.2) can only be performed by a human chef.

In order to capture the different level of specificity of the predicate's agent, early Generative accounts treated the *constructions neutres* as structurally distinct from the *constructions moyennes*. The *constructions neutres* in (7.3) and (7.4) are base generated, while their *moyennes* counterparts in (7.1) and (7.2) are derived by a syntactic operation similar to the one that generates passives (Gross 1968; Ruwet 1972; Zribi-Hertz 1982).[1] Despite the similarities between the *constructions moyennes* and passives and their shared structure (see in particular Zribi-Hertz 1982 for an in-depth evaluation of the similarities and differences between the two, and Stéfanini 1962 for an argument that the *constructions moyennes* originally come from passives diachronically), the passive analysis of the *constructions moyennes* encounters some difficulties. For instance, Jones (1996: 116) notes that unlike passives, the *constructions moyennes* do not, in contemporary French, allow the agent to be specified by the oblique *par* 'by', as illustrated in (7.5) (from Jones 1996: 116):[2]

---

1. Ruwet (1972: 100) provides the following rule to derive the *constructions moyennes*:

$\Delta - V - NP - X$

$1 \quad 2 \quad 3 \quad \quad 4 \quad \rightarrow 3 - se + 2 - \emptyset - 4$

By comparison, the *constructions neutres* are base generated by the rule VP → (*se*) ... V (NP), as well as a lexical redundancy rule (Ruwet 1972: 91).

More recent models also derive middles by movement of the object to the subject position (Wehrli 1986; Lekakou 2003). The main argument in favor of the analysis comes from the fact that middles "are syntactically indistinguishable from (reflexive) passives and thus behave as unaccusatives" (Lekakou 2004: 182).

2. Citing examples from Grevisse (1969) and Wagner and Pinchon (1962), Zribi-Hertz (1982: 351) shows that during earlier periods of French the middle construction accepted the explicit expression of the agent.

(7.5)   *Ce journal est lu par 1 million de personnes*
        *Ce journal se lit par 1 million de personnes
        'This paper is read by 1 million people'

Furthermore, and more importantly for the purposes of this chapter, the treatment of the constructions illustrated in (7.1) and (7.2) as structural passives does little to capture their generalized character because while passives usually report punctual events, "middles can be used to make general or normative statements regarding habitual or hypothetical events" (Jones 1996: 116).[3]

This chapter shows that the structural split between the *constructions neutres* and *moyennes* is untenable because countless examples share characteristics of both of them. Consequently, these two constructions are best analyzed as the two endpoints of a continuum within a much broader "middle domain", namely "a coherent but relatively diffuse category that comprises a set of loosely linked semantic subdomains centering roughly around the direct reflexive" (Kemmer 1993: 15). Within this continuum, the difference between the constructions illustrated in (7.3) and (7.4) and the middle impersonals in (7.1) and (7.2) is explained by (1) a difference in the semantic/conceptual organization of the predicates, which explains why some are better candidates than others for impersonal status, and (2) the responsibility (Van Oosten 1977; see also Dowty 2000 and Lekakou's account of middles as "disposition ascriptions" [Lekakou 2004: 191]) of the subject for the occurrence of the process that the predicate profiles. Subject responsibility accounts for the general availability of that process because it neutralizes the characteristics inherent to individual agents and ensures its stable occurrence. In this analysis, middle impersonals are therefore structurally identical to other middles; they are mainly distinguished by the level of generality of their predicates. Here again, while responsibility and generality are gradual, the presence of two specific contexts within which middle impersonals can reliably be identified makes the analysis tenable. Consistent with the account of demonstrative impersonals presented in Chapter 6, middle impersonals crystallize around two specific

---

3.   Semantic accounts of middles (Condoravdi 1989; Ackema and Schoorlemmer 1994, 1995; Lekakou 2004) capture their general character better. For instance, Lekakou (2004: 183) argues that "since 'middles' are parasitic on independently existing structures – unergatives, passives –, it makes more sense to think of the former as a particular interpretation which the latter may receive." She further argues that middles receive their general interpretation because they are dispositional predicates: "Treating middles as dispositional predicates entails precisely that there is some property inherent to the subject which enables or facilitates the action denoted by the verb" (Lekakou 2004: 191). Except for the fact that the dispositional property is predicated of the syntactic subject of a passive structure, Lekakou's account is basically compatible with the one developed in this chapter.

constructions, but these constructions are identified by the presence of pragmatic rather than morphosyntactic features.

This treatment of middle impersonals better represents the flexibility of usage observed in the data, and complements our current understanding of both middle and impersonal categories. First, the relation between impersonals and middles is well established in other Romance languages. For example, the Italian *si* construction illustrated in (7.6) and (7.7) is uncontroversially recognized as an "impersonal passive (i.e., a construction having passive force but limited to impersonal contexts)" (Kemmer 1993: 178; see also Stéfanini 1962; Zribi-Hertz 1982, among others). While this Italian construction clearly has no direct French equivalent, it nonetheless highlights the semantic proximity of middles and impersonals, and thus the plausible emergence of a more limited, pragmatically based class of middle impersonals:[4]

(7.6) *Si construisce troppe case*   (from Zribi-Hertz 1982: 373)
       'Too many houses are being built'

(7.7) *Qui si leggono troppi libri*
                        (From Stéfanini 1962: 99, also cited in Kemmer 1993: 178)
       'Many books are read here'

Second, the recognition of the impersonal status of the constructions illustrated in (7.1) and (7.2) allows us to better understand the relationship that exists between the middle, passive, and impersonal categories. Middles resemble both passives and impersonals in defocusing the agent of the process that the predicate codes, but different middle situations resemble either passives or impersonals depending on the recoverability of the agent, and hence the general availability of the process it is responsible for. The examples in (7.1) and (7.2) have already been argued to be impersonal because the generalized agent of their profiled process is not recoverable. In the situation described in (7.8), however, the participants in the discussion are not named explicitly, but are nonetheless clearly delineated and could be recovered easily. Consequently, this middle configuration lacks the degree of generality required to be called impersonal, but more closely resembles a passive construction:

(7.8) *Ce point s'est discuté*   (from Zribi-Hertz 1982: 352)
       'This point was discussed [discussed itself]'

---

4. The Italian construction appeared later than the French middle *se* (Stéfanini 1962). Note that its direct translation into French is impossible. In (7.6) it would yield *il se construit trop de maisons*, and in (7.7) the most natural choice would be to use the indefinite pronoun *on* 'one' (*on lit beaucoup de livres ici* 'many books are read here').

This chapter is not directly concerned with the middle/passive connection, but investigates the precise conditions under which *se* constructions acquire the level of generality commensurate with their treatment as impersonals. It is organized in the following manner. Section 2 provides an overview of the different treatments that French *se* constructions have received. As briefly mentioned in this introduction, it shows that the structural separation of the *moyennes* and *neutres* constructions cannot be maintained. The analysis follows Kemmer (1993) in describing *se* impersonals relative to a large functional middle domain, and describes their connections with the neighboring constructions. Section 3 presents the specific section of the middle domain most directly relevant to the concerns of this chapter, namely the continuum between the "spontaneous action or process" and "passive middles" (Kemmer 1993: 206). Section 4 introduces the two constructions in which middle *se* is unquestionably impersonal, and shows that their characteristics are inherited from other middle uses. Section 5 discusses some general issues that the analysis raises particularly with respect to the relation between middle and *il* impersonals. Section 6 recapitulates the results and concludes the chapter.

2.   French pronominal verbs

In the French tradition, the constructions investigated in this chapter are subsumed under the larger morphological category of *verbes pronominaux* 'pronominal verbs' (Melis 1990; Jones 1996, among many others), a term broadly "used to describe constructions containing the clitic *se*" (Jones 1996: 111). This category generally includes the reflexives and reciprocals illustrated in (7.9) and (7.10), as well as a very large group of grooming (*se laver* 'wash oneself'), motion (*se lever* 'get up'), cognitive (*se rappeler* 'remember'), or spontaneous (*se briser* 'break') verbs. Predicates are traditionally divided into the "intrinsically" pronominal verbs described in (7.11) and their "derived" counterparts in (7.12) (Jones 1996: 111). Intrinsic pronominals do not possess a transitive variant while derived pronominals do, as the examples in (7.13) illustrate:[5]

> (7.9)   #*Il s'est regardé dans la glace*
>   'He looked at himself in the mirror'

---

5.   Certain verbs have a transitive variant, but that variant has a different sense. This is illustrated in (i) and (ii):

> (i)   #*Il peut venir ce soir*
>   'He can come tonight'

> (ii) #*Il se peut qu'il vienne ce soir*
>   'It is possible that he will come tonight'

(7.10) #*Ils se battent tout le temps*
        'They fight with each other all the time'

(7.11) a. #*Elle s'est évanouie*
            'She fainted'
        b. #*Elle ne se souvient pas*
            'She cannot remember'
        c. #*Il se peut qu'elle soit venue*
            'It is possible that she came'

(7.12) a. #*La chaise s'est cassée*
            'The chair broke [itself]'
        b. #*Le verre s'est brisé*
            'The glass shattered [itself]'

(7.13) a. #*Jean a cassé la chaise*
            'John broke the chair'
        b. #*Marie a brisé le verre*
            'Mary shattered the glass'

This vast French pronominal area has been investigated in various ways. Grammarians have primarily been interested in documenting the syntactic behavior of the different semantic types of predicates that compose it. Generative linguists have been more concerned with identifying the structure that different predicate classes have in common. Two main issues have received the lion's share of their investigative focus, namely (1) the difference between the intrinsic and derived predicates, and (2) the distinction between the constructions *neutres* and *moyennes* briefly mentioned in the introduction. Functional models, by contrast, have proposed a more comprehensive view of the entire category. For example, Kemmer (1993) posits the existence of a "middle domain" (Kemmer 1993:15) where different constructions describe different event types connected together by semantic relations. In her view, the constructions *neutres* and *moyennes* (spontaneous actions or processes and passive middles in Kemmer's terminology) are not structurally distinct but constitute the opposite endpoints of a semantic continuum (to be considered in detail in Section 3).

This section argues that the comprehensive account of the middle domain that Kemmer proposes affords a better description of the manner in which middle impersonals emerge than a purely syntactic solution. Section 2.1 shows that the Generative analysis that posits a structural separation between the *neutres* and *moyennes* constructions is untenable because of the large number of examples that possess characteristics of both types. Section 2.2 shows that Kemmer's model provides the right framework within which the semantic/pragmatic transition between the two constructions can be investigated.

2.1 Constructions *neutres* and *moyennes*

The introduction already mentioned that Generative analyses (Gross 1968; Ruwet 1972; Zribi-Hertz 1982; Jones 1996) posit a structural distinction between the *constructions moyennes* illustrated in (7.1) and (7.2), and their *neutres* counterparts illustrated in (7.3) and (7.4).[6] The basic idea is that the *neutres* predicates do not specify whether or not an agent is responsible for the change of state that the affected entity undergoes. Jones (1996: 112) expresses their neutrality in the following manner:

> Whereas the transitive verbs ... denote events brought about by an agent (represented by the subject) the pronominal verbs ... simply describe processes which do not involve the participation of an agent. In other words, the examples ... are neutral with respect to the way in which the events are brought about.

Evidence in favor of that position comes from the frequent presence of a transitive variant of the *neutres* predicates with roughly similar meaning, as the examples in (7.12) and (7.13) above illustrate.[7]

The *moyens* predicates share the same surface organization as their *neutres* counterparts, but they imply the necessary presence of a human agent. In the examples in (7.14)–(7.17) taken from Jones (1996: 112), the subject of the transitive variant is always the indefinite *on* 'one' (see Chapter 8), and this indefinite agentive presence is also implicitly attested in the intransitive (*moyenne*) construction. The presence of an agent in both constructions accounts for the semantic equivalence of the pairs in (7.14) / (7.15) and (7.16) / (7.17):[8]

(7.14) **On boit** *ce vin chambré*
'One drinks this wine chilled'

(7.15) *Ce vin* **se boit** *chambré*
'This wine is drunk chilled'

(7.16) **On lit** *ce journal en cinq minutes*
'One reads this newspaper in five minutes'

(7.17) *Ce journal* **se lit** *en cinq minutes*
'This newspaper reads in five minutes'

---

6. The *constructions moyennes* are sometimes also called *mediopassives* (Melis 1990).

7. French possesses another construction in which the predicate is not preceded by pronominal *se*, as in *la chaise a cassé* 'the chair broke', for instance. For a semantic analysis of the difference between this intransitive construction and the pronominal one, see Achard (2009).

8. The relation between the *on* and *se* constructions is considered more specifically in Chapter 8.

One of the reasons most often invoked to keep the two classes of predicates separate is their difference in productivity. *Neutres* predicates are categorized as purely lexical oddities, "an apparently arbitrary set of verbs" (Jones 1996: 119), while the *moyennes* forms are completely productive in the sense that they are derived from any transitive verb that has an agentive subject by a syntactic operation, the exact nature of which has changed through the years but will not be considered here (Jones 1996: 120; see also Ruwet's 1972 analysis introduced in note 1). In addition to their respective productivity, additional diagnostic criteria have been designed to distinguish between the *neutres* and *moyens* predicates. The most exhaustive list comes from Jones (1996: 119–120), who suggests that the presence of the following characteristics should be used to keep the two classes of predicates separate (see also Zribi-Hertz 1982: 352):

Middles:

- Can only be formed with transitive verbs that have an agentive subject. They are possible with all such verbs.
- Always contain a clitic.
- Always imply the participation of a generic agent (even though it cannot be introduced by *par* 'by').
- Can only describe habitual or normative situations and are incompatible with punctual tense forms.
- Allow (and often require) adverbial expressions which involve an agent.

Pronominal verbs:

- May or may not have corresponding transitive forms (Neutral versus Intrinsic).
- Are restricted to an apparently arbitrary set of verbs.
- Do not imply the participation of an implicit agent and thus cannot be modified by adverbial expressions which involve such an agent.
- Can be used with punctual and non-punctual tenses.

Jones's analysis of the two constructions as clearly separate reflects at the same time respect for the French tradition as well as the theoretical concern to point out the structural similarity between the *formes moyennes* and passives (Stéfanini 1962; Ruwet 1972; Zribi Hertz 1982). However, as deeply as it is entrenched in the French and Generative traditions, the distinction between the *neutres* and *moyennes* forms is far from being as straightforward as the literature presents it. In order to make their points in the clearest possible manner, authors are understandably careful to base their analyses on two highly specific, maximally distinctive, and internally consistent sets of situations as representative examples. On the one hand, inanimate objects that undergo a change of state that can be imputed to a variety of causes (*la branche se casse* 'the branch breaks', *le feu s'éteint* 'the fire extinguishes itself', *le verre se brise*'the glass shatters') are chosen to illustrate the *neutres* predicates, while on the other hand stable cultural events that can only be performed by humans (*le champagne se boit frais* 'champagne is drunk chilled', *le fromage se mange à la fin du repas* 'one eats cheese at the end of a meal', *ce journal se lit en cinq minutes* 'this paper is read in five minutes') are taken as emblematic of *constructions moyennes*. These two kinds of situations are, of course, perfectly valid and need to be accounted for, but they do not exhaustively represent the range of situations that *se* constructions cover. In fact, in many cases illustrated such as (7.18), the predicate does not fall neatly into either of the two aforementioned categories because it shares characteristics with both:

(7.18) #*Le diner s'acheva en chantant (dans la bonne humeur)*
        'The dinner finished [itself] in songs'

In (7.18) the predicate *s'achever* figures among the arbitrary small set of *neutres* predicates, but the presence of *en chantant* blatantly violates the condition that such predicates cannot be modified by an adverbial expression that involves an agent. On the other hand, it does not fully satisfy the conditions characteristic of middle predicates because even though it does contain an implicit agent, the latter is not generic, its aspect is punctual, and it does not describe a habitual or normative situation. According to Jones's criteria, the predicate in (7.18) is neither strictly *neutre* nor *moyen*. The problem comes from the fact that the implicit presence of an agent does not come from the predicate but from the noun phrase *le diner* 'the dinner', namely the entity that undergoes the change of state and is coded as subject in the construction. Because the term *diner* appropriately describes only the actions of humans eating, the presence of an abstract human agent is implicit in the subject's lexical semantic structure regardless of the nature of the predicate. Consequently the *neutre* or *moyenne* quality of the situation is determined by the whole construction rather than the nature of the predicate.[9] Note, however, that the implicit presence of an agent does not invalidate the spontaneity of the interruption. The diners' presence does not necessarily indicate that they consciously and willingly interrupted the meal. More likely the latter naturally reached the end of its natural course in a quasi-organic manner (to be elaborated in further detail in Section 3).

The example in (7.18) cannot be dismissed as an idiosyncratic property of a few recalcitrant predicates. A similar analysis can be given for the entire class of creation verbs that describe the coming into existence of an entity, and where consequently the change of state that the predicate profiles can only be performed by human hands, as the examples in (7.19) and (7.20) illustrate:

---

9. Generative linguists, of course, are aware of these constructional effects. See, for example, Ruwet (1972: 118) for discussion.

(7.19) #*Cette maison s'est **construite** en trois mois!*
'This house was built [built itself] in three months'

(7.20) #*En dix ans à peine, au moins cinq entreprises se **sont monté** dans la région.*
'In hardly ten years, at least ten companies opened [themselves] in the area'

Examples like (7.19) and (7.20) clearly show why creation predicates seldom figure in the discussion of change of state predicates, while their destruction counterparts provide the bulk of the examples. If the destruction of an entity can result
from a variety of causes – the very basis for positing a class of *neutres* predicates –
creation is necessarily agentive in the sense that it can only result from human
(animate) effort. As a result, if destruction verbs constitute the prototypical *neutre*
predicates, the creation verbs illustrated in (7.19) and (7.20) are by definition
excluded from the category. Additionally, since they also violate the same middle
requirements as the construction in (7.18), namely their agent is not general and
they describe a punctual rather than habitual or normative kind of situation, they
are not easily accounted for in an analysis that requires a strict separation between
the two constructions.

A final attested example of constructions that do not fit into either category
is given in (7.21).

(7.21) *Jour après jour, nous recouvrons la liberté. La vie, maintenant, reprend peu à
peu. Nos mines travaillent. Nos usines repartent. **Nos ports se rouvrent. Nos
champs se labourent. Nos ruines se déblaient.***

(Gaulle, C. de. *Mémoires de guerre, le salut*: 601)
'Day after day we are recovering our freedom. Life is starting again, little by
little. Our mines are working. Our factories are producing again. Our harbors
are opening [open themselves]. Our fields are being plowed [plow themselves].
Our ruins are being cleaned out [clean themselves out]'.

As was observed in (7.18)–(7.20), the separation of the pronominal predicates
into the *neutres* and *moyennes* forms makes it impossible to analyze the situation
described in (7.21) where the verbs *s'ouvrir* 'be open', *se labourer* 'be plowed', and
se déblayer 'be cleaned out' share characteristics with both classes. They exhibit
the productivity of *formes moyennes* since they are all transitive verbs with human
agents that clearly do not belong to any arbitrary list, but they do not carry the
habitual or normative overtones characteristic of those forms since they all refer
to the highly specific period that follows the end of World War Two in France.

Even if we admit for the time being that the middle impersonals illustrated in
(7.1) and (7.2) are identical to the *constructions moyennes* of the French tradition,
the examples in (7.18)–(7.21) clearly indicate that they are not distinguished from
other middles by their structural properties. In fact, the separation of the domain

that *se* covers into two structurally distinct constructions inadequately represents French usage because the polarization of the data between two diametrically opposed structures provides undue focus on the ends of the continuum that best illustrates them, to the detriment of the countless situations that fall somewhere in between. In order to understand the emergence of middle impersonals, a broader, more-inclusive view of the domain that *se* covers is needed where the relations that exist between the different "middle situation types" (Kemmer 1993: 15) can be brought to light and investigated. The next section presents Kemmer's analysis of the French "middle domain" (Kemmer 1993: 15) where middle impersonals take their natural place.

2.2 The French "middle domain"

For Kemmer (1993: 15), a middle domain is "a coherent but relatively diffuse category that comprises a set of loosely linked semantic subdomains centering roughly around the direct reflexive." This represents a large, difficult to precisely delineate, transitional area between intransitive (one-participant) and transitive (two-participant) events. Semantically, this area can be delimited with reference to two properties: " (1) Initiator as affected entity (Endpoint), and (2) Low degree of elaboration of events. The first property … is subsumed by the second one, since the equating of Initiator and Endpoint effectively makes an event less elaborated than a fully transitive event in which the two entities are completely distinct" (Kemmer 1993: 238). With specific respect to French, the semantic range of the middle domain that the marker *se* morphosyntactically codes is represented in Figure 7.1, adapted from Kemmer (1993: 206).

As the shaded area in Figure 7.1 indicates, the French middle domain covers the broad area between the intransitive and transitive event types. The examination of the entire middle domain is clearly beyond the scope of the concerns of this chapter. For instance, the reflexive and reciprocal structures respectively illustrated in (7.9) and (7.10) as well as the various kinds of event types introduced in (7.11) do not directly relate to impersonals in any obvious manner, and will therefore not be considered any further. The focus of the following sections is thus strictly restricted to the area included in the oblong shape at the right periphery of the category (added to Kemmer's original), where the familiar situation types of "spontaneous actions or processes" (Kemmer's terminology for the *neutres* forms of the French Generative tradition, henceforth SAP) and "passive middles" (the *moyenne* category in the previous section, henceforth PM) can be located. It should be clear that from this point on the term "middle" only refers to *se* constructions

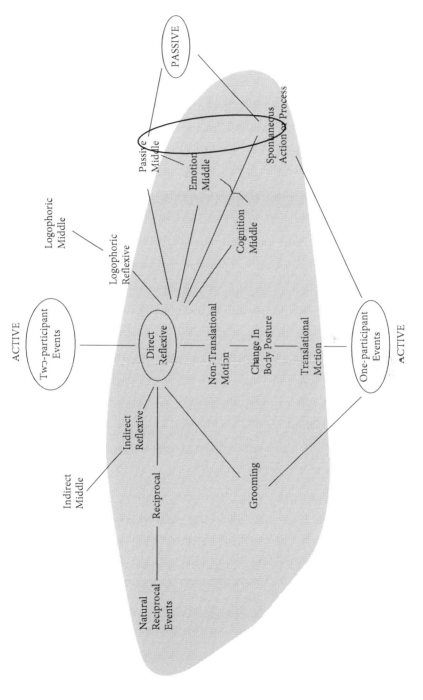

Figure 7.1 The semantic range of French *se* (adapted from Kemmer 1993: 206)

in general, or at least those discussed in this chapter. In particular, it is not used as an English translation of the French *formes moyennes*.

Kemmer's mapping of the French middle domain provides an excellent starting point for the investigation of a class of middle impersonals because of its flexibility and the semantic character of the relations between event types, but in order to clearly understand how that class emerges her analysis needs to be elaborated in the zone of critical interest between the SAP and the PM delineated by the oblong shape in Figure 7.1. Within this smaller domain, some specific semantic relations need to be further elaborated. For one thing, although SAP types are located in the general vicinity of the PM on the map, their semantic relations are not explicitly investigated (note that there is no line connecting them in Figure 7.1). Furthermore, the relation between the passive middles and impersonals is not indicated on the map, perhaps because Kemmer analyzes the middle/impersonal connection as being mediated by passives. For example, she uses the example *cela ne se dit pas* 'this is not said' to illustrate the fact that "passive-like uses that appear with middle marking do not make reference to an inherent characteristic of the Patient, but only to an unknown or generic Agent" (Kemmer 1993: 148). Kemmer rightly recognizes that these examples come remarkably close to impersonals: "this use impinges on the impersonal situation types, in which the Agent is always generic" (Kemmer 1993: 148), but no further analysis of the relation between middles and impersonals is provided.[10]

The analysis in this chapter complements Kemmer's account in that it investigates in closer detail: (1) the relationship that exists between SAPs and PMs, and (2) the conditions under which both types can be considered impersonal. The line between the SAP and the PM defines a continuum along which the profiled process gradually becomes more generally available. In a nutshell, the pragmatic

---

10. Kemmer further notes that "the impersonal situation type subsumes both situations in which there is an affected entity (which is coded as subject or chief nominal participant) as in one should never serve wine/wine should never be served on such occasions, and those in which there is no particular affected entity, as in one can work well here" (Kemmer 1993: 148). Finally, she distinguishes between languages such as Spanish and German, where middles can cover both kinds of situations, and French, where it is restricted to the former: "In some languages, e.g. French, the middle marker is used only for impersonal situations in which there is an expressed Endpoint; in others, the use of the MM has been extended to a general impersonal construction without a necessary reference to an Endpoint (c.f. Spanish *Se hable mucho acquí* 'One talks a lot here, there is a lot of talking here', German *Hier tanzt sich gut = Man tanzt hier gut* 'One can dance well here')" (Kemmer 1993: 148). The distinction between the two kinds of situations is taken up again in Chapter 8 since the second situation type is expressed in French by the indefinite pronoun *on*.

feature of the responsibility (Van Oosten 1977) of the affected entity for the occurrence of the process that the predicate profiles favors an impersonal reading because it increases the stability and predictability of that process so that it can be available to anyone at any given time. The notion of generality is gradual, but middle impersonals can nonetheless reliably be identified within the confines of two constructional islands that possess highly specific semantic/pragmatic properties. In the first, the process that the predicate profiles constitutes a definitional characteristic of the entity coded as subject. In the second, it constitutes a social requirement imposed on that entity.

The analysis developed in the following sections readily accommodates the general character of the French *formes moyennes* and Kemmer's passive middles, but it also shows that middle impersonals cannot be reduced to that type alone because (1) not all passive middles will be general enough to be called impersonals (see example [7.8], for instance) and (2) spontaneous actions or processes types can also be impersonal under specific conditions. It is certainly easier for passive middles than for spontaneous actions and processes types to become impersonal (to be considered in detail in Section 3), but impersonality cannot be equated with any one single situation type. The highly general trademark of impersonals can be a feature of spontaneous actions or processes as well as passive middle types alike, albeit under different circumstances.

3.   From spontaneous events to impersonals

This section focuses on the area between the SAP and the MP on the map in Figure 7.1. It shows that these two event types represent the two endpoints of a continuum of generality of the profiled process. It also shows that the affected entity's responsibility for the occurrence of the event that the predicate profiles greatly determines the latter's general availability.

3.1   Two main groups of predicates

Even though middle constructions have received considerable attention, it is important to carefully consider the whole range of situations that constitute the area contained between the SAPs and the PMs in Figure 7.1 because the examples encountered in the literature are too often polarized in the manner presented in Section 2.

The 969 examples considered for the analysis presented in this section (486 with *s'* from FRANTEXT and AFP, and 483 with *se* from the same sources) neatly divide into two main classes. We already have some degree of familiarity with the first, which we call "spontaneous events" because the predicate primarily profiles the internal change of state that the affected entity endures. The second class describes inherently human activities, namely acts of perception, communication, creation, or social interaction, which can only be performed by humans or, more generally, animates. These two classes present some degree of overlap with previously proposed classifications. The spontaneous events class obviously resembles the *neutres* predicates of the French tradition as well as Kemmer's SAPs, but the class also importantly includes situations that contain a human agent, such as (7.22), and thus cannot be considered *neutres* (this issue will be considered in detail in the next section). The second class is much more inclusive than the French *constructions moyennes* and Kemmer's passive middles because it also includes nonhabitual/deontic situations that lack the degree of generality to warrant inclusion in these groups. The data presented in this section clearly show that if the two classes of *neutres* and *moyennes* forms recognized by a large majority of researchers are indeed attested, they do not provide an exhaustive description of the French middle usage because they fail to include the large number of in-between cases attested between them. The two classes of spontaneous events and inherently human activities are now briefly presented in turn.

Spontaneous predicates profile the specific type of alteration that the affected entity (i.e. the subject) undergoes, namely interruption in (7.22), proliferation in (7.23), degradation in (7.24), amelioration in (7.25), and transformation in (7.26).

(7.22)   *Le dîner s'acheva assez vite. Au moment où ils se levaient de table, Mrs Ferguson demanda à Joseph s'il fumait.*   (Green, J. *Moïra: roman*: 146)
'The dinner ended [finished itself] rather quickly. As they were getting up from the table, Mrs. Ferguson asked Joseph if he smoked'.

(7.23)   *Je n'en finis pas de boucher des trous, on me presse de tous les côtés et **les créanciers se multiplient** comme une portée de souris.* (Aymé, M. *Clérambard*: 19)
'I keep trying to plug holes, I am rushed from all sides and the creditors are proliferating [multiplying themselves] like a litter of mice'.

(7.24)   *Se rendre compte clairement avant chaque travail (ou, pour les travaux tout à fait nouveaux, au bout de quelque temps) des difficultés possibles, notamment comment **la machine** peut **se** dérégler...* (Weil, S. *La condition ouvrière*: 175)
'To realize clearly before any job (or for brand new jobs after some time) what the possible difficulties might be, specifically how the machine can lose its settings [get itself out of tune]...'

(7.25) *Mais seule, sous un ciel inconnu, qu'est-ce qui va m'arriver? Quelles évidences vont soudain m'aveugler? Quels abîmes se découvrir? **Les abîmes se cicatriseront, les évidences s'éteindront**, c'est sûr et certain; j'en ai vu d'autres.*

(Beauvoir, S. de. *Les mandarins*: 179)

'But alone, under a foreign sky, what will happen to me? What certainties will suddenly blind me? Which abysses will appear [reveal themselves]? The abysses will heal themselves, the certainties will fade away [switch themselves off]. I am sure of it. I have been there before'.

(7.26) *Les formes humaines renoncent à leur véhémence musculaire; **elles** aussi **s'amincissent, s'allongent**, aspirent à l'élégance plus qu'à la puissance.*

(Huyghe, R. *Dialogue avec le visible*: 296)

'The human shapes give up their muscular vigor; they also become leaner [thin themselves out], longer [lengthen themselves], in pursuit of elegance rather than strength'.

The processes illustrated in (7.22)–(7.26) all profile the trajectory that their subjects undergo from their initial to their final state. Importantly for our purposes, the profiled process is described as self-initiated, i.e. without the impetus of any specific agent, even though potential agents may be present. The internal dynamics of individual predicates are widely different. For instance, *s'achever* in (7.22), *se cicatriser* and *s'éteindre* in (7.25), as well as *s'amincir* and *s'allonger* in (7.26) represent the natural outcome of the transformation that the predicate profiles, given the nature of the affected entity. *Se multiplier* in (7.23) is somewhat different, because the sentence describes the speaker's interpretation of the situation. Although the affected entity presents some characteristics of agents (creditors need to explicitly request to be paid to be considered as such), their increasing number is presented as inescapable. Given the speaker's financial circumstances, the proliferation of creditors is viewed with the inevitability of any organic process. Even when the agent of the profiled process is not only easily recoverable but also worthy of specific subsequent description as in (7.4) repeated here for convenience, it is not presented as the initiator of the profiled process:

(7.4) *À ce moment, on frappa doucement, et comme tiré d'un rêve, Joseph cria: – Entrez! **La porte s'ouvrit** alors pour livrer passage à une vieille négresse vêtue de noir et la taille ceinte d'un tablier blanc qui lui tombait jusqu'aux pieds.*

(Green, J. *Moïra: roman*: 177)

'At this moment, someone knocked softly, and as if awakening from a dream, Joseph shouted: – Come in! The door then opened [itself] to let in an old black woman dressed in black'.

The second semantic class of middle predicates describes inherently human activities because the profiled process necessarily comes into existence through the specific efforts of a human conceptualizer. It describes events of perception in (7.27), communication in (7.28), mental apprehension in (7.29), creation in (7.30), and social interaction in (7.31):

(7.27)   *on avait cueilli les lavandes **cela se sentait** à plein nez*
                                  (Aragon, L. *Le roman inachevé*: 149)
         'Lavender had been harvested. One could smell it strongly [this smelled itself with full nose]'

(7.28)   *Le geste doit révéler ce qu'il y a au fond de l'âme; c'est son rôle; les phrases ne sont que de l'amplification. On voit cela dans presque tous les romans **qui s'écrivent** aujourd'hui.*   (Green, J. *Journal. T. 5. 1946-1950*: 272)
         'Gestures must reveal the content of the soul; it's their role; sentences merely serve to amplify them. This is visible in almost every novel that is written [writes itself] today'.

(7.29)   ***Une économie refuge se définit** comme telle par la présence ou la combinaison de divers caractères: les règles fondamentales du capitalisme (respect de la propriété privée) ont les moindres chances d'y être violées...*
                                  (Perroux, F. *L'économie du XXe siècle*: 65)
         'A sheltered economy is defined [defines itself] as such by the presence or combination of different characteristics: the fundamental laws of capitalism (respect for private property) are less at risk of being violated...'

(7.30)   *La recherche d'une rigueur aussi cartésienne dans la construction, outre qu'elle se heurte à d'inextricables difficultés instrumentales, n'est pas assurée pour autant d'un effet esthétique. Il serait étrange que **la musique concrète** puisse **se construire** à partir d'une épure de géomètre.*
                                  (Schaeffer, P. *A la recherche d'une musique concrète*: 34)
         'The search for such Cartesian rigor in the design, in addition to the extreme logistical difficulties it faces, presents no aesthetic guarantee. It would be strange to be able to build concrete music [that concrete music could build itself] from a surveyor's outline'.

(7.31)   *On disait aussi qu'à la nuit tombée des arguments moins relevés étaient mis en ligne, et que **l'argent et le vin se distribuaient** à flots...*
                                  (Gracq, J. *Le rivage des Syrtes*: 321)
         'It was also said that at night some less-elevated arguments were being settled, and that large amounts of wine and money were circulating [distributing themselves]...'

The domain of social interaction is extremely eclectic and virtually any initially transitive process can participate in the construction, as previously illustrated in (7.21) and repeated here:

(7.21)   *Jour après jour, nous recouvrons la liberté. La vie, maintenant, reprend peu à peu. Nos mines travaillent. Nos usines repartent. **Nos ports se rouvrent. Nos champs se labourent. Nos ruines se déblaient.***

(Gaulle, C. de. Mémoires de guerre, le salut: 601)

‘Day after day we are recovering our freedom. Life is starting again, little by little. Our mines are working. Our factories are producing again. Our harbors are opening [open themselves]. Our fields are being plowed [plow themselves]. Our ruins are being cleaned out [clean themselves out]’.

3.2   Conceptual structure of the two classes

One of the main claims of the analysis presented in this chapter is that middle impersonals are not structurally different from other middles. Consequently, all middle constructions possess a common semantic/conceptual core, namely they select the affected entity as the focal figure in the profiled relation and thus code the latter as subject (Kemmer 1993; Langacker 1982, 2006). In the spontaneous example in (7.4), for instance, the affected entity *la porte* (underlined in the example) is coded as subject. The agent of the opening process is clearly identifiable as the old woman who entered the room, but her agentive role is not mentioned in the linguistic description of that process (at the clausal level). The same holds true for the middle impersonal form illustrated in (7.32), where the affected entity *un crime* ‘a crime’ is coded as subject and the agent is generic, namely whoever the perpetrator is in any given crime. Consequently, despite their differences, the investigation of which constitutes a significant part of this section, the spontaneous construction in (7.4) and the middle impersonal in (7.32) share the structure represented in Figure 7.2, repeated from Chapter 2 (from Langacker 2008: 385).

(7.32)   *Le crime du roi est en même temps péché contre l'ordre suprême. **Un crime se commet**, puis **se pardonne, se punit** ou **s'oublie**. Mais le crime de royauté est permanent...*   (Camus, A. *L'homme révolté*: 151)

‘The crime of a king is at the same time a sin against the supreme order of things. A crime is committed [commits itself], then it is forgiven [forgives itself], punished [punishes itself] or forgotten [forgets itself]. But the crime of royalty is eternal...’

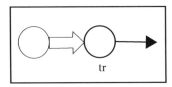

Figure 7.2 Middles (from Langacker 2008: 385)

However, the common middle core illustrated in Figure 7.2 does not suffice to account for the difference between the spontaneous events and human activity predicate classes. The French tradition rightfully points out that the focus of the spontaneous event class is on the affected entity's change of state without any consideration paid to the role of the agent, but it is important to add that this is also the case when the agent is semantically present as part of the predicate itself, such as in the verbs of creation, or as an implicit part of the affected entity (*le diner*). To put it differently, the distinguishing characteristic between the spontaneous event and human activities predicates is not the presence of a human agent but the recognition of that agent as an active participant (a conceptualizer) in the occurrence of the profiled process. For example, in *le diner s'acheva assez vite.* 'the dinner ended rather quickly' in (7.22), the agent of *s'achever* (the diners) is a necessary part of the lexical semantic structure of the noun *diner*, but is not treated as an active internal participant because it is not presented as initiating the termination process. Rather, the affected entity (the dinner) is described as reaching its natural stopping point organically, without any external interference. There is therefore one single conceptualizing presence in the utterance, namely the speaker who constructs the whole scene, but the conceptual organization of the process that *s'achever* profiles includes no internal participating and conceptualizing presence.

The human activity predicates are organized differently because they focus less on the change of state that the affected entity internally undergoes than on the way a given conceptualizer interprets the scene she is witnessing. For instance, in *on avait cueilli les lavandes cela se sentait à plein nez* in (7.27) 'lavender had been harvested. One could smell it strongly', the process that *se sentir* profiles requires an internal active human presence to be realized. That conceptualizing presence is therefore inherent to the conceptual structure of the predicate, and the utterance therefore contains two conceptualizers. The speaker obviously conceptualizes the whole scene, but the profiled process itself contains its own conceptualizing presence that is critical to its realization. In (7.27) that conceptualizer is presented as real (the generalized speaker, to be considered in detail in Chapter 8, also plays that internal role), but it may also be virtual as in (7.28)–(7.31) where arbitrary instances of the relevant participants are conjured up to satisfy the lexical semantic structure of their respective predicates.

Two important points need to be made concerning the two classes of predicates described in this section. The first is that neither of them is coextensive with the middle impersonals that constitute the focus of this chapter. In particular, the verbs of human activity often describe situations not general enough to meet the impersonal requirements. This is illustrated by the contrast in (7.31) and (7.29) repeated here, where (7.31) exhibits some measure of habituality but is too geographically specific to be available to a generalized conceptualizer, and (7.29) alone is general enough to be considered impersonal:

(7.31)   *On disait aussi qu'à la nuit tombée des arguments moins relevés étaient mis en ligne, et que **l'argent et le vin se distribuaient** à flots...*
                                                        (Gracq, J. *Le rivage des Syrtes*: 321)
         'It was also said that at night some less-elevated arguments were being settled, and that large amounts of wine and money were circulating [distributing themselves]...'

(7.29)   ***Une économie refuge se définit** comme telle par la présence ou la combinaison de divers caractères: les règles fondamentales du capitalisme (respect de la propriété privée) ont les moindres chances d'y être violées...*
                                                        (Perroux, F. *L'économie du XXe siècle*: 65)
         'A sheltered economy is defined [defines itself] as such by the presence or combination of different characteristics: the fundamental laws of capitalism (respect for private property) are less at risk of being violated...'

Second, the presence or absence of an internal conceptualizing presence in the conceptual organization of the predicates largely accounts for the manner in which the predicates in those classes acquire their impersonal status. The analysis proposed here therefore captures the fact that the majority of middle impersonals come from the human activity predicates because it is the internal conceptualizing presence that these predicates contain in their lexical semantic structure that makes them good candidates for impersonal status. Consistent with the hypothesis proposed earlier, the human activity predicates gradually approach impersonal status as the conceptualizer that they necessarily contain gets progressively more generalized to incorporate virtually anyone. In other words, human activity impersonals code the inevitable occurrence of the profiled process regardless of the nature of the agent. Taking (7.21) as an illustration, the processes *se rouvrir* 'reopen', *se labourer* 'being plowed', and *se déblayer* 'being cleaned out' necessarily incorporate a conceptualizing presence, an agent in this particular case, but these agents are restricted to the large but highly specific set of people responsible for the recovery period that followed the end of World War Two in France. Therefore the predicates in (7.21) cannot be considered impersonals due to this lack of generality, but they acquire impersonal status as the internal conceptualizing presence gets progressively more general so that the profiled process can be presented as stable, repeatable, and predictable every time the conditions are right. The next section investigates the precise conditions that favor this maximally general construal.

The spontaneous events predicates' exclusive focus on the affected entity's change of state, at the expense of the agent or the entity responsible for the occurrence of the profiled process, makes it difficult to extend the relevance of the situation coded in the construction to other similar situations. In other words, in the absence of a well-isolated cause, the observed change of state cannot be predicted or generalized. This lack of predictability considerably restricts the construction's scope and thus makes it a poor candidate for impersonal status. However, this does not mean that spontaneous event predicates cannot be considered impersonals. For example, the situation that they profile may be broadened to acquire universal relevance if external factors such as the internal structure of the affected entity itself, or particular external conditions account for its predictable and repeatable occurrence. Spontaneous impersonals therefore profile processes that invariably happen if circumstances are right, as illustrated in (7.33) where the degradation the machines undergo predictably affects all the entities that share the same internal structure, or in (7.34) where they face similar adverse circumstances:

(7.33) #*Les machines se dérèglent toujours/ça se dérègle toujours*
'Machines always lose their settings [get themselves out of tune]'

(7.34) #*Même les meilleures machines se dérèglent dans ces conditions extrêmes*
'Even the best machines lose their settings [get themselves out of tune] in these extreme conditions'

This section made it clear that the two classes of predicates observed in the general vicinity outlined by the SAP and MP on the map in Figure 7.1 can reach impersonal status, albeit in rather different ways. The next section investigates how the affected entity's "responsibility" (Van Oosten 1977; see also Dowty 2000; Lekakou 2004) for the occurrence of the profiled process explains the path to impersonals in both cases.

3.3 Generality and responsibility

Van Oosten (1977: 461) shows that the subject of English middles has properties such that it "is understood to be responsible for the action of the verb". Note that this statement does not apply to all French middles with the same degree of relevance. For instance, in (7.35) repeated from Chapter 1 for convenience, the glass can be considered responsible for its own destruction because its internal structure was incapable of sustaining the force applied by the fingers, but the responsible party is nonetheless the agent, as the following context makes clear:

(7.35)   Hero, brusquement: *Tu m'as compris! (Il serrait son verre dans sa main, le verre se casse.* Ils regardent le verre tous deux dans la main de Héro qui dit doucement. *Excuse-moi, mon vieux. J'aime casser.*

(Anouilh, J. *La répétition: ou, l'amour puni:* 75)
'Hero, suddenly: You understood me! (he was holding his glass in his hand, the glass breaks [itself]. Both of them look at the glass in Hero's hand who says softly: Excuse me, Old Man. I like to break things'.

In fact, the previous section showed that with the spontaneous predicates the subject's responsibility for the occurrence of the profiled process is only manifested when additional stipulations make it clear that the change of state expressed by the predicate cannot be attributed to any other cause. This was shown in (7.34) where the habitual *toujours* points to the inherent properties that all machines share, which invariably cause them to lose their initial settings; and in (7.34) where in the presence of extreme conditions the loss of settings can always be expected to occur. In other words, the subject's responsibility for the occurrence of the profiled process is clearest when that process describes one of the characteristics inherent to its type. The example in (7.35) therefore describes an accident that happened in a specific instance, whereas those in (7.33) and (7.34) describe general properties of machines. This process is more generally described as the generic character of (7.33) and (7.34), and its dynamics are not particular to middles. Other predicates, such as the intransitive *aboyer* 'bark' in *un chien ça aboie* 'a dog will bark', can be analyzed in exactly the same way. This kind of spontaneous predicate will not be considered further in this chapter because its generality is subsumed under the more general generic category.[11]

The human activities predicates should also be distinguished along similar lines, even though the added conceptualizer in their lexical semantic structure adds a layer of complexity. In a large number of situations considered in this chapter the agent is uniquely responsible for the process described in the predicate, even though it remains unexpressed. In (7.31), for instance, repeated once again, the entities responsible for the distribution are unquestionably the participants in the gambling and drinking activities. The extent to which money and wine are responsible for their own distribution is questionable beyond the rather-benign observation that both constitute popular commodities during nighttime entertainment. The communicative purpose of the sentence is to present money and wine as the habitual participants in the nightlife of a specific place, not to describe some inherent characteristics that they possess.

---

11. Several researchers (Condoravdi 1989; Lyons 1995; Ackema and Schoorlemmer 1994; Lekakou 2004) treat all middles as generic. Their analysis is generally compatible with that proposed in this chapter. The issue of the relation between middles and generics is discussed in further detail in Chapter 9.

(7.31)   *On disait aussi qu'à la nuit tombée des arguments moins relevés étaient mis en ligne, et que **l'argent et le vin se distribuaient** à flots…*

(Gracq, J. *Le rivage des Syrtes*: 321)

'It was also said that at night some less elevated arguments were being settled, and that large amounts of wine and money were circulating [distributing themselves]…'

As they are described in this monograph, impersonal constructions profile situations that are clearly identified as stable so that future occurrences can be predicted with confidence and hence potentially available to anyone. The middle in (7.31) is therefore not general enough to satisfy this requirement because, even though it can be expected to recur at regular intervals, it is geographically circumscribed and hence only available to the people at that specific location. The basic idea developed in this section is that the more responsibility the subject exhibits toward the profiled process, the greater chance the construction has of reaching impersonal status.

We need to exercise caution here. The agent internal to the lexical semantic structure of human activity predicates represents the entity that brings about the profiled process, but it may be assisted in crucial ways by specific characteristics that the affected entity itself possesses, which renders the occurrence of that process more likely. This is illustrated in (7.36), repeated from Chapter 1, where the agent of the writing process can only be the author but where the very topic of his work strongly contributes to its success. In this sense, one can claim that the book itself is responsible for the easy nature of the writing process:

(7.36)   *Mais tu as eu une critique étonnante, dit Louis d'un ton encourageant; il sourit."Il faut dire que tu es tombé sur un sujet en or; pour ça tu es verni; quand on tient un pareil sujet, **le livre s'écrit** tout seul."* (Beauvoir, S. de. *Les mandarins*: 249)

'But your reviews were surprising, Louis said in an encouraging tone; he smiles. "You have to admit you came across a golden topic; you were lucky that way; with a topic like that, the book writes itself"'.

Crucially for the analysis developed here, the notions of agency and responsibility are intricately connected. Louis' comment in (7.36) points out that the author's achievement is tempered by the quality of his topic, and clearly intimates that other authors may have enjoyed comparable success in similar circumstances. Unlike agency, responsibility does not represent a semantic role but a pragmatic feature associated with the subject of middles (or possibly different participants) with various levels of strength in different situations. For the purposes of this chapter, this pragmatic association plays a critical role in the reliability and predictability of the profiled process because it neutralizes the impact of individual agents on the predicate's outcome and thus favors its more general interpretation. The higher the responsibility of the affected entity, the more accessible the predicate will be to a generalized conceptualizer. From the standpoint of the syntax and semantics represented in the construction's argument structure, middle impersonals are thus perfectly similar to other middles, but the subject's responsibility for the occurrence of the profiled process renders the latter independent from specific agents and thus generally predictable and available to everyone.

The conditions that enhance the affected entity's responsibility therefore need to be considered in further detail. The subject's responsibility for the occurrence of the profiled process may result from its design, as illustrated in (7.37) where the shop windows of the turn of the twentieth century are presented as maximally attractive to the human eye, and could therefore not elicit a different response:

(7.37)   *le monde moderne est ... obsédé par tout ce qui est visuel. Primauté du visuel –* **les vitrines des libraires de 1900 se "lisaient"**: *le groupement compact des couvertures, timidement égayé d'un jaune ou d'un rouge, étalait un damier typographique.*   (Huyghe, R. *Dialogue avec le visible*: 11)
'the modern world is ... obsessed by everything visual. A prime example of visual demands – the shop windows in 1900 were "meant to be read" [read themselves]: the compact grouping of the covers, shyly brightened with red or yellow, was arranged like a typographic chessboard'.

Alternatively, the affected entity may have undergone some transformation that renders the occurrence of the profiled process inevitable, as in (7.38) where the sale and value of Japanese paintings is greatly enhanced if their author previously spent some time in Paris:

(7.38)   *Mais ce passage à Paris va leur permettre de se faire plus facilement un nom au Japon. A leur retour,* **leurs tableaux se vendent** *beaucoup plus ... et beaucoup plus cher.*   (from Achard 2012)
'But their stay in Paris will allow them to be better known in Japan. Upon their return, their paintings sell [themselves] much better ... and for a much higher price'.

Finally, the subject may be the victim of specific circumstances, as in (7.39) where the economic context rather than qualities intrinsic to the animal provide the main reason for predicting the profiled process with confidence:

(7.39)   *On débarquait les crustacés et les poissons de chalut sur le continent, où le bénéfice devenait de jour en jour plus médiocre.* **Les araignées de mer** *– spécialité de l'île –* **se vendaient** *particulièrement mal.*   (Robbe-Grillet, A. *Le Voyeur*: 53)
'The shellfish and fish from the boats were taken to the continent, where the profits were getting worse every day. Spider crabs – the island's specialty – sold [themselves] particularly poorly'.

The responsibility of the affected entity for the occurrence of the profiled process provides that process with some measure of independence from specific agents and thus enhances its predictability. For instance, in (7.38) the boost in sales is predictable for all artists who spent some time in France, and can thus be fully anticipated regardless of the specificity of the artist. Despite the affected entity's responsibility, however, the examples in (7.37)–(7.39) are not impersonals because they do not possess the required degree of generality (the process is predictable within too small a range). Responsibility of the affected entity is thus necessary but not sufficient. The next section considers two situations in which the profiled predicate reaches maximally general status and the construction can therefore be considered impersonal.

4.   Two impersonal constructions

Because the subject's responsibility for the occurrence of the profiled process is a gradual notion, the impersonal status of middle constructions also needs to be evaluated along a continuum. However, in a way that parallels the observation made for *ça* impersonals in the previous chapter, the recognition of middle impersonals is facilitated by the presence of two specific environments within which middles reliably exhibit the generality and predictability representative of impersonals. These two patterns diverge from the rest of the middles because they contain a particular set of semantic/pragmatic features and thus constitute stable constructional islands.

In the first construction the profiled process is inherently contained within the affected entity (the subject) in the sense that it represents a necessary part of its definition, i.e. what it means for that entity to be what it is. This property is illustrated in (7.2) and (7.32) repeated here, (7.40) (already presented in Chapter 1), and (7.41):

(7.2)   *Il note que le pain sans levain est cuit sur des plaques de tôle et ressemble à de la galette ou aux crêpes de carnaval, que **le saucisson d'Arles se fait avec de la viande de mulet**.*   (Durry, MJ. *Gérard de Nerval et le mythe*: 82) 'He notes that yeast-free bread is cooked on flat metal sheets and resembles biscuits or the pancakes of carnival time; that the sausage from Arles is made [makes itself] with mule meat'.

(7.32)   *Le crime du roi est en même temps péché contre l'ordre suprême. **Un crime se commet**, puis **se pardonne, se punit** ou s'oublie. Mais le crime de royauté est permanent…*   (Camus, A. *L'homme révolté*: 151)

'The crime of a king is at the same time a sin against the supreme order of things. A crime is committed [commits itself], then it is forgiven [forgives itself], punished [punishes itself] or forgotten [forgets itself]. But the crime of royalty is eternal...'

(7.40)   *Elle secoua la tête: "j'ai trente-sept ans et je ne connais aucun métier. Je peux me faire chiffonnière; et encore! – Ça s'apprend, un métier; rien ne t'empêche d'apprendre."*   (Beauvoir, S. de. *Les mandarins*: 283)
'She shook her head: "I am thirty-seven years old and I have no trade. I could be a rag picker, if that! – A trade, you can always learn it [that learns itself a trade]; nothing prevents you from learning"'.

(7.41)   *Savoir parler à un enfant est le don rarissime entre tous. Ce qu'on fait quelquefois "pour leur bien" est tout simplement atroce. On ne leur enfoncerait pas un couteau dans la jambe ou le bras, mais on leur poignarde l'âme avec d'autant plus de zèle que **cette espèce d'assassinat se commet** au nom de la vertu.*
(Green, J. *Journal. T. 5. 1946–1950*: 112)
'Knowing how to speak to a child is the rarest of gifts. What we sometimes do "for their own good" is simply awful. One wouldn't stick a knife in their leg or arm, but we stab their soul with all the more fervor that this kind of murder is committed [commits itself] in the name of virtue'.

In the examples above the profiled process is entirely predictable because its occurrence is fully subsumed in the definition of the entity that the subject nominal profiles. For example, in (7.2) mule meat constitutes a necessary ingredient of the *saucisson d'Arles*, without which the latter would not deserve its name. Its presence is thus fully predictable because it constitutes a critical part of the recipe. Similarly, in (7.32), (7.40), and (7.41), each profiled process is completely predictable given the subject's definition or the schemas that are necessarily activated when it is evoked. In (7.40) the term *métier* 'profession' necessarily invokes a set of schemas that includes the kind of training required of its practitioners. In this sense, the process *s'apprendre* 'is learned' constitutes an integral part of the subject's definition, and can thus be considered fully predictable. The examples in (7.32) and (7.41) describe social responses to well-established practices, and each predicate depicts a frequently observed social response. Each one is thus constitutive of the subject because the reaction it profiles is expected to reproduce itself reliably given the nature of our social behavior. Consistent with the hypothesis presented earlier, the subject's responsibility for the occurrence of the profiled process renders the latter fully predictable and thus available to anyone.

In the second constructional cluster, the profiled process is also completely predictable because its occurrence is required by a set of social norms or conventions. In this construction the predicates pertain to the precise way in which things should be done by anyone involved in specific activities. Because social norming applies to everyone, the occurrence of the profiled process is available to any conceptualizer and the construction can rightfully be called impersonal. This cluster is illustrated in (7.42)–(7.45):

(7.42)   *Plutarque déjà disait, avant Machiavel, que **l'occasion s'attrape** par les cheveux.*
         (Jankélévitch, V. *Le je-ne-sais-quoi et le presque-rien*: 119)
         'Before Machiavelli, Plutarque already said that you grab opportunity [opportunity grabs itself] by its hair'.

(7.43)   *mais c'est bien sur les hauteurs du Mont Serrat que le chevalier ingénu fit revivre la lumière du graal. **Cette promenade devrait se faire à pied**, selon la tradition des pèlerinages.*   (T'Serstevens, A. *L'itinéraire espagnol*: 35)
         'but it is on the slopes of Mount Serrat that the ingenuous knight rekindled the grail's light. This hike should be done [do itself] on foot, according to the tradition of pilgrimages'.

(7.44)   *Il n'est pas d'usage de présenter du vin: **il ne se boit qu'aux repas et au cabaret**.*
         (T'Serstevens, A. *L'itinéraire espagnol*: 77)
         'It is not customary to serve wine: it is only drunk [only drinks itself] during meals or in a bar'.

(7.45)   *"**L'apéritif se prend** obligatoirement sur la terrasse du Continental, à même le trottoir", raconte Lucien Bodard dans l'Humiliation.*   (from Achard 2012)
         '"Drinks before meals have to be taken [take themselves] on the Continental's patio, right on the sidewalk", Lucien Bodard tells us in the Humiliation'.

The construction illustrated in (7.42)–(7.45) differs from the one previously considered because of its deontic character. Anyone intending to carry out the profiled process is obliged to follow specific instructions. For example, a possible paraphrase of (7.42) might be *Il faut attraper l'occasion par les cheveux* 'You must catch opportunity by its hair'. This deontic value renders the profiled process fully predictable because everyone is subject to the same social norming, and therefore expected to act in a similar manner. The profiled process is thus general enough to warrant the impersonal label because the social rules that dictate its occurrence, and thus ensure its full predictability, make it available to any conceptualizer.

Although this class of deontic middles includes a variety of verbs, as illustrated in (7.42)–(7.45), the most frequently attested predicates are *dire* 'say' and *faire* 'do', illustrated in (7.46) repeated from Chapter 1:

(7.46)   *Dans les livres, les gens se font des déclarations d'amour, de haine, ils mettent leur cœur en phrases; dans la vie, jamais on ne prononce de paroles qui pèsent. **Ce qui "se dit" est aussi réglé que ce qui "se fait".***
         (Beauvoir, S. de. *Mémoires d'une jeune fille rangée*: 119)

'In books, people claim their love or hatred for each other, they pour their hearts in their words; in life, no one ever pronounces words with any weight. What "is said" is as tightly regulated as what "is done"'.

The quotation marks around *se dire* and *se faire* in (7.46) represent the highly normative character of these predicates, which remind all social participants of the strict codes and conventions that govern words and behaviors in civil society. The example in (7.46) does not describe what people do and say, but what social norms allow them to do or say. The specificity of this deontic construction clearly emerges from the comparison between *se dit* in (7.46) and the identical lexical form in (7.47), also repeated from Chapter 1, which merely describes the surrounding discourse and has no deontic value:

(7.47)   – *Nous sommes en 1920, Jo. Vos idées sont d'un autre temps. Il faut vous réveiller, sortir de vous-même, écouter **ce qui se dit** autour de vous…*

(Green, J. Moïra: roman: 173)

'– We are in 1920, Jo. Your ideas belong to another time. You have to wake up, get out of yourself, listen to what people are saying [says itself] around you…'

The difference in meaning between (7.46) and (7.47) when the two predicates are lexically identical clearly shows that the construction itself contributes the deontic value that the sentence in (7.46) conveys.

The two constructional clusters of middle impersonals have been presented separately for clarity's sake but they are not always easy to distinguish, as the examples in (7.48) and (7.49) illustrate:

(7.48)   *Je n'oserais même pas lui proposer un dédommagement. L'amabilité espagnole est ainsi faite **qu'elle ne se paie d'aucune monnaie sonnante.***

(T'Serstevens, A. L'itinéraire espagnol: 134)

'I wouldn't even dare to offer him compensation. Spanish friendliness is such that it cannot be paid for [doesn't pay itself in cash]'.

(7.49)   *Mais chacun sait aussi, au moins depuis Guy Mollet en 1946, **qu'un congrès socialiste se gagne** à gauche…*   (from Achard 2012)

'But everybody also knows, at least since Guy Mollet in 1946, that a socialist national convention is won [wins itself] from the left…'

The examples in (7.48) and (7.49) are ambiguous between a definitional reading where the nature of the subject explains the predictability of the profiled predicate, and a deontic reading where the latter's occurrence is required by a set of preestablished norms. The origin of this ambiguity is clear. If everyone is compelled to perform a given process in a specific manner, that manner can also be viewed as part of that process's definition. For example, in (7.49) if the method for winning a socialist national convention involves steering the party to the left and flattering its members (the definitional or responsibility reading), the only way of achieving victory is to respect this winning formula (deontic reading). This ambiguity is obviously unproblematic for the analysis developed in this chapter because both readings provide the profiled process with the degree of generality required for impersonals, and both thus qualify as middle impersonals.

5. Discussion

The two middle impersonal constructions discussed in the previous section strongly resemble the *constructions moyennes*, the specificity of which both French grammarians and Generative linguists have long recognized. The similarity between the two construction types clearly emerges from the comparison of the examples presented throughout this chapter, with the most commonly cited examples from Ruwet's (1972: 95–97) seminal study of *constructions moyennes* illustrated in (7.50)–(7.53) (translations mine):

(7.50)   *Ces lunettes se nettoient facilement*
        'These glasses clean [themselves] up easily'

(7.51)   *Ce genre de livres se vend surtout aux bonnes sœurs*
        'This kind of book primarily sells [itself] to sisters'

(7.52)   *Les maximanteaux / un maximanteau, ça se porte sur une minijupe*
        'Extralong coats / an extralong coat are / is worn [that wears itself] over a
        miniskirt'

(7.53)   *Les erreurs / une erreur pareille, ça se paie*
        'Mistakes / such a mistake, you have to pay for them / it [that pays for itself]'

Ruwet's examples in (7.50)–(7.53) clearly meet the conditions for the middle impersonals developed in this chapter because the process expressed in the predicate represents a defining property of the object type that the subject profiles. In (7.50) the ease of the cleaning process represents a distinguishing feature of a specific kind of glasses. In (7.51) the target audience constitutes an important characteristic of the book, and the negative outcome in (7.53) invariably follows mistakes. Similarly, the sentence in (7.52) describes the normatively fashionable way of wearing an extralong coat. Since no one is immune from the rules of fashion, the construction is general enough to be called impersonal. The resemblance between the middle impersonals and the *constructions moyennes* leads one to legitimately wonder if the analysis developed in this chapter merely renamed a well-documented group of constructions without providing much further insight. The first part of this claim obviously has some merit. There is indeed a consensus that the group of constructions illustrated in (7.50)–(7.53) deserves specific attention because of its distinguishing properties, and these properties have been well documented for a long time. On the other hand, I believe that significant insight has been gained in understanding how these constructions naturally emerge from the general ecology of French middle constructions.

First, while the *constructions moyennes* are derived by syntactic movement and are hence structurally different from other middles, the class of middle impersonals discussed in this chapter is structurally identical to all other middles; their distinctiveness resulting from the systematic presence of semantic and pragmatic features.[12] This lack of structural similarity between middle impersonals and passives is important because its purported presence often represents the only motivation for considering the two constructions together. In fact, as was noted already, while the *constructions moyennes* share a defocused agent with passives and impersonals, their generalized character makes them much closer semantically to impersonals than to passives. The discrepancy between the punctual aspect of passives and the much more general *constructions moyennes* has already been pointed out, but it can be summarized by comparing Ruwet's example in (7.50) to its created passive counterpart in (7.54):

(7.54)   #*Ces lunettes ont été nettoyées facilement*
         'These glasses were cleaned easily'

The differences between the *construction moyenne* (i.e., impersonal middle) in (7.50) and the passive in (7.54) are significant. The situation in (7.54) clearly presents a punctual statement about a process performed on the glasses while (7.50) describes how easy it is to clean them, or in other words one of their distinguishing characteristics. As mentioned at several points in this chapter, this general property, available to anyone who attempts to clean the glasses, makes the construction impersonal according to the criteria followed in this monograph. Furthermore, the present marker on the predicate extends its availability as long as the glasses remain in existence.

Ironically, the lexical semantic structure of spontaneous predicates makes them much closer to passives than the human processes, as the tense/aspect marking in the examples introduced previously but repeated here illustrate:

---

12. This is also true for the accounts that do not derive middles by movement because the semantic characteristics that allow the middle interpretation is parasitic on their passive structure (Lekakou 2004).

(7.4) *À ce moment, on frappa doucement, et comme tiré d'un rêve, Joseph cria: –*
  Entrez! **La porte s'ouvrit** *alors pour livrer passage à une vieille négresse vêtue*
  de noir…   (Green, J. *Moïra: roman:* 177)
  'At this moment, someone knocked softly, and as if awakening from a dream,
  Joseph shouted: – Come in! The door then opened [itself] to let in an old black
  woman dressed in black…'

(7.19) #*Cette maison* **s'est construite** *en trois mois!*
  'This house was built [built itself] in three months!'

Beyond their tense/aspect, the constructions in (7.4) and (7.19) possess an easily
recoverable agent, even though it is not explicitly mentioned. In fact, in a way
that is also observed with the indefinite pronoun *on* 'one' in the next chapter,
middle constructions can lean toward the conceptual configuration of passives or
impersonals, depending on the generality of the situation as it is presented in the
construction, and the ease of recoverability of the agent. For example, while (7.19)
is passivelike because it describes a punctual situation whose agents can clearly be
outlined and delineated, the closely related #*une maison se construit en trois mois*
'you can build a house in three months', where the builders are virtual and merely
conjured up for the illustration of a statement about house building in general, can
legitimately be called impersonal. The account presented in this chapter captures
this flexibility by allowing general semantic and pragmatic considerations to orient
middle constructions toward passives or impersonals depending on the situation.

Second, the treatment presented in this chapter highlights the interaction between several semantic and pragmatic factors that need to combine in a precise
manner to allow middle impersonals to emerge. Some of these factors, such as
the presence of an active internal conceptualizer, belong to the predicate's lexical
semantic structure, as the verbs of human activities presented in Section 3 have
illustrated. Others are more diffuse because they belong more generally to the entire construction, but their combined operation is just as critical. For instance, we
saw that the affected entity's responsibility toward the occurrence of the profiled
process only favors an impersonal reading because it decreases the relevance of
individual agents, and thus makes that process generally available to everyone.
Finally, the degree of generality without which no construction can claim impersonal status is provided by the tense and aspectual marking on the predicate itself.
Compare, for example, the situation in (7.36) repeated here to the manipulated
one in (7.55):

(7.36) *Mais tu as eu une critique étonnante, dit Louis d'un ton encourageant; il sourit.*
  "Il faut dire que tu es tombé sur un sujet en or; pour ça tu es verni; quand on
  tient un pareil sujet, **le livre s'écrit** *tout seul."*
                                          (Beauvoir, S. de. *Les mandarins:* 249)

'But your reviews were surprising, Louis said in an encouraging tone; he smiles. "You have to admit you came across a golden topic; you were lucky that way; with a topic like that, the book writes itself"'.

(7.55) #*"Il faut dire que tu es tombé sur un sujet en or; tu avais un tel sujet que **le livre s'est écrit** tout seul"*
'You have to admit you came across a golden topic; you had such a topic that the book wrote itself'.

The construction in (7.55) is not general enough to be impersonal since the situation that *s'écrire* describes is restricted to the hearer's exclusive experience. The presence of the perfect marker restricts the scope of the predicate to the observed situation, and therefore prevents a more general construal. Conversely, in (7.36) the presence of the adverbial *quand on tient un pareil sujet* 'when you came across such a golden topic' and the present tense on the predicate extend the latter's scope beyond the confines of the currently observed situation to all other situations with similar circumstances. The construction is therefore general enough to be called impersonal because the situation it describes is available to anyone if the relevant criteria are met. Importantly, the factors that provide the construction's general character are provided by generalizing adverbials and the presence of a nonperfect aspect, most frequently present tense, but also occasionally *imparfait* 'imperfect'. It is also important to remember that in the analysis developed in this chapter any middle can be considered impersonal if the predicate describes a situation available to a generalized conceptualizer. The two constructions described in Section 4 simply represent stable islands where impersonals are reliably identified.

Finally, it is important to note that if middle predicates can occur with impersonal *il*, middle impersonals do not really compete with these *il* impersonals because the kind of event they code is highly specific. The two constructions are illustrated in (7.56) and (7.57), taken from Zribi-Hertz (1982):

(7.56) #*Une maison **se construit** en trois mois.*
'You can build a house [a house builds itself] in three months'.

(7.57) *Il s'est construit pas mal de maisons dans la région*   (from Zribi-Hertz 1982)
'Quite a few houses have been built in the area [there built itself quite a few houses in the area]'

The presence of a middle predicate with the impersonal pronoun *il* is neither surprising nor problematic for the analysis presented in this monograph. Consistent with the view developed in Chapters 3 to 5, *il* codes the field, namely the mental reach that allows the conceptualizer in (7.57) to identify the newly built houses. The middle predicate has its usual interpretation of focusing on the process itself to the detriment of the agent that remains unexpressed. Also consistent with the treatment of *il* impersonals, the statement in (7.57) pertains to the speaker's interpretation of the way in which the new construction transformed an entire area. By comparison, the example in (7.56) describes a general fact about house building generally available to anyone, in other words, a defining characteristic of a type of object. Consequently, while the two constructions describe the similar conceptual content of the construction of new houses, they access it via different entry points. In the *il* construction the impersonal pronoun provides the reference point through which the entity profiled in the postverbal entity is identified. Conversely, with the middle impersonals the affected entity coded as subject provides the reference point with respect to which one of its defining characteristics can reliably be accessed.

These two different configurations place certain restrictions on their respective syntactic realizations. For instance, the adverbial *en trois mois* 'in three months' in (7.56) evaluates the time frame suitable for building a house, and is thus interpreted as a defining feature of the house itself. Its presence is therefore understandably awkward if not straightforwardly impossible with an *il* impersonal, as illustrated in (7.58), because that construction is more directly concerned with more general properties of the entire scene than with the object itself beyond its mere identification. On the other hand, *il* impersonals are perfectly fine when the adverbials they contain pertain to the nature of the overall scene rather than the entities that transform it, as in (7.59) where *tous les trois mois* 'every three months' profiles the frequency with which new construction repeatedly affects the observed area:

(7.58) #??*Il se construit une maison en trois mois*
      'You can build [there builds itself] a house in three months'

(7.59) #*Il se construit une nouvelle maison tous les trois mois*
      'A new house is built [there builds itself a new house] every three months'

This focus on the field to the detriment of defining characteristics of the identified entity explains why *il* impersonals are generally impossible in the situations prototypically covered by middle impersonals. This is illustrated in (7.60)–(7.63), where the first (a) element of the pair is from Ruwet's examples illustrated in (7.50)–(7.53):

(7.60) a. *Ces lunettes se nettoient facilement*
        b. #**Il se nettoie ces lunettes facilement*
            'These glasses clean up easily'

(7.61) a. *Ce genre de livres se vend surtout aux bonnes sœurs*
        b. #**Il se vend ce genre de livres surtout aux bonnes sœurs*
            'This kind of book primarily sells to sisters'

(7.62) a. *Les maximanteaux / un maximanteau, ça se porte sur une minijupe*
  b. *#*Il se porte les maximanteaux / un maximanteau sur une minijupe*
    'Extralong coats / an extralong coat are / is worn over a miniskirt'

(7.63) a. *Les erreurs / une erreur pareille, ça se paie*
  b. *#*Il se paie les erreurs / une erreur pareille*
    'Mistakes / such a mistake, you have to pay for them / it'

Furthermore, we already saw that *il* impersonals identify or localize a specific instance, real or virtual, of a given type. Consequently, the postverbal expression can contain all the kinds of nominals suitable for describing instances. This includes the partitive article in (7.64) and the indefinite in (7.65), but not the definite article in (7.66) because, in this situation, the unmodified definite profiles a process type:

(7.64) *#Il se boit du bon vin en Italie*
    'You drink good wine [there drinks itself good wine] in Italy'

(7.65) *#Il se boit un vin superbe en Italie*
    'You drink some superb wine [there drinks itself some superb wine] in Italy'

(7.66) *#*Il se boit le bon vin en Italie*
    'You drink the good wine [there drinks itself the good wine] in Italy'

Because the affected entity (i.e., the subject) of the middle impersonal construction represents a process type, the only nominals that can appear in the construction are preceded by the determiners that indicate general entities, namely *le/la* for mass nouns; *un/une* for count nouns, as in (7.62a); and *les* for plurals. Consequently, the distribution in (7.67)–(7.69) is exactly opposite of that in (7.64)–(7.66):

(7.67) *#*Du bon vin se boit en Italie*
    'Some good wine is drunk [drinks itself] in Italy'

(7.68) *#*Un vin superbe se boit en Italie*
    'A superb wine is drunk [drinks itself] in Italy'

(7.69) *#Le bon vin se boit en Italie*
    'The good wine is drunk [drinks itself] in Italy'

The data in (7.67)–(7.69) show that the middle impersonal construction is only possible for making a statement about good wine in general, and the fact that it can only be drunk in Italy. In fact, the example in (7.68) would be perfectly acceptable if being drunk in Italy is interpreted as a defining characteristic of the superb wine type. In this reading all superb wines, including those not produced in Italy, would need to be drunk in that country to be fully appreciated.

6. Recapitulation and conclusion

This chapter argued that the traditional division of middle constructions into constructions *neutres* and *moyennes* fails to account for the French data because many situations share characteristics of the two constructions. By contrast, the area contained between the SAPs and the MP on Kemmer's semantic map of the middle domain is best analyzed as a continuum along which the profiled predicate exhibits different degrees of generality. The main feature that determines generality is the affected entity's responsibility for the occurrence of the profiled process. The spontaneous predicates stand on one end of the continuum because they present a punctual situation that cannot be expected to reoccur in similar conditions. On the other hand, with the human activities predicates the affected entity's responsibility for the occurrence of the profiled process decreases the importance of specific agents, and thus contributes to making that process more generally available. Because generality is gradual, the impersonal status of some constructions is potentially difficult to determine. However, as was observed in Chapter 6 with the *ça* impersonals, the presence of two stable constructional contexts allows us to reliably identify a class of impersonal middles. In the first construction the profiled predicate represents a definitional feature of the affected entity in the sense that it describes a necessary component of that entity. The second construction describes a set of social norms and conventions that need to be performed with respect to the entity that the subject codes. While these two contexts strongly resemble the situations most frequently described by the *constructions moyennes* in the French tradition, the account proposed in this chapter is quite different because these constructions are not structurally different from other middles, and they are only related to passive constructions in the sense that they both share a defocused agent. Furthermore, their classification as impersonals rather than passives better captures their generalized character.

CHAPTER 8

Indefinite impersonals

This chapter focuses on indefinite impersonals, and more specifically structures that contain the indefinite pronoun *on* 'one'. Consistent with the analyses presented in the previous chapters, indefinite impersonals are shown to represent the endpoint of a continuum of generalization of the indefinite subject, to the point where it includes any potential conceptualizer. Along this continuum, the decision to call a structure impersonal is somewhat flexible, but as was the case in the previous chapters the impersonal quality of two specific constructions is consistently predictable. The first is achieved by the lowest possible degree of delimitation of the indefinite pronoun; the second results from the generalization of a specific conceptualizer's experience to everyone because of its virtual quality.

1. Introduction

Historically, the pronoun *on* comes from the Old French *on*, the nominative case of *ome* derived from Latin *homo* 'man' (Le Bidois and Le Bidois 1935: 212). Synchronically, the pronoun possesses both a personal and an indefinite sense.[1] *On*'s personal meaning is often characterized as providing "a colloquial alternative to *nous*" 'we' (Jones 1996: 286) to represent a group of at least two people that includes the speaker. This sense is illustrated in (8.1), where *on* and *nous* are alternatively used to denote the people who spent the night together. One of the most striking differences between the two pronouns concerns their diverging agreement patterns with the following predicate. As the bolded forms attest, *nous* imposes first-person plural agreement on the verb while *on* resembles the personal subject pronouns *il* 'he' and *elle* 'she' in requiring third-person singular agreement:[2]

---

1. Le Bidois and Le Bidois (1935: 212) clearly express the pronoun's dual character: "Ce nominal dont notre langue fait un si grand usage, offre ce caractère singulier d'être en même temps un indéfini et un personnel." 'This nominal our language uses so frequently presents the singularity of being at the same time indefinite and personal'.

2. A careful analysis of the difference between *on* and *nous* in this sense needs to involve several dimensions including, among others, stylistic and sociolinguistic factors. This issue is not examined in further detail in this chapter.

(8.1)   *Une fois, dans un manoir voisin, **nous veillâmes** jusqu'à l'aube; **on confectionna**
        *de la soupe à l'oignon dans la cuisine; **nous allâmes** en auto au pied du mont*
        *Gargan que **nous escaladâmes** pour voir le lever du soleil; **nous bûmes** du café*
        au lait dans une auberge; ce fut ma première nuit blanche.

                    (Beauvoir, S. de. *Mémoires d'une jeune fille rangée*: 165)
        'Once, in a nearby manor, we stayed up until dawn; we made onion soup in
        the kitchen; we drove to the base of Mount Gargan that we climbed to see the
        sunrise; we drank milk and coffee at an inn; it was the first time I stayed up
        all night'.

On's indefinite sense is more difficult to characterize precisely because of the two
highly different meanings it possesses. In the first, the pronoun is best viewed as
an existential with the meaning of an "indefinite roughly equivalent to *quelqu'un*
['someone']" (Jones 1996: 286, insertions in brackets mine). This use of the pronoun is illustrated in (8.2) where its presence indicates that a human agent, as
opposed to other possible forces such as the wind or rain, is responsible for the
opening of the window, even though that agent is not precisely identified:

(8.2)   *La fête de Vanessa ne faisait pas mentir sa réputation de prodigalité somptueuse.*
        ***On** avait ouvert toutes grandes les baies à arcades qui donnaient directement*
        sur la lagune...   (Gracq, J. *Le rivage des Syrtes*: 94)
        'Vanessa's reception did not betray her reputation for extravagant generosity.
        The large vaulted French doors that overlooked the lagoon had been opened
        [one had opened the large vaulted French doors that overlooked the lagoon]...'

In its second indefinite meaning, *on* can be analyzed as a "generic referencing
people in general" (Jones 1996: 286). This is illustrated in (8.3) where the pronoun
refers to any member of the French community aware of what the term *création*
means when it is applied to the greatest artists:

(8.3)   *Ce qu'**on** appelle création dans les grands artistes n'est qu'une manière particulière*
        à chacun de voir, de coordonner et de rendre la nature.

                          (Huyghe, R. *Dialogue avec le visible*: 266)
        'What one calls creation among the great artists is only their own particular
        way of seeing, arranging, and depicting nature'.

A convincing semantic analysis of the pronoun crucially depends on the identification of clear distinctions between its different senses. The difference between
personal and indefinite *on* is easily noticeable, and thus universally recognized
in the literature. However, the internal organization of the semantic domain that
indefinite *on* covers is much more controversial, and several classification proposals have been suggested. For example, and directly relevant to the concerns
of this chapter, Creissels (2008b: 7) considers all indefinite senses as impersonal:
"'impersonal *on*' refers to all the uses of *on* in which *on* does not substitute for

the 1st person plural clitic *nous* of Standard French". In his analysis both existentials, illustrated in (8.2), and generics (gnomics in his terminology), presented in (8.3), represent instances of the pronoun's impersonal use.[3] Cabredo Hofherr (2003, 2008) retains the same impersonal label for all of *on*'s indefinite uses, but distinguishes between the pronoun's "lectures épisodiques" 'episodic readings' illustrated in (8.2), and its "lectures génériques" 'generic readings' illustrated, for instance, in La Fontaine's famous *on a souvent besoin d'un plus petit que soi* 'one often needs someone smaller than one's self'. The impersonal definition in these two analyses does not conform to the one used throughout this monograph. Existentials – episodics in Cabredo Hofherr's terminology – constitute a problem in particular because if the agent of the process profiled by the predicate is properly defocused, the event that predicate profiles does not possess the level of generality that makes it available to a generalized conceptualizer. In (8.2), for example, the event that *ouvrir* 'open' codes is strictly restricted to the precise circumstances of the speech situation, and thus strictly available to its participants, with no indication that it can be experienced by anyone else at any other time. Consequently by our definition it cannot be considered an impersonal; Section 3.1 shows that these cases resemble functional passives more than impersonals.

If the pronoun's indefinite reference does not necessarily guarantee its impersonal status, different criteria need to be considered if we want to delineate a class of *on* impersonals. This chapter investigates the conditions under which indefinite *on* possesses the degree of generality compatible with impersonals as they were defined in Chapter 1.[4] Consistent with the analysis developed in the previous chapters, it shows that two separate indefinite impersonal constructions can be isolated, each corresponding to a specific cognitive configuration. In the first, the pronoun's delimitation (Langacker 2008; to be defined more precisely in the next section) is minimal and thus includes all possible conceptualizers. In the second, the pronoun's referent is presented as a virtual instance specifically conjured up to illustrate the type of process expressed in the following predicate. Importantly, these two constructions naturally emerge from the continuum of generality along which all the senses of *on*, including the personal ones, can be evaluated. Here again, these two processes of homogenization and virtualization define two stable constructional islands within which *on* impersonals are reliably delineated. The analysis of indefinite impersonals is organized in the following

---

3. This is not to say that Creissels views impersonal *on* as a unified category. He argues that gnomic (generic) uses of the pronoun should be distinguished from existential uses based on their different referential properties in discourse.

4. This chapter does not seek to provide an exhaustive analysis of *on*. Such an investigation would involve a large number of issues pertaining, among others, to sociolinguistic distribution and reference properties. The range of these topics falls well outside the scope of this chapter.

manner. Section 2 introduces the standard analysis of personal pronouns in Cognitive Grammar and considers *on*'s distinguishing characteristics. Section 3 presents an overview of the pronoun's usage patterns based on 500 random examples from the FRANTEXT corpus. Section 4 describes two different paths to generality, namely the processes of homogenization and virtualization, which define the two constructions where *on* is always impersonal. Section 5 summarizes the results and concludes the chapter.

2. Pronouns and other nominals: Semantic functions

Personal pronouns are rightfully considered nominals because they can always be used in the same syntactic positions as other nominals. In order to understand *on*'s specific character as well as the precise conditions under which it can be considered impersonal, this section presents the semantic structure that all personal pronouns share with other nominals before focusing on its idiosyncratic qualities.

2.1   Layered semantic functions

The semantic function of nominals has already been briefly mentioned in Chapters 4 and 5. While verbal grounding assesses the existence of events and propositions, nominals narrow all the possible choices to the very entity on which the speaker and hearer jointly focus. Different constructions in different languages perform this function in a variety of ways, and even within the same language different kinds of nominals exhibit some degree of variation. However, in prototypical cases this focus can be broken down into two main steps. The first involves the selection of the proper type of entities, and the second its grounding (Langacker 2009: Chapter 6). These two functions are examined in turn.

Humans have potential conceptual access to an infinite variety of objects, so narrowing these possibilities begins with the selection of a particular type. Lexemes perform this narrowing function by "making *type specifications*" (Langacker 2008: 265, emphasis in original). For example, the lexeme *table* 'table' limits the range of investigation to objects of a similar nature by excluding other types of objects grouped together under other lexemes such as *bureau* 'desk' or *chaise* 'chair'. However, this initial type specification does not suffice to identify a specific member of the category. This is accomplished by selecting a particular instance of the relevant type. Within the same type, different instances are distinguished by the different locations they occupy in space, or in any other relevant domain, so consequently a specific instance is one that "*is thought as having a particular location in the domain of instantiation* which serves to distinguish it from other instances"

(Langacker 2008: 268, emphasis in original). It is important to note that instantiation does not represent an objectively separate level of representation where the presence of objects at a certain location is directly observed; rather, it is a mental operation that may be quite remote from actual existence. In particular, it is often considered as an instance of entities that only exist "virtually" (Langacker 2008: 270) and thus do not occupy a specific geographical location. For example, in the example in (8.4) the noun *endroit* (*pour camper*) 'place (to camp)' cannot be located in reality since the predicate *trouve pas toujours* 'does not always find' challenges its possible existence, but it does exist virtually as an instance specifically conjured up to express the traveler's desires and difficulties. Its virtual status is perfectly compatible with its being considered a specific instance, even though the domain of instantiation is restricted to the traveler's conception:

(8.4)   *On ne trouve pas toujours facilement, en Espagne, **un endroit pour camper**, à cause de l'absence de bois, et de la culture intensive.*

(T'Serstevens, A. *L'itinéraire espagnol*: 16)

'One cannot always easily find a place to camp in Spain, because of the lack of forests, and extensive agriculture'.

It is fundamental to realize that the two notions necessary to identify a given entity, namely its consideration as a type and an instance, are inherent in each other because they merely represent different ways of structuring the same conceptual base. Figure 8.1 (from Langacker 2008: 268) clearly shows that the type conception of the entity illustrated in (a) contains the potential for that entity's being instantiated at different locations, even though these different locations are not profiled. Conversely, the instance conception illustrated in (b) also contains as an unprofiled part of the base the idea of a type, i.e. the conception that emerges once one abstracts away from the particularities specific to each instance.

The semantic function of a nominal is to identify a specific entity. To that effect, the instance that the speaker has in mind needs to be made accessible to the other participants in the speech situation so that the proper referent can be "singled out" (Langacker 2008: 277).[5] As mentioned earlier, grounding refers to

---

5. This process of shared attention by which different people express interest in the same entity is remarkably complex and central to our cultural and linguistic experience. For Tomasello (1999, 2003), it represents an important foundation of human cultural learning and is made possible by "a single very special form of human cognition, namely, the ability of individual organisms to understand conspecifics as being *like themselves* who have intentional and mental lives like their own" (Tomasello 1999: 5, italics in the original). With respect to the concerns of this chapter, the speaker's recognition that the hearer's aspirations and desires are similar to hers not only allows her to anticipate which entities may be of interest to others, but also how she can help her interlocutors make contact with them.

a. Type Conception   b. Instance Conception

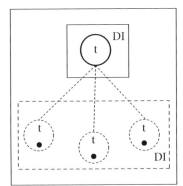
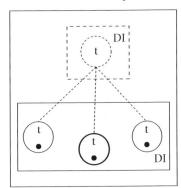

Figure 8.1 Types and instances (from Langacker 2008: 268)

the "epistemic relationship between the ground and the profiled thing" (Langacker 2008: 275) that allows the speaker and hearer to examine a specific entity together by pointing to it unequivocally among a large set of potential competitors. In that sense, it represents "the final step in putting together a nominal or finite clause" (Langacker 2008: 275).

The grounding function is performed differently in different kinds of nominals, but for expository purposes it is easier to focus on the canonical cases in which it is provided by a specific class of elements reserved for that sole purpose. French, as well as English and a variety of other languages, possesses a class of determiners whose single function is to epistemically relate the instance of the entity that the noun profiles to the speech situation. As an illustration, consider the example in (8.5) where the feminine definite article *la* indicates that the square is deemed identifiable by the interlocutor, and thus presented as such. In this case this identifiability can be imputed to a general schema of European towns, cities, and villages organized around a church surrounded by a square. The definite article therefore indicates the epistemic position of the speaker with respect to the existence of the church, and its possible identification by the interlocutor.

(8.5) *À la fin de l'office on forme la procession, et je descends sur **la place**, parmi les fidèles, portant un cierge de la main gauche, comme tous ceux de la file de gauche, car on marche sur deux files parallèles, selon le rite traditionnel qu'on voit déjà dans les autodafés.* (T'Serstevens, A. *L'itinéraire espagnol*: 203)
'At the end of the service a procession is formed, and I go down onto the square, among the faithful, a candle in my left hand, just like everyone in the left line, since we are forming two parallel lines, according to the traditional rite already observed during the autodafés'.

2.2   Grounding: Subjectivity and dynamicity

Two separate aspects of nominal grounding need to be emphasized. The first is the subjective nature of the grounding expressions. It has already been mentioned at several points of the analysis that the subjective or objective construal of an entity is based on the basic asymmetry that exists between the conceptualizing subject and the entity conceptualized. The person who entertains a conceptual experience is only present in that experience as a subject, and thus subjectively construed. Conversely, the entity she focuses on is placed on a metaphorical stage and thus objectively construed (Langacker 1985, 1990). The subjective construal of the ground is illustrated in Figure 8.2, where the conceptualized entity (represented by the bold circle) is prominently profiled onstage, the region of maximal acuity, while the speaker, hearer, and speech circumstances are kept offstage and thus "subjectively construed" (Langacker 2008: 274).[6]

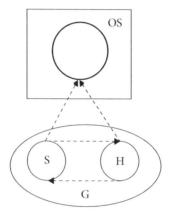

Figure 8.2 Grounding asymmetry (based on Langacker 2007: 174)

The second aspect of nominals that directly bears on the semantic description of pronouns is the dynamic nature of the conceptual activity by which the relevant entity is apprehended. In a nutshell, reference or mental access can be accomplished by successively invoking a series of entities. This conceptual path between entities results in one of them being used as a reference point to locate the other. For example, in the phrase "John's pen", the pen is accessed via the conception of its owner used as a reference point from which the entities in his dominion can be located. The reference point model is illustrated in Figure 8.3:

---

6. The subjective construal of grounding expressions explains why these expressions profile the grounded entity and not the grounding relation (Langacker 2008: 274).

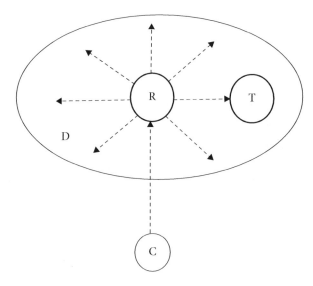

Figure 8.3 Reference point model (from Langacker 2008: 84)

In "John's pen", John represents the reference point R, which constitutes an intermediate station in the conceptual path (indicated by the dashed lines) leading to
the pen (the target T). As a human, John represents a naturally salient entity from
which the location of a variety of other entities can also be accessed. The group of
things that can be accessed from John used as a reference point (represented by the
oblong shape) is called John's dominion (D). In this case, the relationship between
the reference point and the target is made specific by the possessive marker's functions as a grounding expression.

2.3   Pronouns as nominals

In the canonical cases presented up to this point – the ones in (8.4) and (8.5),
for example – the grounding function is performed by a specialized element (a
determiner in these cases) that is separate from the noun that denotes the specific
instance under consideration. However, this is not the case for all nominals. Proper
nouns and personal pronouns have the characteristic of possessing "intrinsic"
grounding in the sense that the singling out of a specific referent is not performed
by a separate element but by part of the noun itself (Langacker 2008: 272). Obviously
proper nouns and pronouns achieve this identifying function in very different ways.
Proper nouns "incorporate an idealized cognitive model pertaining to the role of
that name in the relevant speech community" (Langacker 2007: 176). In that model,

because each name refers to one single individual there is no need for an external device such as a determiner to identify it. In other words, proper nouns essentially define "a type conceived as having just a single instance" (Langacker 2007: 176), and the very mention of that type provides enough information for successful identification. It is important to note that the very mention of a proper name uncovers a potentially large amount of information about its referent. At the very least, it provides the fact that the referent bears that name (Langacker 2007: 176), as well as whether s/he is male or female, if the hearer is familiar with the naming conventions of the relevant speech community. Any additional information depends on the hearer's degree of familiarity with the referent's life. For example, the fact that "Michael Jordan" refers to a male character is readily available to anyone with a passing knowledge of the naming conventions of English-speaking communities, but any further information depends on the level of acquaintance with the person's life. Basketball fans will be aware of Jordan's public achievements and career landmarks, while personal friends will know many aspects of his life that the general public ignores. The important aspects of the meaning of proper nouns are (1) they do not place any boundaries on the amount of information they make available, and (2) the information they provide is solely contained within the noun itself and thus relatively independent from the context of the interaction.

Personal pronouns represent the opposite case in the sense that they only reveal fragmentary information about their referent, the precise nature of which varies from language to language. In English it incorporates their human versus nonhuman status, gender, and number. In French it is restricted to its gender and number, as well as the degree of familiarity between the speaker and hearer in the case of the second-person singular pronoun. Consequently, unlike proper nouns, pronouns are potentially compatible with an open-ended set of possible referents. The first- and second-person pronouns can only be defined relative to their common discursive function (Benveniste 1966: 252):

> Il faut donc souligner ce point: *je* ne peut être identifié que par l'instance de discours qui le contient et par là seulement. Il ne vaut que dans l'instance où il est produit. Mais parallèlement, c'est aussi en tant qu'instance de forme *je* qu'il doit être pris; la forme *je* n'a d'existence linguistique que dans l'acte de parole qui la profère. Il y a donc dans ce procès une double instance conjuguée: instance de *je* comme référent, et instance de discours contenant *je*, comme référé. La définition peut alors être précisée ainsi: *je* est l'"individu qui énonce la présente instance de discours contenant *je*". Par conséquent, en introduisant la situation d'"allocution", on obtient une définition symétrique pour *tu*, comme l'"individu allocuté dans la présente instance de discours contenant l'instance linguistique *tu*".

'We therefore need to underline this point: *je* can only be identified by the utterance that contains it. It only exists within the occurrence where it is produced. But conversely, it must also be understood as an instance of the form *je*; the form *je* only exists linguistically in the act of speech where it is uttered. This process thus contains two different forms: an instance of *je* as the referent, and an instance of the utterance containing *je* as the referred entity. The definition can thus be specified as follows: *je* is "the person who utters the current instance of discourse that contains *je*". Consequently, if we introduce the notion of "allocution", we get a symmetrical definition for *tu*, as the "allocated person in the current utterance that contains the linguistic form *tu*"'.

The third person pronouns *il* 'he', *elle* 'she', and *ils* 'they' are somewhat more re-stricted because they carry their referents' gender and number. Despite this under-specification of their referent, pronouns refer to a single, possibly plural referent. In other words, they "carry the presupposition that their minimal descriptive content is sufficient to single out an intended referent" (Langacker 2007: 177).[7]

The minimal information that pronouns provide is sufficient because they rely heavily on the context to perform their referring function. In other words, reference is strongly tied to a specific speech event where the minimal information provided will be sufficient to access a specific entity. The first- and second-person pronouns represent particularly obvious cases. Benveniste's definition makes it clear that there is only one speaker and one listener in any given utterance, so these two entities are inherently salient and uniquely identifiable in the current discourse space. Third-person pronouns are not as straightforward, but "as an inherent as-pect of its meaning, a third-person pronoun presupposes that its referent can be identified with a particular entity sufficiently salient in the linguistic or extralin-guistic context to offer itself as the only obvious candidate with the appropriate specifications" (Langacker 2007: 177). In anaphoric cases, the immediate discourse proximity and hence cognitive availability suffices to unambiguously determine the pronoun referent, as illustrated in (8.6) where *il* 'he' obviously refers to Ballester because of its proximity in the discourse despite its being potentially compatible with a very large number of male characters:

(8.6)   *Ballester hocha la tête et eut un geste vague vers l'atelier; mais **il** avait l'air bou-*
         leversé.   (Camus, A. *L'exil et le royaume*: 1605)
         'Ballester shook his head and made a vague gesture toward the workshop, but
         he seemed upset'.

---

7. Benveniste (1966: 255) considers third-person pronouns as fundamentally different from first- and second-person pronouns because they refer to an objective situation rather than to empty positions in discourse that can only be filled in specific utterances.

These characteristics of personal pronouns are summarized in Figure 8.4, which illustrates their semantic structure:

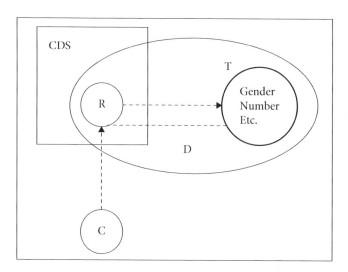

Figure 8.4 Semantic structure of personal pronouns (from Langacker (2007:178)

As a noun, a pronoun profiles a thing, indicated in Figure 8.4 by the bold circle. This thing is only characterized for highly schematic information such as gender, and number, as well as the familiarity between the speaker and hearer for the *tu/ vous* 'you' distinction. This profiled noun also includes a reference-point relationship where it functions as a target (T). The reference point (R) is a salient entity in the current discourse space (CDS), i.e. the base on common knowledge that the speaker and hearer rely on to communicate at any given point of the flow of the interaction, and thus presumed to be easily accessible to both of them. The dashed arrows represent the conceptual path leading the conceptualizer (C) to the target via the reference point, and the dashed line between the reference point and the target indicates that these two entities are identical. The semantic structure illustrated in Figure 8.4 indicates that a pronoun is presumed to be interpretable in the reference point's dominion (D) or, more specifically, that R is to be equated with T's referent. When R is an entity of extralinguistic discourse, the interlocutors are obvious candidates and they, or any group that contains/excludes them, function as R with respect to the first- and second-person pronouns. With third-person pronouns, R can be identified as a salient entity clearly established as a shared center of attention at this particular time of the interaction. In (8.6), for example, Ballester is active in the current discourse space because of its recent mention, and since it represents the only character that satisfies the gender and number restrictions imposed by the third-person masculine singular pronoun *il*, it can safely be identified as the pronoun's referent.

Cases such as that presented in (8.6), where the pronoun's referent is a clearly delineated and easily identified single entity, might be canonical but they do not exhaust all possibilities. In fact, the "delimitation" of most pronouns or, in other terms, their "projection to the world" (Langacker 2007: 179) may vary greatly from a single entity to a group of various sizes that can extend to notions as vague as people in general.[8] This is illustrated in (8.7) and (8.8), where the second-person pronouns *tu* and *vous* 'you' do not refer to the hearer/reader, but to everyone who finds themselves in a similar position:

(8.7)   *Au Quinté plus, quand **tu** gagnes, ça déforme les poches*
                                    (Gadet 1992: 78, cited in Coveney 2003: 167)
         'At Quinté plus [betting on the first four horses], when you win, it makes your pockets bulge'

(8.8)   *C'est quelque chose de bien terrible qu'une tempête: Il est bien difficile de ne pas craindre, lorsque **vous** voyez les flots soulevés qui vènent* [sic] *fondre sur vous…*
                                    (François 1933: 1664, cited in Coveney 2003: 170)
         'A storm is indeed a terrible thing: It is hard not to be afraid when you see the waves swelling up and then swooping down on you…'

The examples in (8.7) and (8.8) clearly show that the second-person pronoun's delimitation is not restricted to the hearer, but includes anyone who plays *Quinté plus* or finds themselves in a middle of a storm at sea.[9]

2.4   *On*: Minimal specification

On's extreme level of generality distinguishes it from all the other pronouns. The type of information it provides does not even include the considerations of person, gender, or number that other French pronouns generally incorporate. This characteristic is often presented in the French tradition as the pronoun's *omnipersonnel* 'multipersonal' character (Wilmet 1997: 273). Le Bidois and Le Bidois (1935: 212) express its high level of schematicity in the following way:

---

8. First-person singular pronouns constitute a notable exception to this observation because their delimitation is usually restricted to the speaker.

9. Langacker (2007: 179) claims that 'you' "designates a group of any size that includes the hearer but not the speaker…" It is not clear that this statement holds in the case of *tu* and *vous* in (8.7) or (8.8), where the outcome described in the predicate would be equally relevant to the speaker if she is in the right position to experience it.

On offre plusieurs nuances de sens et se prend dans une extension variable. Il peut signifier tous les hommes en général … ou un nombre de personnes indéterminées … ou encore une seule personne que pour une raison ou pour une autre on ne détermine pas.

'*On* presents several nuances of meaning and can have variable extension. It can denote people in general … or an undetermined number of people … or even a single person that for one reason or other remains undetermined'.

As a consequence of its multipersonal character, *on* can refer to any participant in the speech situation and thus stand in the place of most other personal pronouns. This is illustrated in (8.9) and (8.10) where it refers to the author (first person), and in (8.11) and (8.12) where it refers to the reader (second person):

(8.9)   *Pour donner sa force à la thèse libérale **on** admettra que le pays emprunteur est en régime d'étalon-or.*   (Perroux, F. *L'économie du XXe siècle*: 381)
'To give the liberal position all its force, we [one] will posit that the borrowing country is using the gold standard'.

(8.10)   *Ces faits fondamentaux sont observés et ils nous sont devenus sensiblement moins inintelligibles après les explications qui précèdent. C'est le moment de les interpréter à l'échelle de la nation. **On** décomposera donc et classera les raisons pour lesquelles certaines régions sont motrices, tandis que d'autres ne le sont pas...*   (Perroux, F. *L'économie du XXe siècle*: 233)
'These fundamental facts have been observed and they have become noticeably more understandable following the earlier explanations. It is now time to interpret them in the context of a nation. We [one] will thus analyze and classify the reasons why some countries lead and some don't…'

(8.11)   *Je parle ici d'expérience, qu'**on** ne l'oublie pas.*
                  (Teilhard de Chardin. *Le milieu divin*: 36)
'I am speaking from experience here, let's not forget it [may one not forget it]'.

(8.12)   *Qu'**on** ne s'y trompe pas. Quand **on** emploie pour la première fois la tierce, ou la seconde, ou la septième de dominante, **on** ne crée pas une musique entièrement neuve.*   (Schaeffer, P. *A la recherche d'une musique concrète*: 130)
'Let's [that one] make no mistake. When one uses the dominant third, or second, or seventh for the first time, one does not create a totally new music'.

The use of the indefinite in (8.9)–(8.12) represents a well-established convention in written French where the use of the first and second persons is strongly discouraged. Consequently, *on* is selected instead of *je* in (8.9) and (8.10), even though the author is clearly solely responsible for the assumptions he makes and the organization he follows. Similarly, *on* is found in place of the (formal) second-person *vous* in (8.11) and (8.12) despite the author's unambiguous direct addresses to the reader. These conventions are deeply rooted in tradition. Gougenheim (1963: 237) notes that in the seventeenth century *on* frequently replaced *je* so that the "moi haïssable" 'hateful self' could be avoided. Consequently at the Court the proper form for *je vous en serai obligé* 'I will be thankful for it' was *on vous en sera obligé*. Even today, French students are often taught that the first person denotes an unfortunate lack of modesty and that the directness of the second-person pronoun lacks the required formality of written usage. The conventional character of these strategies, however, should not undermine the relevance of *on*'s presence in contexts where other pronouns might be predicted. In fact, their very existence is obviously predicated on the pronoun's multipersonal character. Furthermore, similar substitutions are also attested outside the literary domain where they produce entirely different semantic effects, as the example in (8.13) illustrates:

(8.13)   *Et ça ne te gêne pas de penser que des types ont écrit des trucs tellement supérieurs à ce que tu pondras, toi? Dit Nadine d'un ton vaguement irrité. – Au début, je ne le pensais pas, dit Henri en souriant; on est arrogant tant qu'on n'a rien fait. Et puis une fois qu'on est dans le coup, on s'intéresse à ce qu'on écrit et on ne perd plus de temps à se comparer. – Oh! Bien sûr, on s'arrange! Dit-elle d'une voix boudeuse en se laissant retomber de tout son long sur le sol.*

(Beauvoir, S de. *Les mandarins*: 92)

'And it does not bother you to think that some guys have written things so superior to what you'll come up with? Nadine said in a slightly irritated voice. – At the beginning, I didn't think so Henri said with a smile; you are arrogant when you haven't done anything. And then once you get started, you get interested in what you write and you waste no time comparing yourself to other people. Oh! Of course, that's convenient [one makes things easy for oneself]! she said in a pouty voice, letting herself fall to the ground'.

In (8.13) the presence of indefinite *on* cannot be imputed to literary convention about authors and readers since the scene describes an interaction between two characters. Nadine believes that Henri's stance toward his stature in the literary world is fake and self-serving, and there is no question he constitutes *on*'s referent. Some possible reasons for the pronoun's presence instead of a more-probable first person will be examined shortly, but at this point it suffices to note that the conventionalized cases of first and second person illustrated in (8.9)–(8.13) are highly representative of *on*'s particularity to derive its semantic import precisely from its ambiguous reference.

On also obviously (and more frequently) refers to a third person entity. This is illustrated in (8.14) and (8.15) where the pronoun's referent is identified as the unmentioned agent of the relation the predicate describes:

(8.14)   *Aujourd'hui, **on** me remet cette lettre. Avez-vous lu comment il me traite à la fin?*   (Camus, A. *Les possédés; pièce en trois actes*: 996)
'Today this letter is delivered to me [one gives me this letter]. Did you see how he talks to me at the end?'

(8.15)   ***Les gens** vous montreront du doigt en ricanant. **Ils** diront que vous avez épousé une putain de la ruelle aux brebis. **On** vous insultera.*
                                                                (Aymé, M. *Clérambard*: 97)
'People will sneer and point at you. They will say you married a whore from the gutter. You will be insulted [one will insult you]'.

The referent of the pronoun *on* in (8.14) is obviously the courier. Although the latter could easily be identified, her relevance to the story does not extend beyond her delivery of the letter, and no further specification (gender for instance) is therefore required to satisfy the author's narrative purpose.[10] The example in (8.15) provides further illustration of the substitutions mentioned earlier because both *ils* and *on* refer to the nominal *les gens* 'people'.[11] The examples in (8.14) and (8.15) also show that *on* is not sensitive to number since the agent in (8.14) is a single person, while the insults in (8.15) most likely involve numerous separate agents.

The semantic structure of the indefinite pronoun *on* is illustrated in Figure 8.5. It is obviously quite similar to the structure of other pronouns presented in Figure 8.4, since *on* competes with the other pronouns in various contexts:[12]

Just like other pronouns, *on* profiles a target (T) with which the conceptualizer (C) makes contact via a reference point (R). The conceptual path that leads C to R and ultimately to T is indicated by the dotted arrows, and the dotted line between R and T indicates that the two entities are identical. This section examines in turn the two main differences between *on* and the other pronouns, namely (1) the singular agreement it imposes on the following predicate, and (2) the pronoun's high degree of generality or, to put it differently, the very limited set of restrictions it imposes on its referent.

---

10. *On*'s referential properties are different from those of the other pronouns. For example, in (8.14), the third-person singular *il* 'he' or *elle* 'she' would only be possible if their referent were available from the immediate context. The indefinite pronoun construction in (8.14) functions very much like a passive (to be considered in further detail in Section 3.1).

11. Alternatively, one could argue that in (8.15) *on* does not refer to *les gens* 'people' but to an undefined human collective. Because of the maximally general meaning of *les gens*, however, the two analyses are essentially similar.

12. Recall that *on* cannot replace third-person pronouns in directly anaphoric contexts. This particularity is examined in further detail in this section.

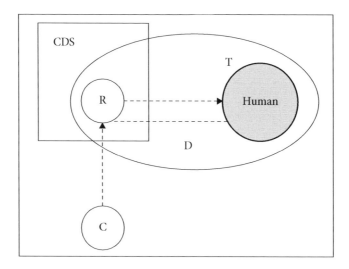

Figure 8.5 *On*'s semantic structure

As the previous examples have illustrated, perhaps the most striking difference between *on* and the other pronouns concerns the third-person singular agreement it imposes on the following predicate, even when the latter's referent is unquestionably composed of multiple individuals. In a nutshell, the pronoun exhibits this specific agreement pattern because it treats its referent as a homogenous mass of individuals who share the characteristic described by the predicate. In Figure 8.5 the cross-hatching inside the profiled target represents the mass construal that the pronoun imposes. The example in (8.3) repeated here provides a clear illustration of this characteristic:

(8.3)   *Ce qu'on appelle création dans les grands artistes n'est qu'une manière particulière*
        à chacun de voir, de coordonner et de rendre la nature.

                                        (Huyghe, R. *Dialogue avec le visible*: 266)
        'What one calls creation among the great artists is only their own particular
        way of seeing, arranging, and depicting nature'.

The predicate *appeller* 'call' describes the linguistic convention shared by every French-speaking person who knows the meaning of the term. The sum of these individuals constitutes a community of equals with respect to the state of affairs that the predicate describes. Because of their equal status, those individuals can be likened to the different yet homogenous constituents that constitute the substance that mass nouns profile (Langacker 2008: 128). To take just one example, a noun such as *sable* 'sand' determines singular agreement on the accompanying predicate (*le sable est chaud* 'the sand is hot') because its internal components – the individual grains – are considered too similar to be treated as separate entities, and consequently the substance they compose is construed as a homogenous mass. The third-person singular marking on the predicate that follows *on* underscores the analogy between indefinite pronouns and mass nouns. To come back to the example in (8.3), French speakers are treated as a homogenous mass with respect to their knowledge of what *création* means. It is that undistinguished mass and not its individual components that is profiled, and the singular agreement on the predicate reflects this specific construal.[13]

The construal of the referent as a homogenous mass represents one of *on*'s constant traits and is thus attested in all its uses, including its personal sense. This is illustrated in (8.1), repeated here:

(8.1)   *Une fois, dans un manoir voisin, **nous veillâmes** jusqu'à l'aube; **on confectionna** de la soupe à l'oignon dans la cuisine; **nous allâmes** en auto au pied du mont Gargan que **nous escaladâmes** pour voir le lever du soleil; **nous bûmes** du café au lait dans une auberge; ce fut ma première nuit blanche.*
(Beauvoir, S. de. *Mémoires d'une jeune fille rangée*: 165)
'Once, in a nearby manor, we stayed up until dawn; we made onion soup in the kitchen; we drove to the base of Mount Gargan that we climbed to see the sunrise; we drank milk and coffee at an inn; it was the first time I stayed up all night'.

We can safely assume that the same number of young people constitutes the referent of all the predicates in the sentence, but the different agreement patterns on those predicates reflect the different ways in which it is constructed. With *veiller* 'stay up', *aller* 'go', *escalader* 'climb', and *boire* 'drink', the plural on the predicate indicates that the group is construed as a collection of individuals who participate in the activity that the predicate profiles. With *confectionner*, however, the group is treated as a homogenous mass composed of similar elements, and the singular agreement on the predicate reflects this mass construal. Such construal variations should not surprise us since they are commonly attested in other areas of grammar. For example, the difference in agreement between *tous les gens sont partis* 'all persons left' and *tout le monde est parti* 'everyone left' can be analyzed

---

13. The individual elements that compose that mass are recoverable and can be used for anaphoric reference. In *on a souvent besoin d'un plus petit que soi* 'one often needs someone smaller than oneself' (La Fontaine: *Fables. Livre 2*, XI, *Le lion et le rat*), *on* evokes a homogenous mass but the anaphoric *soi* denotes each specific individual that composes that mass. The referential properties of indefinite *on* is not considered in detail; they are addressed in Koenig (1999), Koenig and Mauner (1999), and Creissels (2008b).

in a similar manner where the singular reflects the mass construal of the noun *monde*, despite its complex internal structure.[14]

The second distinguishing characteristic between *on* and the other pronouns concerns the level of schematicity of the restrictions placed on the pronoun's referent. As indicated in Figure 8.5, *on* does not specify the gender and number of its referent, only its human character. This stands in sharp contrast with the other pronouns that specify their referent's gender and number but not its animacy (in French inanimates are necessarily marked masculine or feminine). Just like the other pronouns, *on* crucially depends on the linguistic and extralinguistic context to isolate within the current discourse space the entity that satisfies its specifications. Additionally, however, because of both its similarity to the other pronouns and its higher degree of generality, *on*'s use is often blocked by the presence of a more-specific form whose own restrictions better match the intended referent. The competition from the other more-specific pronouns therefore accounts for *on*'s highly specific distribution. The remainder of this section examines the pronoun's use as a first- or second-person separately from its third-person usage because they are markedly different.

In order to understand *on*'s referent as a first- or second-person entity, it is necessary to understand the precise nature of its competition, namely *je* and *tu/vous*. *Je* and *tu* (the analysis also applies to its formal variant *vous*) are obviously characterized against the background of a very complex model of social interaction. This model incorporates several dimensions, among which two are particularly relevant for our purposes and act as input domains (Fauconnier and Turner 2002) to the blended space that constitutes the pronouns' meaning (Langacker 2007: 182–185). The first is a canonical speech-event scenario in which interlocutors alternatively assume the roles of speaker and hearer (Benveniste 1966). This model states that every conception of a speaker or a hearer involves the backstage conception of two separate speech events where both participants play the part of speaker and hearer respectively. The resulting conception recapitulates the intersubjective nature of the ground where the conceptions of speaker and hearer mutually evoke each other. The blended space that describes the dual role of the speaker and hearer is illustrated in Figure 8.6:

---

14. The alternation between *on* and *nous* can serve a stylistic purpose. For instance, Victor Hugo uses it to evoke the personal consequences of collective experience in the following: "**On est un peuple, on est un monde, on est une âme.** *Chacun se donne à tous et nul ne songe à soi.* **Nous sommes** *sans soleil, sans appui, sans effroi*" 'We are one people, we are one world. Each gives himself to all, and no one thinks of himself. We are without sun, without support, without fear' (Hugo, V. *L'année terrible, janvier,* II [cited in Gougenheim 1963:237, emphasis in Gougenheim]).

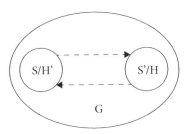

Figure 8.6 Dual role of the speaker and hearer (adapted from Langacker 2007:182)

The second model concerns another similar asymmetry between the subject and object of conception. These two roles are also "reversible" in that "when one person (S) conceives of another (O), the former usually recognizes the possibility of being conceptualized by the latter as well" (Langacker 2007:183). The two events where the two participants alternatively occupy the roles of subject and object provide the input for the conception of the ground as both subject and object of conception. The blended space that results from these complementary conceptions is illustrated in Figure 8.7:

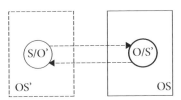

Figure 8.7 Dual role of the ground as subject and object of conception (adapted from Langacker 2007:183)

The meaning of the first- and second-person pronouns incorporates these two facets of our interactive conception of a verbal exchange as the input of a higher-level blend. The second-person *tu/vous* identifies "the speaker with the subject of conception, and the hearer with the object of conception". By contrast, the first-person *je* "results from identifying the speaker with the object of conception, and the hearer with the subject" (Langacker 2007:183). The brief description of the meaning of the first- and second-person pronouns given here suffices to show the extent to which these pronouns are embedded both in the speech event itself and in the models of interaction between the speaker and the hearer more generally. Because (1) both speaker and hearer are always available in interaction by definition, and (2) *je* and *tu /vous* are so intricately connected to those respective roles, the presence of any other pronoun such as *on* in their place requires especially strong pragmatic justification. This justification is often provided by a severe discrepancy between the kind of interaction described and the canonical model introduced in this overview. The basic idea is that *on* can occur as a possible substitute for either the speaker/author or the hearer/listener if the exchange in which it is involved deviates from the communicative norm. The highly specific semantic import of first- and second-person (personal) *on* can therefore be analyzed as marking the unconventional character of the protagonists in the described speech event.

Understandably, even unconventional speech-event participants fall within well-established norms, and *on* is most frequently attested in predictable environments. The literary conventions presented at the beginning of this chapter can be analyzed in this manner. One might suggest that *on*'s presence marks the unconventional nature of the author/reader interaction where both roles are set for the duration of the reading, and no exchange per se occurs. In this context *on*'s presence highlights the difference between a literary exchange and a canonical speech event. The avoidance of first- and second-person pronouns decreases the asymmetry between the author and the reader as specific and separate roles, and thus depicts the writing/reading act as a communal exchange around the text. The second context in which *on* is attested is what we may call caregiving *on* where the indefinite pronoun marks highly specific interactions between a hearer who is being attended to and a speaker who sees to her needs in a cheerful, caring, yet slightly condescending manner. These exchanges illustrated in (8.16) and (8.17) are often attested with small children or patients who have not yet recovered their full capacity:

(8.16) #*Alors, **on** va bien ce matin*?
        'So are we [one] doing well this morning?'

(8.17) #***On** a bien mangé son dessert*?
        'Did we [one] eat our [his] dessert?'

Exchanges such as those described in (8.16) and (8.17) clearly do not conform to the full intersubjective model described at the beginning of this section because the speaker and hearer are not presented as equal and thus equally capable of fulfilling the same alternative roles. *On*'s presence codes this highly specific exchange and marks its departure from the canonical interactional model by retaining the human nature of the interlocutor, but not granting her full participation in the interaction. In yet another kind of well-attested pattern, *on*'s presence in the interaction illustrated in (8.13) and repeated here also codes the hearer's unconventional status:

(8.13)   *Et ça ne te gêne pas de penser que des types ont écrit des trucs tellement supérieurs à ce que tu pondras, toi? Dit Nadine d'un ton vaguement irrité. – Au début, je ne le pensais pas, dit Henri en souriant; on est arrogant tant qu'on n'a rien fait. Et puis une fois qu'on est dans le coup, on s'intéresse à ce qu'on écrit et on ne perd plus de temps à se comparer. – Oh! Bien sûr, **on** s'arrange! Dit-elle d'une voix boudeuse en se laissant retomber de tout son long sur le sol.*

(Beauvoir, S de. *Les mandarins*: 92)

'And it does not bother you to think that some guys have written things so superior to what you'll come up with? Nadine said in a slightly irritated voice. – At the beginning, I didn't think so, Henri said with a smile; you are arrogant when you haven't done anything. And then once you get started, you get interested in what you write and you waste no time comparing yourself to other people. Oh! Of course, that's convenient [one makes things easy for oneself]! she said in a pouty voice, letting herself fall to the ground'.

This example is considered in further detail later, but it is nonetheless useful to note at this point that Nadine's statement goes beyond the evocation of Henri's actions to include other people's similar behaviors in comparable situations. *On*'s presence therefore codes a level of relevance that goes beyond the canonical interaction between two interlocutors to reach more general conclusions. The conditions under which *on* can refer to the speaker or the hearer needs to be pragmatically justified, and the justifications primarily come from highly specific cases in which the described interaction deviates from the intersubjective norm. The important point for our purposes is that these cases make use of the pronoun's underspecification to mark the unconventional character of the interaction.

Third-person referents are not so fundamentally embedded within the interaction itself, but *on*'s presence also needs to be justified due to the presence of the well-entrenched *il(s)* and *elle(s)*. In the context of people external to the speaker and hearer, this justification comes primarily from the difficulty of precisely identifying and delineating the referent. This is obviously the case if the referent is unidentified as in (8.15), or simply irrelevant beyond its participation in the event that the predicate profiles as in (8.14):

(8.15)   *Les gens vous montreront du doigt en ricanant. Ils diront que vous avez épousé une putain de la ruelle aux brebis. **On** vous insultera.*   (Aymé, M. *Clérambard*: 97)

'People will sneer and point at you. They will say you married a whore from the gutter. You will be insulted [one will insult you]'.

(8.14)   *Aujourd'hui, **on** me remet cette lettre. Avez-vous lu comment il me traite à la fin?*

(Camus, A. *Les possédés; pièce en trois actes*: 996)

'Today this letter is delivered to me [one gives me this letter]. Did you see how he talks to me at the end?'

Most importantly for the purposes of this chapter, this is also the case in situations where the pronoun's referent is a large group of people, perhaps even inclusive of humanity at large. This kind of situation was already described in (8.3) where the pronoun's referent comprises all French speakers who know what *création* means. With respect to their participation in the process that the predicate codes, the reference point from which the pronoun is accessed has the lowest possible level of delimitation because the projection of the pronoun onto the world yields the totality of French speakers (Langacker 2007: 179). This kind of situation where R is minimally delimited (maximally general) is considered impersonal.[15] It is important to note, however, that the pronoun's impersonal sense is closely related to its other senses but nonetheless relatively easy to delineate. Consistent with the analyses presented in previous chapters, this minimal delimitation of the reference point via which the pronoun is accessed occurs in the context of specific constructions. This should not be a surprise. The clues that inform the hearer that the intended referent is highly general are often provided by very specific contexts, including the immediate speech situation; the general structure of the world as it conforms to our expectations; or, more generally, the schemas and conventions that regulate our everyday physical, intellectual, and emotional experience. These cognitive constructs, along with their grammatical correlates such as specific patterns of tense, aspect, or modality markers, for example, define highly recognizable environments where the access to the pronoun's referent are clearly defined. Each of these environments represents a particular construction in the sense used throughout this monograph, so once again constructions represent the working construct that allows us to define impersonal constructions. The key point here is that the possibilities of access to *on*'s referent are not random but organized into highly recognizable patterns. The next section shows that impersonal *on* can be found in two specific constructions that present the pronoun's referent as a homogenous mass exhaustive of every potential conceptualizer. It shows that this minimal delimitation can be accomplished in two different manners, namely by homogenization and virtualization.

---

15. The minimal delimitation of the personal pronouns is particularly clear in English since 'it' functions at the same time as a third-person neuter and an impersonal pronoun (Langacker 2007: 179).

3.   Patterns of use: From personal to indefinite

This chapter is primarily concerned with the identification of a class of indefinite impersonals. As was the case with the middle impersonals in Chapter 7, there are no set morphological or syntactic criteria to facilitate the task, but stable specific environments can be identified where *on* undeniably has impersonal meaning. As was also the case with the other aforementioned constructions, the pronoun's meaning in these environments exhibits striking similarities with its meaning in other contexts. This section briefly introduces the specific patterns that emerged from the corpus; shows that *on* can be evaluated along a continuum of generality and identifiability of its referent; and that the endpoint of that continuum, i.e., when the pronoun's referent is minimally delimited, constitutes its impersonal sense. While our focus is unquestionably on the indefinite senses, the personal sense also needs to be briefly considered to present the entire semantic range that the pronoun covers.

In the pronoun's personal sense, the referent is identified by its participation in the event or activity profiled by the predicate. This is most typically illustrated in (8.18), where the referents of *on* are clearly identified as the narrator and Bresson who met at the café:

(8.18)   *J'envoyai un mot au jeune Bresson que je retrouvai un soir vers six heures au*
         Stryx; **on** *parla de Jacques, qu'il admirait; mais le bar était désert et il n'arriva*
         rien.   (Beauvoir, S. de. *Mémoires d'une jeune fille rangée*: 268)
         'I sent a note to young Bresson whom I met one evening around 6 o'clock at
         the Stryx; we talked about Jack whom he admired; but the bar was empty and
         nothing happened'.

Unlike its indefinite counterpart, personal *on* in (8.18) is directly anaphoric because it refers back to the two previously mentioned participants. While the configuration illustrated in (8.18) cannot be considered impersonal, it is nonetheless worth examining because it constitutes the conceptual blueprint from which the impersonal sense emerges. Two related yet separate aspects of this configuration need to be distinguished. The first is obviously the identifiability of the participants, clearly available in (8.18) by the explicit mention of their names. The second characteristic concerns the extent to which participation in the event that the predicate profiles is restricted to the pronoun's referents or available to other potential participants. In (8.18) the discussion mentioned in the passage is exclusively carried out by the two protagonists, whose role relative to the conversation can be called equal and exclusive since no one else took part in it. This configuration represents perhaps the most specific situation the pronoun participates in because (1) the participants in the profiled process are identified and specifically mentioned, and (2) they constitute the only possible participants in that process. Other configurations can be gradually more general if the participants cannot be identified with precision, or their participation in the event that the predicate codes cannot easily be ascertained. The situation described in (8.19) departs from the highly specific one in (8.18), because if the participants in the profiled process (*mise en avant* 'positioned in front') bear the sole responsibility for its occurrence they cannot be identified with precision among the occupants of the boat. In (8.20) we know that the harvesting has been carried out by specific participants who bear exclusive responsibility for its accomplishment, but nonetheless remain unidentified.

(8.19)   *Tout ça, je me rappelais tout ça sur le bateau. Toi, c'était le pilote, **on** t'avait mise en avant pour nous trouver la route, c'était toi, le pilote. Et moi, à ta place, je m'étais posté en arrière, la figure tournée vers le vieux pays.*
                                            (Claudel, P. *L'échange: deuxième version*: 737)
         'All that, I remembered all that on the boat. You, you were the pilot, you had been placed [one had placed you] in front to show us the way, you were the pilot. And me, in your place, I had positioned myself in the back, my head turned toward the old country'.

(8.20)   ***on** avait cueilli les lavandes cela se sentait à plein nez*
                                            (Aragon, L. *Le roman inachevé*: 149)
         'Lavender had been harvested [one had harvested lavender], you could smell it strongly'

The identifiability of the referent and her exclusive responsibility for the realization of the event described by the predicate constitute two independent paths of extension for the pronoun's indefinite senses, and they each take the pronoun in different directions. When the agent is left implicit as in (8.19) and (8.20) but its exclusive responsibility for the profiled process is unquestionable, the ensuing construction performs the function of a passive, as the additional examples in (8.21)–(8.23) illustrate:

(8.21)   *Me parle d'un jeune homme qui n'a pas pu continuer la lutte et qui s'est tué en absorbant une grosse quantité de gardénal, trop grosse, semble-t-il, car la mort a été longue à venir. **On** a trouvé dans sa poche des lettres et un chapelet...*
                                            (Green, J. *Journal. T. 5. 1946–1950*: 221)
         '[He] talks to me about a young man who couldn't continue the fight and killed himself by taking a large quantity of gardenal, too large a dose it seems, because it took a long time for him to die. Some letters and a rosary were found [one found some letters and a rosary] in his pocket...'

(8.22)   *Au jour fixé pour leur retour, ils s'arrêtèrent pour déjeuner dans un petit port à trois heures de Lisbonne; ils laissèrent la voiture devant l'auberge pour escalader une des collines qui dominaient la mer; au sommet se dressait un moulin blanc, coiffé de tuiles vertes;* **on** *avait fixé à ses ailes de petites jarres de terre cuite au col étroit où le vent chantait.*   (Beauvoir, S. de. *Les mandarins*: 91)
          'On the day of their return, they stopped at a little harbor three hours from Lisbon for lunch. They left the car in front of the inn to climb one of the hills that overlooked the sea; at the top was a little white mill with a green tiled roof; some little clay jars with narrow necks had been attached [one had attached some little clay jars with narrow necks] to its wings, and the wind was singing through them'.

(8.23)   La Femme Malade: *moi, aussi, je riais quand je suis entrée ici pour la première fois.* Le Monsieur Gros *pour la première opération?* La Femme Malade *exactement.* Mascherini **on** *vous a endormie?*
                                                        (Camus, A. *Un cas intéressant*: 643)
          'The sick woman: I too was laughing the first time I came here. The fat man: for the first surgery? The sick woman: exactly. Mascherini: did they put you under [one put you under]?'

The indefinite constructions in (8.21)–(8.23) share important functional characteristics with passives. First, the presence of the indefinite pronoun as the subject constitutes a way of defocusing the agent (Shibatani 1985) because the pronoun's referent is not made specific beyond its human character. Second, the predicates are transitive, and finally, the patient – the character that would be the subject in a morphosyntactic passive – is either specifically mentioned or easily recoverable.

With some intransitive predicates illustrated in (8.24), the indefinite construction represents the only way of achieving the function of a passive since the morphosyntactic passive construction is not possible:

(8.24)   **On frappe, et on entrouvre la porte.** *L'abbé De Pradts, qui voit le visiteur (invisible au public,) dit:* Monsieur Prial, je vais vous voir un instant.
                              (Montherlant, H. de. *La ville dont le prince est un enfant*: 918)
          'There is a knock [one knocks] and someone pushes the door ajar [one pushes the door ajar]. Abbott De Pardts, who sees the visitor (whom the public can't see) says: Mister Prial, I will see you for a minute'.

With other intransitive predicates or predicates used intransitively, indefinite constructions do not resemble passives to the same extent because they do not include an agent that can unquestionably be held responsible for carrying out the profiled process. This is illustrated in (8.25) and (8.26) where the agents of the profiled process do exist but cannot be recovered easily:[16]

(8.25)   *J'ai déjà parcouru la moitié du chemin. Que dira-t-on de moi si je m'en retourne?*
         (Camus, A. *Le chevalier d'Olmedo adaptation*: 806)
         'I have already gone halfway. What will people say [one say] of me if I turn back?

(8.26)   *Le nouveau monde semblait d'abord plus inquiétant que l'ancien: on y pillait, on y tuait; le sang coulait à flots.*   (Sartre, JP. *Les mots*: 58)
         'At first, the new world seemed more worrisome than the old one. There was pillaging [one pillaged], there was killing [one killed], blood was flowing in the streets'.

Although this chapter is not primarily concerned with indefinite passives, the data presented in (8.21)–(8.26) are interesting because they clearly illustrate the path of semantic extension between the pronoun's personal sense and its functional passive usage, and a similar trajectory can be outlined in the direction of impersonals. In this section we saw that *on* takes on a passive function when its referent is not identified but nonetheless remains solely responsible for the event coded by the predicate. In a similar fashion, the following section shows that indefinite *on* takes on an impersonal function when the pronoun's referent is not only unidentified, but also cannot be held solely responsible for the occurrence of the profiled process. This is the case particularly when its delimitation is minimal, i.e., includes everyone, because in this case the profiled event is generally available. In this sense, impersonal *on* occupies the opposite endpoint on a continuum of specificity from personal *on*. The scale of specificity from *on*'s personal sense to its impersonal sense is recapitulated in Figure 8.8.

Consistent with the analysis developed in the previous chapters, the minimal delimitation of the pronoun's referent is accomplished in systematic ways, and it reliably occurs in specific contexts. The next section examines these two issues in turn. We first consider the two processes of homogenization and virtualization by which *on*'s referent acquires its minimal delimitation before turning to the semantic and syntactic contexts where these processes can reliably be observed.

---

16. In fact, the function of the indefinite construction in (8.26) is closer to some impersonals in languages such as German, where examples like *Es wurde getanzt* (Smith 2006) are generally translated into English by an existential 'there' construction ('there was dancing'). In other languages the same constructions are translated by middles (see Chapter 7).

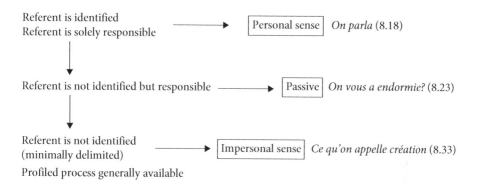

Figure 8.8 From personal to impersonal *on*

4.   Indefinite impersonals

One can legitimately wonder how statements can be made at a level of generality that involves every single member of a given group, and even potentially every human being on the planet. As we will see here, the answer is complex and involves many closely related facets of several cognitive models in different impersonal constructions, but it ultimately resides in the deeply social nature of human cognition (Tomasello 1999, 2003). This section shows that the different usage patterns of indefinite impersonals reflect two alternative manners of constructing maximally general statements based on different aspects of our social models of cognition. The first involves the homogenization of experience, the second, the virtualization of individual experience.

4.1   Minimal delimitation by homogenization

According to Tomasello (1999, 2003), the cognitive breakthrough that enabled human culture to distinguish itself from that of other mammals and primates stems from the realization that conspecifics are sentient beings very similar to the self. Consequently all sorts of analogical conclusions can be drawn concerning others on the basis of what each of us experiences for her/himself. Our own internal landscape therefore constitutes a legitimate guide to predict, and possibly influence, other people's reactions, aspirations, motivations, and fears. This shared conceptualization of the world inside and outside of us allows us to recognize shared circumstances and express them as common experience. This ability is particularly important to the characterization of indefinite impersonals, as the example in (8.27) illustrates, where the presence of the indefinite *on* reflects the understanding that the seasonal cycle affects everyone in a similar manner and that it is best described as a collective experience, even though it may momentarily be observed by a single person such as the artist who may be uniquely affected by it:

(8.27)   *Pendant quelque temps, il s'arrêta de travailler et réfléchit. Il aurait peint sur le motif si la saison s'y était prêtée. Malheureusement, **on** allait entrer dans l'hiver, il était difficile de faire du paysage avant le printemps.*
                                            (Camus, A. *L'exil et le royaume*: 1646)
         'He stopped working and thought for a while. He would have painted on the motif if the season had been right. Unfortunately, winter was coming [one was about to enter winter], it was hard to paint landscapes before the spring'.

This possibility of analyzing the reactions, aspirations, and behaviors of entire groups on the basis of the internal mental state of a single conceptualizer allows humans to reflect on their past, analyze their present, and predict future events with different degrees of confidence. This conception of reality, articulated in Langacker's elaborated reality model, in which the events that have already occurred constrain future outcomes to different degrees (Langacker 2008: 306), was presented in earlier chapters. Chapter 5 emphasized the epistemic pursuit of individual conceptualizers, but the collective nature of our cognition, based on the similarity of others to the self, also allows any observer to provide a snapshot of the past, current, or future state of the knowledge, aspirations, fears, accomplishments, and so on of a group of any size on any topic. The examples in (8.28) and (8.29) illustrate statements made by one community member about the entire community's state of knowledge on a variety of subjects, ranging from the highly specific in (8.28), to the most general in (8.29):

(8.28)   *La cour, indignée, voulait chasser de France cet homme dangereux. **On** ne sait si les musiciens de l'opéra pensèrent, comme il s'en vante, à l'assassiner.*
                                            (Guéhenno, J. *Jean-Jacques. T. 2*: 67)
         'The indignant court wanted to expel this dangerous man from France. We don't [one doesn't] know if the opera musicians were thinking about killing him, as he is proud to report'.

(8.29)   *il s'agit des choses qu'**on** ne peut pas maintenant, mais qu'**on** peut pouvoir un jour et plus tard, qu'**on** pourra…*
                                            (Jankélévitch, V. *Le je-ne-sais-quoi et le presque-rien*: 231)
         'These are things that we [one] cannot do now, but that we [one] may be able to do one day and that we [one] will later be able to do…'

The conceptualizers' role in the construction of reality goes well beyond mere observation. This sounds trivial but should not be overlooked. Numerous statements pertaining to a variety of subjects reflect some conceptualizer's analysis of a (possibly overwhelmingly) large number of events, behaviors, and circumstances, as the examples in (8.30) and (8.31) illustrate:

(8.30) *Oui, **on** sait ce que ça coûte la résignation, l'égoïsme: mais il y a longtemps qu'**on** le sait, sans profit. **On** n'a jamais réussi à arrêter le malheur, **on** n'y réussira pas de si tôt, en tout cas pas de notre vivant.* (Beauvoir, S. de. *Les mandarins*: 205)
'Yes, we know [one knows] the price of resignation, selfishness: but we have [one has] known that for a long time, without any benefit. We have [one has] never succeeded in stopping misfortune, we [one] won't succeed anytime soon, at least not in our lifetime'.

(8.31) *Le progrès, de Sade à nos jours, a consisté à élargir de plus en plus le lieu clos où, selon sa propre règle, régnait farouchement l'homme sans dieu. **On** a poussé de plus en plus les frontières du camp retranché, face à la divinité, jusqu'à faire de l'univers entier une forteresse contre le dieu déchu et exilé.*
(Camus, A. *L'homme révolté*: 131)
'Progress from Sade until today has consisted in increasingly broadening the secluded space where godless man reigned according to his own rule. The boundaries of the fortified camp against divinity have been pushed further and further [one pushed the boundaries of the fortified camp against divinity further and further], until the entire universe became a fortress against the fallen and exiled God'.

A statement such as *on n'a jamais réussi à arrêter le malheur* 'we have never succeeded in stopping misfortune' in (8.30) represents a conclusion that can only be formulated following the examination of countless episodes of human history. It is also clear that it only applies indirectly to individual members of society – few can be said to have consciously tried to stop misfortune. However, it possesses universal value because it proposes a framework through which every human action can be analyzed. The statement presented in (8.31) can obviously be described in the same manner since it interprets a large number of events and behaviors within a specific model.

In the examples presented in (8.27)–(8.31), the agent of the event that the predicate describes cannot be identified with precision, and the participation in that predicate is shared by an unspecified number of people, possibly all of them. Importantly, the speaker is part of that community. Despite the large number of potential referents, the third-person singular marking on the verb reflects the construal of all these referents as a homogenous mass where the individual differences of the various constituents are overlooked to focus on their similarity. Just as the individual kernels of corn are homogenized to yield the mass noun "corn", the referents of indefinite *on* in the configuration described in (8.27)–(8.31) are also considered identical with respect to their relation to the following predicate. For example, in (8.27) all members of the community described by the predicate *aller* 'go' necessarily share similar geographical circumstances, however significant their individual characteristics might be. Consequently, with respect to an event as general as the cycle of seasons, they can rightfully be described as a human mass in which all component parts are identical and representative of the whole.

These homogenizing statements can also describe a community's linguistic or cultural habits that are shared by every member, as previously presented in (8.3) and further illustrated in (8.32) and (8.33):

(8.32)   *Nous sommes oublieux, et nous avons oublié, parmi beaucoup d'autres choses, quelle terreur entourait il n'y a pas tant d'années, dans ce qu'on nomme les milieux bourgeois, le nom de la Russie.*   (Weil, S. *Écrits historiques et politiques*: 44)
'We forget easily, and we have forgotten, among many other things, the terror that the name of Russia struck among what one calls the bourgeois society until fairly recently'.

(8.33)   *J'ai envie de la prendre tout de suite dans mes bras, mais il y a vraiment trop de spectateurs. **On** dit que l'éléphant se cache au plus profond des forêts pour se livrer à ses ébats. J'ai de cette pudicité de pachyderme.*
(T'Serstevens, A. *L'itinéraire espagnol*: 120)
'I want to take her in my arms right away, but there are too many onlookers. It is said [one says] that elephants hide deep in the forest to mate. I share the elephant's modesty'.

So far, in all the examples considered the speaker has been included in the homogenous mass that constitutes the pronoun's referent so the close similarity between the pronoun's personal and indefinite senses is clearly apparent.[17] However, *on* is also attested in a configuration in which the speaker does not belong to the community described and is thus not a part of the referred mass, as the examples in (8.34)–(8.36) illustrate:

(8.34)   *En tout cas, je m'efforce de ne pas contrarier le fonctionnement des services par un emploi du temps mal réglé. En principe, à "Carlton Gardens", **on** ne travaille pas la nuit, excepté au bureau du chiffre.*
(Gaulle, C. de. *Mémoires de guerre, l'appel*: 239)
'In any case, I try not to disturb the services with a poorly timed schedule. Usually, at Carlton Gardens, they don't [one doesn't] work at night, except in the coding office'.

---

17. There are two main differences between the pronoun's personal sense and this configuration. The group that constitutes the indefinite's referent is minimally delimited, and consequently responsibility for the event that the predicate profiles is maximally shared. Second, the mass of the referents is homogenous rather than particulate.

(8.35) *Si M. Churchill envoyait le coup de semonce à propos d'un renfort de 2500 soldats*
français, expédié dans un territoire où se trouvaient 60000 britanniques, qui
allaient être rejoints par 15000 autres et que 2000 avions de combat se tenaient
*prêts à appuyer, c'est qu'**on** allait, du côté anglais, provoquer une forte secousse.*
(Gaulle, C. de. *Mémoires de guerre, le salut*: 188)
'If Mr. Churchill was so eager for a reinforcement of 2,500 French soldiers to
be sent to a place where there were 60,000 Englishmen assisted by 2,000 fighter
jets with another 15,000 soldiers on the way, it was because on the English
side, they were [one was] about to launch a major offensive'.

(8.36) *Toutes les familles, femmes et enfants, ont suivi les moissonneurs, et pendant*
que ceux-ci travaillent, elles somnolent, bavardent, font la cuisine ou la lessive,
tout comme chez elles. **On** *étale les gerbes sur une aire d'argile durcie et l'**on** y*
fait passer un traîneau de bois tiré par trois ou quatre mules que le conducteur
mène en rond.   (T'Serstevens, A. *L'itinéraire espagnol*: 264)
'All the families, women, and children followed the harvesters, and while the
men work, they nap, chat, cook or do the laundry, as they would do at home.
The wheat is spread [one spreads the wheat] on a hard clay platform, and a
wooden sleigh pulled by three or four mules led in a circle runs over it [one
runs a wooden sleigh pulled by three or four mules over it]'.

The homogenous mass of people that constitutes *on*'s referent in these three examples is clearly identifiable. In (8.34) the adverbial *à Carlton Gardens* indicates
that it is composed of the members of the British headquarters. In (8.35) the presence of *du côté anglais* makes it clear that it includes anyone in an English uniform.
Even though it is not specifically mentioned in (8.36), it is nonetheless obviously
composed of the families who take part in the harvest activities. Importantly, the
speaker is never part of the community that these groups define. As a French officer, De Gaulle remains an outsider to Carlton Gardens, and he is similarly not privy
to British strategy. In the same manner in (8.36), the narrator does not directly
participate in the harvest ceremonies.

The external position of the speaker relative to the pronoun's referent is reminiscent of a third-person arrangement (coded by *ils/elles*), so further consideration
is required to explain the presence of indefinite *on*. The basic idea is that this
configuration reflects an alternative viewpoint from which the referent mass is
considered. More specifically, the context defines a search domain within which
the collections of individuals present should be considered homogenous relative
to the event profiled by the predicate. This search domain can be specifically mentioned as in (8.34) and (8.35), or pragmatically available as in (8.36). Second, the
speaker sets up a virtual member of the community, specifically conjured up for
the purpose of presenting that process from within. This virtual conceptualizer
C' constitutes the vantage point from which the referred mass is conceptualized.

Because C' is a member of the community whereas C is not, all the other aspects of the configuration are identical to the one illustrated in (8.27)–(8.33). *On* has minimal delimitation within the relevant search domain. In other words, all the individuals that meet the conditions that the domain imposes (working at Carlton Gardens or being part of the British strategy team) are conceptualized together as a homogenous mass with respect to the event that the predicate describes.

This configuration with an alternative viewpoint frequently describes prototypical generalizations about specific groups, as the examples in (8.37) and (8.38) illustrate:

(8.37)   *En Italie on sait préparer les pâtes*   (from Creissels 2008b: 15)
         'In Italy they know [one knows] how to prepare pasta'

(8.38)   *J'ai des raisons toutes personnelles d'aller à Cadix. C'est là que mon ami le père*
         Labat débarqua en revenant des Antilles et vécut plusieurs mois en 1705. C'est là
         aussi qu'on mange les meilleures gambas, ces grandes crevettes roses qu'on vend
         jusqu'à Madrid mais qui ne sont vraiment délicieuses que sur le port de Cadix.
                                           (T'Serstevens, A. *L'itinéraire espagnol*: 143)
         'I have very personal reasons to go to Cadiz. This is where my friend, father
         Labat, arrived and lived for several months when he came back from the
         Caribbean in 1705. It is also where you can eat [one eats] the best gambas,
         these big pink shrimps that you can find as far as Madrid but that are only
         truly delicious in the Cadiz harbor'.

It is important to note that in (8.37) and (8.38) there is no way of knowing if the narrator is part of the homogenous referred community defined by the search domain. The statement in (8.37) is equally felicitous whether it is uttered by an Italian or merely someone else aware of Italy's reputation, and while we may assume the author has tasted the gambas his observation would still take the same form if he was simply reporting common knowledge.

At this point the indefinite pronoun *on* has been attested in four separate yet related configurations relative to the relation between the pronoun's referent and the predicate, namely personal, passive, homogenous mass, and homogenous mass with an alternative viewpoint. The obvious question concerns the possible identification of these configurations. Is it possible to know if a given instance of *on* represents a passive or an impersonal, or, more generally, does it need to be an instance of any particular type of construction? In the view defended in this monograph, it is illusory to attempt to define each and every instance of *on* as a member of a specific functional class such as impersonal or passive, for example. *On* is first and foremost an indefinite pronoun; although in specific situations it participates in constructions that approach the semantic characteristics of these classes, in a large number of cases it does not. In fact, there is no particular semantic trait that reliably indicates a particular sense of the pronoun. The latter's meaning is exclusively determined by the pragmatic availability of its referent, as illustrated in (8.39) where the interpretation primarily depends on who the speaker is:[18]

(8.39)   #*En Suisse on fait de l'horlogerie de qualité*
            'In Switzerland, they make [one makes] quality timepieces'

To briefly recapitulate the results obtained in this section, impersonal *on* stands at the exact opposite end from the pronoun's personal sense because (1) the pronoun's referent is composed of a minimally delimited group (all the relevant participants in a given search domain), and (2) each member of the group has equal responsibility (access) for the realization of the event or process that the predicate codes. The configuration considered in this section describes a stable characteristic of a given community. It meets the impersonal definition by treating all members of the community as a homogenous mass. The speaker can be part of that mass, but she can also set up an alternative viewpoint inside the community to present its characteristic as if she were part of it. Some semantic or grammatical traits may be related to specific configurations. For example, the most general statements illustrated in (8.29) tend to include verbs of cognition or perception in the present tense. Similarly, the construction of an alternative viewpoint is often accompanied by the specific mention of the search domain within which the referred mass is homogenous. However, neither of these features, nor many others not discussed here, is systematic enough to be considered a valid diagnostic. Perhaps most importantly, in this construction the pronoun's minimal delimitation is achieved by the homogenization of the individuals who potentially participate in the profiled event and only available pragmatically. Consistent with the definition of impersonals proposed in Chapter 1, this mass construal of the pronoun's referent provides the event that the predicate profiles with the highest degree of generalization and availability because its realization is independent from being carried out by a specific agent.

---

18. Certain semantic properties are indicative of specific senses. For example, the perfect aspect in (i) contributes to the pronoun's personal sense but is not consistent enough to be considered reliable:

(i)   #*En Italie on a mangé de bonnes pâtes*
         'In Italy we ate good pasta'

4.2   Delimitation by generalization of individual experience (virtualization)

The homogenization of the indefinite pronoun's potential referents into one mass of minimal delimitation does not represent the only path to the kind of generalization that the *on* construction demands to be considered impersonal. A second possible way of achieving the required level of generality and predictability comes from the generalization of individual experience. For the purposes of this chapter, it is interesting and expected to note that this generalization occurs within the confines of strict linguistic (syntactic and semantic) contexts. The first of these contexts is illustrated in the examples in (8.40)–(8.42):

(8.40)   *La lettre de Voltaire était légère, aimable et malicieuse à son habitude: "j'ai reçu, monsieur, votre nouveau livre contre le genre humain, je vous en remercie … on n'a jamais tant employé d'esprit à vouloir nous rendre bêtes. Il prend envie de marcher à quatre pattes quand **on** lit votre ouvrage..."*

(Guéhenno, J. *Jean-Jacques. T. 2*: 112)

'Voltaire's letter was customarily light, friendly and witty: "Sir, I have received your new book against humanity, I appreciate it … no greater wit has ever been used making us look like animals. One feels like walking on all fours when one reads your work..."'

(8.41)   *Pour tout esprit impartial, il est évident qu'un territoire qui est à la France depuis 1911 est français de droit pour l'éternité. C'est ce qui apparaît d'ailleurs encore plus clairement si **on** se reporte à l'histoire du Maroc.*

(Weil, S. *Écrits historiques et politiques*: 58)

'For any objective mind, it is obvious that a place that has belonged to France since 1911 is rightfully French for all eternity. This appears ever more clearly if one considers the history of Morocco'.

(8.42)   *Je me méfie toujours des histoires que je n'ai pas contrôlées de visu; si l'**on** devait croire, par exemple, toutes celles que des écrivains aveugles ont racontées sur la Polynésie, **on** se ferait de ses archipels une idée complètement fausse.*

(T'Serstevens, A. *L'itinéraire espagnol*: 248)

'I am always suspicious of stories I haven't checked for myself; if one were to believe, for example, all that blind authors have said about Polynesia, one would have a totally false idea of what these islands are like'.

From a formal standpoint, the examples in (8.40)–(8.42) all contain the same kind of construction, namely a subordinate clause introduced by *si* 'if' or *quand* 'when' clause accompanied by a main clause where *on* is the subject of the predicate. Semantically, they all indicate that the situation coded in the main clause will take place provided that the conditions described in the subordinate clause are met. Furthermore, they can also all be considered impersonal because any unidentified individual who experiences the trigger that the subordinate clause codes cannot help but experience the situation the predicate describes. The kind of general statement the examples in (8.40)–(8.42) present, however, differ from those considered earlier in that they do not describe an observed stable characteristic representative of a community but the natural and therefore predictable consequence of a given action. In other words, their generality is not achieved by the homogenization of the relevant referents into a masslike entity, but by making one conceptualizer's experience representative for that of the entire community. For example, Voltaire's criticism of Rousseau's stance on human nature presented in (8.40) is based on his own reaction; his desire to walk on all fours is triggered by his own reading of Rousseau's work. Perhaps the most straightforward coding of this individual reaction would use the pronouns *je* and *me* to produce the first-person #*Il me prend envie de marcher à quatre pattes quand je lis votre livre* 'I feel like walking on all fours when I read your book', but Voltaire did not adopt this solution because the alternative use of indefinite *on* provides his commentary with a level of generality that strengthens his argument. The use of the first-person *je* would limit the scope of his assertion by reducing the number of referents of the predicate *prendre l'envie de marcher à quatre pattes* 'feel like walking on all fours' to himself alone, and thus depict him as accepting sole responsibility for the interpretation of Rousseau's book. By contrast, his selection of *on* indicates that anyone in a similar position would invariably arrive at the same position. Because it is shared with the rest of the community, the author's reaction therefore acquires the unassailable force of inescapable conclusion. The selection of the indefinite *on* in (8.40) allows the author to transcend the limitations of individual experience by presenting his own reaction with the certainty that accompanies universal recognition. The other two examples function in essentially the same manner, even though they may not share the rhetorical power of Voltaire's assertion. In (8.41) anyone reading the history of Morocco will invariably confirm the author's interpretation of that country's privileged relationship with France. Similarly, in (8.42) the author contrasts his own beliefs to the reported accounts of other travelers by using a counterfactual construction. The mental space introduced by the "if" clause *si l'on devait croire, par exemple, toutes celles que des écrivains aveugles ont racontées sur la Polynésie* sets the stage for the necessary conclusion that our ideas about Polynesia would be false. In this strategy, the import of the indefinite pronoun is to make it clear that the author's sole reliance on personal accounts of foreign lands is justified by the erroneous conclusions that secondhand descriptions unfailingly provide.

The generality of the examples in (8.40)–(8.42) is therefore not achieved by the amalgamation of all possible referents into a homogenous mass, but by the systematic and predictable replication of the cause-and-effect relation that exists between a trigger and a resulting event – the reading of Rousseau's book and the desire to walk on all fours in (8.40), for example. This path to generality requires some explanation because at first sight, a single individual's reaction to a highly specific event that occurs only once seems a poor candidate for universality. Here again, this kind of generalization is made possible by the human ability to confidently predict other people's reactions on the basis of one's own (Tomasello 1999, 2003). As indicated earlier, because each individual views her conspecifics as basically identical to herself and therefore driven by similar needs, fears, feelings, and emotions, any person's individual response to any kind of stimulus can be calibrated relative to a norm of expected behavior and thus possibly accepted as universal. *On*'s primary semantic import in the examples in (8.40)–(8.42) precisely consists of transcending the specificity of individual response by presenting it as universal.

But how does it work conceptually? How can specific experience be generalized to the point of being considered universal? The key point is the human capacity for imagination, which enables speakers to talk about things that do not currently exist by conjuring up different kinds of virtual entities (objects and situations) to describe them. The concept of "virtual entities" (Langacker 1999) is perhaps best illustrated by the difference between definite and indefinite nominals. Langacker (2008: 289) argues that "a definite nominal of any sort is presumed capable of identifying its referent independently of the clause containing it." Conversely, "an indefinite standing alone fails to identify any specific individual as its referent." Consequently the discourse referents that indefinites introduce need to be conjured up for this purpose. For example, in #*j'aimerais bien avoir un chien* 'I would really like to have a dog', the referent of the indefinite nominal *un chien* 'a dog' cannot be located in reality. Its existence is virtual, i.e. it is created for the specific purpose of expressing the speaker's desires.

Closer to the concerns of this chapter, indefinites and the virtual entities they conjure up represent a possible expression of generics, as the example in (8.43b), repeated from Chapter 6, illustrates:

(8.43) a. *Les gosses, ça se lève tôt le matin* (from Carlier 1996)
            'Kids, that gets up early in the morning'
        b. #*Un gosse, ça se lève tôt le matin*
            'A kid, that gets up early in the morning'

Both sentences in (8.43) present a stable and general characteristic of kids, but that generality is achieved in different ways. In (8.43a) the plural marker indicates a "particulate" mass (Langacker 2008: 130) where all instances of the kid category are considered as homogenous relative to the event described in the predicate (getting up early). The presence of the indefinite article in (8.43b) indicates a single referent but a virtual one, namely a representative sample specifically conjured up to illustrate the process coded in the predicate. This sample has no independent existence in reality, and is manufactured by the speaker for the narrative purpose of describing one of its characteristics. The singular noun *gosse* in (8.43b) gains its generic value from the fact that it is not tied to a specific referent with its own idiosyncrasies but specifically designed for the illustration described by the predicate.

In the examples in (8.40)–(8.42), indefinite *on* functions in essentially the same way. To take just one example, the pronoun's referent in *quand on lit votre livre* 'when one reads your book' in (8.40) is a virtual reader conjured up to illustrate the predictable causal relation that exists between reading Rousseau's book and feeling like an animal. As mentioned previously, that reader is not independently attested in reality and can therefore not be understood as the speaker himself. The power of this conceptual configuration is obvious. Using a first-person pronoun to describe his own experience would restrict its scope to one single individual, but setting up a virtual reader as the pronoun's referent allows the author to emphasize the predictable and replicable aspect of the reaction, and hence present it as universal. In this second conceptual configuration of the indefinite pronoun, generality is achieved by the virtualization of the referent.

The highly specific formal structure of the examples in (8.40)–(8.42) reflects a rather specialized cognitive operation, namely the kind of reaction that specific triggers necessarily entail. The subordinate clause codes the trigger, and the main predicate expresses the predictable outcome. In other words, the specificity of the task itself explains the construction's syntactic rigidity. The same virtualization of behavior is also exhibited in more general areas of human experience, such as the analysis of specific input that we can be confident all humans will process in the same manner in similar circumstances. There are no constraints on the expression of this type of generalized behavior beyond the necessary presence of a perception or cognition predicate. Three separate situations have been observed that depend on which kind of cognitive manipulation is considered universal. In the first, illustrated in (8.44)–(8.46), the perception verbs do not describe the perceiver's experience but the properties of the scene examined. Because it is structured in a specific and predictable way, the scene is potentially processed in a similar manner by everyone in a situation to do so. This sense of perception is particularly well suited to the potential experience that the presence of the indefinite *on* indicates. For example, in (8.44) the scene is clearly processed by the narrator alone, as the presence of the first-person *je* attests in *je m'approchai de la fenêtre*. The shift from *je* to *on* reflects a change in focus to the general properties of the scene, which remain identical for any person observing it from the same position. Here again, *on*'s referent is a virtual observer whose presence guarantees the similarity, predictability, and hence generality of the experience.

(8.44) *Pendant qu'elle déballait les tissus brodés, je m'approchai de la fenêtre; on aper-*
cevait, comme d'habitude, Notre-Dame et ses jardins.

(Beauvoir, S. de. *Les mandarins*: 493)

'While she was unloading the embroidered fabrics, I walked to the window;
as usual, one could see Notre Dame and its gardens'.

A similar shift occurs in (8.45) where the experience described (the content of the
paintings) reaches beyond the small group of people present in the room at the
time of narration to include all potential viewers:

(8.45) *L'ambassadeur des États-Unis et le chargé d'affaires britannique étaient présents.*
Nous étions montés par l'escalier monumental, décoré des mêmes tableaux qu'au
temps du tsar. On y voyait représentés quelques sujets terrifiants: la furieuse
bataille de l'Irtych, Ivan le terrible étranglant son fils, etc.

(Gaulle, C. de. *Mémoires de guerre, le salut*: 73)

'The United States ambassador and the British representative were present.
We had walked up the enormous staircase, decorated with the same paintings
as during the tsar's regime. Some terrifying subjects were represented [one
could see some terrifying subjects]: the ferocious Irtych battle, Ivan the terrible
choking his son to death, etc.'.

It is important to notice that in (8.45) *nous* and *on* have different referents. *Nous*
refers to a small, well-delineated group of people that includes the American ambassador and the British representative in addition to the future French president.
These visitors all enter the room at the same time and thus discover the paintings
together, but their common experience is not what the narrator chooses to focus
on. His choice of the indefinite pronoun reflects his desire to present the paintings'
internal structure and content, which makes them available to everyone, including
but not restricted to the people currently experiencing them. The focus on the
work itself as a potential experience makes it independent from each individual's
actual viewing experience, and provides the situation with a degree of generality
comparable to an *il* impersonal construction (*il y avait...* 'there was'). The shift
between *nous* and *on* reflects the shift in referent from the actual viewers of the
paintings to the virtual observer conjured up for the sole purpose of describing
the immortalized scenes. The generalization of the viewing experience is complete
in (8.46). The scene does not include any episode of actual perception, but merely
describes the visual impression the author constructs and presents as the only one
available in this orientation. The virtual observer, which *on* conjures up, serves
her purposes perfectly by extending that vision to any potential viewer:

(8.46) *Vailland se plaisait à choquer et son physique même étonnait ...: de face, on ne*
voyait qu'une pomme d'Adam.

(Beauvoir, S. de. *Mémoires d'une jeune fille rangée*: 260)

'Vailland enjoyed shocking people and even his physical appearance was surprising …: from the front, all you could see [one only saw] was his Adam's apple'.

The second group of predicates illustrated in (8.47) and (8.48) are more directly concerned with the cognitive reaction to an observed situation. The speaker evaluates that situation and analyzes it, perhaps by comparing it to other similar episodes in her experience or according to her own expectations. In (8.47) the narrator observes the behavior of prostitutes in a foreign country, and locates the reasons for their passivity in the overall relationship between men and women in Spanish society. However, this analysis is not offered as his own, but as the inescapable conclusion that anyone who knows Spanish society and the expected behavior of prostitutes would reach.

(8.47)   *Elles sont pleines de discrétion, ces filles andalouses. Depuis une heure que nous sommes là, pas une seule ne m'a entrepris, ne m'a proposé de monter avec elle. **On** sent bien que cette initiative leur est refusée ou qu'elles n'y pensent même pas, habituées depuis l'enfance à subir l'autorité des mâles.*

(T'Serstevens, A. *L'itinéraire espagnol*: 152)

'These Andalusian girls are very discreet. We have been here for one hour, and not one of them has approached me and asked me to go up with her. One clearly sees that they are not permitted such initiative or that they don't even think about it, accustomed as they have been since childhood to accept male authority'.

In (8.48) the narrator's attempts to cheer up a sick person include comparing his appearance to that of even-sicker patients. The act of perception of those patients that the predicates *se demande* and *se dit* describe thus involve cognitively complex processes of evaluation, comparison, and assessment to come up with a general impression.

(8.48)   *Son visage était désarmé soudain par une sincérité presque insupportable; la tristesse confiante de sa voix m'alla au cœur; je dis avec élan: "il y a plus malade que vous. – Comment ça? – Il y a des gens, **on** se demande en les voyant comment ils peuvent se supporter; **on** se dit qu'à moins d'être gâteux ils devraient se faire horreur: ce n'est pas l'effet que vous produisez."*

(Beauvoir, S. de. *Les mandarins*: 71)

'His face was suddenly rendered defenseless by an almost unbearable sincerity; the trusting sadness of his voice went straight to my heart; "some people are sicker than you are, I said earnestly. – What do you mean? – There are some people, when you see them [one sees them], you wonder [one wonders] how they can stand themselves; you say to yourself [one says to oneself] that unless they are senile, they must terrify themselves: you don't look that way"'.

The reactions presented in (8.47) and (8.48) are considerably more cognitively complex than those presented in (8.44)–(8.46) and therefore much harder to consider predictable and universal, but they are nonetheless presented that way. The narrator's attitude toward very sick people in (8.48) seems a little harsh to be considered commonplace, but it is introduced as the one anyone would be expected to have in the same situation. The use of the indefinite *on* and its virtual referent allows the narrator to portray the most individual, idiosyncratic, and possibly controversial reaction as if it were necessarily and predictably expected of everyone.

Finally, the examples in (8.49) and (8.50) present the processing and analysis of the resemblance that the observed scene exhibits with another kind of entity. In (8.49) a small pivoting fan is reanalyzed as a giant eye scanning the room from left to right.

(8.49)   *elle fixa le petit ventilateur dont l'hélice pivotait sur un axe. Il se tournait posément vers la droite, attendait une seconde, puis avec la même lenteur se tournait vers la gauche, et à force de le considérer, Mrs Dare finissait par lui prêter des sentiments humains;* **on** *eût dit, en effet, un gros œil noir qui cherchait quelqu'un d'un côté et de l'autre, en vain: personne à droite, personne à gauche.*
(Green, J. *Moïra: roman*: 36)
'She stared at the little fan whose blade pivoted on an axis. It turned to the right, waited for a second, then just as slowly turned to the left, and after staring at it for so long, Mrs. Dare ended up attributing human feelings to it; indeed, it looked like [one would have thought it was] a big black eye looking for someone on either side of the room in vain: nobody to the right, nobody to the left'.

In (8.50) the main character interprets the crowd's behavior as a response to his internal state:

(8.50)   *mon arrivée, écrit-il, fit sensation. Je n'ai jamais reçu d'accueil plus caressant.* **On** *eût dit que toute la compagnie sentait combien j'avais besoin d'être rassuré.*
(Guéhenno, J. *Jean-Jacques. T.* 3: 17)
'my arrival, he wrote, created a stir. I have never received such pleasing welcome. It was like [one would have thought that] everyone in the company knew how much I needed to be comforted'.

The processes described in these examples are even more personal and idiosyncratic than the ones presented earlier, and yet they are also presented as if the interpretation they describe were predictable and universal. In this sense, the impersonal value of the indefinite *on* is clear since the construction it participates in constitutes a very close paraphrase to another impersonal construction, namely *il semble* 'it seems'. While the emphasis in both constructions rests on properties intrinsic to the scene, the difference between them essentially pertains to the degree of objectivity of the conceptualizing presence. It is completely subjective in the *il* construction where the situation that the predicate codes is truly presented as a property of the field (see Chapter 3). It is construed more objectively in the indefinite construction where *on* is coded as the subject of the sentence. However, the virtual quality of that conceptualizing presence does not deter from its general value, and the construction meets the criteria, outlined in Chapter 1, to be considered impersonal.

The final generalization pattern observed in the data reflects a rather complex conceptual process of classification and evaluation. Consider the examples in (8.13), repeated once again, as well as (8.51)–(8.53):

(8.13) *Et ça ne te gêne pas de penser que des types ont écrit des trucs tellement supérieurs à ce que tu pondras, toi? Dit Nadine d'un ton vaguement irrité. – Au début, **je** ne le pensais pas, dit Henri en souriant; **on** est arrogant tant qu'**on** n'a rien fait. Et puis une fois qu'**on** est dans le coup, **on** s'intéresse à ce qu'**on** écrit et **on** ne perd plus de temps à se comparer. – Oh! Bien sûr, **on** s'arrange! Dit-elle d'une voix boudeuse en se laissant retomber de tout son long sur le sol.*

(Beauvoir, S. de. *Les mandarins*: 92)

'And it does not bother you to think that some guys have written things so superior to what you'll come up with? Nadine said in a slightly irritated voice. – At the beginning, I didn't think so Henri said with a smile; you are arrogant when you haven't done anything. And then once you get started, you get interested in what you write and you waste no time comparing yourself to other people. Oh! Of course, that's convenient [one makes things easy for oneself]! She said in a pouty voice, letting herself fall to the ground'.

(8.51) *il était plutôt gauche; et **je** n'étais même pas sûre d'avoir plaisir à le revoir; **je** n'avais passé qu'un après-midi avec lui, **je** risquais les pires déceptions. Aucun doute, ce projet était stupide; **j'**avais envie de bouger, de m'agiter pour me masquer ma déconvenue, c'est comme ça qu'**on** fait de vraies sottises.*

(Beauvoir, S. de. *Les mandarins*: 310)

'he was rather awkward; and I am not ever sure I had any pleasure seeing him again; I had only spent one afternoon with him, I could easily be very disappointed. There is no doubt, this project was stupid; I just wanted to do something, to act in order to hide my disillusion, that's how you make [one makes] real mistakes'.

(8.52) *Réveil brusque: combien est-ce que **j'**en fais? Ça ne doit pas être assez. Ne pas rêver. Forcer encore. Si seulement **je** savais combien il faut en faire! **Je** regarde autour de moi! Personne ne lève la tête, jamais. Personne ne sourit. Personne ne dit un mot. Comme **on** est seul! **je** fais 400 pièces à l'heure.*

(Weil, S. *La condition ouvrière*: 249)

'I wake up suddenly: how many am I doing? That cannot be enough. Do not daydream. Keep going. If only I knew how many I must make! I look around me! No one looks up, ever. Nobody smiles. Nobody says a word. How alone one is! I make 400 pieces an hour'.

(8.53)   *Je me recouche, pardonnez-moi. Je crains de m'être exalté; je ne pleure pas, pour-*
         tant. **On** *s'égare parfois,* **on** *doute de l'évidence, même quand* **on** *à découvert les*
         secrets d'une bonne vie. **Ma** *solution, bien sûr, ce n'est pas l'idéal. Mais quand* **on**
         n'aime pas sa vie, quand **on** *sait qu'il faut en changer,* **on** *n'a pas le choix, n'est-ce*
         pas? Que faire pour être un autre? Impossible. Il faudrait n'être plus personne,
         s'oublier pour quelqu'un, une fois au moins.   (Camus, A. *La chute*: 1548)
         'I go back to bed, forgive me. I am afraid I am overexcited; I don't cry, though.
         You [one] sometimes lose your [one's] way; you deny [one denies] evidence,
         even when you [one] have discovered the secret of a good life. Of course, my
         solution isn't ideal. But when you don't like your life [when one doesn't like
         one's life], when you know you need to change it [when one knows one needs
         to change it], you don't have a choice, do you [one doesn't have a choice, does
         one]? What can you [one] do to be someone else? Nothing. It would be nice
         to no longer be anybody, to forget oneself for someone, at least once'.

The examples in (8.13) and (8.51)–(8.53) share a universal value with all the other
impersonal configurations described in this chapter, but they reach this universality by reanalyzing a situation experienced by one specific individual into an
instance of a higher-level category that can be recognized by anyone. This complex
cognitive process is reflected in the linguistic forms used in all these examples. The
event or situation that provides the initial input experienced by a specific person,
usually the narrator, is coded by the first-person singular pronoun *je*, but that event
is analyzed as an instance of a higher-level category coded by the predicate that
follows the indefinite *on*. This shift between *je* and *on* represents the most important characteristic of this configuration, and is attested in some fashion in all its
instances. For example, in (8.13) the predicate *penser* 'think' describes Henri's position with respect to his own assessment of the way in which his writing compares
to that of other authors. The presence of the first-person *je* restricts the scope of
the predicate to his sole person. However, Henri's assessment is used as an instance
of a higher-level category, namely that of acts of arrogance and self-evaluation.
Interestingly, the subject of the predicate that codes this category (*être arrogant*)
is the indefinite *on*. The shift between *je* and *on* clearly indicates that Henri is not
the only subject of *être arrogant*, but that the predicate describes a general situation applicable to anyone in the appropriate situation. Here again, the pronoun's
referent is virtual but it is not specifically conjured up to illustrate the higher-level
category, rather, the referent of the initial, more-specific experience is reanalyzed
as an arbitrary instance of the higher-level category it exemplifies. The juxtaposition between *je* and *on* therefore clearly reflects the shift in categories where the
initial individual experience is reinterpreted as a virtual instance of a higher-level
category universally applicable to anyone in the relevant position.

All the examples in (8.13) and (8.51)–(8.53) function in a similar manner. Example (8.51) is very similar to (8.13) in that the narrator's specific behavior is reanalyzed as an instance of the *vraies sottises* 'real mistakes' category. Here the presence of the other indefinite pronoun *ça* contributes to the shift between individual experience and universal assessment and thus deserves some attention. The author is describing a careless romance that she explains by her desire to "do something" to hide her disappointment. The referent of *ça* is difficult to delineate with precision, but can generally be described as the abstract region composed of all the behaviors that can result from a similar ill-advised desire for action (see Chapter 6). Importantly, that region does not merely represent the precise behavior that the sentence describes, but the higher-level category of ill-advised actions. In other words, the narrator's behavior exemplifies dangerous behavior. It is thus interesting to notice that both indefinite pronouns *ça* and *on* reflect very similar shifts from the individual to the more generally predictable. *Ça* subsumes the romance that the narrator describes into an indistinguishable mass of potentially dangerous actions and *on* refers to the universal subject of these actions, a virtual subject established by virtualizing the narrator as the referent of the initial action. The result is a higher-level category derived from the highly specific initial ill-advised romance, where anyone who indulges in careless behavior can be expected to face serious consequences.

In (8.52) the narrator describes her feeling of loneliness among a crowd of fellow workers. Importantly, the *on* in *comme on est seul* 'how alone one is' does not represent that community of workers but the generalization over the narrator's individual sensation. The indefinite pronoun refers to a virtual conceptualizer conjured up by reanalyzing her own feeling as a universal experience of alienation, which anyone would sense if placed in a similar situation. In a similar manner, in (8.53) *on*'s presence marks the generalization of the narrator's experience to the universal situation encountered by anyone who wants to change their life. Here again, the individual experience is analyzed as a valid instance of a higher category, and the indefinite pronoun codes the virtual referent obtained by the reanalysis of the narrator's experience as an instance of that category.

5. Recapitulation and conclusion

This chapter investigated the conditions under which indefinite *on* possesses the degree of generality compatible with impersonals as they have been defined throughout this monograph. Consistent with the analysis developed in the preceding chapters, it showed that impersonal *on* inherits its characteristics from its personal sense. Personal *on* is distinguished by (1) the identifiability of its referent, and (2) that referent's exclusive responsibility for the performance of the process that the predicate codes. The absence of one or both of these characteristics steers the pronoun in two different directions. If the referent is not identified but nonetheless remains responsible for the occurrence of the profiled process, the pronoun takes on a passive meaning. If, on the other hand, both properties of personal *on* are missing, namely if the pronoun's referent is not identifiable and the responsibility for the occurrence of the profiled process cannot be traced to anyone in particular, the pronoun can be considered impersonal. The third-person singular agreement that *on* determines on the following predicate shows that when its referent is composed of multiple individuals it is treated as a uniform (particulate) mass. In order for the indefinite pronoun to be considered impersonal that mass has to be minimally delimited, namely maximally inclusive of all possible conceptualizers. This chapter showed that this minimal delimitation is achieved in two different contexts. In the first, the experience of a given community is presented as homogenous because every member is equally responsible for the occurrence of the profiled process, given the structure of the universe they share. In the second context the experience of a specific conceptualizer is virtualized so that the insight, reaction, or conclusion that it proposes can be applied to everyone. These two stable environments provide the anchor point for a class of French indefinite impersonals.

CHAPTER 9

Concluding remarks

1. Recapitulation

The main goal of this monograph was to introduce French impersonals as a functional class. This view contrasts sharply with the purely syntactic definition these constructions usually receive in the literature. Syntactically, French possesses a pleonastic impersonal *il*, which gets inserted to fulfill the structural requirement that all French clauses have a subject. This structural definition of impersonals clearly delineates the category members. In particular, it isolates *il* constructions from other structures with which they share important semantic characteristics. Perhaps most strikingly, while *il* and *ça* are mutually interchangeable in (9.1) and (9.2) (repeated from Chapter 1), they are analyzed very differently. Whereas *il* is semantically empty, *ça* is treated as a full-fledged cataphoric pronoun that refers forward to the upcoming clause. This difference in the pronouns yields two distinct structures for the constructions in which they participate. The clause that contains *il* in (9.1) is impersonal and derived by syntactic movement, but the one that contains *ça* in (9.2) is analyzed as a dislocation construction.

(9.1) *Pour la première fois je sentais qu'**il était possible** que ma mère vécût sans moi*
                               (Proust, M. *A l'ombre des jeunes filles en fleurs*: 648)
       'For the first time I felt it was possible for my mother to live [that my mother live] without me'

(9.2) *Dubreuilh t'attend avec impatience. Ne te laisse pas embarquer dans son machin … – j'y suis déjà plus ou moins embarqué, dit Henri. – eh bien! Dépêche-toi de t'en sortir. Henri sourit: non. **Ça n'est plus possible** aujourd'hui de rester apolitique.*   (Beauvoir, S. de. *Les mandarins:* 101)
       'Dubreuilh is waiting for you impatiently. Don't let him drag you into his plan … – I am already more or less part of it, Henry said. – well get out of it as soon as you can. Henry smiled: no. It [this] is no longer possible to remain outside of politics these days'.

Chapters 3 and 6 argued that this structural distinction between the two constructions is untenable because (1) *il* is not semantically vacuous, and (2) *ça* does not behave as a cataphoric pronoun in contexts such as (9.2). Chapter 3 showed that *il* impersonals are presentational constructions that identify or locate the entity coded in the postverbal expression with respect to a specific domain, and the pronoun profiles the field or the mental range which allows the conceptualizer to assess that identification or location. For instance, in (9.1) the pronoun profiles the knowledge base that allows the narrator to understand that his mother can live without him. Chapter 6 showed that *ça* never behaves as a true cataphoric because it never unambiguously refers forward to the upcoming entity. One of the semantic specificities of *ça* is precisely that it refers in equal parts to the preceding discourse context from which the event or proposition described in the postverbal entity is extracted because a more specific or synthetic reformulation of some aspect of that context is required to supplement the more holistic construal that the preceding discourse provides. Consequently in situations such as (9.2) *ça* constructions are true abstract setting constructions where *ça* profiles the setting, namely the abstract region composed of the interconnected entities from the current discourse context. For instance, in (9.2) *ça* profiles the elements of the discourse concerning the ability to remain politically independent (*Ne te laisse pas embarquer dans son machin ... – j'y suis déjà plus ou moins embarqué, dit Henri. – eh bien! Dépêche- toi de t'en sortir.* 'Don't let him drag you into his plan ... – I am already more or less part of it, Henry said – well get out of it as soon as you can') from which the more synthetic postverbal expression *de rester apolitique* 'to remain outside of politics' is extracted.

Given that *il* impersonals are meaningful structures and that *ça* is not strictly cataphoric in similar contexts, the semantic distinction posited between the two pronouns vanishes and the structural distinction between the two constructions in which they participate is also unwarranted. In the contexts illustrated in (9.1) and (9.2) French therefore possesses two kinds of impersonals respectively introduced by *il* and *ça*, and the syntactic competition between these two pronouns reflects their semantic proximity. The analysis of *ça* constructions as demonstrative impersonals is important because it invalidates the claim that French impersonals are structurally specific and can be restricted to *il* constructions. The only possible alternative consists of treating impersonals as a functional category and therefore opening it to a wider range of constructions.

Any functional domain is composed of a set of constructions that may or may not share morphosyntactic characteristics, bound together by a number of shared semantic functions. In French any structure is considered impersonal provided that (1) it defocuses or backgrounds the agent of the predicate, and (2) its predicate describes a situation at a degree of stability and prediction that makes it available to a generalized conceptualizer or, in other words, virtually anyone in the appropriate situation. This monograph argued that while the list is certainly not exhaustive, in addition to the *il* and demonstrative (*ça*) impersonals illustrated in (9.1) and (9.2) the middle (*se*) constructions illustrated in (9.3) and the indefinite *on* 'one' structures illustrated in (9.4) also deserve the impersonal label because they satisfy the two aforementioned criteria.

(9.3)   *Il note que le pain sans levain est cuit sur des plaques de tôle et ressemble à de la galette ou aux crêpes de carnaval, que **le saucisson d'Arles se fait avec de la viande de mulet**.*   (Durry, MJ. *Gérard de Nerval et le mythe*: 82)
'He notes that yeast-free bread is cooked on flat metal sheets and resembles biscuits or the pancakes of carnival time; that the sausage from Arles is made [makes itself] with mule meat'.

(9.4)   ***On** ne trouve pas toujours facilement, en Espagne, un endroit pour camper, à cause de l'absence de bois, et de la culture intensive.*
(T'Serstevens, A. *L'itinéraire espagnol*: 16)
'One cannot always easily find a place to camp in Spain, because of the lack of forests, and extensive agriculture'.

The constructions in (9.3) and (9.4) are general enough to be impersonal, but many other middle or indefinite structures are not. An important aspect of the analysis presented in this monograph is that the identification of impersonal constructions is rendered possible by their clustering into specific constructions that can be reliably distinguished from the other members of their morphosyntactic class by the presence of specific properties. Chapter 6 showed that while *ça* impersonals may occur in other environments they can only be reliably identified within the confines of the copular complement construction, namely the [*c'* + *être* + ADJECTIVE + COMPLEMENT CLAUSE] observed in (9.2). In a similar manner, middle impersonals can also only be readily identified within two specific constructions, even though their characteristic features are semantic/pragmatic rather than morphosyntactic. Chapter 7 showed that in the first middle impersonal construction the profiled process is part of the definition of the affected entity coded as subject. For instance, in (9.3) mule meat constitutes a necessary part of the *saucisson d'Arles* recipe and will therefore be present regardless of the chef executing it. The presence of this semantic/pragmatic property increases the generality of the profiled process, and thus its impersonality, because it minimizes the potential impact of individual agents and thus makes it available to everyone. Chapter 8 provided a similar type of analysis of the indefinite (*on*) constructions. It showed that impersonal *on* emerges when the two characteristics of the pronoun's personal sense are missing, namely its referent is not only unidentified but also maximally inclusive of all relevant conceptualizers. As was the case with *ça* and the middles, indefinite impersonals obtain the degree of generality required of its impersonal status in two contexts, namely when the pronoun's delimitation is minimal and therefore inclusive of any potential conceptualizer, and when one person's experience is virtualized and thus applicable to everyone. These constructional islands identified for demonstratives, middles, and indefinite impersonals are crucial for the analysis presented in this monograph. Because of the fluid nature of the two proposed impersonal criteria, they provide areas of stability within which impersonals can reliably be identi-fied, and therefore constitute one of the main organizing principles of the French impersonal category.

In order to recapitulate the analyses developed in the earlier chapters, Figure 9.1 illustrates the way in which the French functional impersonal category borrows from different morphosyntactic categories to express stable and predictable events whose occurrence cannot be imputed to a specific source.

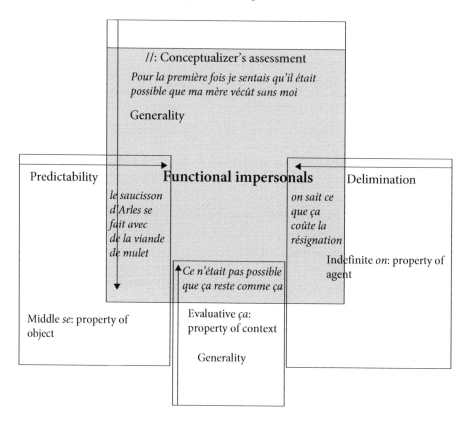

Figure 9.1 The French functional impersonal category

In Figure 9.1 the individual boxes represent the morphosyntactic categories of *il*, *on*, *ça*, and *se* constructions. The shaded box represents the functional impersonal category, i.e. the class of maximally general events whose occurrence cannot be imputed to a specific source. Each morphosyntactic category provides a specific entry point – property of the object (*se*), the agent (*on*), the context (*ça*), concep-tualizer's assessment (*il*) – from which that general event can be accessed. The dis-crepancy between the different boxes indicates that no morphosyntactic category is entirely impersonal functionally. Even though *il* constructions are predominantly impersonal, Chapter 4 has shown that in certain cases the situation described in the predicate fails to reach the level of generality commensurate with impersonal status. An example considered in detail in one of the previous chapters is included for each type of impersonal.

The arrow within each morphosyntactic category represents the specific dimension along which the impersonal subsection emerges. For instance, *on* indefinites acquire their impersonal status when their delimitation is minimal and thus potentially includes every conceptualizer. Similarly, middle *se* constructions become impersonal when the specific nature of the object renders the event that the predicate describes entirely predictable. Importantly, even though it is not represented in Figure 9.1 the impersonal subsections of the *on, ça*, and *se* impersonals occur in the context of well-delineated constructional islands. These islands provide the functional impersonal category with the stability that makes it useful to language users and analysts alike.

2.   Do we need a French impersonal class?

We are now in a position to revisit the issue of whether the notion of impersonal constitutes a useful notion to describe the grammar of individual languages. Recall from Chapter 1 Helasvuo and Vilkuna's suggestion that "impersonality may be a useful tool for cross-linguistic comparison because it directs the analyst's attention to a broad field of phenomena that share the same properties; but it does not seem to us to be a necessary notion in the description of individual languages" (Helasvuo and Vilkuna 2008: 242). This manuscript has shown that impersonals describe an important aspect of French grammar because it allows us to group together a coherent kind of event. In a nutshell, impersonal events stand at the opposite end from transitive events on a continuum of all their respective characteristics. Whereas a prototypical transitive situation represents an energetic punctual interaction that occurs at a given time and place between two well-differentiated participants (Hopper and Thompson 1980), impersonal situations describe stable and predictable states, in the loosest possible sense, that are available to everyone in appropriate circumstances because they represent various aspects of the structure of our environment. Importantly, the origin of these stable configurations is not imputable to any identifiable source, as they merely represent different facets of the world as we know it. Important as it is, the recognition of a class of impersonal events does not prove the relevance of the impersonal category for the French language if that category is not linguistically stable enough for speakers to use and analysts to describe. To that effect, the identification of specific impersonal constructions, which share the structure of their respective morphosyntactic categories but are nonetheless distinguished by morphological, semantic, or pragmatic features, is of critical importance because it provides the necessary stability without which the impersonal class would have no descriptive power.

The analysis developed in the previous chapters emphasized the way in which demonstrative, middle, and indefinite impersonals not only emerge from the ranks of their own morphosyntactic categories but also retain the characteristics they exhibit in their other uses. In Chapter 6 demonstratives were shown to acquire impersonal status in great part due to the flexible nature of *ça*'s referent, the dual nature of its anaphoric/cataphoric reference, and the inherent subjective construal that it imposes on the scene it profiles. In Chapter 7 we saw that human activity middle predicates alone are candidates for impersonal status because their lexical semantic structure includes an internal conceptualizer, and how the affected entity's responsibility for the profiled process – a pragmatic feature present in many middle constructions – plays a major part in the determination of a class of middle impersonals. Indefinite *on* in Chapter 8 was also shown to represent the ultimate stage on a continuum of delimitation of the pronoun's referent where it is maximally inclusive of every potential conceptualizer.

The systematic emergence of a specific type of construction in different morphosyntactic environments represents a highly relevant feature of the French language because it shows how speakers not only designed elaborate ways of capitalizing on the resources that each category provides to discuss highly general and predictable events or situations, but also made them stable enough to be reliably counted on. The analyst therefore has no choice. Each of these constructions needs to be described individually, whether or not the whole group they constitute is subsumed under the same label. In other words, the general demonstratives in Chapter 6, the middles in Chapter 7, and their indefinite counterparts in Chapter 8 need to be independently accounted for whether or not they are recognized as part of the same impersonal category. The recognition that this group of constructions belongs to the impersonal category reflects its functional equivalence with the unequivocally recognized *il* impersonals, and captures French speakers' consistent desire to symbolically represent a class of similar events via different access points.

The functional equivalence of the constructions described in the preceding chapters has been mentioned at different points of the analysis, but it is appropriate in this recapitulating chapter to provide a final example to illustrate how the different impersonals presented in this monograph afford functionally comparable construals of the same conceptual content by using different strategies. The situation illustrated in (9.5) describes an acoustic configuration that anyone can experience if they stand at the right location. In other words, the indefinite *on* describes a virtual hearer and the middle predicate *se dire* includes, as part of its lexical-semantic structure, the abstract speaker whose voice will inevitably be heard:

(9.5) *Tu sais bien que je serai contente de t'avoir ici. Je craignais seulement que pour*
vous ça ne manque d'intimité. Je te préviens entre autre que de ma chambre **on**
entend <u>*tout ce qui se dit*</u> *au jardin.*   (Beauvoir, S. de. *Les mandarins*: 332)
'You know I will be happy to have you here. I was simply afraid that the two
of you wouldn't have enough privacy. Let me warn you for instance that from
my bedroom you [one] can hear everything that people say [says itself] in the
garden'.

The indefinite and middle impersonals in (9.5) achieve the desired degree of generality in different ways. Consistent with the analysis in Chapter 8, the indefinite
on construction profiles the agent as subject, but that agent is at the same time defocused and general because the delimitation of the pronoun's referent is minimal
and thus excludes no one. The middle predicate *se dire* accesses the same situation
differently, namely from the access point of the process itself. The affected entity (a
virtual conversation) is selected as subject, and the conceptualizers required to carry
out the profiled process are part of the scope of predication of the predicate. In other
words, indefinite impersonals reach the required level of generality via the participant in the profiled process, while middles achieve the same result by presenting a
characteristic of the affected entity and using the described object as an entry point.
Note, however, that these two strategies are not determined by objective properties
of the situation because they can be interchanged with little change in meaning. In
the constructed variant of (9.5) in (9.6) the situation is identical, but the respective
generality of the hearing and saying is achieved by the alternative strategy since
dire occurs with an indefinite subject and *entendre* is part of a middle construction:

(9.6) #*Tu sais bien que je serai contente de t'avoir ici. Je craignais seulement que pour*
vous ça ne manque d'intimité. Je te préviens entre autre que **tout ce qu'on dit** *au*
jardin **s'entend** *de ma chambre.*
'You know I will be happy to have you here. I was simply afraid that the two of
you wouldn't have enough privacy. Let me warn you for instance that everything that people say [one says] in the garden can be heard [hears itself] from
my bedroom'.

Alternatively, the same situation can also be described with an *il* impersonal, as in
another constructed variant of (9.5) presented in (9.7):

(9.7) #**Il est possible** *d'entendre* **tout ce qui se dit**/**tout ce qu'on dit** *dans le jardin.*
'It is possible to hear everything that people say [that says itself/that one says]
in the garden'.

However, the notion of functional equivalence does not mean that all constructions are interchangeable in all contexts. In fact, the *il* impersonal in (9.7) seems
less natural than the indefinite and middle constructions respectively illustrated in

(9.5) and (9.6). The preference of certain contexts for specific constructions is to be expected, given the intrinsic properties of the chosen predicates as well as more general characteristics of the described situation. The important point is that the four constructions presented in this monograph provide four alternative strategies to describe maximally generalized and predictable events whose occurrence describes stable characteristics of our environment. As abstract locational constructions, both *il* and *ça* impersonals treat such events as a defining characteristic of the context itself and thus give focal prominence to the abstract location (field or setting) within which their existence can be ascertained. Middle (*se*) impersonals access these events as inescapably determined by the structure of the affected entity. Consequently, that entity is coded as the main figure in the profiled relation. Finally, indefinite *on* presents these predictable events as the unambiguous response that anyone would provide in a given context. The minimally delimited subject reflects the emphasis placed on the only expected human response to the stimulus given in the context. In this view, the circumstances of the world or the context, the intrinsic nature of objects and situations, and the predictable behavior of humans in specific conditions provide different reference points via which general properties of our environment can be reliably accessed.

This focus on events that are exhibited by the *ça*, middle, and indefinite impersonals also explains the imbalance between these constructions and *il* impersonals, because *il* consistently codes the field in both simple (Chapter 4) and complex (Chapter 5) cases, and *il* constructions are consequently far more frequent. Additionally, whereas *il* constructions are predominantly functionally impersonal, all other structures emerge from the ranks of their respective morphosyntactic categories to fulfill their impersonal function. However, I do not believe that this imbalance constitutes a problem for the analysis presented in this monograph. To the contrary, as mentioned earlier, the emergence of several functionally equivalent yet morphosyntactically unrelated constructions attests to the importance of the events they systematically code to French speakers, and thus argues in favor of positing a French impersonal class. Importantly, however, the analysis provided in this monograph is so deeply anchored in the ecology of French that it cannot easily be extended cross-linguistically. The impersonal category may be organized quite differently in some languages or be completely irrelevant to the grammar of others.

3.   Advantages of the analysis

In addition to delineating a class of French impersonals, the analysis presented in this monograph offers two main advantages. The first is that it allows us to clearly examine the close relationships that connect these constructions to other related morphosyntactic or semantic categories, and more precisely to the passives and middles. The relation between middles and impersonals has been considered at some length in Chapter 7. Middle constructions generally profile the process that an affected entity (the term is used in the most general sense) undergoes, without specific mention of the agent responsible for its occurrence. The category is neutral as to the level of specificity of the process that the predicate profiles. Chapter 7 showed that middle impersonals represent a small group of middles where the profiled process is completely stable and thus predictable. This process is made available to any conceptualizer due to the affected entity's responsibility for its occurrence. Middle impersonals are therefore perfectly integrated among other middles because they are structurally identical to them, and also because they share most of their semantic features. Their sole distinctive characteristic comes from the pragmatic connections that exist between the profiled process and the entity that its occurrence affects, namely definitionality and necessity.

The relation between impersonals and passives has been mentioned at several points in this monograph but not explored in any significant depth. Perhaps the most unexpected aspect of the analysis proposed in the previous chapters concerns the interpretation of the *constructions moyennes* as impersonals rather than passives, as the French tradition has generally done. As discussed in Chapter 7, however, the precise label assigned to this very specific group of constructions is of little matter when their structural similarity with passives – namely the presence of their logical object in subject position – is no longer part of the analysis. From a purely semantic standpoint, these *constructions moyennes* are much closer to impersonals than to passives. In fact, both *se* and *on* impersonals provide good examples of the way in which the two categories intersect. Both impersonals and passives possess a category core identified by the presence of stable morphosyntactic traits. Chapter 3 argued that *il*'s systematic and distinguishing presence makes the construction in which it participates the core of the impersonal category, with the other constructions considered in the subsequent chapters forming a periphery. Passives are organized in essentially the same way. The construction marked by exclusively passive morphosyntax, namely the presence of the [AUXILIARY + PP] marking on the predicate and the selection of the patient as the main figure in the profiled relation (Langacker 1982), constitutes the core but members of other morphosyntactic classes also participate in the extended category when they share its basic semantic function. Chapters 7 and 8 showed how both middle (*se*) and indefinite (*on*) constructions align with passives or impersonals depending on the type of configuration they describe.

The analyses presented in Chapters 7 and 8 showed that the difference between passive and impersonal middles and indefinites essentially pertains to the recoverability of the agent of the profiled process. For instance, in Chapter 7 we saw that the presence of the perfect marker on the predicate in (9.8) and (9.9) renders the middle construction incompatible with the impersonal criteria, but aligns it perfectly with a passive interpretation where the agent of the profiled process is either specified later on in the discourse as in (9.8), or easily recoverable as in (9.9) where it can only be the people who built the house:

(9.8)   *À ce moment, on frappa doucement, et comme tiré d'un rêve, Joseph cria: –*
        Entrez! **La porte s'ouvrit** *alors pour livrer passage à une vieille négresse vêtue*
        de noir...   (Green, J. *Moïra: roman*: 177)
        'At this moment, someone knocked softly, and as if awakening from a dream,
        Joseph shouted: – Come in! The door then opened [itself] to let in an old black
        woman dressed in black...'

(9.9)   #*Cette maison* **s'est construite** *en trois mois!*
        'This house was built [built itself] in three months!'

In a parallel manner, Chapter 8 showed that the indefinite (*on*) constructions illustrated in (9.10)–(9.12) also serve a passive function because even though the agent of the profiled process is not specifically mentioned, it bears the entire responsibility for the occurrence of that process and could possibly be recovered. More specifically, the agent of the finding process in (9.10) can only be the person who searched the dead man's pockets. Similarly in (9.11) and (9.12), the respective agents of the giving and knocking processes can only be the courier and the visitor respectively:

(9.10) *Me parle d'un jeune homme qui n'a pas pu continuer la lutte et qui s'est tué en*
        absorbant une grosse quantité de gardénal, trop grosse, semble-t-il, car la mort
        a été longue à venir. **On a trouvé** *dans sa poche des lettres et un chapelet...*
                                    (Green, J. *Journal. T. 5. 1946–1950*: 221)
        '[He] talks to me about a young man who couldn't continue the fight and killed
        himself by taking a large quantity of gardenal, too large a dose it seems, because
        it took a long time for him to die. Some letters and a rosary were found [one
        found some letters and a rosary] in his pocket...'

(9.11) *Aujourd'hui,* **on me remet** *cette lettre. Avez-vous lu comment il me traite à la*
        fin?   (Camus, A. *Les possédés; pièce en trois actes*: 996)
        'Today this letter is delivered to me [one gives me this letter]. Did you see how
        he talks to me at the end?'

(9.12) **On frappe**, *et* **on entrouvre** *la porte. L'abbé De Pradts, qui voit le visiteur (invisible*
        au public,) dit: Monsieur Prial, je vais vous voir un instant.
                           (Montherlant, H. de. *La ville dont le prince est un enfant*: 918)
        'There is a knock [one knocks] and someone pushes the door ajar [one pushes
        the door ajar]. Abbott De Pardts, who sees the visitor (whom the public can't
        see) says: Mister Prial, I will see you for a minute'.

Alternatively, when middle and indefinite constructions describe a more general situation available to everyone they serve the semantic function of impersonals. Since this point constitutes a large part of the analysis presented in Chapters 6 through 8, one example suffices to illustrate it in this conclusion. The passive middle (9.9) describes a punctual situation that strictly pertains to a single building act performed by specific easily recoverable agents, but the closely related construction in (9.13) is best analyzed as impersonal because the builders are virtual, merely conjured up for their role in a statement about construction in general. The described situation is therefore not restricted to a specific time, place, and construction crew, but applicable to any instance of house building anywhere:

(9.13)   #*Une maison **se construit** en trois mois*
         'It takes three months to build a house [a house builds itself in three months]'

Middle and indefinite constructions therefore possess the flexibility to receive either a passive or impersonal interpretation, and the account presented in this monograph captures this flexibility by allowing general semantic and pragmatic considerations to steer them toward passives or impersonals depending on the specific configuration they code. While an analysis of the reasons why middles and indefinites receive passive interpretation is well beyond the scope of this conclusion, it is interesting to note that with intransitive predicates, such as *frapper* in (9.12), indefinites represent the only way of defocusing the agent. This is also the case when the described situation is too general for specific participants to be distinguished, as in (9.14) where the *on* construction can be viewed as the French equivalent to the existential constructions used in languages such as German or English (*there was killing*). These examples clearly illustrate the functional flexibility of this middle/passive/impersonal area where speakers use different constructions to express similar conceptual content, depending on the resources made available to them by their language of choice:

(9.14)   *Le nouveau monde semblait d'abord plus inquiétant que l'ancien:* **on** *y pillait,* **on** *y tuait; le sang coulait à flots.*   (Sartre, JP. *Les mots*: 58)
         'At first the new world seemed more worrisome than the old one. There was pillaging [one pillaged], there was killing [one killed], blood was flowing in the streets.'

Second, with its emphasis on the meaning of the constructions themselves, the account developed in this monograph allowed us to assess their semantic compatibility with the various predicates that participate in the construction, and thus describe French impersonal usage with some degree of precision. Chapter 3 showed that *il* impersonals are presentational constructions in the sense that their semantic function is to identify or locate the entity coded in the postverbal expression with respect to a specific domain, and that function explains its semantic range established by the predicates that participate in it. The most frequently attested predicates saliently invoke the setting in their scope of predication because knowledge about the setting within which it can be located figures prominently among the mental resources drawn on to locate the conceptualized target, and thus provides an area of overlap with the semantic content that the pronoun *il* profiles. Furthermore, the examination of individual predicates in Chapter 4 revealed the surprisingly systematic fine-grained associations they develop with impersonals. *Exister* 'exist', *rester* 'remain, and *manquer* 'lack' almost obligatorily occur with the impersonal construction in one of their senses, even though other constructions are potentially available. The usage of the less-frequent *arriver* 'arrive', *venir* 'come', and *passer* 'pass' is heavily constrained and essentially formulaic. The usage of *il* (simple) impersonals clearly illustrates one of the most basic principles of the usage-based model, namely the importance of lower-level schemas to the mental representation of language.

The meaning of the constructions also provided useful insight into the distribution of the different types of impersonals investigated in this monograph. For instance, Chapter 6 showed that while *il* and *ça* are in competition in a large number of cases, their respective semantic import accounts for their selection in particular situations once we consider their reinterpretation in the domain of discourse coherence. With *être vrai* 'be true', for instance, the use of *il*, which locates the proposition coded in the postverbal expression in reality, serves to temper the overall scope of an argument by pointing to the existence of a fact that diminishes its strength. In (9.15), for instance, the author's argument about the importance of the rebellion at his geographical location is weakened by his further consideration of his companions' particular temperament. Conversely, as a direct reflex of *ça*'s profiling the abstract setting within which the proposition coded in the postverbal expression is extracted, the selection of *c'* with *être vrai* often indicates that the proposition that follows the predicate directly corresponds to some element of the immediate context. In (9.16) the proposition *Farnese était seul* 'Farnese was alone' is repeated from the earlier context:

(9.15) *À voir cela, il me semble que la révolte est plus loin de nous que je ne croyais d'*
        abord. **Il est vrai** *que je suis avec des montagnards, écartés des centres industriels*
        et très fatalistes.   (Alain-Fournier, H. *Correspondance avec J. Rivière*: 120)
        'When I see this, it seems to me that the rebellion is further from us than I
        first thought. It is true that I am with mountain men, remote from industrial
        areas, and very fatalistic'.

(9.16) *Je sais: il a tué un pauvre vieil homme sans défense: Farnese était seul, – pas un laquais, – et le coup de revolver a été tiré par derrière. Je sais tout ça … mais écoutez un peu: ce n'est pas vrai que Farnese était seul.*

(Farrère, C. L'homme qui assassina: 280)

'I know: he killed a poor defenseless man: Farnese was alone – not a servant – and the shot was fired from behind. I know all that … but listen for a minute: it [this] is not true that Farnese was alone'.

Finally, the account of French impersonals presented in this monograph is necessarily preliminary and incomplete. Several of the issues it raises are worthy of much more attention than they can be given at the moment. The first is the true range of French impersonals. The four constructions presented in the previous chapters constitute at the same time a useful starting point and a possible investigative methodology, but they are certainly not exhaustive of all French constructions that could receive the impersonal label. Second, while these four constructions have been shown to compete in specific contexts, a more exhaustive examination of their distribution is required before French impersonal usage can be really understood. Lastly, the relation between impersonals and generics has been mentioned at several points of the analysis, but it needs to be explored further since both constructions describe highly general events and situations. The remainder of this conclusion briefly evokes the main issues that a more thorough analysis would necessarily develop.

Generics and impersonals describe highly general events and situations, but the two categories exhibit a relatively limited amount of overlap. *Il* and *ça* constructions can produce general statements (*Il faut toujours faire attention* 'one should always be careful'), but the two categories are not inherently generic because they also frequently describe highly specific situations (*il y a trois livres sur la table* 'there are three books on the table'). These constructions are impersonal because the entity coded in the postverbal expression is generally available, but that entity may be very specific. There is no a priori reason to believe that the conditions under which *il* and *ça* impersonals are generic are fundamentally different from those that produce other kinds of generics, such as the intransitive *un chien, ça aboie* 'a dog will bark', even though they will not be considered further here. Similarly, the indefinite impersonal in (9.17) is indeed generic but its related counterpart in (9.18) is not. Additionally, the impersonal cases that achieve maximal levels of generality by the virtualization of individual experience (see Chapter 8, Section 4.2) illustrated in (9.19) are generally not generic:

(9.17) *En Italie on sait préparer les pâtes*   (from Creissels 2008b: 15)
        'In Italy they know [one knows] how to prepare pasta'

(9.18)   *J'ai des raisons toutes personnelles d'aller à Cadix. C'est là que mon ami le père*
         Labat débarqua en revenant des Antilles et vécut plusieurs mois en 1705. C'est là
         *aussi qu'**on** mange les meilleures gambas, ces grandes crevettes roses qu'on vend*
         jusqu'à Madrid mais qui ne sont vraiment délicieuses que sur le port de Cadix.
                                        (T'Serstevens, A. *L'itinéraire espagnol*: 143)
         'I have very personal reasons to go to Cadiz. This is where my friend, father
         Labat, arrived and lived for several months when he came back from the
         Caribbean in 1705. It is also where you can eat [one eats] the best gambas,
         these big pink shrimps that you can find as far as Madrid but which are only
         truly delicious in the Cadiz harbor'.

(9.19)   *La lettre de Voltaire était légère, aimable et malicieuse à son habitude: "j'ai reçu,*
         monsieur, votre nouveau livre contre le genre humain, je vous en remercie … on
         n'a jamais tant employé d'esprit à vouloir nous rendre bêtes. Il prend envie de
         *marcher à quatre pattes quand **on** lit votre ouvrage…*
                                        (Guéhenno, J. *Jean-Jacques. T. 2*: 112)
         'Voltaire's letter was customarily light, friendly and witty: "Sir, I have received
         your new book against humanity, I appreciate it … no greater wit has ever been
         used making us look like animals. One feels like walking on all fours when
         one reads your work…'

The overlap between the impersonal and generic categories therefore predominantly concerns middle constructions. The analysis developed in Chapter 7
follows a number of researchers (Condoravdi 1989; Lyons 1995; Ackema and
Schoorlemmer 1994; Lekakou 2004) in treating impersonal middles as generic because they describe stable social configurations that apply to everyone. Importantly,
merely recognizing these constructions as generic does not suffice to distinguish
them from other middles because other members of the category, which we did
not treat as impersonals, can also have a generic reading. Recall that in Chapter 7
spontaneous predicates were distinguished from their human activity counterparts
because they do not include an internal conceptualizer in their lexical semantic
structure. These predicates were not considered impersonal in any situation even
though, as the example in (9.20) illustrates, they also occur in statements that
express highly general events:

(9.20)   #*Les machines **se dérèglent** toujours/ça **se dérègle** toujours*
         'Machines always lose their settings [get themselves out of tune]'

The construction in (9.20), which describes a general property of machines, was
not considered impersonal in Chapter 7 because the process by which the generalization occurs is common to a large number of distinct constructions that are
not usually described as impersonal but rather as generic (*un chien ça aboie* 'a dog
will bark', *un enfant, ça dort toute la nuit* 'a child will sleep all night').

The problem therefore consists in distinguishing between impersonals and generics in a principled manner in the contexts where they overlap. This complex issue cannot be resolved here, but one might tentatively suggest as a starting point that impersonals are distinguished from generics by the necessary presence of an active conceptualizer in the scope of predication of the profiled predicate. In this view, generic statements such as *un chien, ça aboie* 'a dog will bark', or *une machine, ça se dérègle toujours* 'a machine always loses its settings' are not impersonals because the predicates *aboyer* and *se dérégler* contain no conceptualizing presence, the speaker being the only conceptualizer in the sentence. Conversely, the four constructions described in the preceding chapters all contain an active conceptualizer in the scope of predication of their predicate. In the *il* (and to a lesser extent *ça*) constructions, that conceptualizer was shown to be evoked by the field, since the latter represents the mental reach within which the target can be identified. In the indefinite construction it is explicitly mentioned in the inherent human presence that the pronoun *on* profiles, and in the middle impersonal construction it is located in the internal semantic structure of the predicate since the category was restricted to verbs of human activity. The middle and indefinite constructions become impersonal when that internal conceptualizing presence reaches the required level of generality. This line of argumentation certainly requires a great deal of work to be convincing, but it seems rather promising because it provides at the same time a possible avenue for capturing the essence of impersonals, namely a defocused agent and a maximally general process, and a principled way of distinguishing them from generics, which also describe maximally general events or situations.

References

Achard, Michel. (1998). *Representation of cognitive structures: Syntax and semantics of French complements.* Cognitive Linguistics Research 11. Berlin: Mouton de Gruyter. DOI: 10.1515/9783110805956

Achard, Michel. (2000). The distribution of French raising constructions. *BLS*, 26, 1–12.

Achard, Michel. (2001). French *ça* and the dynamics of reference. In Ruth Brend, Alan Melby, & Arle Lommel (Eds.), *LACUS Forum 27: Speaking and understanding* (pp. 49–62). Fullerton, CA: LACUS.

Achard, Michel. (2002). The meaning and distribution of French mood inflections. In Frank Brisard (Ed.), *Grounding: The epistemic footing of deixis and reference* (pp. 197–249). Berlin: Mouton de Gruyter.

Achard, Michel. (2007). Usage-based semantics: Body parts with three French breaking verbs. In Marja Nenonen & Sinikka Niemi (Eds.), *Collocations and Idioms* 1 (pp. 1–13). Joensuu: Joensuu University Press.

Achard, Michel. (2009). The distribution of French intransitive predicates. *Linguistics*, 47(3), 513–558. DOI: 10.1515/LING.2009.018

Achard, Michel. (2010). Fields and settings: French *il* and *ça* impersonals in copular complement constructions. *Cognitive Linguistics*, 21(3), 441–498. DOI: 10.1515/COGL.2010.016

Achard, Michel. (2012). The impersonals value of demonstrative and middle constructions. In Myriam Bouveret & Dominique Legallois (Eds.), *French constructions* (pp. 177–200). Amsterdam: John Benjamins. DOI: 10.1075/cal.13.11ach

Achard, Michel. (in press). Abstract locational subjects: Field and settings in French and English. In Marja-Liisa Helasvuo & Tuomas Huumo (Eds.), *Subjects in constructions: Canonical and non canonical.* Amsterdam: John Benjamins.

Ackema, Paul, & Schoorlemmer, Maaike. (1994). The middle construction and the syntax-semantics interface. *Lingua*, 93, 59–90. DOI: 10.1016/0024-3841(94)90353-0

Ackema, Paul, & Schoorlemmer, Maaike. (1995). Middles and nonmovement. *Linguistic Inquiry*, 26(2), 173–197.

Afonso, Susana. (2008). Existentials as impersonalizing devices: The case of European Portuguese. *Transactions of the Philological Society*, 106(2), 180–215. DOI: 10.1111/j.1467-968X.2008.00192.x

Bally, Charles. (1932). *Linguistique générale et linguistique française.* Bern: Francke.

Barlow, Michael, & Kemmer, Suzanne. (2000). *Usage-based models of language.* Stanford: CSLI.

Benveniste, Emile. (1966). *Problèmes de linguistique générale.* Paris: Gallimard.

Blevins, James. (2003). Passives and impersonals. *Journal of Linguistics*, 39, 473–520. DOI: 10.1017/S0022226703002081

Blinkenberg, Andreas. (1960). *Le problème de la transitivité en français moderne.* Copenhagen: Munksgaard.

Bolinger, Dwight. (1973). Ambient *it* is meaningful too. *Journal of Linguistics*, 9, 261–270. DOI: 10.1017/S0022226700003789

Bolinger, Dwight. (1977). *Meaning and form*. London & New York: Longman.

Bruneau, Charles, & Heulluy, Marcel. (1937). *Grammaire pratique de la langue française à l'usage des honnêtes gens*. Paris: Delagrave.

Brunot, Ferdinand. (1936). *La pensée et la langue*. Paris: Masson.

Bybee, Joan. (2001). *Phonology and language use*. Cambridge & New York: Cambridge University Press. DOI: 10.1017/CBO9780511612886

Cabredo Hofheer, Patricia. (2003). Arbitrary readings of third person plural pronominals. In Mattias Weisgerber (Ed.), *Proceedings of the Conference Sinn und Beudetung 7*. FB Sprachwissenschaft. Germany: Universität Konstanz.

Cabredo Hofheer, Patricia. (2008). Les pronoms impersonnels humains – syntaxe et interprétation. *Modèles Linguistiques*, XXIX-1(57), 35–56.

Cadiot, Pierre. (1988). De quoi *ça* parle? A propos de la référence de *ça* pronom-sujet. *Le français Moderne*, 65, 174–192.

Carlier, Anne. (1996). 'Les Gosses *ça* se lève tôt le matin': L'interprétation générique du syntagme nominal disloqué au moyen de *ce* ou *ça*. *Journal of French Language Studies*, 6, 133–162. DOI: 10.1017/S0959269500003045

Carnie, Andrew, & Harley, Heidi. (2005). Existential impersonals. *Studia Linguistica*, 59(1), 45–65. DOI: 10.1111/j.1467-9582.2005.00119.x

Chomsky, Noam. (1981). *Lectures on government and binding*. Dordrecht: Foris.

Chomsky, Noam. (1995). *The minimalist program*. Cambridge, MA: MIT Press.

Corblin, Francis. (1995). *Les formes de reprise dans le discours: Anaphores et chaînes de références*. Rennes: Presses Universitaires de Rennes.

Condoravdi, Cleo. (1989). The middle: Where semantics and morphology meet. *MIT Working Papers in Linguistics*, 11, 18–30.

Coveney, Aidan. (2003). "Anything *you* can do, *tu* can do better": *Tu* and *vous* as substitutes for indefinite *on* in French. *Journal of Sociolinguistics*, 7(2), 164–191. DOI: 10.1111/1467-9481.00218

Creissels, Denis. (2008a). Impersonal and related constructions: A typological approach. Manuscript, University of Lyon. Downloaded from: http://www.deniscreissels.fr/public/Creissels-impers.constr.pdf.

Creissels, Denis. (2008b). Impersonal pronouns and coreference: The case of French *on*. Manuscript, University of Lyon. Downloaded from: http://www.deniscreissels.fr/public/Creissels-ON.pdf.

Croft, William. (2001). *Radical construction grammar: Syntactic theory in typological perspective*. Oxford: Oxford University Press. DOI: 10.1093/acprof:oso/9780198299554.001.0001

Cummins, Sarah. (2000). The unaccusative hypothesis and the impersonal construction in French. *Canadian Journal of Linguistics*, 45(3/4), 227–251.

Diessel, Holger. (1999). Demonstratives: Form, function and grammaticalization. *Typological Studies in Language*, 42. Amsterdam: John Benjamins.

Divjak, Dagmar, & Janda, Laura. (2008). Ways of attenuating agency in Russian. *Transactions of the Philological Society*, 106(2), 138–179. DOI: 10.1111/j.1467-968X.2008.00207.x

Dowty, David. (2000). The semantic asymmetry of "argument alternations" (and why it matters). *Groninger Arbeiten zur germanistischen Linguistik*. Available at: http://www.ling.ohio-state.edu/~dowty.

Fauconnier, Gilles. (1985). *Mental spaces: Aspects of meaning construction in natural language*. Cambridge, MA: MIT Press, & London: Bradford.

Fauconnier, Gilles, & Turner, Mark. (2002). *The way we think: Conceptual blending and the mind's hidden complexities*. New York: Basic Books.

Fillmore, Charles. (1982). Frame semantics. In The linguistics society of Korea (Ed.), *Linguistics in the morning calm* (pp. 111–137). Seoul: Hanshin Publishing Company

Fillmore, Charles, Kay, Paul, & O'Connor, Mary Catherine. (1988). Regularity and idiomaticity in grammatical constructions: The case of *let alone. Language*, 64(3), 501–538. DOI: 10.2307/414531

François, Alexis. (1933). *Histoire de la langue française (tome VI, partie IIB: La langue post-classique)*. Paris: Colin.

Gadet, Françoise. (1992). *Le français populaire*. Paris: Presses Universitaires de France.

Galichet, Georges. (1968). *Grammaire structurale du français moderne*. Paris & Limoges: Editions Charles-Lavauzelle.

Gavioli, Laura. (2005). *Exploring corpora for ESP learning*. Amsterdam: John Benjamins. DOI: 10.1075/scl.21

Gledhill, Christopher. (2003). *Fundamentals of French syntax*. München LINCOM EUROPA.

Goldberg, Adele. (1995). *Constructions: A construction grammar approach to argument structure*. Chicago: The University of Chicago Press.

Goldberg, Adele. (2006). *Constructions at work: The nature of generalizations in language*. Oxford: Oxford University Press.

Gougenheim, Georges. (1963). *Système grammatical de la langue française*. Paris: Editions d'Artrey.

Grammaire larousse du XXe siècle. (1936). Paris: Librairie Larousse.

Grevisse, Maurice. (1936). *Le bon usage. Cours de grammaire française et de langage français*. Gembloux: Duculot.

Grevisse, Maurice. (1969). *Le bon usage* (9ème édition). Gembloux: Duculot.

Grevisse, Maurice. (1986). *Le bon usage* (12ème édition). Paris, Louvain-la-Neuve: Duculot.

Gries, Stefan, & Divjak, Dagmar. (2009). Behavioral profiles: A corpus-based approach towards cognitive semantic analysis. In Vyvyan Evans, & Stephanie Pourcel (Eds.), *New directions in cognitive linguistics* (pp. 57–75). Amsterdam: John Benjamins. DOI: 10.1075/hcp.24.07gri

Gries, Stefan, & Stefanowitsch, Anatol (Eds.). (2006). *Corpora in cognitive linguistics: Corpus-based approaches to syntax and lexis*. Berlin & New York: Mouton de Gruyter. DOI: 10.1515/9783110197709

Grimshaw, Jane. (1980). *Argument structure*. Cambridge, MA: MIT Press.

Gross, Maurice. (1968). *Grammaire transformationnelle du français: Syntaxe du verbe*. Paris: Larousse.

Guénette, Louise. (1996). *Le démonstratif en français*. Paris: Honoré Champion.

Guéron, Jacqueline. (1980). On the syntax and semantics of PP extraposition. *Linguistic Inquiry*, 11, 637–678.

Heluasvo, Marja-Liisa, & Vilkuna, Maria. (2008). Impersonal is personal: Finnish perspectives. *Transactions of the Philological Society*, 106(2), 216–245. DOI: 10.1111/j.1467-968X.2008.00208.x

Hériau, Michel. (1980). *Le verbe impersonnel en français moderne*. Lille: Atelier de reproductions de thèses, Université de Lille III.

Herschensohn, Julia. (1982). The French impersonal as a base generated structure. *Studies in Language*, 6, 193–219. DOI: 10.1075/sl.6.2.03her

Herschensohn, Julia. (1996). *Case suspension and binary complement structure in French*. Amsterdam: John Benjamins. DOI: 10.1075/cilt.132

Hilty, Gerold. (1959). *Il* impersonnel: Syntaxe historique et interprétation littéraire. *Le Français Moderne*, 27, 241–251.

Hopper, Paul, & Thompson, Sandra. (1980). Transitivity in grammar and discourse. *Language*, 56, 251–299. DOI: 10.1353/lan.1980.0017

Johnson-Laird, Philip. (1993). Foreword. In Cristina Cacciari, & Patrizia Tabossi (Eds.), *Idioms: Processing, structure, and interpretation* (pp. vii–x). Hillsdale, NJ: Lawrence Erlbaum.

Jones, Michael. (1996). *Foundations of French syntax*. Cambridge: Cambridge University Press. DOI: 10.1017/CBO9780511620591

Karttunnen, Laurie. (1971). Some observations on factivity. *Papers in Linguistics*, 4, 55–70. DOI: 10.1080/08351817109370248

Kayne, Richard. (1979). Rightward NP movement in French and English. *Linguistic Inquiry*, 10, 710–719.

Keenan, Edward, & Dryer, Matthew. (2007). Passive in the world's languages. In Timothy Shopen (Ed.), *Clause structure, language typology and syntactic description*, Vol. 1, (2nd Edition). Cambridge: Cambridge University Press.

Kemmer, Suzanne. (1993). *The middle voice*. Amsterdam: John Benjamins. DOI: 10.1075/tsl.23

Kiparsky, Paul, & Kiparsky, Carol. (1970). Fact. In Manfred Bierwisch, & Karl E. Heidolph (Eds.), *Progress in linguistics* (pp. 143–173). The Hague: Mouton.

Kirsner, Robert. (1979). *The problem of presentative sentences in modern Dutch*. North-Holland Linguistic Series 43. Amsterdam: North-Holland.

Koenig, Jean-Pierre. (1999). *On a tué le président!* The nature of passives and ultra-indefinites. In Barbara Fox, Dan Jurafsky, & Laura Michaelis (Eds.), *Cognition and function in language* (pp. 256–272). Stanford: CSLI.

Koenig, Jean-Pierre, & Mauner, Gail. (1999). A-definites and the discourse status of implicit arguments. *Journal of Semantics*, 16(3), 207–236. DOI: 10.1093/jos/16.3.207

Labelle, Marie. (1992). Change of state and valency. *Journal of Linguistics*, 28, 375–414. DOI: 10.1017/S0022226700015267

Lakoff, George. (1987). *Women, fire, and dangerous things: What categories reveal about the mind*. Chicago & London: The University of Chicago Press. DOI: 10.7208/chicago/9780226471013.001.0001

Lakoff, George, & Johnson, Mark. (1980). *Metaphors we live by*. Chicago: The University of Chicago Press.

Lambrecht, Knud. (1994). *Information structure and sentence form: Topic, focus, and the mental representation of discourse referents*. Cambridge: Cambridge University Press. DOI: 10.1017/CBO9780511620607

Langacker, Ronald. (1982). Space grammar, analyzability, and the English passive. *Language*, 58, 22–80. DOI: 10.2307/413531

Langacker, Ronald. (1985). Observations and speculations on subjectivity. In John Haiman (Ed.), *Iconicity in syntax* (pp. 109–150). Amsterdam: John Benjamins. DOI: 10.1075/tsl.6.07lan

Langacker, Ronald. (1987a). *Foundations of cognitive grammar, Vol. 1: Theoretical prerequisites*. Stanford: Stanford University Press.

Langacker, Ronald. (1987b). Nouns and verbs. *Language*, 63, 53–94. DOI: 10.2307/415384

Langacker, Ronald. (1988). A usage-based model. In Brygida Rudzka-Ostyn (Ed.), *Topics in cognitive linguistics* (pp. 127–161). Amsterdam: John Benjamins. DOI: 10.1075/cilt.50.06lan

Langacker, Ronald. (1990). Subjectification. *Cognitive Linguistics*, 1, 5–38. DOI: 10.1515/cogl.1990.1.1.5

Langacker, Ronald. (1991). *Foundations of cognitive grammar, Vol. 2: Descriptive application.* Stanford: Stanford University Press.

Langacker, Ronald. (1993). Reference point constructions. *Cognitive Linguistics, 4*, 1–38. DOI: 10.1515/cogl.1993.4.1.1

Langacker, Ronald. (1995). Raising and transparency. *Language, 71*(1), 1–62. DOI: 10.2307/415962

Langacker, Ronald. (1999). Virtual reality. *Study in the Linguistic Sciences, 29*(2), 77–103.

Langacker, Ronald. (2000). A dynamic usage-based model. In Michael Barlow & Suzanne Kemmer (Eds.), *Usage-based models of language* (pp. 1–63). Stanford: CSLI.

Langacker, Ronald. (2002). The control cycle: Why grammar is a matter of life and death. *Proceedings of the Annual Meeting of the Japanese Cognitive Linguistics Association, 2*, 193–220.

Langacker, Ronald. (2004). Aspects of the grammar of finite clauses. In Michel Achard, & Suzanne Kemmer (Eds.), *Language, culture, and mind* (pp. 535–577). Stanford: CSLI.

Langacker, Ronald. (2005). Construction grammars: Cognitive, radical, and less so. In Francisco J. Ruiz de Mendoza Ibáñez, & M. Sandra Peña Cevel (Eds.), *Cognitive linguistics: Internal dynamics and interdisciplinary interaction* (pp. 101–159). Berlin: Mouton de Gruyter.

Langacker, Ronald. (2006). Dimensions of defocusing. In Masayoshi Shibatani, & Taro Kageyama (Eds.), *Voice and grammatical relations: In honor of Masayoshi Shibatani* (pp. 115–137). Amsterdam: John Benjamins. DOI: 10.1075/tsl.65.08lan

Langacker, Ronald. (2007). Constructing the meanings of personal pronouns. In Günter Radden, Klaus-Michael Köpcke, Thomas Berg, & Peter Siemund (Eds.), *Aspects of meaning construction* (pp. 171–197). Amsterdam: John Benjamins. DOI: 10.1075/z.136.12lan

Langacker, Ronald. (2008). *Cognitive grammar: A basic introduction* Oxford: Oxford University Press. DOI: 10.1093/acprof:oso/9780195331967.001.0001

Langacker, Ronald. (2009). *Investigations in cognitive grammar.* Berlin & New York: Mouton de Gruyter. DOI: 10.1515/9783110214369

Lauwers, Peter. (2004). *La description du français entre la tradition grammaticale et le modernité linguistique.* Leuven, Paris, & Dudley, MA: Peeters.

Lazard, Gilbert. (1998). *Actancy.* Berlin & New York: Mouton de Gruyter. DOI: 10.1515/9783110808100

Lazdina, Tereza Budina. (1966). *Teach yourself Latvian.* London: The English Universities Press.

Le Bidois, Georges, & Le Bidois, Robert. (1935). *Syntaxe du français moderne*, Vol. 1. New York: Strechert.

Le Bidois, Georges, & Le Bidois, Robert. (1938). *Syntaxe du français moderne*, Vol. 2. New York: Strechert.

Legendre, Géraldine. (1989). Unaccusativity in French. *Lingua, 79*, 95–164. DOI: 10.1016/0024-3841(89)90067-3

Legendre, Géraldine. (1990). French impersonal constructions. *NLLT, 8*, 81–128.

Lekakou, Marika. (2003). Greek passives on the middle interpretation. *Proceedings of the 6th International Conference on Greek Linguistics.* Downloaded from: https://www.academia.edu/884778/Greek_passives_on_the_middle_interpretation.

Lekakou, Marika. (2004). Middles as disposition ascriptions. In Cécile Meier, & Mattias Weisgerber (Eds.), *Proceedings of the conference "sub8 – Sinn und Beudetung" Arbeitpapier 117*, (pp. 181–195). FB Sprachwissenschaft. Germany: Universität Konstanz.

Lyons, Christopher. (1995). Voice, aspect and arbitrary arguments. In John Charles Smith, & Martin Maiden (Eds.), *Linguistic theory and the Romance languages* (pp. 77–114). Amsterdam: John Benjamins. DOI: 10.1075/cilt.122.04lyo

Malchukov, Andrej, & Siewierska, Anna. (2011). *Impersonal constructions: A cross-linguistic perspective.* Amsterdam: John Benjamins. DOI: 10.1075/slcs.124

Malchukov, Andrej, & Ogawa, Akio. (2011). Towards a typology of impersonal constructions. In Andrej Malchukov, & Anna Siewierska (Eds.), *Impersonal constructions: A cross-linguistic perspective* (pp. 19–56). Amsterdam: John Benjamins.

Martin, Robert. (1970). La transformation impersonnelle. *Revue de Linguistique Romane, 34,* 377–394.

Martinon, Philippe. (1927). *Comment on parle en français.* Paris: Larousse.

Melis, Ludo. (1990). *La voie pronominale.* Louvain-la-Neuve: Duculot.

Mendikoetxea, Amaya. (2008). Clitic impersonal constructions in Romance: Syntactic features and semantic interpretation. *Transactions of the Philological Society,* 106(2), 290–336. DOI: 10.1111/j.1467-968X.2008.00210.x

Michaelis, Laura. (2005). Entity and event coercion in a symbolic theory of syntax. In Jan-Ola Östman, & Mirjam Fried (Eds.), *Construction grammars: Cognitive grounding and theoretical extensions* (pp. 45–88). Amsterdam: John Benjamins. DOI: 10.1075/cal.3.04mic

Michaelis, Laura. (2004). Type shifting in construction grammar: An integrated approach to aspectual coercion. *Cognitive Linguistics,* 15, 1–67. DOI: 10.1515/cogl.2004.001

Moignet, Gérard. (1974). *Etudes de psycho-systématique française.* Paris: Klincksieck.

Olsson, Hugo. (1986). *La concurrence entre il, ce et cela (ça) comme sujet d'expressions impersonnelles en français contemporain.* Stockholm: Almqvist & Wiksell.

Perlmutter, David. (1978). Impersonal passives and the unaccusative hypothesis. *BLS,* 4, 157–189.

Perlmutter, David (Ed.). (1983). *Studies in relational grammar 1.* Chicago & London: The University of Chicago Press.

Perlmutter, David, & Rosen, Carol (Eds.). (1984). *Studies in relational grammar 2.* Chicago & London: The University of Chicago Press.

Perlmutter, David, & Postal, Paul. (1983). Some proposed laws of basic clause structure. In David Perlmutter (Ed.), *Studies in relational grammar 1* (pp. 81–129). Chicago & London: The University of Chicago Press.

Perlmutter, David, & Postal, Paul. (1984). Impersonal passives and some relational laws. In David Perlmutter, & Carol Rosen (Eds.), *Studies in relational grammar 2* (pp. 126–171). Chicago & London: The University of Chicago Press.

Pollock, Jean-Yves. (1978). Trace theory and French syntax. In Jay Keyser (Ed.), *Recent transformational studies in European languages* (pp. 65–112). Cambridge, MA: MIT Press.

Postal, Paul. (1982). Arc pair grammar descriptions. In Pauline Jacobson, & Geoffrey Pullum (Eds.), *The nature of syntactic representation* (pp. 341–425). Dordrecht: Kluwer. DOI: 10.1007/978-94-009-7707-5_9

Postal, Paul. (1984). French indirect object cliticization and SSC/BT. *Linguistic Analysis,* 14, 111–172.

Pustejovsky, James. (1989). Type coercion and selection. Paper presented at *West Coast Conference on Formal Linguistics,* Vancouver.

Pustejovsky, James. (1995). Linguistic constraints on type coercion. In Patrick Saint-Dizier, & Evelyn Viegas (Eds.), *Computational lexical semantics* (pp. 71–97). Cambridge, New York, & Melbourne: Cambridge University Press. DOI: 10.1017/CBO9780511527227.007

Radford, Andrew. (2004). *Minimalist syntax: Exploring the structure of English.* Cambridge: Cambridge University Press. DOI: 10.1017/CBO9780511811319

Rice, Sally. (1987). *Towards a cognitive model of transitivity.* Unpublished Ph.D. dissertation, University of California San Diego.

Rowlett, Paul. (2007). *The syntax of French*. Cambridge: Cambridge University Press. DOI: 10.1017/CBO9780511618642

Ruwet, Nicolas. (1972). *Théorie syntaxique et syntaxe du français*. Paris: Éditions du Seuil.

Ruwet, Nicolas. (1989). Weather-verbs and the unaccusative hypothesis. In Carl Kirschner, & Janet De Cesaris (Eds.), *Studies in Romance linguistics* (pp. 313–345). Amsterdam: John Benjamins. DOI: 10.1075/cilt.60.20ruw

Ruwet, Nicolas. 1991. *Syntax and human experience*. Chicago: University of Chicago Press.

Sandfeld, Kristian. (1929). *Syntaxe du français contemporain*. Paris: Champion.

Sansó, Andrea. (2005). Semantic maps in action, a discourse-based approach to passive and impersonal constructions. In Annalisa Baicchi, Cristiano Broccias, & Andrea Sansó (Eds.), *Modelling thought and constructing meaning* (pp. 89–106). Milan: Angeli.

Sechehaye, Albert. (1950). *Essai sur la structure logique de la langue*. Paris: Champion.

Shibatani, Masayochi. (1985). Passive and related constructions: A prototype analysis. *Language*, 61, 821–848. DOI: 10.2307/414491

Siewierska, Anna. (2008a). Ways of impersonalizing: Pronominal vs. verbal strategies. In Maria de los Angeles Gómez González, J. Lachlan MacKenzie, & Elsa M. González Alvarez (Eds.), *Current trends in contrastive linguistics, functional and cognitive perspectives* (pp. 3–26). Amsterdam: John Benjamins. DOI: 10.1075/sfsl.60.03sie

Siewierska, Anna. (2008b). Introduction, impersonalization: An agent-based vs. a subject-based perspective. *Transactions of Philological Society*, 106(2), 115–137. DOI: 10.1111/j.1467-968X.2008.00211.x

Sinclair, John. (1991). *Corpus, concordance, collocation*. Oxford. Oxford University Press.

Sinclair, John. (1996). The search for units of meaning. *Textus*, 9, 75–106.

Słoń, Anna. (2007). The 'impersonal' impersonal construction in Polish: A cognitive grammar analysis. In Dagmar Divjak, & Agata Kochańska (Eds.), *Cognitive paths through the Slavic domain* (pp. 257–287). Berlin: Mouton de Gruyter. DOI: 10.1515/9783110198799.3.257

Smith, Michael. (1985). An analysis of German dummy subject constructions in cognitive grammar. In Scott DeLancey, & Russell Tomlin (Eds.), *Proceedings of the First Annual Meeting of the Pacific Linguistics Conference* (pp. 412–425). Eugene: Department of Linguistics, University of Oregon.

Smith, Michael. (2000). Cataphors, spaces, propositions: Cataphoric pronouns and their function. *Proceedings from the Meeting of the Chicago Linguistic Society*, 36(1), 483–500.

Smith, Michael. (2004). Cataphoric pronouns as mental space designators. In Robert Kirsner, Ellen Contini-Morava, & Betsy Rodriguez-Bachiller (Eds.), *Cognitive and communicative approaches to linguistic analysis* (pp. 61–90). Amsterdam: John Benjamins. DOI: 10.1075/sfsl.51.04smi

Smith, Michael. (2006). The conceptual structure of German impersonal constructions. *Journal of Germanic Linguistics*, 17(2), 79–138.

Stéfanini, Jean. (1962). *La voix pronominale en ancien et en moyen français*. Aix-en-Provence: Ophrys.

Stefanowitsch, Anatol, & Gries, Stefan. (2003). Collostructions: On the interaction between verbs and constructions. *International Journal of Corpus Linguistics*, 8(2), 209–243. DOI: 10.1075/ijcl.8.2.03ste

Tesnière, Lucien. (1959). *Eléments de syntaxe structurale*. Paris: Klincksieck.

Tomasello, Michael. (1999). *The cultural origins of human cognition*. Cambridge, MA: Harvard University Press.

Tomasello, Michael. (2003). *Constructing a language: A usage-based theory of language acquisition*. Cambridge, MA: Harvard University Press.

Van Oosten, Jeanne. (1977). Subjects and agenthood in English. *Chicago Linguistic Society*, 13, 451–471.

Wagner, Robert Léon, & Pinchon, Jacqueline. (1962). *Grammaire du français classique et moderne*. Paris: Hachette.

Wartburg, von Walter, & Zumthor, Paul. (1958). *Précis de syntaxe du français contemporain*. Bern: Francke.

Wilmet, Marc. (1997). *Grammaire critique du français*. Louvain-la-Neuve: Duculot.

Wehrli, Eric. (1986). On some properties of the French clitic *se*. In Hagit Borer (Ed.), *The syntax of pronominal clitics* (pp. 263–283). San Francisco: Academic Press.

Yoon, Soyeon. (2012). *Constructions, semantic compatibility, and coercion: An empirical usage-based approach*. Unpublished Ph.D. dissertation, Rice University.

Zribi-Hertz, Anne. (1982). La construction "se-moyen" du français et son statut dans le triangle moyen, passif réfléchi. *Lingvisticæ Investigationes*, VI(2), 345–401. DOI: 10.1075/li.6.2.05zri

Index